Study Guide for

Weiten's

Psychology
Themes and Variations
Fifth Edition

Richard B. Stalling
Bradley University

Ronald E. Wasden
Bradley University

WADSWORTH

THOMSON LEARNING ™

Australia • Canada • Mexico • Singapore • Spain • United Kingdom • United States

For permission to use material from this text, contact us by **Web**: http://www.thomsonrights.com **Fax:** 1-800-730-2215 **Phone:** 1-800-730-2214

For more information, contact
Wadsworth/Thomson Learning
10 Davis Drive
Belmont, CA 94002-3098
USA

For more information about our products, contact us:
Thomson Learning Academic Resource Center
1-800-423-0563
http://www.wadsworth.com

International Headquarters
Thomson Learning
International Division
290 Harbor Drive, 2nd Floor
Stamford, CT 06902-7477
USA

UK/Europe/Middle East/South Africa
Thomson Learning
Berkshire House
168-173 High Holborn
London WC1V 7AA
United Kingdom

Asia
Thomson Learning
60 Albert Complex, #15-01
Singapore 189969

Canada
Nelson Thomson Learning
1120 Birchmount Road
Toronto, Ontario M1K 5G4
Canada

ISBN 0-534-36716-x

Contents

To the Student

The two of us have written about eight study guides in our careers and we've used a number of them written by others as well. Our goal in writing this study guide was to make it the best that we have ever written or used. We're pleased with the organization, the clear way in which each component parallels each part of the text, the fact that the practice material is in close proximity to the learning objectives, and the variety of the examples. We hope you find it as helpful a resource as we have tried to make it.

The first and major section of each chapter in the study guide is the Review of Key Ideas, consisting of 20 to 30 learning objectives and several questions or exercises relating to each objective. The learning objectives tell you what you are expected to know; the exercises quiz you, sometimes tutor you, and occasionally provide additional information. Answers are presented at the end of each set of exercises.

The second section is the Review of Key Terms, which asks you to match 20 to 60 terms from the chapter with their definitions. The third section is the Review of Key People, a matching exercise confined to the major researchers and theorists presented in each chapter. Finally, the Self-Quiz for each chapter gives you some idea of whether or not your studying has been on target.

What's the best way to work with this book? We suggest that you try this: (1) read each learning objective; (2) read the part of the textbook that relates to that learning objective; (3) complete the exercises for that learning objective; (4) check your answers. After you finish the objectives, do the matching exercises and take the self-quiz. Of course, you may find a different procedure that works better for you. Whatever method you use, the learning objectives will serve as an excellent review. At the end of your study of a particular chapter you can quiz yourself by reading over the learning objectives, reciting answers aloud, and checking your answers. This procedure roughly parallels the SQ3R study technique introduced in the Application section of Chapter 1 of the text.

We wish to acknowledge the help of a few people. First, we wish to thank Wayne Weiten, our former student at Bradley University. Across five editions of this study guide Wayne, by now recognized as one of America's outstanding teachers, has been our teacher as well. It has been a pleasure to work with him. His guidance has made our task much easier, and we owe much of the success of this project to him. Our thanks also to Annie Berterretche of Brooks/Cole, whose delightful voice on the end of the phone encouraged us, and to Gail Reynolds, who transformed our copy into its final form.

Rick Stalling and Ron Wasden

Study Guide for

Weiten's

Psychology
Themes and Variation
Fifth Edition

The Evolution of Psychology

REVIEW OF KEY IDEAS

FROM SPECULATION TO SCIENCE: HOW PSYCHOLOGY DEVELOPED

1. Summarize Wundt's accomplishments and contributions to psychology.

   1-1.   If you ask most college graduates to name the founder of psychology they might mention the name of a famous psychologist (for example, maybe Sigmund Freud), but they almost certainly would *not* say Wilhelm Wundt. Yet among psychologists Wundt is generally acknowledged to be the "_____" of our field.

   1-2.   Wundt established the first experimental psychology _____ , in Leipzig, Germany, in 1879. He also established the first _____ devoted to publishing psychological research.

   1-3.   The subject matter of Wundt's psychology was (<u>consciousness/behavior</u>).

   1-4.   Wundt's major contributions to the evolution of psychology may be summarized as follows: He is the _____ of psychology as an independent academic field, and he insisted that psychology can and must use the _____ method.

Answers: 1-1. founder **1-2.** laboratory, journal **1-3.** consciousness **1-4.** founder, scientific (experimental). (Personal note from RS: I visited Leipzig in the former East Germany during summer 1996 and looked for the famous founding laboratory. It wasn't there! I found Wundt Street, but no lab. Had I read World War II history more carefully I would have known that an English-U.S. bombing raid destroyed the laboratory in 1943.)

2. Summarize Hall's accomplishments and contributions to psychology.

   2-1.   Wundt had many important students, among them the G. Stanley Hall, an American. In 1883, just four years after Wundt created his laboratory in Leipzig, Hall established the first American psychological _____ at Johns Hopkins. Hall also founded America's first _____ devoted to publishing material in the field of psychology.

2-2. In 1892, with 26 of his colleagues, Hall began the American Psychological Association, known by the initials _____. Hall also became the first _____ of the Association. The APA now includes more than 80,000 members.

Answers: **2-1.** laboratory, journal **2-2.** APA, president.

3. Describe structuralism and its impact on the subsequent development of psychology.

3-1. Another of Wundt's students, Edward Titchener, developed the school of psychology known as _____. The major tenet of this viewpoint was that psychology should study the structure of _____ by breaking it down into its basic components or _____.

3-2. These basic elements of consciousness were thought to be the sensations (or images or feelings) that people reported when they observed some object. Subjects were first trained to observe (or listen to) something and then, after careful introspection, report on their conscious experience. Thus, the subject matter of structuralism was _____, and its method involved training observers in the technique of _____.

Answers: **3-1.** structuralism, consciousness, elements **3-2.** consciousness, introspection.

4. Describe functionalism and its impact on the subsequent development of psychology.

4-1. Rather than breaking down consciousness into basic elements, the _____ school emphasized determining the _____ or purpose of consciousness.

4-2. The origins of functionalism are associated with William James. Influenced by the Darwin's concept of natural selection, James concluded that psychology should study the basic (underline: elements/purpose) of consciousness.

4-3. Which "school" is characterized by each of the following descriptions? Place an "S" for structuralism or "F" for functionalism in the appropriate blanks.

_____ Concerned with the purpose (or function) of consciousness.

_____ Trained observers to introspect about consciousness.

_____ Assumed that consciousness could be broken down into basic elements (in the same way that physical matter is comprised of atoms).

_____ Interested in the flow of consciousness.

_____ Focused on the adaptive (evolutionary) value of consciousness.

_____ Emphasized sensation and perception in vision, hearing, and touch.

4-4. While neither structuralism nor functionalism survived as viable theories of psychology, functionalism had a more lasting impact. The emphasis of functionalism on the practical (or the adaptive or purposeful) led to the development of these two areas of modern psychology: _____ and _____ psychology.

5. **Summarize Watson's view on the appropriate subject matter of psychology, nature versus nurture, and animal research.**

    5-1.   A literal translation of the root words of psychology (*psyche* and *logos*) suggests that psychology is the study of the _____. For both Wundt and James, this was the case: they studied human _____. For Watson, however, the subject matter of psychology was _____.

    5-2.   Watson believed that psychology could not be a science unless it, like the other sciences, concentrated on _____ rather than unobservable events.

    5-3.   Which of the following are observable behaviors? Place an "O" in the blank if the event is observable and an "N" if it is not.

        _____ writing a letter

        _____ feeling angry

        _____ saying "Please pass the salt"

        _____ passing the salt

        _____ perceiving a round object

        _____ experiencing hunger

        _____ walking rapidly

    5-4.   Watson largely discounted the importance of genetic inheritance. For Watson, behavior was governed by the _____.

    5-5.   Watson also made a shift away from human introspection by using _____ as the subjects for research. Why the change in orientation? First, animal behavior is observable; human consciousness is not. Second, the environment of laboratory animals, in contrast to that of humans, is subject to much more _____.

    5-6.   Let's briefly review structuralism and behaviorism:

        (a) As defined by the structuralists, what was the <u>subject matter</u> of psychology?

        (b) For behaviorists, what was the subject matter of psychology?

        (c) While structuralists and behaviorists differed in their views of the subject matter of psychology, their approach to the new field was similar in one major respect. In what way were the two systems similar?

6. Summarize Freud's principal ideas and why they inspired controversy.

6-1. For Wundt, the subject matter of psychology was human consciousness. For Freud, a major subject of study was what he termed the _____. With this concept, Freud asserted that human beings are (<u>aware/unaware</u>) of most of the factors that influence their thoughts and behavior.

6-2. There is a word beginning with *s* that means the same thing as feces. This word, however, may be more likely to cause laughter, embarrassment, or anger than the word feces. Why do two words that mean the same thing produce such differing reactions? Freud would assert that our more emotional response to one of the words would be caused by the _____.

6-3. Although generally not accessible to us, the unconscious is revealed in several ways, according to Freud. Freud thought, for example, that the unconscious is revealed in mistakes, such as "_____ of the tongue," or the symbolism in nighttime _____.

6-4. Freud's ideas were (and still are) considered quite controversial. The general public tended to find Freud's ideas unacceptable because of his emphasis on _____. And scientific psychologists, with their increasing emphasis on observable behavior, rejected Freud's notion that we are controlled by _____ forces. Nonetheless, Freud's theory gradually gained prominence and survives today as an influential theoretical perspective.

7. Summarize Skinner's work, views, and influence.

7-1. While he did not deny their existence, Skinner said that (<u>mental/environmental</u>) events are not observable and cannot be studied scientifically.

7-2. The fundamental principle of behavior, according to Skinner, is that organisms will tend to _____ behaviors that lead to positive outcome (and tend not to repeat responses that lead to neutral or negative outcomes).

7-3. Skinner asserted that because behavior is under the lawful control of the environment, our feeling of _____ is an illusion.

7-4. According to Skinner, to adequately account for and predict behavior psychologists must understand

a. the relationship between thinking and behavior

b. the physiological basis of action

c. the way environmental factors affect behavior

d. all of the above

8. **Summarize Rogers's and Maslow's ideas and the contributions of humanistic psychology.**

   8-1.   Both Rogers and Maslow, like other _____ psychologists, emphasized the (<u>similarities/ differences</u>) between human beings and other animals.

   8-2.   While Freud and Skinner stressed the way in which behavior is *controlled* (by unconscious forces or by the environment), Rogers and Maslow emphasized human beings' _____ to determine their own actions.

   8-3.   Rogers and Maslow also asserted that human beings have a drive to express their inner potential, a drive toward personal _____.

   8-4.   Perhaps the greatest contribution of the humanistic movement has been in producing (<u>scientific findings/ new approaches</u>) in psychotherapy.

   Answers: **8-1.** humanistic, differences **8-2.** freedom **8-3.** growth (expression) **8-4.** new approaches.

9. **Explain how historical events since World War I have contributed to the emergence of psychology as a profession.**

   9-1.   World War I ushered in the field of applied psychology, primarily the extensive use of _____ testing of military recruits.

   9-2.   World War II brought an increased need for screening recruits and treating emotional casualties. With the increased demand, the Veterans Administration began funding many new training programs in the field of _____ psychology.

   9-3.   In contrast to its founding in the 19th century as a research or academic endeavor, psychology in the 20th century developed a prominent _____ branch devoted to solving practical problems. These applied fields, which emerged in large part as a result of two world wars, included psychological _____ and _____ psychology.

   Answers: **9-1.** intelligence (psychological, mental) **9-2.** clinical **9-3.** applied (or professional), testing, clinical.

10. **Describe two recent trends in research in psychology that reflect a return to psychology's intellectual roots.**

   10-1.   Two recent trends in research in psychology involve the reemergence of areas largely discarded or ignored by the behaviorists. What are these two areas?

   10-2.   Think about sucking on a lemon. When you do, the amount of saliva in your mouth will increase measurably. While it would be enough to describe your observable response as a function of my observable instruction, it is also obvious that thinking, or cognition, is involved: My instruction changed your _____ image, which was accompanied by a change in salivation.

10-3. The study of mental imagery, problem solving, and decision making involves _____ processes. The second more recent trend also concerns "internal" processes: Research on electrical stimulation of the brain, brain specialization, and biofeedback involves _____ processes.

Answers: **10-1.** cognition (consciousness or thinking) and physiological (or biological) processes **10-2.** mental **10-3.** cognitive, physiological (biological).

11. Explain why Western psychology traditionally had scant interest in other cultures and why this situation has begun to change.

11-1. Several factors contributed to the narrow focus of Western, and especially United States, psychology:

(a) First, studying other cultures is expensive and time consuming. It's much _____ for researchers to study people in their own country (and especially middle-class students at their own schools).

(b) Second, psychology has traditionally been more interested in the study of _____ than groups.

(c) Third, some psychologists may worry that study of diverse groups may foster _____ of those groups.

(d) Fourth, there may be a tendency among Western psychologists to view their own group as superior, the group tendency referred to as _____.

11-2. The situation has begun to change in recent years for two primary reasons: (1) increased communication and trade worldwide, the so-called _____ economy or global interdependence; and (2) increased diversity of ethnic groups within the countries of the Western World, including the _____ mosaic characteristic of the United States.

Answers: **11-1.** (a) cheaper (easier), (b) individuals, (c) stereotypes, (d) ethnocentrism **11-2.** global; multicultural.

12. Summarize the basic tenets of evolutionary psychology.

12-1. According to evolutionary psychologists, all aspects of human behavior—including not only aggression and mate selection but perception, language, personality, and cognition—are strongly influenced by the _____ value that these factors have had for the human species.

12-2. While Darwin's influence is clear in other psychological theories (e.g., James, Freud, and Skinner), the new emphasis on natural selection is (less/more) comprehensive and widely researched than the earlier versions.

12-3. The viewpoint has its critics. Some charge that the theory is not subject to scientific _____ and that evolutionary conceptions are simply post hoc accounts rather than explanations. Nonetheless, _____ psychology has gained a high degree of acceptance as the first major new perspective in psychology since the 1960s.

Answers: **12-1.** survival (adaptive) **12-2.** more **12-3.** test (evaluation, disconfirmation, proof), evolutionary.

PSYCHOLOGY TODAY: VIGOROUS AND DIVERSIFIED

13. **Discuss the growth of psychology and the most common work settings for contemporary psychologists.**

13-1. Psychology is a thriving field that has experienced a remarkable growth since its founding in 1879. Which of the following statements about that growth are true? (Use a T or F to indicate true or false for the following statements.)

_____ APA membership now numbers more than 80,000.

_____ 10 percent of all doctoral degrees awarded in science and the humanities are in psychology.

_____ Psychology is the second most popular undergraduate major.

_____ Over 1000 journals worldwide publish articles in psychology.

13-2. Psychology was founded in a University, and earlier in this century almost all psychologists were employed as academics. Today, however, more than two-thirds of psychologists are employed in (university/non-academic) settings that include hospitals, business and industry, schools, and government agencies.

Answers: **13-1.** T, T, T, T **13-2.** non-academic.

14. **List and describe seven major research areas in psychology.**

14-1. Read over the descriptions of the research areas in Figure 1.9. Then match the names of the areas with the sampled research topics by placing the appropriate letters in the blanks. (Note that the separation between these areas is not always perfect. For example, a personality theorist might also be a psychometrician who has a physiological focus in explaining behavior. Nonetheless, the following topics have been chosen so that one answer is correct for each.)

A. Experimental _____ attitude change, group behavior

B. Physiological _____ personality and intelligence assessment, test design, new statistical procedures

C. Cognitive _____ personality assessment, personality description

D. Developmental _____ "core" topics (e.g., perception, conditioning, motivation)

E. Psychometrics _____ influence of the brain, bodily chemicals, genetics

F. Personality _____ child, adolescent, and adult development

G. Social _____ memory, decision making, thinking

14-2. In case you want to remember the list of seven research areas, here's a mnemonic device: _Peter Piper Picked Some Exquisite California Dills._ List the seven research areas by matching them with the first letter of each word.

15. List and describe the four professional specialties in psychology.

15-1. Review Figure 1.10. Then match the following specialties with the descriptions by placing the appropriate letter in the blanks.

A. Clinical _____ Treatment of less severe problems and problems involving family, marital, and career difficulties.

B. Counseling _____ Treatment of psychological disorders, behavioral and emotional problems

C. Educational and school _____ Involves work on curriculum design and achievement testing in school settings.

D. Industrial and organizational _____ Psychology applied to business settings; deals with personnel, job satisfaction, etc.

15-2. What is the difference between psychology and psychiatry? The major difference is a matter of degree (this is a pun, folks). Psychiatrists have _____ degrees. Clinical psychologists generally have _____ degrees (although some clinical psychologists have Ed.D. or Psy.D. degrees).

15-3. The major portion of psychiatrists' training occurs in _____ schools and in the residency programs in psychiatry that follow medical school. Clinical psychologists' training occurs in _____ schools.

15-4. While clinical psychologists and psychiatrists frequently use the same psychotherapeutic treatment procedures, only _____, as physicians, are licensed to prescribe drugs and engage in other medical treatment.

PUTTING IT IN PERSPECTIVE: SEVEN KEY THEMES

16. Summarize the text's three unifying themes relating to psychology as a field of study.

16-1. When my (R. S.'s) older daughter Samantha was about three years old, she pulled a sugar bowl off a shelf and broke it while I was not present. Later, when I surveyed the damage, I said, "I see you've broken something." She said, "How do yer know, did yer see me do it?" I was amused, because while it was obvious who had broken it, her comment reflected psychology's foundation in direct observation. **Theme 1** is that psychology is _____. Empiricism is the point of view that knowledge should be acquired through _____.

16-2. My daughter's comment caused me to think about one other aspect of empiricism: she expressed *doubt* (albeit somewhat self-serving with regard to the sugar bowl). One can describe belief systems along a continuum from *credulity*, which means ready to believe, to *skepticism*, which means disposed toward doubt. Psychology, and the empirical approach, is more disposed toward the _____ end of the continuum.

16-3. We would ordinarily think that if one theory is correct, any other theory used to explain the same data must be wrong. While scientists do pit theories against each other, it is also the case that apparently contradictory theories may both be correct—as with the explanation of light in terms of both wave and particle theories. Thus, **Theme 2** indicates that psychology is theoretically _____.

16-4. Psychology tolerates and in fact encourages) different theoretical explanations because:

16-5. As is the case with science in general, psychology does not evolve in a vacuum. It is influenced by and influences our society. For example, the current interest in cultural diversity has prompted increased interest in cross-cultural research, which in turn affects the viewpoints in our society. As stated in **Theme 3**, psychology evolves in a _____ context.

Answers: **16-1.** empirical, observation **16-2.** skepticism **16-3.** diverse **16-4.** more than one theory may be correct; or, one theory may not adequately explain all of the observations **16-5.** sociohistorical.

17. Summarize the text's four unifying themes relating to psychology's subject matter.

17-1. When looking for an explanation of a particular behavior, someone might ask: "Well, why did he do it? What was *the reason*? Was it greed or ignorance?" The question implies that if one cause is present another cannot be, and it illustrates the human tendency to reason in terms of (one cause/multiple causes).

17-2. What influences the course of a ball rolled down an inclined plane? Gravity. And also friction. And the presence of other objects, and a number of other factors. That is the point of **Theme 4**: even more than is the case for physical events, behavior is determined by _____ _____.

17-3. Among the multiple causes of human behavior is the category of causes referred to as *culture*. Cultural factors include the customs, beliefs, and values that we transmit across generations—what we eat, how we walk, what we wear, what we say, what we think, and so on. **Theme 5** indicates that our behavior is shaped by our _____ heritage.

17-4. For example, I have observed that many American students traveling abroad initially think that their European lecturers talk down to them; the lecturers, in turn, may regard our students as spoiled and insolent. Perhaps closer to the truth is that there is a clash of customs invisible to both cultures. While we are shaped by our _____ _____ we are often _____ (aware/unaware) of the precise rules and customs that affect us.

17-5. **Theme 6** relates to the influence of heredity and environment. What is the consensus among psychologists about the effect of heredity and environment on behavior?

17-6. The scientific method relies on observation, but observation by itself isn't sufficient. Why isn't it?

17-7. **Theme 7** indicates that our experience is subjective. What does this mean?

Answers: 17-1. one cause **17-2.** multiple causes **17-3.** cultural **17-4.** cultural heritage, aware **17-5.** Theme 6 states that heredity and environment *jointly* affect behavior. While the relative influence of each is still debated, theorists no longer assert that behavior is entirely a function of one or the other. **17-6.** Because (Theme 7) people's experience of the world is highly subjective. **17-7.** Different people experience different things; even if we observe the same event at the same time, we do not "see" the same things; we selectively focus on some events and ignore others.

APPLICATION: IMPROVING ACADEMIC PERFORMANCE

18. Discuss three important considerations in designing a program to promote adequate studying.

18-1. Three features of successful studying are listed below. Elaborate on them by providing some of the details asked for.

(a) A schedule: When should you plan your study schedule? Should you write it down?

(b) A place: What are the major characteristics of a good study place?

(c) A reward: When should you reward yourself? What kinds of rewards are suggested?

Answers: 18-1. (a) It's probably useful to set up a general schedule for a particular quarter or semester and then, at the beginning of each week, plan the specific assignments you intend to work on during each study session. Put your plans in writing. (b) Find one or two places to study with minimal distractions: little noise, few interruptions. (c) Reward yourself shortly after you finish a particular amount of studying; snacking, watching TV, or calling a friend are suggested. **Suggestion:** You are studying now. Is this a good time for you? If it is, why not *write out your weekly schedule now.* Include schedule preparation as part of your study time.

19. Describe the SQ3R method and explain what makes it effective.

19-1. Below are descriptions of an individual applying the five steps of the SQ3R method to Chapter 1 of your text. The steps are not in the correct order. Label each of the steps and place a number in the parentheses which indicates the correct order.

( ) _____ Vanessa looks at the title of the first subsection of the chapter. After wondering briefly what it means for psychology to have "parents," she formulates this question: How was the field of psychology influenced by philosophy and physiology?

( ) _____ Vanessa turns to the back of Chapter 1 and notes that there is a chapter review. She turns back to the first page of the chapter, sees that the outline on that page matches the review at the end, and browses through some of the other parts of the chapter. She has a rough idea that the chapter is going to define the field and discuss its history.

( ) _____ Keeping in mind the question she has posed, Vanessa reads the section about the meeting of psychology's "parents" and formulates a tentative answer to her question. (She also formulates some additional questions: "Who was Descartes?" and "What method did philosophers use?")

( ) _____ Vanessa answers her first question as follows: "Philosophy (one of the parents) posed questions about the mind that made the study of human thinking and actions acceptable; physiology (the other parent) contributed the scientific method." She decides to note down her answer for later review.

( ) _____ When she has finished step 4 for all sections, Vanessa looks over the entire chapter, section by section. She repeats the questions for each section and attempts to answer each one.

19-2. What makes the SQ3R technique so effective?

Answers: 19-1. (2) Question (1) Survey (3) Read (4) Recite (5) Review **19-2.** It breaks the reading assignment into manageable segments; it requires understanding before you move on.

20. Summarize advice provided on how to get more out of lectures.

20-1. Using a few words for each point, summarize the four points on getting more out of lectures.

Answers: 20-1. Listen actively; focus full attention on the speaker and try to anticipate what's coming. For complex material, read ahead. Take notes in your own words and attend to clues about what is most important. Consider asking questions during lectures (to keep involved and to clarify points presented).

21. Summarize advice provided on improving test-taking strategies.

21-1. Is it better to change answers on multiple-choice tests or to go with one's first hunch?

21-2. Following are situations you might encounter while taking a test. Reread the section on general test-taking tips and then indicate what you would do in each situation.

(a) You run into a particularly difficult item:

(b) The answer seems to be simple, but you think you may be missing something:

(c) The test is a timed test:

(d) You have some time left at the end of the test:

21-3. Following are samples of the situations mentioned under the discussion of tips for multiple-choice and essay exam questions. Based on the suggestions, what would you do?

(a) In a multiple-choice test, item c seems to be correct, but you have not yet read items d and e: What would you do next?

(b) You know that items a and b are correct, are unsure of items c and d, and item e is an "all of the above" option. Which alternative (a, b, c, d, or e) would you choose?

(c) You have no idea which multiple-choice alternative is correct. You note that option a has the word "always" in it, items b and c use the word "never," and item d says "frequently."

(d) You have read the stem of a multiple-choice item but you have not yet looked at the options.

(e) Faced with an essay, you wonder whether to simply begin writing and let the ideas flow or to spend a few minutes in organization.

Answers: 21-1. In general, changing answers seems to be better. Available research indicates that people are more than twice as likely to go from a wrong answer to a right one as from a right answer to a wrong one. **21-2.** (a) Skip it and come back to it it if time permits. (b) Maybe the answer is simple! Don't make the question more complex than it was intended to be. (c) Budget your time, checking the proportion of the test completed against the time available. (d) Review, reconsider, check over your answers. **21-3.** (a) Read all options. (b) Answer *e*. (c) Answer *d*. (Still good advice and generally the best procedure to follow. But note that some professors, aware of the strategy, may throw in an item in which "always" is part of a correct answer! It's sort of like radar detectors: someone builds a better detector and someone else tries to build radar that can't be detected.) (d) Try to anticipate the correct answer *before* reading the options. (e) Spend a few minutes looking over the questions and allocating time, planning, organizing, and possibly even outlining. Many examiners will appreciate your use of headings or numbers to identify points made.

22. Explain the nature of critical thinking skills and why they need to be taught.

22-1. The previous section on test-taking strategies asked whether or not it is better to change answers or go with one's first hunch. Actually, that is a critical thinking question. While our hunches are often pretty good, sometimes they don't lead to the desired outcome. When we use critical thinking we use the same principles that we would use in a _____ investigation, apply the formal and informal rules of _____, and analyze events in terms of likelihood or _____.

22-2. Critical thinking is not something that we come by naturally, and it (<u>is/is not</u>) a normal part of instruction in most subject areas. So, for people to develop the skill of critical thinking, it has to be deliberately and consciously _____.

Answers: 22-1. scientific, logic, probability **22-2.** is not, taught.

23. Discuss some weaknesses in evolutionary explanations for gender differences in spatial abilities.

23-1. Some evidence suggests that males tend to have better visual-spatial perception than females and that females have better memories for locations. The reason for these gender differences, according to evolutionary psychologists, is that in our evolutionary past natural selection favored a division of labor in which men were _____ and women were _____. Hunting (aiming a projectile, traveling long distances) required _____ perception, while gathering required _____ for locations of food.

23-2. As previously discussed, evolutionary psychology is a major new theoretical perspective in psychology. While the interpretation of the evolutionary psychologists is certainly plausible, critical thinking urges us to consider the following questions when assessing a truth claim: Are there _____ explanations for these results? And, are there data that _____ the evidence provided?

23-3. It turns out that the answer to both of these questions is a qualified "yes." For example, it may be the case that male children are encouraged to engage in sex-typed activities, such as playing with blocks, that provide more experience with visual-spatial tasks. The possibility of such gender-based differences in experience provides an _____ interpretation to one based on evolutionary principles. Some scholars have also suggested that women in these early societies often did, in fact, travel long distances to gather food and were also involved in hunting. While far from established, this type of evidence _____ data collected by evolutionary psychologists.

Answers: 23-1. hunters, gatherers, visual-spatial, memory **23-2.** alternative, contradict **23-3.** alternative, contradicts (challenges, disputes).

REVIEW OF KEY TERMS

Applied psychology
Behavior
Behaviorism
Clinical psychology
Cognition
Critical thinking
Culture
Empiricism

Ethnocentrism
Evolutionary psychology
Functionalism
Humanism
Introspection
Natural selection
Phi phenomenon
Psychiatry

Psychoanalytic theory
Psychology
SQ3R
Stimulus
Structuralism
Testwiseness
Theory
Unconscious

_____   **1.** Any detectable input from the environment.

_____   **2.** The branch of psychology concerned with practical problems.

_____   **3.** School of thought based on notion that the task of psychology is to analyze consciousness into its basic elements.

_____   **4.** Observation of one's own conscious experience.

_____   **5.** School of thought asserting that psychology's major purpose was to investigate the function or purpose of consciousness.

_____   **6.** The theoretical orientation asserting that scientific psychology should study only observable behavior.

_____   **7.** An observable activity or response by an organism.

_____   **8.** Examines behavioral processes in terms of their adaptive or survival value for a species.

_____   **9.** The use of cognitive skills and strategies to increase the probability of a desirable outcome.

_____   **10.** The illusion of movement created by presenting visual stimuli in rapid succession.

_____   **11.** Freudian theory that explains personality and abnormal behavior in terms of unconscious processes.

_____   **12.** According to psychoanalytic theory, that portion of the mind containing thoughts, memories, and wishes not in awareness but nonetheless exerting a strong effect on human behavior.

_____   **13.** The psychological theory asserting that human beings are unique and fundamentally different from other animals.

_____   **14.** The tendency to view one's own group as superior to other groups.

_____   **15.** Widely shared customs, beliefs, values, norms, and institutions that are transmitted socially across generations.

_____   **16.** The branch of psychology concerned with the diagnosis and treatment of psychological disorders.

_____   **17.** Mental processes or thinking.

_____   **18.** The science that studies behavior and the physiological and cognitive processes that underlie it, and it is the profession that applies this knowledge to solving various practical problems.

_____   **19.** The branch of medicine concerned with the diagnosis and treatment of psychological problems and disorders.

_____   **20.** The point of view that knowledge should be based on observation.

_____   **21.** A system of ideas used to link together or explain a set of observations.

_____ **22.** A five-step procedure designed to improve study skills.

_____ **23.** Ability to use the characteristics and formats of a test to maximize one's score.

_____ **24.** The Darwinian principle that characteristics that have a survival advantage for a species are more likely to be passed on to subsequent generations.

Answers: 1. stimulus **2.** applied psychology **3.** structuralism **4.** introspection **5.** functionalism **6.** behaviorism **7.** behavior **8.** evolutionary psychology **9.** critical thinking **10.** phi phenomenon **10.** psychoanalytic theory **12.** unconscious **13.** humanism **14.** ethnocentrism **15.** culture **16.** clinical psychology **17.** cognition **18.** psychology **19.** psychiatry **20.** empiricism **21.** theory **22.** SQ3R **23.** testwiseness **24.** natural selection.

REVIEW OF KEY PEOPLE

Sigmund Freud   Carl Rogers   John B. Watson
G. Stanley Hall   B. F. Skinner   Wilhelm Wundt
William James

_____ **1.** Founded experimental psychology and the first experimental psychology laboratory.

_____ **2.** Established the first American research laboratory, launched America's first psychological journal, was first president of the APA.

_____ **3.** Chief architect of functionalism; described a "stream of consciousness."

_____ **4.** Founded behaviorism.

_____ **5.** Devised the theory and technique known as psychoanalysis.

_____ **6.** Identified operant conditioning.

_____ **7.** A major proponent of "humanistic" psychology.

Answers: 1. Wundt **2.** Hall **3.** James **4.** Watson **5.** Freud **6.** Skinner **7.** Rogers.

SELF-QUIZ

1. Structuralism is the historical school of psychology that asserted that the purpose of psychology was to:
   a. study behavior
   b. discover the smaller elements that comprise consciousness
   c. explore the unconscious
   d. examine the purposes of conscious processes

2. Of the two parents of psychology, physiology and philosophy, which provided the method? What is the method?
   a. philosophy; logic, reasoning
   b. philosophy; intuition, introspection
   c. physiology; observation, science
   d. physiology; anatomy, surgery

3. Who is Wilhelm Wundt?
   a. He founded the first experimental laboratory.
   b. He founded the American Psychological Association.
   c. He discovered the classically conditioned salivary reflex.
   d. He founded behaviorism.

4. For John B. Watson, the appropriate subject matter of psychology was:
   a. animal behavior
   b. the unconscious
   c. consciousness
   d. human physiology

5. Which of the following represents a major breakthrough in the development of applied psychology?
   a. the use of the method of introspection
   b. Binet's development of the intelligence test
   c. establishment of the first animal laboratory
   d. Wundt's founding of experimental psychology

6. Within the field of psychology, Freud's ideas encountered resistance because he emphasized:
   a. human consciousness
   b. human behavior
   c. introspection
   d. the unconscious

7. Which of the following would be considered the major principle of operant conditioning?
   a. Human behavior derives in part from free will; animal behavior is determined by the environment.
   b. Humans and other animals tend to repeat responses followed by positive outcomes.
   c. The majority of human behavior is based on thoughts, feelings, and wishes of which we are unaware.
   d. Human beings are fundamentally different from other animals.

8. Which of the following theorists would tend to emphasize explanations in terms of freedom and potential for personal growth?
   a. Carl Rogers
   b. Sigmund Freud
   c. B. F. Skinner
   d. all of the above

9. Recent research trends in psychology involve two areas largely ignored by early behaviorists. These two areas are:
   a. observable and measurable responses
   b. cognition (thinking) and physiological processes
   c. classical and operant conditioning
   d. the effect of environmental events and the behavior of lower animals

10. Which core psychological research area is primarily devoted to the study of such topics as memory, problem solving, and thinking?
    a. physiological
    b. social
    c. cognitive
    d. personality

11. Critical thinking refers to:
    a. analysis of problems in terms of scientific principles
    b. making decisions based on formal and informal logic
    c. thinking that includes consideration of probabilities
    d. all of the above

12. The assertion that "psychology is empirical" means that psychology is based on:
    a. introspection
    b. logic
    c. observation
    d. mathematics

13. In looking for the causes of a particular behavior, psychologists assume:
   a. one cause or factor
   b. multifactorial causation
   c. free will
   d. infinite causation

14. Contemporary psychologists generally assume that human behavior is determined by:
   a. heredity
   b. environment
   c. heredity and environment acting jointly
   d. heredity, environment, and free will

15. What does SQ3R stand for?
   a. search, question, research, recommend, reconstitute
   b. silence, quietude, reading, writing, arithmetic
   c. summarize, quickly, read, research, reread
   d. survey, question, read, recite, review

Answers: 1. b **2.** c **3.** a **4.** a **5.** b **6.** d **7.** b **8.** a **9.** b **10.** c **11.** d **12.** c **13.** b **14.** c **15.** d.

Chapter Two

The Research Enterprise in Psychology

REVIEW OF KEY IDEAS

LOOKING FOR LAWS: THE SCIENTIFIC APPROACH TO BEHAVIOR

1. **Explain science's main assumption and describe the goals of the scientific enterprise in psychology.**

   1-1. A major assumption of science is that events occur in a(an) _____ manner.

   1-2. The three interrelated goals of psychology and the other sciences are: (a) measurement and description, (b) understanding and prediction, and (c) application and control. Match each of the following descriptions with the goal it represents by placing the appropriate letters in the blanks. (There is considerable overlap among these goals; pick the closest match.)

   _____ Muscle relaxation techniques are found to be useful in reducing anxiety and improving concentration and memory.

   _____ A psychologist develops a test or procedure that measures anxiety.

   _____ Researchers find that participants in an experiment conform more to the judgments of someone similar to themselves than to someone who is dissimilar.

   Answers: **1-1.** lawful (predictable, consistent, regular, orderly) **1-2.** c, a, b.

2. **Explain the relations between theory, hypotheses, and research.**

   2-1. What's a theory? Your text defines a theory as a system of ideas that is used to explain a set of observations. So, a theory is a *system*, which means that it integrates (or organizes or classifies) a series of observations; and it helps _____ those observations. And, it does one thing more: it suggests ideas, or predictions, or _____, to be tested in research.

2-2. Researchers can't test a theory all at once, but they can test one or two hypotheses derived from the theory. This is the relationship between theory, hypothesis, and research: theories suggest _____ (questions or predictions), which are then tested in _____. If the hypotheses are supported, confidence in the concepts of the _____ is strengthened.

Answers: **2-1.** explain, hypotheses (questions) **2-2.** hypotheses, research, theory.

3. Outline the steps in a scientific investigation.

3-1. Following are the five steps generally used in performing a scientific investigation. Fill in the missing key words.

a. Formulate a testable _____.

b. Select the research _____ and design the study.

c. _____ the data.

d. _____ the data and draw conclusions.

e. _____ the findings.

3-2. Following are descriptions of various phases in the study by Cole and his co-workers (Cole et al., 1996). Indicate which step of this study is being described by placing a letter from the previous question (1, 2, 3, 4, or 5) in the appropriate blank.

_____ The authors prepared a report of their findings that was accepted for publication in a technical journal.

_____ The patients' responses were expressed as numbers and analyzed with statistics. The data indicated that higher scores on closetedness were associated with higher incidences of physical illness.

_____ Cole and his co-workers thought that concealment of homosexual identify might be associated with increased illness. Before they began they made precise operational definitions of both concealment (closetedness) and illness.

_____ The researchers decided to use a survey procedure involving administering questionnaires to a large number of people.

_____ The researchers gathered questionnaire and medical data from gay men over a period of several years.

Answers: **3-1.** (a) hypothesis (b) method (c) collect (d) analyze (e) report (publish, write up) **3-2.** e, d, a, b, c.

4. Discuss the advantages of the scientific approach.

4-1. We all tend to agree with the idea that "haste makes waste." We are also likely to agree with a commonsense saying that has the opposite implication: "a stitch in time saves nine." What are the two major advantages of the scientific approach over the commonsense approach?

LOOKING FOR CAUSES: EXPERIMENTAL RESEARCH

5. **Describe the experimental method, explaining independent and dependent variables, experimental and control groups, and extraneous variables.**

   5-1.   Schachter proposed that affiliation is caused (in part) by level of anxiety. What was his independent variable? _____ Dependent variable? _____

   5-2.   The variable that is manipulated or varied by the experimenter is termed the _____ variable. The variable that is affected by, or is dependent on, the manipulation is termed the _____ variable.

   5-3.   What is the name of the variable that *results from* the manipulation? _____ What is the name of the variable that *produces* the effect? _____

   5-4.   The group of subjects that receives the experimental treatment is known as the _____ group; the group that does not is known as the _____ group.

   5-5.   Control and experimental groups are quite similar in most respects. They differ in that the experimental group receives the experimental _____ and the control group does not. Thus, any differences found in the measure of the _____ variable are assumed to be due to differences in manipulation of the _____ variable.

   5-6.   In Schachter's study, the experimental group was given instructions that produced a high level of _____. Results were that the experimental group, the high anxiety group, had a greater tendency to _____ with others than did the control group.

   5-7.   An extraneous variable is any variable other than the _____ variable that seems likely to cause a difference between groups as measured by the _____ variable.

   5-8.   To review the parts of an experiment: Suppose a researcher is interested in the effect of a drug on the running speed of rats. The _____ group is injected with the drug and the _____ group is not. Whether or not the rats received the drug would be the _____ variable, and running speed would be the _____ variable.

   5-9.   Suppose also that the average age of the experimental rats is two years while the average age of the control rats is 3 months. What is the extraneous variable in this experiment? _____ Why does this variable present a problem?

   5-10. Researchers generally control for extraneous variables through random _____ of subjects to groups. Write a definition of this procedure:

6. **Describe the Featured Study on the efficacy of subliminal self-help audiotapes.**

    6-1. The purpose of the study was to examine whether or not commercially sold tape recordings presented at a _____ level, below the threshold of hearing, would enhance either self-esteem or memory.

    6-2. Several manufacturers claim that subliminal audiotapes will help people lose weight, stop smoking, sleep better, and so on. The tapes used in the present study were supposed either to augment listeners' memory or else to improve their _____.

    6-3. Participants were 237 university students and community members who listened either to a memory tape or to a self-esteem tape. The experimenters labeled the tapes randomly, however, so that roughly half of the *self-esteem* tapes were mislabeled as _____ tapes. Similarly, half of the memory tapes were mislabeled as self-esteem tapes.

    6-4. Thus, the study manipulated two _____ variables. One was the actual purpose of the tape as described by the manufacturer, which was to enhance either _____ or _____ . The second was the labeling of the tapes. Half of the tapes were labeled accurately (i.e., memory tapes were labeled as memory tapes) and half were labeled _____.

    6-5. The major _____ variable was any <u>improvement</u> in memory and self-esteem that may have occurred. A second dependent variable was subjects' _____ about whether or not they had improved.

    6-6. Results were as follows: there were (<u>strong/negligible</u>) differences between the means of the group that had listened to the correctly labeled memory tapes and the group that had listened to the mislabeled memory tapes. And, there were (<u>strong/negligible</u>) differences between the those who had listened to the correctly labeled self-esteem tapes and those who had listened to the mislabeled self-esteem tapes.

    6-7. With regard to the second dependent variable, approximately _____ of the subjects believed that the tapes had improved their memories or self-esteem. Thus, although many subjects thought that the tapes had helped them, in fact the tapes had produced no differences.

7. **Explain the major advantages and disadvantages of the experimental method.**

    7-1. What is the major advantage of the experimental method?

    7-2. What are the two major disadvantages of the experimental method?

7-3.   Suppose a researcher is interested in the effect of drinking large amounts of alcohol on health (e.g., 15 glasses of wine per day over an extended period of time). What would be a major *disadvantage* of using the experimental method to examine this particular question?

Answers: **7-1.** The major advantage is that it permits researchers to make cause-effect conclusions. **7-2.** The major disadvantages are that (a) precise experimental control may make the situation so artificial that it does not apply to the real world, and (b) ethical or practical considerations may prevent one from manipulating independent variables of interest. **7-3.** To the extent that excessive coffee drinking is a suspected factor in health problems, it would be unethical and perhaps impossible to require an experimental group to drink that much per day.

LOOKING FOR LINKS: DESCRIPTIVE RESEARCH

8. **Discuss three descriptive/correlational methods: naturalistic observation, case studies, and surveys.**

   8-1.   Naturalistic observation involves study of human beings or animals in their natural environments conducted (<u>with/without</u>) direct intervention from the observer.

   8-2.   A case study is an in-depth and generally highly subjective or impressionistic report on (<u>a group of people/a single individual</u>) that may be based on interviews, psychological testing, and so on.

   8-3.   The third descriptive procedure is the survey technique. Surveys use _____ to find out about specific aspects of human attitudes or opinions.

   8-4.   List the three descriptive/correlational methods in the space below.

   Answers: **8-1.** without **8-2.** a single individual **8-3.** questionnaires (or interviews) **8-4.** naturalistic observation, case studies, surveys.

9. **Explain the major advantages and disadvantages of descriptive/correlational research.**

   9-1.   The major difference between the experimental method and descriptive research is that with descriptive/correlational research the experimenter cannot _____ variables. For this reason, the descriptive methods do not permit one to demonstrate _____ relationships between variables.

   9-2.   For example, suppose you have data indicating that people who happen to drink a lot of coffee tend to have cardiovascular problems. Is this experimental or descriptive/correlational research? _____ Would it be correct to conclude (from these data) that coffee drinking causes cardiovascular problems? _____

   9-3.   An advantage of the descriptive/correlational methods is that they allow researchers to study phenomena that they could not study with experimental methods. Thus, the descriptive/correlational methods (<u>narrow/broaden</u>) the scope of phenomena studied. A major disadvantage of these techniques is that one generally cannot make _____ conclusions from the resulting data.

LOOKING FOR CONCLUSIONS: STATISTICS AND RESEARCH

10. Describe three measures of central tendency and one measure of variability.

10-1. To review the meaning of the three measures of central tendency, determine the mean, median, and mode of the following scores: 3, 5, 5, 5, 6, 6, 7, 9, 80.

Mean: _____

Median: _____

Mode: _____

10-2. One can describe a group of data with a single number by using one of the measures of central tendency. In the blanks below indicate which measure of central tendency is being described.

_____ The score that occurs most frequently.

_____ The sum of all scores divided by the total number of scores.

_____ Half the scores fall above this measure and half below.

_____ Very sensitive to extreme scores.

_____ Usually the most useful because it may be used in further statistical manipulations.

_____ The middle score.

10-3. What is the median of data set A, below? _____ of set B? _____ Which of these sets is more variable, A or B? _____

A. 30, 40, 50, 60, 70   B. 10, 30, 50, 70, 90

10-4. What is the name of the statistic used as a measure of variability? _____

_____.

11. Distinguish between positive and negative correlations.

11-1. Some examples help illustrate the difference between positive and negative correlations. Which of the following relationships are positive (direct) and which are negative (inverse)? (Indicate with a + or − sign.)

_____ The better students' grades are in high school, the better their grades tend to be in college.

_____ The more alcohol one has drunk, the slower his or her reaction time.

_____ The higher the anxiety, the poorer the test performance.

_____ The greater the fear, the greater the need for affiliation.

11-2. Which of the following indicates the *strongest correlational relationship*?

    a. 1.12

    b. −.92

    c. .58

    d. .87

Answers: 11-1. +, −, −, + **11-2.** b (not *a*, because correlations cannot exceed +1.00 or −1.00).

12. Discuss correlation in relation to prediction and causation.

12-1. Suppose you have data indicating that the more money people make (i.e., the higher their annual incomes), the less depressed they report being on a mood survey. Thus, if you know the incomes of people in that group you should be able to _____, with some degree of accuracy, their self-reported depressed mood.

12-2. The accuracy of your prediction will depend on the size of the correlation coefficient. Which of the following correlation coefficients would allow you to predict with the greatest accuracy?

    a. +.41

    b. +.54

    c. −.65

12-3. What kind of conclusion is justified on the basis of the previous relationship, a conclusion involving prediction or one involving a statement about causation? _____

12-4. Consider the relationship described in an earlier question: You discover that the more money people make, the greater their happiness. Which of the following conclusions is justified? Explain why.

    a. Money makes people happy.

    b. Happiness causes people to earn more money.

    c. Both happiness and money result from some unknown third factor.

    d. none of the above

12-5. Again consider the relationship between money and happiness. Assume that money does not cause happiness and happiness does not cause money. What possible *third factor* can you think of that could cause both? (I'm asking you to make a wild speculation here just to get the idea of how third variables may operate.)

12-6. We aren't justified in making causal conclusions from a correlation, but we can predict. Let's examine what prediction means in the case of our hypothetical example. If the relationship really exists, what prediction would you make about people who are rich? What prediction would you make concerning people who are unhappy?

Answers: 12-1. predict 12-2. c 12-3. prediction (Generally, one can't make causal conclusions from a correlation.) 12-4. d. Any of the statements is a possible *causal* explanation of the relationship, but we don't know which one(s) may be correct because the data are correlational. Therefore, *no causal conclusions* are justified. 12-5. For example, poor health might cause one to be both unhappy *and* poverty stricken (while good health would cause one to be both happy and wealthy). Intelligence or aggressiveness or stubbornness or a number of other physiological or behavioral factors could be causally related *both* to income and to happiness without those two factors being causes of one another. 12-6. You would predict that a group that was rich would also be happy and that a group that was unhappy would be poor. No causation is implied in these statements.

13. **Explain the logic of hypothesis testing and the meaning of statistical significance.**

   13-1.   In the hypothetical experiment described in your text there are two groups, largely equivalent except that the _____ group receives the computerized tutoring sessions and the _____ group does not. What is the hypothesis of this experiment?

   13-2.   Researchers statistically evaluate the hypothesis by comparing means and determining the likelihood or probability that a difference between means of the size obtained (or larger) would occur by _____. If the probability that such a difference would occur by chance is very low, say less than 5 times in 100, the researchers would conclude that the difference (is/is not) due to chance. They would declare the difference statistically _____ at the _____ level of significance.

   13-3.   Statistically significant does not mean important or significant in the usual sense of that word. What does statistically significant mean?

   13-4.   How do we reach a conclusion when the results of different studies often produce contradictory results? One method for doing so is the relatively new technique known as _____. What is meta-analysis?

Answers: 13-1. experimental, control. The hypothesis is that special tutoring would increase reading scores. 13-2. chance, is not, significant, .05 13-3. It means that a difference that large would be rare on a chance basis, so it is assumed *not* to be due to chance; or, more simply, it is assumed that the difference between means is due to treatment. 13-4. Meta-analysis is a statistical technique for combining results from many different studies.

LOOKING FOR FLAWS: EVALUATING RESEARCH

14. **Explain what makes a sample representative and discuss the problem of sampling bias.**

   14-1.   Sampling bias exists when the sample is not representative of the _____ from which it was drawn.

   14-2.   Suppose that Professor Brutalbaum distributes a questionnaire in an attempt to find out how the students react to his teaching. The day that he chooses for the evaluation is the day before a scheduled vacation, and about half the students are absent. He is aware that he does not have to test the entire class, that he may use a representative sample. The question is: is the sample that attended class that day a representative sample of the class? _____ Why or why not?

Answers: 14-1. population **14-2.** No. A representative sample is one that is similar in composition to the population from which it is drawn. In this case, it seems likely that students who attend are different from those who do not (e.g., perhaps more enthusiastic, harder working, more fearful, etc.). Since the sample is not representative, the flaw illustrated is *sampling bias*.

15. Explain when placebo effects are likely to be a problem.

15-1. A student in Brutalbaum's class orders some audio tapes that promise to produce sleep learning. (Brutalbaum is dubious, because from his observations students sleep a lot in class but still don't seem to learn very much. Nonetheless . . .)

The student runs the experiment in Brutalbaum's class. She describes the anticipated sleep-learning benefits to the class and then gives the sleep tapes to a random half of the students and nothing to the other half. After the next test she analyzes the results. The mean test score of the experimental group is statistically significantly higher than that of the control group. What is the flaw in this experiment?

(a) sampling bias

(b) possible placebo effects

(c) distortions in self-report

(d) none of the above

15-2. What are placebo effects?

15-3. How would you change the study described above to reduce or eliminate the possibility of placebo effects?

Answers: 15-1. b **15-2.** Placebo effects: the tendency for people's behavior to change because of their expectation that the treatment will have an effect **15-3.** Include a placebo treatment. For example, the experimenter might have given the control group a placebo tape that was the same as the sleep tape in every respect except for the supposedly critical information.

16. Describe the typical kinds of distortions that occur in self-report data.

16-1. Brutalbaum is now concerned about class attendance and decides to find out what proportion of students miss class regularly. He distributes a questionnaire asking students to indicate how many classes they have missed. Which of the four common flaws is he likely to encounter? _____

16-2. For a number of reasons, people may not answer questions correctly, including the fact that they may not understand the question or may not remember accurately. Respondents also frequently want to create a favorable impression, the response tendency known as the social _____ bias. People may also be predisposed to respond in particular ways regardless of the question, for example, to agree or disagree regardless of content. This type of response tendency is known as a response _____.

Answers: **16-1.** distortions in self-report **16-2.** desirability, set.

17. Describe Rosenthal's research on experimenter bias.

17-1.   When we ask a question, we frequently expect a particular answer. When scientists form a hypothesis, they also may expect a particular answer, and in some cases the scientist's hypotheses or expectations may influence the answers that they obtain. When a researcher's expectations about the outcome of a study influence the results, then the flaw in procedure known as _____ has occurred.

17-2.   Experimenter bias or influence may occur in subtle ways. Rosenthal has repeatedly demonstrated that when the experimenter merely knows which treatment condition a subject is in, the fact of that knowledge or expectation alone may influence the subject's behavior. For this reason it is extremely important in research to maintain the _____ procedure, in which neither subjects nor experimenters know which treatment condition the subject is in.

Answers: **17-1.** experimenter bias **17-2.** double-blind

LOOKING AT ETHICS: DO THE ENDS JUSTIFY THE MEANS?

18. Discuss the pros and cons of deception in research with human subjects.

18-1.   In the space below present one or two of the arguments in favor of using deception and one or two arguments against.

Answers: **18-1.** On the con side, deception is, after all, lying; it may undermine people's trust in others; it may cause distress. On the pro side, many research issues could not be investigated without deception; the "white lies" involved are generally harmless; research indicates that deception studies are not actually harmful to subjects; the advances in knowledge obtained may improve human well-being.

19. Discuss the controversy about the use of animals as research subjects.

19-1.   What is the major reason that some people object to using animal subjects in research? In view of this objection, what moral considerations are raised by those who favor using animals in research?

Answers: **19-1.** Many people believe that it is morally wrong to use animals in research, especially in painful or harmful treatments that would be unacceptable for human subjects. In defense of the practice, others cite the significant advances in treatment of a variety of mental and physical disorders that have resulted from animal research. The question to some degree involves the issue of whether or not saving human lives or finding remedies for human illnesses justifies the sacrifice of or pain inflicted on research animals.

PUTTING IT IN PERSPECTIVE

20. **Explain how this chapter highlighted two of the text's unifying themes.**

    20-1. One of the text's unifying themes is that psychology is _____ , which means that its conclusions are based on systematic _____ and that it tends to be (<u>skeptical/credulous</u>).

    20-2. In what way did the discussion of methodology suggest that psychology tends to be skeptical of its results?

    20-3. Which two methodological problems discussed point up psychology's awareness of the subjective nature of our experience?

Answers: 20-1. empirical, observation (experience, research), skeptical **20-2.** The field pays attention only to results considered highly unlikely to have occurred by chance; it constantly searches for methodological flaws; it subjects results to critical scrutiny by other scientists. **20-3.** Scientists try to guard against subjective reactions, their own as well as those of the participants, by building controls into their experiments. Particularly important is the double-blind procedure for minimizing *placebo effects* and *experimenter bias*.

APPLICATION: FINDING AND READING JOURNAL ARTICLES

21. **Describe the nature of technical journals.**

    21-1. A journal publishes technical material in a field, generally the results of research or other scholarly activity. Since journal articles are written primarily for (<u>the layman/other professionals</u>), they frequently contain technical language that makes it difficult for people outside the field to understand.

    21-2. Journals represent the core intellectual activity of a field and are generally highly (<u>inclusive/selective</u>) about what they publish. Some of the more prestigious journals reject more than 90% of the manuscripts submitted.

    21-3. In psychology, most journal articles are reports of research or other empirical studies. Some journals also publish articles that summarize findings from a large number of studies; these articles are known as _____ articles. Some review articles employ the statistical technique of _____, a procedure that combines the results of many different studies.

Answers: 21-1. other professionals **21-2.** selective **21-3.** review, meta-analysis.

22. **Explain how to use *Psychological Abstracts* and discuss the advantages of computerized literature searches.**

    22-1. *Psychological Abstracts* contains abstracts or concise _____ of articles published in psychological journals. To find information about a particular article, consult either the author index or the _____ index found at the back of each monthly issue of the *Abstracts*. Cumulative _____ are published annually.

22-2. If you know the author's name you can easily find the article. Next to the author's name, each article he or she has published within the period is identified by a particular number, its _____ number.

22-3. Once you know the index number you can find the abstract. As you can see in Figure 2.20 in your text, the abstract provides not only a summary but the exact reference for the article, including publication date, page numbers, and name of the _____ in which the article was published.

22-4. The subject index works the same way as the author index, but it's a little more like looking through the yellow pages of a phone book (e.g., do you look under cars, automobiles, or rental?). As with the author index, you can locate the abstract once you find the index _____ of a particular article. A quick glance at the abstract will then tell you whether the article is likely to be of interest.

22-5. The availability of personal computers has made the search easier. The information contained in *Psychological Abstracts* from 1887 on is now stored in the _____ databases PsycINFO and PsychLIT.

22-6. The advantages of computerized over manual searches include:

a. speed or power

b. decreased likelihood of missing relevant articles

c. the option of pairing topics in a search

d. all of the above

Answers: **22-1.** summaries, subject, indexes **22-2.** index **22-3.** journal **22-4.** number **22-5.** computerized **22-6.** d.

23. **Describe the standard organization of journal articles reporting on empirical research.**

23-1. In the blanks below list the six parts of the standard journal article in the order in which they occur. (The initial letters of each section are listed on the left.)

A _____

I _____

M _____

R _____

D _____

R _____

23-2. In the blanks below match the name of the sections of the standard journal article with the descriptions.

_____ States the hypothesis and reviews the literature relevant to the hypothesis.

_____ A list of all the sources referred to in the paper.

_____ A summary.

_____ Presents the data; may include statistical analyses, graphs, and tables.

_____ Describes what the researchers did in the study; includes participants, procedures, and data collection techniques.

_____ Interprets or evaluates the data and presents conclusions.

Answers: 23-1. abstract, introduction, method, results, discussion, references **23-2.** introduction, references, abstract, results, method, discussion.

24. Explain why anecdotal evidence is flawed and unreliable.

24-1. Anecdotal evidence consists of personal stories that support a particular point of view. Anecdotes are frequently persuasive because they are concrete and vivid and, therefore, easy to _____.

24-2. What's wrong with anecdotal evidence? First, one cannot generalize from a single case. Although a political candidate's story about a coal minor named Bob (or a physician named Alice, etc.) may be memorable, Bob's experiences cannot be _____ to other people or situations.

24-3. Second, people tend to represent themselves in the most favorable light. To the extent that Bob is the source of the anecdote, the information he supplies may reflect the social _____ bias.

24-4. In addition, stories change with the telling, so that later versions may bear little resemblance to the original event. Stories one has heard second- or third-hand, so-called _____ evidence, are likely to be particularly unreliable.

24-5. Nor is it likely that Bob, or the story about Bob, was picked randomly. The candidate selects an anecdote to make a particular point, a process similar to _____ bias in a research setting. The clear alternative to anecdotal evidence is to solve problems based on data, the so-called _____-based decision-making process.

Answers: 24-1. remember **24-2.** generalized **24-3.** desirability **24-4.** heard **24-5.** sampling, evidence.

REVIEW OF KEY TERMS

Anecdotal evidence
Case study
Confounding of variables
Control group
Correlation
Correlation coefficient
Data collection techniques
Dependent variable
Descriptive statistics
Double-blind procedure
Experiment
Experimental group
Experimenter bias
Extraneous variables

Hypothesis
Independent variable
Inferential statistics
Journal
Mean
Median
Meta-analysis
Mode
Naturalistic observation
Operational definition
Participants
Placebo effects
Population
Random assignment

Replication
Research methods
Response set
Sample
Sampling bias
Social desirability bias
Statistical significance
Statistics
Subjects
Survey
Theory
Variability
Variables

_____ 1. Any of the factors in an experiment that are controlled or observed by an experimenter or that in some other way affect the outcome.

_____ 2. A tentative statement about the expected relationship between two or more variables.

_____ 3. Precisely defines each variable in a study in terms of the operations needed to produce or measure that variable.

_____ 4. Persons or animals whose behavior is being studied; means the same thing as *participants*.

_____ 5. Differing ways of conducting research, which include experiments, case studies, surveys, and naturalistic observation.

_____ 6. A research method in which independent variables are manipulated and which permits causal interpretations.

_____ 7. A condition or event that an experimenter varies in order to observe its impact.

_____ 8. The variable that results from the manipulation in an experiment.

_____ 9. The group in an experiment that receives a treatment as part of the independent variable manipulation.

_____ 10. The group in an experiment that does not receive the treatment.

_____ 11. Any variables other than the independent variables that seem likely to influence the dependent measure in an experiment.

_____ 12. Distribution of subjects in an experiment in which each subject has an equal chance of being assigned to any group or condition.

_____ 13. A link or association between variables such that one can be predicted from the other.

_____ 14. The statistic that indicates the degree of relationship between variables.

_____ 15. A research method in which the researcher observes behavior in the natural environment without directly intervening.

_____ 16. An in-depth, generally subjective, investigation of an individual subject.

_____ 17. A questionnaire or interview used to gather information about specific aspects of subjects' behavior.

_____ 18. Procedures for making empirical observations, including questionnaires, interviews, psychological tests, and physiological recordings.

_____ 19. Mathematical techniques that help in organizing, summarizing, and interpreting numerical data.

_____ 20. Statistics helpful in organizing and summarizing (but not interpreting) data.

_____ 21. Statistical procedures used to interpret data in an experiment and draw conclusions.

_____ 22. A statistical procedure that combines the results of many studies.

_____ 23. A descriptive statistic and measure of central tendency that always falls in the exact half-way point of a distribution of data.

_____ 24. The arithmetic average.

_____ 25. The score that occurs most frequently.

_____ 26. The spread or dispersion of data, including the extent to which scores vary from the mean.

_____ 27. A measure of variability in data.

_____ 28. A judgment inferred from statistics that the probability of the observed findings occurring by chance is very low.

	29.	A repetition of a study to determine whether the previously obtained results can be duplicated.
_____	30.	A group of subjects taken from a population.
_____	31.	A larger group from which a sample is drawn and to which the researcher wishes to generalize.
_____	32.	Exists when a sample is not representative of the population from which it was drawn.
_____	33.	Also known as subjects, the persons or animals whose behavior is systematically observed in a study.
_____	34.	Occurs when a researcher's expectations influence the results of the study.
_____	35.	Effects that occur when subjects experience a change due to their expectations (or to a "fake" treatment).
_____	36.	The tendency to respond in a particular way (e.g., agreeing) that is unrelated to the content of questions asked.
_____	37.	Occurs when an extraneous variable makes it difficult to sort out the effects of the independent variable.
_____	38.	The tendency to answer questions about oneself in a socially approved manner.
_____	39.	A research strategy in which neither the subjects nor experimenters know which condition or treatment the subjects are in.
_____	40.	A periodical that publishes technical and scholarly material within a discipline.
_____	41.	A system of interrelated ideas used to explain a set of observations.
_____	42.	Support for a particular point of view through the use of personal (and frequently vivid) stories.

Answers: 1. variables **2.** hypothesis **3.** operational definition **4.** subjects **5.** research methods **6.** experiment **7.** independent variable **8.** dependent variable **9.** experimental group **10.** control group **11.** extraneous variables **12.** random assignment **13.** correlation **14.** correlation coefficient **15.** naturalistic observation **16.** case study **17.** survey **18.** data collection techniques **19.** statistics **20.** descriptive statistics **21.** inferential statistics **22.** meta-analysis **23.** median **24.** mean **25.** mode **26.** variability **27.** standard deviation **28.** statistical significance **29.** replication **30.** sample **31.** population **32.** sampling bias **33.** participants **34.** experimenter bias **35.** placebo effects **36.** response set **37.** confounding of variables **38.** social desirability bias **39.** double-blind procedure **40.** journal **41.** theory **42.** anecdotal evidence.

REVIEW OF KEY PEOPLE

Neal Miller   Robert Rosenthal   Stanley Schachter

	1.	Studied the effect of anxiety on affiliation.
_____	2.	Studied experimenter bias, a researcher's unintended influence on the behavior of subjects.
_____	3.	Asserted that the benefits of animal research (e.g., the resulting treatments for mental and physical disorders) far outweigh the harm done.

Answers: 1. Schachter **2.** Rosenthal **3.** Miller.

1. Which of the following is a major assumption of science?
   a. Events occur in a relatively orderly or predictable manner.
   b. Cause and effect is indicated by correlational relationships.
   c. In contrast to the behavior of lower animals, human behavior is in part a function of free will.
   d. Events are largely randomly determined.

2. An experimenter tests the hypothesis that physical exercise helps people's mood (makes them happier). Subjects in the experimental group participate on Monday and Tuesday and those in the control group on Wednesday and Thursday. What is the *independent* variable?
   a. the hypothesis
   b. day of the week
   c. the exercise
   d. the mood (degree of happiness)

3. Regarding the experiment described in the previous question: What is the *dependent* variable?
   a. the hypothesis
   b. day of the week
   c. the exercise
   d. the mood (degree of happiness)

4. Regarding the experiment described above: What is an *extraneous* (confounding) variable?
   a. the hypothesis
   b. day of the week
   c. the exercise
   d. the mood (degree of happiness)

5. The major advantage of the experimental method over the correlational approach is that the experimental method:
   a. permits one to make causal conclusions
   b. allows for prediction
   c. is generally less artificial than correlational procedures
   d. permits the study of people in groups

6. In looking through some medical records you find that there is a strong relationship between depression and chronic pain: the stronger the physical pain that people report, the higher their scores on an inventory that measures depression. Which of the following conclusions are justified?
   a. Depression tends to produce chronic pain.
   b. Chronic pain tends to produce depression.
   c. Both chronic pain and depression result from some unknown third factor.
   d. none of the above

7. What is the mode of the following data? 2, 3, 3, 3, 5, 5, 7, 12
   a. 3
   b. 4
   c. 5
   d. 6

8. What is the median of the following data? 1, 3, 4, 4, 5, 6, 9,
   a. 3
   b. 4
   c. 4.57
   d. 6

9. Researchers find a negative relationship between alcohol consumption and speed of response: the more alcohol consumed, the slower the response speed. Which of the following fictitious statistics could possibly represent that correlation?
   a. –4.57
   b. –.87
   c. .91
   d. .05

10. The term *statistical significance* refers to:
    a. how important the data are for future research on the topic
    b. the conclusion that there are no reasonable alternative explanations
    c. the inference that the observed effects are unlikely to be due to chance
    d. the representativeness of the sample

11. An instructor wishes to find out whether a new teaching method is superior to his usual procedures, so he conducts an experiment. Everyone in his classes is quite excited about the prospect of learning under the new procedure, but of course he cannot administer the new teaching method to everyone. A random half of the students receive the new method and the remaining half receive the old. What is the most obvious flaw in this experiment?
    a. Subjects should have been systematically assigned to groups.
    b. The sample is not representative of the population.
    c. Placebo effects or experimenter bias are likely to affect results.
    d. Distortions in self-report will affect results.

12. What procedure helps correct for experimenter bias?
    a. extraneous or confounding variables
    b. sleep learning or hypnosis
    c. a higher standard for statistical significance
    d. use of the double-blind procedure

13. With regard to the topic of deception in research with human subjects, which of the following is true?
    a. Researchers are careful to avoid deceiving subjects.
    b. Some topics could not be investigated unless deception was used.
    c. It has been empirically demonstrated that deception causes severe distress.
    d. All psychological research must involve some deception.

14. Which of the following is among the six standard parts of a psychological journal article?
    a. conclusions
    b. bibliography
    c. data summary
    d. results

15. The Author Index in the *Psychological Abstracts* provides:
    a. names of current APA members
    b. registration and biographical information about frequent authors
    c. index numbers that locate article summaries
    d. names of authors who specialize in abstractions

Answers: 1. a **2.** c **3.** d **4.** b **5.** a **6.** d **7.** a **8.** b **9.** b **10.** c **11.** c **12.** d **13.** b **14.** d **15.** c.

Chapter Three

The Biological Basis of Behavior

COMMUNICATION IN THE NERVOUS SYSTEM

1. **Describe the main functions of the two types of nervous tissue.**

    1-1. One of the major types of nervous tissue provides very important services to the other type: such removing waste, supplying nutrients, insulating, and providing structural support. Individual members of this kind of nervous tissue are called _____.

    1-2. The other type of nervous tissue receives, integrates, and transmits information. Individual members of this type of tissue are called _____.

    1-3. Most neurons communicate with (select the correct alternative) (a) only with other neurons (b) with the sensory organs and muscles.

    Answers: **1-1.** glia **1-2.** neurons **1-3.** (a).

2. **Describe the various parts of the neuron and their functions.**

    2-1. The neuron has three basic parts, the dendrites, the cell body or soma, and the axon. The major mission of the average neuron is to receive information from one neuron and pass it on to the next neuron. The receiving part is the job of the branch-like parts called _____. They then pass the message along to the nucleus of the cell, called the cell body, or _____. From there the message is sent down the _____ to be passed along to other neurons.

    2-2. Many axons are wrapped in a fatty jacket called the _____ _____, which permits for faster transmission of information and prevents messages from getting on to the wrong track. Like the covering on an electrical cord, myelin acts as an _____ material.

2-3. When the neural message reaches the end of the axon it excites projections called terminal _____, which then release a chemical substance into the junction that separates them from other neurons. This junction between neurons is called the _____.

2-4. Identify the major parts of a neuron in the figure below. Note that the arrow indicates the direction of the flow of information.

(a) _____ (b) _____ (c) _____ (d) _____

Answers: **2-1.** dendrites, soma, axon **2-2.** myelin sheath, insulating **2-3.** buttons, synapse **2-4.** (a) dendrites, (b) cell body or soma, (c) axon, (d) terminal buttons.

3. Describe the neural impulse.

3-1. When it is at rest, the neuron is like a tiny battery in that it contains a weak (<u>negative/positive</u>) charge. When the neuron is stimulated, the cell membrane becomes more permeable. This allows positively charged _____ ions to flow into the cell, thus lessening the cell's negative charge.

3-2. The change in the charge of the cell caused by the inflow of positively charged sodium ions, called an _____ potential, travels down the _____ of the neuron. After the firing of an action potential, there is a brief period in which no further action potentials can be generated. This brief period is called the absolute _____ period.

3-3. The text likens the neuron to a gun in that it either fires or it does not fire. This property of the neuron is called the _____ law. Neurons transmit information about the strength of a stimulus by variations in the number of action potentials generated. For example, in comparison to a weak stimulus, a strong stimulus will generate a (<u>higher/lower</u>) rate of action potentials.

Answers: **3-1.** negative, sodium **3-2.** action, axon, refractory **3-3.** all or none, higher.

4. Describe how neurons communicate at chemical synapses.

4-1. A neuron passes its message on to another neuron by releasing a chemical messenger into the gap or _____ that separates it from other neurons. The sending neuron, called the _____, releases a chemical messenger into the synaptic cleft, which then excites the _____ neuron.

4-2. The chemical messenger that provides this transmitting service is called a _____. The chemical binds with specifically tuned receptor sites on the postsynaptic neurons. In other words, the receptor sites accept some neurotransmitters and reject _____.

Answers: **4-1.** synaptic cleft, presynaptic, postsynaptic **4-2.** neurotransmitter, others.

5. Describe the two types of postsynaptic potentials and how cells integrate these signals.

5-1. When the neurotransmitter combines with a molecule at the receptor site it causes a voltage change at the receptor site called a _____potential (PSP). One type of PSP is excitatory and (<u>increases/decreases</u>) the probability of producing an action potential in the receiving neuron. The other type is inhibitory and _____the probability of producing an action potential.

5-2. Whether or not a neuron fires depends on the number of excitatory PSPs it is receiving and the number of _____ PSPs it is receiving. PSPs (<u>do/do not</u>) follow the all or none law.

5-3. Put the five steps of communication at the synapse in their correct order (by using the numbers 1 through 5):

_____ (a) The reuptake of transmitters by the presynaptic neuron.

_____ b) The enzyme inactivation or drifting away of transmitters in the synapse

_____ (c) The synthesis and storage or transmitters

_____ (d) The binding of transmitters at receptor sites on the postsynaptic membrane.

_____ (e) The release of transmitters into the synaptic cleft.

5-4. If enough excitatory PSPs occur in a neuron, the electrical currents can add up causing the neuron to generate an action potential. Excitatory PSPs can add up in two ways. When several PSPs follow one another in rapid succession at a receptor site, _____ summation can occur. When several PSPs occur simultaneously at different receptor sites, _____ summation can occur.

Answers: **5-1.** postsynaptic, increases, decreases **5-2.** inhibitory, do not **5-3.** (a) 5, (b) 4, (c) 1, (d) 3, (e) 2
5-4. temporal, spatial.

6. Discuss some of the functions of acetylcholine and the monoamine neurotransmitters.

6-1. Our moods, thoughts and actions all depend on the action of neurotransmitters. For example, the movement of all muscles depends on _____ (ACh). Like other neurotransmitters, ACh can only bind to specific sites, much like a lock and _____. However, the receptor sites can be fooled by other chemical substances. For example, an agonist like nicotine can (<u>block/mimic</u>) the action of ACh, while an antagonist like curare can (<u>block/mimic</u>) the action of ACh.

6-2. Three neurotransmitters, dopamine, norepinephrine, and serotonin, are collectively known as

_____. Both Parkinsonism and schizophrenia have been linked with alterations in

_____ activity, while the mood changes found in depression have been linked to receptor sites for

norepinephrine and _____. Serotonin also plays a key role in the regulation of

_____and wakefulness and perhaps _____ behavior in animals.

Answers: **6-1.** acetylcholine, key, mimic, block **6-2.** monoamines, dopamine, serotonin, sleep, aggressive.

7. Explain what endorphins are how they are related to behavior.

7-1. Endorphins are chemicals internally produced by the body that have effects similar to those produced by

the drug _____and its derivatives. That is, they are able to reduce pain and also induce

_____, such as the "runner's high" sometimes experienced by joggers.

Answers: **7-1.** opium, pleasure (or euphoria).

ORGANIZATION OF THE NERVOUS SYSTEM

8. Provide an overview of the peripheral nervous system, including its subdivisions.

With approximately 85 to 180 billion individual neurons to control, it is important that the central nervous system
have some kind of organizational structure. This organizational structure is depicted in Figure 3.5 of the text, and
it will prove helpful if you have this figure in front of you while answering the following questions.

8-1. Answer the following questions regarding the organization of the peripheral nervous system.

(a) What constitutes the peripheral nervous system?

(b) What two subdivisions make up the peripheral nervous system?

(c) What is the role of the afferent and efferent nerve fibers?

(d) What two subdivisions make up the autonomic nervous system?

(e) Describe the opposing roles of the sympathetic and parasympathetic nervous systems.

Answers: 8-1. (a) All of the nerves that lie outside of the brain and spinal cord. (b) The somatic nervous system and the autonomic nervous system. (c) Afferent fibers carry information inward from the periphery, while efferent fibers carry information outward to the periphery. (d) The sympathetic nervous system and the parasympathetic nervous system. (e) The sympathetic system prepares the body for fight or flight, and the parasympathetic system conserves the body's resources.

9. **Distinguish between the central nervous system and the peripheral nervous system.**

   9-1.   What are the two parts of the central nervous system?

   9-2.   What is the name given to all of the nerves that lie outside of the central nervous system?

   Answers: 9-1. The brain and the spinal cord. **9-2.** The peripheral nervous system.

LOOKING INSIDE THE BRAIN: RESEARCH METHODS

10. **Describe how the EEG, lesioning, and ESB are used to investigate brain function.**

   10-1.   The electroencephalograph, or _____, is a device that can measure the brain's _____ activity. Electrodes are placed on the scalp and the brain's electrical activity is then monitored by the EEG machine and transformed into line tracings called _____ waves.

   10-2.   Answer the following questions regarding the use of lesioning and ESB to investigate brain function.

   (a) What technique involves the actual destruction of brain tissue in order to examine the resulting effect on behavior?

   (b) What technique would most likely be employed by a neurosurgeon to map the brain of a patient?

   (c) Which techniques employ the use of electrodes and electrical currents?

   (d) In what fundamental way does lesioning differ from ESB?

   Answers: 10-1. EEG, electrical, brain **10-2.** (a) lesioning (b) ESB (c) lesioning and ESB (d) Lesioning is used to actually destroy tissue, whereas ESB is used to merely elicit behavior.

11. Describe the new brain imaging methods that are used to study brain structure and function.

11-1. There are three new kinds of brain-imaging procedures that have come into recent use. One of these procedures consists of a computer enhanced X-ray machine that compiles multiple X-rays of the brain into a single vivid picture. The resulting images are called _____ scans. An even newer device that produces clearer three dimensional images of the brain goes by the name of magnetic resonance imaging scanner, and the images it produces are known as _____ scans.

11-2. Unlike CT and MRI scans, which can only show the structure of the brain, the positron emission tomography scanner can portray the brain's actual _____ across time. The images produced by this procedure are called _____ scans. Newer variations of MRI scans can also monitor brain activity, such as blood and oxygen flow, and thus provide both functional and structural information. These scans are called _____ magnetic images (fMRI).

Answers: **11-1.** CT, MRI **11-2.** activity, PET, functional.

THE BRAIN AND BEHAVIOR

12. Summarize the key functions of the medulla, pons, and cerebellum.

12-1. Three separate structures make up the hindbrain: the cerebellum, the pons, and the medulla. Identify these structures from the descriptions given below.

(a) This structure is essential for executing and coordinating physical movement.

(b) This structure attaches to the top of the spinal cord and controls many essential functions such as breathing and circulation.

(c) This structure forms a bridge of fibers between the brainstem and cerebellum and plays an important role in both sleep and arousal.

Answers: **12-1.** (a) cerebellum (b) medulla (c) pons.

13. Summarize the key functions of the midbrain.

13-1. Helping to locate objects in space is one of the major roles of the _____. In addition, dopamine releasing neurons originate here and help to regulate the performance of _____ movements carried out by higher brain centers. It also shares a structure with the hindbrain that is essential for the regulation of sleep and wakefulness as well as modulation of muscular reflexes, breathing, and pain perception. This structure is called the _____ formation.

14. Summarize the key functions of the thalamus and hypothalamus.

14-1. The structure which serves as a way station for all sensory information headed for the brain is called the
_____. The thalamus also appears to play an active role in _____ sensory information.

14-2. In addition to its role in controlling the autonomic nervous system and linking the brain to the endocrine
system, the hypothalamus also plays a major role in regulating basic biological drives such as fighting,
_____, feeding, and _____.

Answers: **14-1.** thalamus, integrating **14-2.** fleeing, mating.

15. Describe the nature and location of the limbic system and summarize some of its key functions.

15-1. An interconnected network of structures involved in the control of emotion, motivation, and memory are
collectively known as the _____ system. The hippocampus, for example, appears to play a key
role in the formation of _____. However, the limbic system is best known for its role as the seat
of _____. Electrical stimulation of particular areas of the limbic system in rats (particularly in
the medial forebrain bundle) appears to produce intense _____. These "pleasure centers"
appear to actually be neural circuits that release the neurotransmitter _____.

Answers: **15-1.** limbic, memories, emotion, pleasure, dopamine.

16. Name the four lobes in the cerebral cortex and identify some of their key functions.

16-1. The cerebrum is the brain structure that is responsible for our most complex _____activities. Its
folded outer surface is called the _____ cortex. The cerebrum is divided into two halves,
known as the right and _____ cerebral hemispheres. The two hemispheres communicate with
each other by means of a wide band of fibers called the _____ _____.

16-2. Each cerebral hemisphere is divided into four parts called lobes. Match these four lobes (occipital,
parietal, temporal, and frontal) with their key function:

_____ (a) Contains the primary motor cortex that controls the movement of muscles.

_____ (b) Contains the primary visual cortex which initiates the processing of visual information.

_____ (c) Contains the primary auditory cortex which initiates the processing of auditory information.

_____ (d) Contains the primary somatosensory cortex that registers the sense of touch.

16-3. The prefrontal cortex seems to play an active role in higher order functions involving working memory
and relational reasoning, suggesting to some that it serves an "executive _____ system".

Answers: **16-1.** mental, cerebral, left, corpus callosum **16-2.** (a) frontal (b) occipital (c) temporal (d) parietal
16-3. control.

17. Summarize evidence that led scientists to view the left hemisphere as the dominant hemisphere and describe how split-brain research changed this view.

17-1. Until recent years, it was believed that the left hemisphere dominated a submissive right hemisphere. Evidence for this belief came from several sources which all seemed to indicate that the left hemisphere played the dominant role with respect to the use of _____. For example, damage to an area in the frontal lobe known as _____ area was associated with speech deficits. Also, damage to another area located in the temporal lobe was found to be associated with difficulty in speech comprehension. This area is called _____ area. Both of these areas are located in the _____ cerebral hemisphere.

17-2. Answer the following questions regarding split-brain research.

(a) What was the result of severing the corpus callosum in these patients?

(b) Which hemisphere was found to be primarily responsible for verbal and language tasks in general?

(c) Which hemisphere was found to be primarily responsible for visual and spatial tasks?

17-3. What can be concluded with respect to hemispheric domination from split-brain studies?

Answers: **17-1.** language, Broca's, Wernicke's, left **17-2.** (a) The two cerebral hemispheres could no longer communicate with each other. (b) The left cerebral hemisphere. (c) the right cerebral hemisphere **17-3.** Neither hemisphere dominates, rather each has its own specialized tasks.

18. Describe how neuroscientists conduct research on cerebral specialization in normal subjects and what this research has revealed.

18-1. Researchers have looked at left-right imbalances in the speed of visual or auditory processing in the two hemispheres and (have/have not) observed perceptual asymmetries in normal subjects.

18-2. Answer the following questions regarding the conclusions that can be drawn from the research on hemispheric asymmetry.

(a) Are you more likely to identify quickly and accurately verbal stimuli when presented to the right visual field (left hemisphere), or when presented to the left visual field (right hemisphere).

(b) Are you more likely to identify quickly and accurately visual-spatial information, such as recognizing a face, when the stimuli are presented to the right visual field (left hemisphere) or when presented to the left visual field (right hemisphere).

(c) What conclusions can be drawn from the research on normal subjects regarding hemispheric specialization with respect to cognitive tasks?

Answers: **18-1.** have **18-2.** (a) When presented to the right visual field (left hemisphere). (b) When presented to the left visual field (right hemisphere). (c) The two hemispheres are specialized to handle different cognitive tasks.

THE ENDOCRINE SYSTEM: ANOTHER WAY TO COMMUNICATE

19. Describe some of the ways in which hormones regulate behavior.

    19-1.   Answer the following questions regarding the workings of the endocrine system.

        (a) What is the role played by the hormones in the endocrine system?

        (b) While many glands comprise the endocrine system, which one functions as a master gland to control the others?

        (c) What structure is the real power behind the throne here?

    19-2.   Fill in the boxes in the diagram below showing the role of the pituitary gland in the "fight or flight" response to stress.

    19-3.   What is the role of sexual hormones:

        (a) Prior to birth?

(b) At puberty?

HEREDITY AND BEHAVIOR: IS IT ALL IN THE GENES?

20. Describe the structures and processes involved in genetic transmission.

20-1.   When a human sperm and egg unite at conception they form a one-celled organism called a

_____. This cell contains 46 chromosomes, half of which are contributed by each _____, thus making 23 pairs. Each member of a pair operates in conjunction with its _____ member. The zygote then evolves to form all of the cells in the body, each of which have _____ pairs of chromosomes.

20-2.   Each chromosome is actually a threadlike strand of a _____ molecule, and along this threadlike structure are found the individual units of information, called _____, that determine our biological makeup. Like chromosomes, genes operate in _____. For example, type of ear lobe is determined by a pair of genes. If both parents contribute a gene for the same type, the child will inherit this type, and the two genes are said to be _____. If the parents contribute two different genes for the type of ear lobe, the genes are said to be _____, and the child will inherit the type carried by the dominant gene. When heterozygous genes are paired, the dominant gene masks the _____ gene.

21. Explain the difference between genotype and phenotype and the meaning of polygenic inheritance.

21-1.   Answer the following questions about the difference between genotype and phenotype.

(a) What are the two genes that make up your ear lobe type said to be?

(b) What is your resulting ear lobe type said to be?

(c) Can your genotype or phenotype change over time?

21-2. What is meant when it is said that most human traits are polygenic?

Answers: 21-1. (a) your genotype (b) your phenotype (c) Only your phenotype can change. **21-2.** They are determined by two or more pairs of genes.

22. Explain the special methods used to investigate the influence of heredity on behavior.

22-1. If a trait is due to heredity, then more closely related members of a family should show (<u>lesser/greater</u>) resemblance on this trait than less closely related family members. Studies using this method are called _____ studies. Data gathered from family studies (<u>can/cannot</u>) furnish conclusive proof as to the heritability of a specific trait. Even when it is demonstrated that a particular trait is highly related to the degree of family relationship, the cause for this relationship could be either heredity or _____.

22-2. A second method in this line of investigation is to compare specific traits across identical twins and fraternal twins. This method, called _____ studies, assumes that inherited traits are much more likely to be found among (<u>identical/fraternal</u>) twins. These studies do in fact show that for many characteristics, such as intelligence and extraversion, the resemblance is closest for _____ twins. However, since identical twins are far from identical on these characteristics, _____ factors must also play a role here.

22-3. A third method in this line of investigation is to study children who have been separated from their biological parents at a very early age and raised by adoptive parents. The idea behind these _____ studies is that if the adoptive children more closely resemble their biological parents with respect to a specific trait, then it can be assumed that _____ plays a major role. On the other hand, if the adoptive children more closely resemble their adoptive parents with respect to a specific trait it would indicate that _____ plays a major role. Studies using this method to study the heritabilty of intelligence have found that adoptive children _____ resemble their biological and adoptive parents on this particular trait. This would indicate that a trait such as intelligence is influenced by both heredity and _____.

Answers: 22-1. greater, family, cannot, environment **22-2.** twin, identical, identical, environmental **22-3.** adoption, heredity, environment, equally, environment.

THE EVOLUTIONARY BASES OF BEHAVIOR

23. Explain the four key insights that represent the essence of Darwin's theory.

23-1. Darwin's four key insights are listed below. Match each one with the statement that best reflects the essence of the insight.

1. Organisms vary in endless ways.

2. Some of these characteristics are heritable.

3. Organisms tend to reproduce faster than the available resources necessary for their survival.

4. If a specific heritable trait contributes to survival or reproductive fitness its prevalence will increase over generations.

_____ (a) The gazelle that runs the fastest is most likely to leave offspring behind.

_____ (b) The members of most species die from starvation or other side effects of overcrowding.

_____ (c) Birds fly, fish swim, and lions roar.

_____ (d) We all have some traits that are very similar to our grandparents.

Answers: 23-1. 1 (c), 2 (d), 3 (b), 4 (a).

24. Describe some subsequent refinements to evolutionary theory.

24-1. While contemporary theorists accept Darwin's basic theory of natural selection, they have found that natural selection operates on a gene pool that is also influenced by genetic drift, mutations, and gene flow. Match these terms with the definitions given below.

(a) Spontaneous, heritable changes in a piece of DNA can occur in an individual organism.

_____

(b) Gene frequencies in a population can shift because of emigration (out flow) and immigration (in flow). _____

(c) There can be random fluctuations in a gene pool. _____

Answers: 24-1. (a) mutation (b) gene flow (c) genetic drift.

25. Provide some examples of animal behavior that represent adaptations.

25-1. Answer the following questions about behavioral adaptations.

(a) What advantage do gazelles that stot (we humans call it mooning) gain when spotting a cheetah?

(b) What advantage do rats gain by only eating a small amount when they encounter a new food?

Answers: 25-1. (a) It increases their chances of escaping. (b) It decreases their chances of being poisoned.

26. Explain the relationship between parental investment and species' mating systems.

26-1. In general, the sex that makes the smaller paternal investment will compete for mating opportunities with the sex that makes the larger investment, and the sex with the larger investment will tend to be more discriminating in selecting partners. Which of the following, monogamy, polyandry, or polygyny, is likely to be displayed when:

(a) Parental investment is high for females and low for males?

(b) Parental investment is high for males and low for females?

(c) Parental investment is roughly equally for both sexes?

Answers: **26-1.** (a) polygyny (b) polyandry (c) monogamy.

27. **Discuss some common misconceptions about evolution.**

    27-1.   The evolution of species (<u>is</u>/is not) a well established fact. The numerous propositions, natural selection, fitness, genetic drift, and so forth, put forward to account for the evolution of species constitute (facts/ <u>theories</u>).

    27-2.   Evolutionary analyses (does/<u>does not</u>) assume that organisms have a motive to maximize reproductive fitness. It only assumes that organisms have a motive to copulate.

    27-3.   Evolutionary analyses (does/<u>does not</u>) embrace genetic determinism. Rather it is all about how organisms adapt to their _____ and get changed by it.

Answers: **27-1.** is, theories **27-2.** does not **27-3.** does not, environment.

PUTTING IT IN PERSPECTIVE

28. **Explain how this chapter highlighted three of the texts unifying themes.**

    28-1.   Indicate which of the three unifying themes (heredity and environment jointly influence behavior, behavior is determined by multiple causes, and psychology is empirical) is particularly illustrated in each of the following situations.

(a) The discovery of the factors that lead to the development of schizophrenic disorders.

(b) The development of many new techniques and instruments that led to the discovery of cerebral specialization.

(c) A new look at the two major factors that influence the development of personal characteristics such as intelligence and temperament.

Answers: **28-1.** (a) Behavior is determined by multiple causes. (b) Psychology is empirical. (c) Heredity and environment jointly influence behavior.

EVALUATING THE CONCEPT OF "TWO MINDS IN ONE"

29. **Critically evaluate each of the five ideas on cerebral specialization and cognitive processes discussed in the chapter.**

    29-1. Your text lists five popular ideas that have found support among some neuroscientists and psychologists. These ideas are:

        (a) The two hemispheres are _____ to process different cognitive tasks.

        (b) Each hemisphere has its own independent stream of _____.

        (c) The two hemispheres have _____ modes of thinking.

        (d) People vary in their _____ on one hemisphere as opposed to the other.

        (e) Schools should place more emphasis on teaching the _____ side of the brain.

Answers: 29-1. (a) specialized (b) consciousness (c) different (d) reliance (dependence) (e) right.

    29-2. We will now proceed through each of these five assumptions to show how each has to be qualified in light of currently available evidence.

        (a) The idea that the left and right brains are specialized to handle different kinds of information (is/is not) supported by research. However, there is evidence that this specialization hardly occurs in some persons, while in other persons the specialization is reversed, particularly among _____handed persons. Moreover, most tasks require the ongoing cooperation of _____ hemispheres.

        (b) The evidence that each hemisphere has its own mind, or stream of consciousness, is actually very weak, except for persons who have undergone _____-_____surgery. The resulting "two minds" in these patients appears to be a byproduct of the surgery.

        (c) The assertion that each hemisphere has its own mode of thinking is (plausible/confirmed). A big problem here, however, is that mode of thinking, or cognitive style, has proven difficult to both define and _____.

        (d) The assertion that some people are left-brained while other are right-brained (is/is not) conclusive at this time. Abilities and personality characteristics (do/do not) appear to be influenced by brainedness.

        (e) The notion that most schooling overlooks the education of the right brain (does/does not) really make sense. Since both hemispheres are almost always sharing in accomplishing an ongoing task, it would be _____ to teach only one hemisphere at a time.

Answers: 29-2. (a) is, left, both (b) split-brain (c) plausible, measure (d) is not, do not (e) does not, impossible.

30. **Explain how neuroscience research Ha been overextrapolated by some education and child care advocates who have campaigned for infant schooling.**

 30-1. Answer the following questions regarding neuroscience research.

 (a) What happened to kittens deprived of light to one eye for the first 4-6 weeks of life?

 (b) What happened to kittens deprived of light to one eye for the same amount of time after 4 months of age?

 (c) What is the name given to that early period in the kitten's life when light is essential for the normal development of vision?

 (d) What difference was found in synapses in rats that were raised in "enriched" environments when compared to rats raised in "impoverished" environments?

 30-2. Answer the following questions regarding the overextrapolation of neuroscience findings.

 (a) What findings argue against the notion that brain development is more malleable during the first three years of life?

 (b) There are findings that argue against the notion that greater synaptic density is associated with greater intelligence. Which of the following is correct?

 1. Infant animals and human beings begin life with an overabundance of synaptic connections.

 2. Infant animals and human beings begin life with an insufficient number of synaptic connections.

 3. Learning involves the pruning of inactive synapses and reinforcing heavily used neural pathways.

Answers: 30-1. (a) They became blind in the light-deprived eye. (b) They did not suffer blindness in that eye. (c) critical period (d) They had more synapses. **30-2.** (a) It has been found that the brain remains malleable throughout life. (b) 1 and 3 are correct.

REVIEW OF KEY TERMS

Absolute refractory period
Action potential
Adaptation
Adoption studies
Afferent nerve fibers
Agonist
Antagonist
Autonomic nervous system (ANS)
Axon
Behavioral genetics
Blood-brain barrier
Central nervous system (CNS)
Cerebral cortex
Cerebral hemispheres
Cerebrospinal fluid (CSF)
Chromosomes
Corpus callosum
Critical period
Dendrites
Dominant gene
Efferent nerve fibers
Electrical stimulation of the brain (ESB)
Electroencephalograph (EEG)
Endocrine System
Endorphins
Excitatory PSP

Family studies
Family studies
Fitness
Forebrain
Fraternal (dizygotic) twins
Genes
Genetic mapping
Genotype
Heterozygous condition
Hindbrain
Homozygous condition
Hormones
Hypothalamus
Identical (monozygotic) twins
Inclusive fitness
Inhibitory PSP
Lesioning
Limbic system
Midbrain
Monogamy
Mutation
Myelin sheath
Natural selection
Nerves
Neuromodulators
Neurons
Neurotransmitters

Parasympathetic division
Parental investment
Perceptual asymmetries
Peripheral nervous system
Phenotype
Pituitary gland
Polyandry
Polygenic traits
Polygyny
Postsynaptic potential (PSP)
Recessive gene
Resting potential
Reuptake
Soma
Somatic nervous system
Split-brain surgery
Stereotaxic instrument
Sympathetic division
Synapse
Synaptic cleft
Temporal summation
Terminal buttons
Thalamus
Twin studies
Zygote

_____ **1.** An inherited characteristic that increased in a population (through natural selection) because it helped solve a problem of survival or reproduction during the time it emerged.

_____ **2.** A limited time span the development of an organism that is optimal for certain capacities to emerge because the organism is especially responsive to certain experiences.

_____ **3.** Refers to the reproductive success of an individual organism relative to the average reproductive success in the population.

_____ **4.** Individual cells in the nervous system that receive, integrate, and transmit information.

_____ **5.** Neuron part that contains the cell nucleus and much of the chemical machinery common to most cells.

_____ **6.** Branchlike parts of a neuron that are specialized to receive information.

_____ **7.** A long, thin fiber that transmits signals away from the soma to other neurons, or to muscles or glands.

_____ **8.** An insulating jacket, derived from glia cells, that encases some axons.

_____ **9.** Small knobs at the end of the axon that secrete chemicals called neurotransmitters.

_____ **10.** A junction where information is transmitted between neurons.

_____ **11.** The stable, negative charge of an inactive neuron.

_____ **12.** A brief change in a neuron's electrical charge.

_____ **13.** The minimum length of time after an action potential during which another action potential cannot begin.

_____ **14.** A microscopic gap between the terminal buttons of the sending neuron and the cell membrane of another neuron.

_____ **15.** Chemicals that transmit information from one neuron to another.

_____ **16.** A voltage change at the receptor site of a neuron.

_____ **17.** An electric potential that increases the likelihood that a postsynaptic neuron will fire action potentials.

_____ **18.** An electric potential that decreases the likelihood that a postsynaptic neuron will fire action potentials.

_____ **19.** A technique for assessing hereditary influence by examining blood relatives to see how much they resemble each other on a specific trait.

_____ **20.** A chemical that mimics the action of a neurotransmitter.

_____ **21.** A chemical that opposes the action of a neurotransmitter.

_____ **22.** An entire family of internally produced chemicals that resemble opiates in structure and effects.

_____ **23.** Chemicals that increase or decrease (modulate) the activity of specific neurotransmitters.

_____ **24.** System that includes all those nerves that lie outside the brain and spinal cord.

_____ **25.** Bundles of neuron fibers (axons) that travel together in the peripheral nervous system.

_____ **26.** System made up of the nerves that connect to voluntary skeletal muscles and sensory receptors.

_____ **27.** Axons that carry information inward to the central nervous system from the periphery of the body.

_____ **28.** Axons that carry information outward from the central nervous system to the periphery of the body.

_____ **29.** System made up of the nerves that connect to the heart, blood vessels, smooth muscles and glands.

_____ **30.** The branch of the autonomic nervous system that mobilizes the body's resources for emergencies.

_____ **31.** The branch of the autonomic nervous system that generally conserves bodily resources.

_____ **32.** System that consists of the brain and spinal cord.

_____ **33.** A solution that fills the hollow cavities (ventricles) of the brain and circulates around the brain and spinal cord.

_____ **34.** A semipermeable membranelike mechanism that stops some chemicals from passing between the bloodstream and brain cells.

_____ **35.** A device that monitors the electrical activity of the brain over time by means of recording electrodes attached to the surface of the scalp.

_____ **36.** Assessing hereditary influence by comparing the resemblance of identical twins and fraternal twins on a trait.

_____ **37.** Method that involves destroying a piece of the brain by means of a strong electric current delivered through an electrode.

_____ **38.** A device used to implant electrodes at precise locations in the brain.

_____ 39. Method that involves sending a weak electric current into a brain structure to stimulate (activate) it.

_____ 40. Part of the brain that includes the cerebellum and two structures found in the lower part of the brainstem—the medulla and the pons.

_____ 41. The segment of the brainstem that lies between the hindbrain and the forebrain.

_____ 42. Part of the brain encompassing the thalamus, hypothalamus, limbic system, and cerebrum.

_____ 43. A structure in the forebrain through which all sensory information (except smell) must pass to get to the cerebral cortex.

_____ 44. A structure found near the base of the forebrain that is involved in the regulation of basic biological needs.

_____ 45. A densely connected network of structures located beneath the cerebral cortex, involved in the control of emotion, motivation and memory.

_____ 46. The convoluted outer layer of the cerebrum.

_____ 47. The right and left halves of the cerebrum.

_____ 48. The structure that connects the two cerebral hemispheres.

_____ 49. Assessing hereditary influence by examining the resemblance between adopted children and both their adoptive and biological parents.

_____ 50. Surgery in which the corpus callosum is severed to reduce the severity of epileptic seizures.

_____ 51. System of glands that secrete chemicals into the bloodstream that help control bodily functioning.

_____ 52. The chemical substances released by the endocrine glands.

_____ 53. The "master gland" of the endocrine system.

_____ 54. Threadlike strands of DNA molecules that carry genetic information.

_____ 55. A one-celled organism formed by the union of a sperm and an egg.

_____ 56. DNA segments that serve as the key functional units in hereditary transmission.

_____ 57. A gene that is expressed when the paired genes are different (heterozygous).

_____ 58. A gene that is masked when paired genes are heterozygous.

_____ 59. A person's genetic makeup.

_____ 60. The ways in which a person's genotype is manifested in observable characteristics.

_____ 61. Characteristics that are influenced by more than one pair of genes.

_____ 62. The sum of an individuals' own reproductive success, plus the effects the organism has on the reproductive success of related others.

_____ 63. A mating system in which one male and one female nate exclusively, or almost exclusively, with one another.

_____ 64. Left-right imbalances between the cerebral hemispheres in the speed of visual or auditory processing.

_____ 65. A spontaneous, inheritable change in a piece of DNA that occurs in an individual organism.

_____ 66. An interdisciplinary field that studies the influence of genetic factors on behavioral traits.

_____ 67. The two genes in a specific pair are the same.

_____ **68.** The two genes in a specific pair are different.

_____ **69.** Twins that emerge from one zygote that splits.

_____ **70.** Twins that result when two eggs are fertilized simultaneously by different sperm cells, forming two separate zygotes.

_____ **71.** The process of determining the location and chemical sequence of specific genes on specific chromosomes.

_____ **72.** Posits that heritable characteristics that provide a survival or reproductive advantage are more likely than alternative characteristics to be passed on to subsequent generations and thus come to be "selected" over time.

_____ **73.** Refers to what each sex has to invest, in the way of time, energy, survival risk, and forgone opportunities to produce and nurture offspring.

_____ **74.** A mating system in which each female seeks to mate with multiple males, whereas each male mates with only one female.

_____ **75.** A mating system in which each male seeks to mate with multiple females, whereas each female mates with only one male.

_____ **76.** A process in which neurotransmitters are sponged up from the synaptic cleft by the presynaptic neuron.

Answers: 1. adaptation **2.** critical period **3.** fitness **4.** neurons **5.** soma **6.** dendrites **7.** axon **8.** myelin sheath **9.** terminal buttons **10.** synapse **11.** resting potential **12.** action potential **13.** absolute refractory period **14.** synaptic cleft **15.** neurotransmitters **16.** postsynaptic potential (PSP) **17.** excitatory PSP **18.** inhibitory PSP **19.** family studies **20.** agonist **21.** antagonist **22.** endorphins **23.** neuromodulators **24.** peripheral nervous system **25.** nerves **26.** somatic nervous system **27.** afferent nerve fibers **28.** efferent fibers **29.** autonomic nervous system (ANS) **30.** sympathetic division **31.** parasympathetic division **32.** central nervous system (CNS) **33.** cerebrospinal fluid (CSF) **34.** blood-brain barrier **35.** electroencephalograph (EEG) **36.** twin studies **37.** lesioning **38.** stereotaxic instrument **39.** electrical stimulation of the brain (ESB) **40.** hindbrain **41.** midbrain **42.** forebrain **43.** thalamus **44.** hypothalamus **45.** limbic system **46.** cerebral cortex **47.** cerebral hemispheres **48.** corpus callosum **49.** adoption studies **50.** split-brain surgery **51.** endocrine system **52.** hormones **53.** pituitary gland **54.** chromosomes **55.** zygote **56.** genes **57.** dominant gene **58.** recessive gene **59.** genotype **60.** phenotype **61.** polygenic traits **62.** inclusive fitness **63.** monogamy **64.** perceptual asymmetries **65.** mutation **66.** behavioral genetics **67.** homozygotic condition **68.** heterozygotic condition **69.** identical (monozygotic) twins **70.** fraternal (dizygotic) twins **71.** genetic mapping **72.** natural selection **73.** parental investment **74.** polyandry **75.** polygyny **76.** reuptake.

REVIEW OF KEY PEOPLE

Charles Darwin

Alan Hodgkin & Andrew Huxley

James Olds & Peter Milner

Candice Pert & Solomon Snyder

Robert Plomin

Roger Sperry & Michael Garzzaniga

_____ **1.** Unlocked the mystery of the neural impulse.

_____ **2.** Known for their work with the split-brain.

_____ **3.** Showed that morphine works by binding to specific receptors.

_____ **4.** Discovered "pleasure-centers" in the limbic system.

_____ **5.** One of the leading behavior genetics researchers in the last decade.

_____ **6.** Identified natural selection as the mechanism that orchestrates the process of evolution.

Answers : 1. Hodgkin & Huxley **2.** Sperry & Garzzaniga **3.** Pert & Snyder **4.** Olds & Milner **5.** Plomin **6.** Darwin.

SELF-QUIZ

1. Most neurons are involved in transmitting information:
   a. from one neuron to another
   b. from the outside world to the brain
   c. from the brain to the muscles
   d. none of the above

2. Which part of the neuron has the responsibility for receiving information from other neurons?
   a. the cell body
   b. the soma
   c. the axon
   d. the dendrites

3. The myelin sheath serves to:
   a. permit faster transmission of the neural impulse
   b. keep neural impulses on the right track
   c. both of the above
   d. none of the above

4. The change in the polarity of a neuron that results from the inflow of positively charged ions and the outflow of negatively charged ions is called the:
   a. presynaptic potential
   b. postsynaptic potential
   c. synaptic potential
   d. action potential

5. The task of passing a message from one neuron to another is actually carried out by:
   a. the myelin sheath
   b. the glia cells
   c. the action potential
   d. neurotransmitters

6. Which of the following techniques is often used by neurosurgeons to map the brain when performing brain surgery?
   a. EEG recordings
   b. ESB
   c. lesioning
   d. all of the above

7. The seat of emotion is to be found in the:
   a. reticular formation
   b. hindbrain
   c. limbic system
   d. forebrain

8. Persons having difficulty with language and speech following an accident that resulted in injury to the brain are most likely to have sustained damage in the:
   a. right cerebral hemisphere
   b. left cerebral hemisphere
   c. right cerebral hemisphere if they are a male and left cerebral hemisphere if they are a female
   d. I have no idea what you are talking about

9. In carrying out the "fight or flight" response, the role of supervisor is assigned to the:
   a. adrenal gland
   b. pituitary gland
   c. hypothalamus
   d. parasympathetic nervous system

10. A person's current weight and height could be said to exemplify his or her:
    a. genotype
    b. phenotype
    c. both of the above
    d. none of the above

11. Which of the following kinds of studies can truly demonstrate that specific traits are indeed inherited?
    a. family studies
    b. twin studies
    c. adoption studies
    d. none of the above

12. Current evidence indicates that schizophrenia results from:
    a. genetic factors
    b. environmental factors
    c. multiple causes that involve both genetic and environmental factors
    d. completely unknown factors

13. Psychology as a science can be said to be:
    a. empirical
    b. rational
    c. analytic
    d. both b and c

14. Which of the following statements is/are correct?
    a. The right side of the brain is the creative side.
    b. The right and left brains are specialized to handle different kinds of information.
    c. Language tasks are always handled by the left side of the brain.
    d. all of the above

15. Which of the following is not one of Darwin's four key insights?
    a. Some characteristics are heritable.
    b. Organisms vary in endless ways.
    c. Genetic drift is a major factor in the evolution of species.
    d. Organisms tend to reproduce faster than available resources.

16. Which mating pattern is likely to develop when the males have far more parental involvement than females?
    a. monogamy
    b. polyandry
    c. polygyny
    d. No species shows this mating pattern.

17. The evolution of species is:
    a. a fact
    b. a theory with a few flaws
    c. a theory with many flaws
    d. a speculation not open to empirical verification

18. Evolutionary analyses assumes that:
    a. organisms are controlled by genetic determinism
    b. organisms have a motive to maximize reproductive fitness
    c. only the physically strongest organisms will survive
    d. organisms have a motive to copulate

19. Which of the following is correct?
    a. Human beings begin life with an insufficient number of synapses.
    b. Human beings begin life with an overabundance off synapses.
    c. Synaptic density is associated with intelligence.
    d. Brain development is only malleable during the first 3 years of life.

Answers: 1. a **2.** d **3.** c **4.** d **5.** d **6.** b **7.** c **8.** b **9.** c **10.** b **11.** d **12.** c **13.** a **14.** b **15.** c **16.** b **17.** a **18.** d **19.** c.

Chapter Four

Sensation and Perception

REVIEW OF KEY IDEAS

PSYCHOPHYSICS: BASIC CONCEPTS AND ISSUES

1. Explain how stimulus intensity is related to absolute thresholds.

    1-1.   You are sitting on a secluded beach at sundown with a good friend. You make a bet as to who can detect the first evening star. Since you have just recently covered this chapter in your text, you explain to your friend that doing so involves the detection of a stimulus threshold. In this case, the first star that provides the minimal amount of stimulation which can be detected is said to have crossed the _____. All of our senses have thresholds, but research clearly shows that the minimal amount of stimulation necessary to be detected by any one of our senses (<u>is/is not</u>) always the same. Therefore, the absolute threshold is defined as the stimulus intensity that can be detected _____ percent of the time.

    Answers: **1-1.** threshold, is not, 50.

2. Explain Weber's law and Fechner's law.

    2-1.   Weber's law states that the size of a just noticeable difference (JND) is a constant proportion of the intensity (size) of the initial stimulus. This means that as a stimulus increases in intensity, the JND increases proportionally as well. Therefore, it would be more difficult to detect a slight increase in the length of a (<u>1-inch/20-inch</u>) line, a slight decrease in a (<u>quiet/loud</u>) tone, or a slight increase in the weight of a (<u>30-ounce/90-ounce</u>) object.

    2-2.   Fechner's law states that larger and larger increases in stimulus intensity are required to produce perceptible increments, or _____, in the magnitude of sensation. What this means is that as the intensity of a stimulus increases, the size of the JND we are able to detect (<u>decreases/increases</u>).

    Answers: **2-1.** 20-inch, loud, 90-ounce **2-2.** JNDs, increases.

3. **Explain the basic thrust of signal-detection theory.**

    3-1.   The major idea behind signal detection theory is that our ability to detect signals depends not only on the initial intensity of a stimulus, but also on other sensory and decision processes as well. One factors that is particularly important here is the criterion you set for how certain you must feel before you react (what are the gains from being correct and what are the losses from being incorrect). What other factor is particularly important here?

    3-2.   Thus, according to signal detection theory, the concepts of absolute thresholds and JNDs need to be replaced by the notion that the probability of detecting any given stimulus will depend on all of the above factors; this is called the concept of _____.

    Answers: 3-1. background noise **3-2.** detectability.

4. **Describe some evidence on perception without awareness and discuss the practical implications of subliminal perception.**

    4-1.   Answer the following questions about the study conducted by Jon Krosnick and his colleagues.

        (a) What two different kinds of emotion arousing subliminal stimuli accompanied the slides of the target person?

        (b) Which group rated the target group in a more favorable manner?

    4-2.   What general conclusions can be drawn from the research on subliminal perception with respect to its potential persuasive effects?

    Answers: 4-1. (a) Stimuli that would elicit either positive or negative emotions. (b) The group exposed to positive emotional stimuli. **4-2.** The effects are very weak.

5. **Discuss the meaning and significance of sensory adaptation.**

    5-1.   Which of the following examples best illustrates what is meant by sensory adaptation?

(a) You are unable to clearly hear the conversation at the next table even though it sounds intriguing and you are straining to listen.

(b) The strawberries you eat at grandma's farm at the age of 20 seem not to taste as good as when you ate them at the age of 6.

(c) The wonderful smell you encounter upon first entering the bakery seems to have declined considerably by the time you make your purchase and leave.

5-2. If you answered c to the above question you are right on track and understand that sensory adaptation involves a gradual _____ in sensitivity to prolonged stimulation. This automatic process means that we are not as likely to be as sensitive to the constants in our sensory environments as we are to the _____.

Answers: **5-1.** c **5-2.** decrease, changes.

OUR SENSE OF SIGHT: THE VISUAL SYSTEM

6. List the three properties of light and the aspects of visual perception that they influence.

6-1. Before we can see anything, _____ must be present. There are three characteristics of lightwaves that directly effect how we perceive visual objects; match each of these characteristics with its psychological effect.

_____ (a) wavelength   1. color

_____ (b) amplitude   2. saturation (or richness)

_____ (c) purity   3. brightness

Answers: **6-1.** lightwaves or light, (a) 1 (b) 3 (c) 2.

7. Describe the role of the lens and pupil in the functioning of the eye.

7-1. Getting light rays entering the eye to properly focus on the retina is the job of the _____. It accomplishes this task by either thickening or flattening its curvature, a process called _____. Controlling the amount of light entering the eye is the job of the _____. It accomplishes this task by opening or closing the opening in the center of the eye called the _____.

Answers: **7-1.** lens, accommodation, iris, pupil.

8. Describe the role of the retina in light sensitivity and in visual information processing.

8-1. The structure that transforms the information contained in light rays into neural impulses that are then sent to the brain is called the _____. All of the axons carrying these neural impulses exit the eye at a single opening in the retina called the optic _____. Since the optic disk is actually a hole in the retina, this part of the retina cannot sense incoming visual information and for this reason it is called the _____ spot.

8-2. The specialized receptor cells that are primarily responsible for visual acuity and color vision are called the _____. The cones are mainly located in the center of the retina in a tiny spot called the _____. The specialized receptor cells that lie outside of the fovea and towards the periphery of the retina are called the _____. The rods are primarily responsible for peripheral vision and for _____vision.

8-3. Both dark and light adaptation are primarily accomplished through _____ reactions in the rods and cones. This chemical reaction occurs more quickly in the _____, so they are quicker to show both dark adaptation and light adaptation.

8-4. Light rays striking the rods and cones initiate neural impulses that are then transmitted to _____ cells and then to _____cells. From here the visual information is transmitted to the brain via the axons running from the retina to the brain, collectively known as the _____ nerve.

8-5. The processing of visual information begins within the receiving area of a retinal cell called the _____ field. Stimulation of the receptive field of a cell causes signals to be sent inward towards the brain and sideways, or _____, to nearby cells, thus allowing them to interact with one another.

Answers: 8-1. retina, disk, blind **8-2.** cones, fovea, rods, night **8-3.** chemical, cones **8-4.** bipolar, ganglion, optic **8-5.** receptive, laterally.

9. Describe the routing of signals from the eye to the brain and the brain's role in visual information processing.

9-1. Visual information from the right side of the visual field (Figure 4-12 in the text) exits from the retinas of both eyes via the optic nerves and meet at the _____ chiasm, where it is combined and sent to the _____ side of the brain. Visual information from the left side of the visual field follow a similar pattern, meeting at the optic chiasm, and then on to the _____ side of the brain.

9-2. After leaving the optic chiasm on their way to the visual cortex, the optic nerve fibers diverge along two pathways. Fill in the missing parts of these pathways in the figures below.

Main pathway

(a) Optic chiasm _____ Visual cortex _____

Secondary pathway

(b) Optic chiasm _____ Visual cortex _____

9-3. The main pathway is subdivided into the magnocellular and parvocellular pathways which simultaneously extract _____ kinds of information from the same input.

(a) Which channel processes the details of "what" objects are out there?

(b) Which channel processes the details of "where" the objects are?

9-4. Because the cells in the visual cortex respond very selectively to specific features of complex stimuli, they have been described as _____ detectors. There are two major types of cells in the visual cortex: simple cells and complex cells. Identify them from their descriptions below.

(a) These cells are particular about the width and orientation of a line but respond to any position in their receptive field.

(b) These cells are very particular about the width, orientation, and position of a line.

9-5. As signals move further long in the visual processing system the neurons become (less/more) specialized as to what turns them on and the stimuli that will activate them become (less/more) complex. For example, cells in the temporal lobe along the "what" pathway best respond to pictures of human _____.

Answers: 9-1. optic, left, right **9-2.** (a) thalamus, lateral geniculate nucleus (b) superior colliculus, thalamus **9-3.** different, (a) parvocellular (b) magnocellular **9-4.** feature, (a) complex cells (b) simple cells **9-5.** more, more, faces.

10. Discuss the trichromatic and opponent process theories of color vision, and the modern reconciliation of these theories.

10-1. The trichromatic theory of color vision, as its name suggests, proposes three different kinds of receptors (channels) for the three primary colors red, _____, and _____. The opponent process theory of color vision also proposes three channels for color vision, but these channels are red versus _____, yellow versus _____, and black versus _____.

10-2. These two theories of color vision can be used to explain different phenomenon. Use T (trichromatic) or O (opponent process) to indicate which theory best explains the following phenomena.

_____ (a) The color of an afterimage is the complement of the original color.

_____ (b) The different kinds of color blindness suggest three different kinds of receptors.

_____ (c) Any three appropriately spaced colors can produce all other colors.

_____ (d) People describing colors often require at least four different names.

10-3. The evidence is now clear that both theories are (incorrect/correct). Each is needed to explain all of the phenomena associated with color vision. Three different kinds of cones have been found in the retina which are sensitive to each of the three primary colors; this supports the _____ theory. It has also been found that visual cells in the retina, the LGN, and the visual cortex respond in opposite (antagonistic) ways to complementary colors, thus supporting the _____ theory.

Answers: 10-1. green, blue, green, blue, white **10-2.** (a) O (b) T (c) T (d) O **10-3.** correct, trichromatic, opponent process.

11. Distinguish between top-down processing and bottom-up processing.

11-1. Answer the following questions regarding top-down and bottom-up processing.

(a) Which process appears to assume feature analysis, the process of detecting specific elements in visual input and assembling them into a more complex whole?

(b) Which process appears to account for our ability to rapidly recognize and read long strings of words?

(c) What does the text conclude about which theory is correct?

Answers: 11-1. (a) bottom-up processing (b) top-down processing (c) Both theories have a place in form perception.

12. Explain the basic premise of Gestalt psychology and describe Gestalt principles of visual perception.

12-1. The Gestalt view of form perception assumes that form perception is not constructed out of individual elements; rather the form, or whole, is said to be _____ than the sum of its individual elements. The illusion of movement, called the _____ phenomenon, is used to support the Gestalt view of form perception because the illusion of movement (is/is not) completely contained in the individual chunks of stimuli that give rise to it. In other words, the illusion, or whole, appears to be _____ than the sum of its parts.

12-2. Five Gestalt principles of visual perception are illustrated below. Match each illustration with its correct name.

Proximity

Similarity

Continuity

Closure

Simplicity

(a) _____

(b) _____

(c) _____

(d) _____

(e) _____

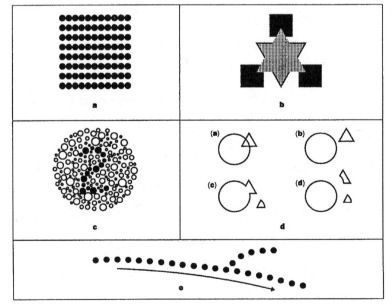

12-3. What Gestalt principle is illustrated by:

(a) The words printed on this page appear to stand out from the white paper they are printed on?

(b) Things moving in the same direction together get grouped together?

Answers: 12-1. greater (more), phi, is not, greater (more) **12-2.** (a) proximity (b) closure (c) similarity (d) simplicity (e) continuity **12-3.** (a) figure and ground (b) common fate.

13. Explain how form perception can be a matter of formulating perceptual hypotheses.

13-1. The objects that surround us in the world outside of our bodies are called _____stimuli; the images the objects project on our retinas are called _____ stimuli. When perceived from different angles or distances, the same distal stimulus projects (<u>similar/different</u>) proximal images on the retina. This forces us to make perceptual _____ about the distal stimulus.

Answers: 13-1. distal, proximal, different, hypotheses or guesses.

14. Describe the monocular and binocular cues employed in depth perception and cultural variations in depth perception.

14-1. There are two general kinds of cues that allow us to perceive depth and they are easy to remember because one kind involve the use of both eyes and are called _____ cues; the other kind require the use of only one of the eyes and are called _____ cues. Depth perception (<u>does/does not</u>) require the use of both binocular and monocular cues.

14-2. Here are examples of two different kinds of binocular cues, retinal disparity and convergence. Identify each from these examples:

(a) As a person walks towards you your eyes turn inward.

(b) The images are slightly different on each retina and the differences change with distance.

14-3. There are two general kinds of monocular cues. One kind involves the active use of the eye, such as the accommodation used for focusing the eye. The other general kind are used to indicate depth in flat pictures and thus are called _____ depth cues.

14-4. Identify the following pictorial cues below:

(a) Parallel lines grow closer as they recede into the distance.

(b) More distant objects are higher in the field than nearer objects.

(c) When objects appear to be of the same size, closer ones appear larger than more distant ones.

(d) Near objects block or overlap more distant ones.

(e) Texture appears to grow finer as viewing distance increases.

(f) Patterns of light and dark suggest shadows that can create an impression of three-dimensional space.

14-5. What differences have been found in a few cultures without previous experience in viewing two-dimensional figures and photographs?

Answers: 14-1. binocular, monocular, does not **14-2.** (a) convergence (b) retinal disparity **14-3.** pictorial **14-4.** (a) linear perspective (b) height in plane (c) relative size (d) interposition (e) texture gradients (f) light and shadow **14-5.** They have difficulty in perceiving depth (using only pictorial depth cues).

15. Summarize the Featured Study and follow-up research on the perception of geographical slant.

15-1. After reading the Featured Study you should be able to answer the following questions.

(a) Which method of judgment of geographical slant, verbal, visual, or haptic (based on touch), was the most accurate?

(b) In what way might overestimates of geographical slant by the visual and verbal methods be of value?

(c) In what way might the better accuracy of haptic estimates be of value?

15-2. Answer the following questions regarding the follow-up research.

(a) The overestimates of geographical slant were even more pronounced when the hills were viewed from the top than from the bottom. What functional purpose would this serve?

(b) What effect did fatigue have on the overestimation bias?

Answers: 15-1. (a) haptic (b) They prevent people from undertaking climbs they are not equipped to handle. (c) It prevents stumbling (when climbing or descending a geographical slant). **15-2.** (a) Steep hills are harder to descend than ascend. (b) It increased the bias.

16. Describe perceptual constancies and illusions in vision, and discuss cultural variations in susceptibility to certain illusions.

16-1. The tendency to experience stable perceptions in spite of constantly changing sensory input is called perceptual _____. For example, even though the retinal image shrinks as a friend walks away, she continues to appear her usual height. This is an example of _____ constancy.

16-2. Being fooled by the discrepancy between the appearance of a visual stimulus and its physical reality is what is meant by an optical _____. Both perceptual constancies and optical illusions illustrate the point we are continually formulating _____ about what we perceive and also that these perceptions can be quite (<u>subjective/objective</u>).

16-3. What do the variations in cultural susceptibility to certain illusions tell us about our perceptual inferences?

Answers: 16-1. constancy, size **16-2.** illusion, hypotheses, subjective **16-3.** They can be shaped by our experience.

OUR SENSE OF HEARING: THE AUDITORY SYSTEM

17. List the three properties of sound and the aspects of auditory perception that they influence.

17-1. Name the perceived qualities that are associated with the following properties of sound waves.

Physical property	Description	Perceived Quality
(a) purity	kind of mixture	_____
(b) amplitude	wave height	_____
(c) wavelength	wave frequency	_____

18. **Summarize the information on human hearing capacities and describe how sensory processing occurs in the ear.**

    18-1.   Below are questions concerning human hearing capacities. Match the questions with their correct answers.

Answers	Questions
1. 90 to 120 decibels (dB).	____ (a) What is the frequency range of human hearing?
2. 1,000 to 5,000 Hz.	____ (b) How loud do sounds have to be to cause damage to human hearing?
3. 20 to 20,000 Hz.	____ (c) To what frequency range is human hearing the most sensitive?

    18-2.   Below is a scrambled sequence of events that occurs when a sound wave strikes the ear. Put these events in their correct order using the numbers 1 through 4.

        _____ Fluid waves travel down the cochlea causing the hair cells on the basilar membrane to vibrate.

        _____ The pinna directs air to the eardrum.

        _____ The hair cells convert fluid motion into neural impulses and send them to the brain.

        _____ The motion of the vibrating eardrum is converted to fluid motion by the ossicles.

19. **Compare and contrast the place and frequency theories of pitch perception and discuss the resolution of the debate.**

    19-1.   One theory of pitch perception assumes that the hair cells respond differentially to pitch depending on their location along the basilar membrane. This is the main idea of the _____ theory of pitch perception. A second theory assumes a one to one correspondence between the actual frequency of the sound wave and the frequency at which the entire basilar membrane vibrates. This is the main idea of the _____ theory of pitch perception.

    19-2.   Below are several facts uncovered by research. Tell which theory of pitch is supported by each of these facts.

    (a) The hair cells vibrate in unison and not independently.

    (b) Even when they fire in volleys, auditory nerves can only handle up to 5000 Hz.

    (c) A wave pattern caused by the vibrating basilar membrane peaks at a particular place along the membrane.

19-3. The above facts mean that the perception of pitch depends on both _____ and _____ coding.

Answers: 19-1. place, frequency 19-2. (a) frequency theory (b) place theory (c) place theory 19-3. place, frequency.

20. Discuss the cues employed in auditory localization.

20-1. The sound shadow cast by the head is in a large part responsible for enhancing two important cues used for auditory localization. What are these two cues?

Answers: 20-1. The differences in the intensity and time of arrival of sound waves reaching each ear.

OUR CHEMICAL SENSES: TASTE AND SMELL

21. Describe the stimulus and receptors for taste and discuss individual differences in taste perception.

21-1. The stimuli for taste perception are _____ absorbed in the saliva that stimulate taste cells located in the tongue's _____ _____. It is generally thought that there are four fundamental tastes; these are _____, _____, _____, and _____.

21-2. What accounts for much of the wide variations in taste preferences among people?

21-3. What appears to account for the difference between supertasters and nontasters; is it a learned or genetic characteristic?

Answers: 21-1. chemicals, taste buds, sweet, sour, salty, bitter (in any order). 21-2. What they have been exposed to. 21-3. It is a genetic characteristic.

22. Describe the stimulus and receptors for smell and human olfactory capabilities.

22-1. The stimuli for the sense of smell are _____ molecules floating in the air. The receptors for smell are hairlike structures located in the nasal passages called _____ _____. If there are any primary odors, they must be (large/small) in number. Human sensitivity to smell (does/does not) compare favorably with that of many other animals, although some animals surpass us in this respect.

Answers: 22-1. chemical, olfactory cilia, large, does.

23. Describe processes involved in the perception of pressure and temperature.

23-1.   The statements below pertain to either the sense of pressure (P) or the sense of temperature (T). Indicate the correct answers below using the letters P or T.

_____ (a) The somatosensory area of the cortex is the primary receiving area for this sense.

_____ (b) Has receptors specific for either warmth or cold.

_____ (c) The free nerve endings in the skin are in patches that act like receptive fields in vision.

_____ (d) The free nerve endings in the skin fire spontaneously when no stimulus change is being experienced

Answers: 23-1. (a) P (b) T (c) P (d) T.

24. Describe the two pathways along which pain signals travel and discuss evidence that the perception of pain is subjective.

24-1.   Pain signals travel to the brain by two slightly different pathways. One pathway sends signals directly and immediately through myelinated neurons to the cortex and is called the _____ pathway. The other sends signals to the cortex through unmyelinated neurons and is called the _____ pathway. Lingering, less localized pain is mediated by the _____ pathway.

24-2.   Many studies have demonstrated that the perception of pain can be affected by factors such as mood, ethnicity, and culture. Thus, the perception of pain is _____.

Answers: 24-1. fast, slow, slow **24-2.** subjective.

25. Explain the gate-control theory of pain perception and recent findings related to it.

25-1.   Answer the following questions regarding the perception of pain.

(a) What phenomenon did the gate-control theory of pain perception attempt to explain?

(b) What effect do endorphins have with respect to pain?

(c) What seems to be the role of the descending neural pathway that appears to originate in the periaqueductual gray (PAG) area in the midbrain?

Answers: 25-1. (a) Why the perception of pain is so subjective. (b) An analgesic, or pain-relieving, effect.
(c) It mediates the suppression of pain.

OUR OTHER SENSES

26. Describe the perceptual experiences mediated by the kinesthetic and vestibular senses.

26-1. The system that monitors the positions of various parts of the body is called the _____ system. This systems sends information to the brain about body position and movement obtained from receptors located in the joints and _____.

26-2. The system that monitors the body's location in space is called the _____ system. The receptors for the vestibular system are primarily hair cells contained within the _____ canals in the inner ear.

26-3. What point does the text make about the kinesthetic and vestibular systems, and indeed all sensory systems, in carrying out their tasks?

Answers: **26-1.** kinesthetic, muscles **26-2.** vestibular, semicircular **26-3.** They integrate information from other senses (in carrying out their tasks).

PUTTING IT IN PERSPECTIVE

27. Explain how this chapter highlighted three of the text's unifying themes.

27-1. The fact that competing theories of both color vision and pitch were eventually reconciled attests to the value of theoretical diversity. Why is this?

27-2. Why must our experience of the world always be highly subjective?

27-3. What do cultural variations in depth perception, taste preferences, and pain tolerance tell us about the physiological basis of perception?

Answers: **27-1.** They drove and guided the research that resolved the conflicts. **27-2.** The perceptual processes themselves are inherently subjective. **27-3.** That it is subject to cultural influences.

28. Discuss how the impressionists, Cubists, and Surrealists used various principles of visual perception.

28-1. After reading the Application section in your text, try and answer the following questions by only looking at the paintings.

_____ (a) Which cubist painting depends particularly on the Gestalt principles of continuity and common fate for its effect?

_____ (b) Which surrealist painting makes use of a reversible figure to enhance a feeling of fantasy?

_____ (c) Which two impressionists paintings make use of color mixing to illustrate how different spots of colors can be blended into a picture that is more than the sum of its parts?

_____ (d) Which cubist painting uses proximity, similarity, and closure to allow you see its abstract subject (feature analysis applied to canvas)?

Answers: 28-1. (a) Figure 4.60 (b) Figure 4.61 (c) Figures 4.57 and 4.58 (d) Figure 4.59.

29. Discuss how Escher, Vasarely, and Magritte used various principles of visual perception.

29-1. After reading the Application section in your text, try and answer the following questions by only looking at the paintings?

_____ (a) Which painting uses variations in context to make identical triangles appear very different?

_____ (b) Which two paintings incorporate impossible figures to achieve their effect?

_____ (c) Which painting manipulates the figure and ground relationship to achieve its special effect?

_____ (d) Which painting makes particular use of texture gradient and light and dark shadow to convey the impression of depth?

Answers: 29-1. (a) Figure 4.66 (b) Figures 4.63 and 4.64 (c) Figure 4.62 (d) Figure 4.65.

30. Explain how contrast effects can be manipulated to influence or distort judgments.

30-1. Which of the following contrast strategies, the door in the face technique or employing comparitors, is being illustrated in the following situations.

(a) You want to hit the Florida beaches for Spring Break, but you need extra money from home. Realizing this is going to be a hard sell, you first ask for a week in Paris and then try and settle for the beaches.

(b) When your lover catches you in an indiscretion, you quickly point out many more serious infractions by friends and acquaintances.

30-2. Both of these strategies illustrate the point that our perceptions and judgments are _____.

Answers: 30-1. (a) the foot in the door technique (b) employing comparitors **30-2.** subjective.

REVIEW OF KEY TERMS

Absolute threshold
Additive color mixing
Afterimage
Auditory localization
Basilar membrane
Binocular depth cues
Bottom-up processing
Cochlea
Color blindness
Comparitors
Complimentary colors
Cones
Convergence
Dark adaptation
Depth perception
Distal stimuli
Door-in-the-face technique
Farsightedness
Feature analysis
Feature detectors
Fechner's law
Fovea
Frequency theory

Gate-control theory
Gustatory system
Impossible figures
Just noticeable difference (JND)
Kinesthetic system
Lens
Light adaptation
Monocular depth cues
Motion parallax
Nearsightedness
Olfactory system
Opponent process theory of color vision
Optic chiasm
Optic disk
Optical illusion
Parallel processing
Perception
Perceptual constancy
Perceptual hypothesis
Perceptual set
Phi phenomenon
Pictorial depth cues

Place theory
Prosopagnosia
Proximal stimuli
Psychophysics
Pupil
Receptive field of a visual cell
Retina
Retinal disparity
Reversible figure
Rods
Sensation
Sensory adaptation
Signal-detection theory
Subliminal perception
Subtractive color mixing
Threshold
Top-down processing
Trichromatic theory of color vision
Vestibular system
Visual agnosia
Volley principle
Weber's law

_____ 1. The stimulation of sense organs.

_____ 2. The selection, organization, and interpretation of sensory input.

_____ 3. The study of how physical stimuli are translated into psychological (sensory) experience.

_____ 4. A dividing point between energy levels that do and do not have a detectable effect.

_____ 5. The minimum amount of stimulation that can be detected by an organism for a specific type of sensory input.

_____ 6. The smallest amount of difference in the amount of stimulation that can be detected in a sense.

_____ 7. States that the size of a just noticeable difference is a constant proportion of the size of the initial stimulus.

_____ 8. Proposes that sensory sensitivity depends on a variety of factors besides the physical intensity of the stimulus.

_____ 9. Involves a gradual decline in sensitivity to prolonged stimulation.

_____ 10. States that larger and larger increases in stimulus intensity are required to produce perceptible increments in the magnitude of sensation.

_____ 11. The transparent eye structure that focuses the light rays falling on the retina.

_____ 12. The opening in the center of the iris that helps regulate the amount of light passing into the rear chamber of the eye.

_____ 13. The neural tissue lining the inside back surface of the eye that absorbs light, processes images, and sends visual information to the brain.

_____ 14. Specialized receptors that play a key role in daylight vision and color vision.

_____ **15.** Specialized receptors that play a key role in night vision and peripheral vision.

_____ **16.** A tiny spot in the center of the retina that contains only cones, where visual acuity is greatest.

_____ **17.** The process in which the eyes become more sensitive to light in low illumination.

_____ **18.** The process in which the eyes become less sensitive to light in high illumination.

_____ **19.** A variety of deficiencies in the ability to distinguish among colors.

_____ **20.** The retinal area that, when stimulated, affects the firing of a particular cell.

_____ **21.** A hole in the retina where the optic nerve fibers exit the eye (the blind spot).

_____ **22.** Neurons that respond selectively to very specific features of more complex stimuli.

_____ **23.** Works by removing some wavelengths of light, leaving less light than was originally there.

_____ **24.** Works by superimposing lights, leaving more light in the mixture than in any one light by itself.

_____ **25.** Proposes that the human eye has three types of receptors with differing sensitivities to different wavelengths.

_____ **26.** Pairs of colors that can be added together to produce gray tones.

_____ **27.** A visual image that persists after a stimulus is removed.

_____ **28.** Proposes that color is perceived in three channels, where an either-or response is made to pairs of antagonistic colors.

_____ **29.** A drawing compatible with two different interpretations that can shift back and forth.

_____ **30.** A readiness to perceive a stimulus in a particular way.

_____ **31.** A process in which we detect specific elements in visual input and assemble these elements into a more complex form.

_____ **32.** A progression from individual elements to the whole.

_____ **33.** A progression from the whole to the individual elements.

_____ **34.** An apparently inexplicable discrepancy between the appearance of a visual stimulus and its physical reality.

_____ **35.** The illusion of movement created by presenting visual stimuli in rapid succession.

_____ **36.** Stimuli that lie in the distance (in the world outside us).

_____ **37.** The stimulus energies that impinge directly on our sensory receptors.

_____ **38.** An inference about what distal stimuli could be responsible for the proximal stimuli sensed.

_____ **39.** Involves our interpretation of visual cues that tell us how near or far away objects are.

_____ **40.** Clues about distance that are obtained by comparing the differing views of two eyes.

_____ **41.** Clues about distance that are obtained from the image in either eye alone.

_____ **42.** A tendency to experience a stable perception in the face of constantly changing sensory input.

_____ 43. Locating the source of a sound in space.

_____ 44. A fluid-filled, coiled tunnel that makes up the largest part of the inner ear.

_____ 45. A membrane running the length of the cochlea that holds the actual auditory receptors, called hair cells.

_____ 46. Holds that our perception of pitch corresponds to the vibration of different portions, or places, along the basilar membrane.

_____ 47. Holds that our perception of pitch corresponds to the rate, or frequency, at which the entire basilar membrane vibrates.

_____ 48. Holds that groups of auditory nerve fibers fire neural impulses in rapid succession, creating volleys of impulses.

_____ 49. Our sense of taste.

_____ 50. Our sense of smell.

_____ 51. Objects that can be represented in two-dimensional figures but cannot exist in three-dimensional space.

_____ 52. Holds that incoming pain sensations pass through a ìgateîin the spinal cord that can be opened or closed.

_____ 53. The sense that monitors the positions of the various parts of the body.

_____ 54. The system that provides the sense of balance.

_____ 55. The point at which the optic nerves from the inside half of each eye cross over and then project to the opposite half of the brain.

_____ 56. Clues about distance that can be given in a flat picture.

_____ 57. The registration of sensory input without conscious awareness.

_____ 58. Involves simultaneously extracting different kinds of information from the same input.

_____ 59. A case in which close objects are seen clearly but distant objects appear blurry.

_____ 60. A case in which distant objects are seen clearly but close objects are blurry.

_____ 61. A depth cue which refers to the fact that objects within 25 feet project images to slightly different locations on your right and left retinas, so the right and left eyes see slightly different images.

_____ 62. A binocular cue which involves sensing the eyes converging toward each other as they focus on closer objects.

_____ 63. A monocular depth cue which involves images of objects at different distances moving across the retina at different rates.

_____ 64. An inability to recognize a familiar face.

_____ 65. An inability to recognize familiar objects.

_____ 66. Holds that groups of auditory nerve fibers fire neural impulses in rapid succession, creating volleys of impulses.

_____ 67. People, objects, events, and other standards that are used as a baseline for comparison in judgments.

_____ 68. Involves making a very large request that is likely to be turned down to increase the chances that people will agree to a smaller request.

Answers: 1. sensation **2.** perception **3.** psychophysics **4.** threshold **5.** absolute threshold **6.** just noticeable difference (JND) **7.** Weber's law **8.** signal detection theory **9.** sensory adaptation **10.** Fechner's law **11.** lens **12.** pupil **13.** retina **14.** cones **15.** rods **16.** fovea **17.** dark adaptation **18.** light adaptation **19.** color blindness **20.** receptive field of a visual cell **21.** optic disk **22.** feature detectors **23.** subtractive color mixing **24.** additive color mixing **25.** trichromatic theory of color vision **26.** complementary colors **27.** afterimage **28.** opponent process theory of color vision **29.** reversible figure **30.** perceptual set **31.** feature analysis **32.** bottom-up processing **33.** top-down processing **34.** optical illusions **35.** phi phenomenon **36.** distal stimuli **37.** proximal stimuli **38.** perceptual hypothesis **39.** depth perception **40.** binocular cues **41.** monocular cues **42.** perceptual constancy **43.** auditory localization **44.** cochlea **45.** basilar membrane **46.** place theory **47.** frequency theory **48.** volley principle **49.** gustatory system **50.** olfactory system **51.** impossible figures **52.** gate-control theory **53.** kinesthetic sense **54.** vestibular system **55.** optic chiasm **56.** pictorial depth cues **57.** subliminal perception **58.** parallel processing **59.** nearsightedness **60.** farsightedness **61.** retinal disparity **62.** convergence **63.** motion parallax **64.** prosopagnosia **65.** visual agnosia **66.** volley principle **67.** comparitors **68.** door-in-the-face technique.

REVIEW OF KEY PEOPLE

Linda Bartoshuk   Herman von Helmholtz   Ronald Melzack and Patrick Wall
Gustav Fechner   David Hubel and Torston Wiesel   Max Wertheimer

_____   **1.**   Pioneered the early work in the detection of thresholds.

_____   **2.**   These two men won the Nobel prize for their discovery of feature detector cells in the retina.

_____   **3.**   One of the originators of the trichromatic theory of color vision.

_____   **4.**   Made use of the phi phenomenon to illustrate some of the basic principles of gestalt psychology.

_____   **5.**   A leading authority on taste research.

_____   **6.**   Proposed a gate-control theory of pain.

Answers: 1. Fechner **2.** Hubel and Wiesel **3.** Helmholtz **4.** Wertheimer **5.** Bartoshuk **6.** Melzack and Wall.

SELF-QUIZ

1. We have gathered 50 people together to determine the absolute threshold on a particular tone. The absolute threshold will have been reached when:
   a. the first person reports hearing the tone
   b. all persons report hearing the tone
   c. 25 persons report hearing the tone
   d. no persons are able to hear the tone

2. Research shows that subliminal perception:
   a. cannot be reliably demonstrated
   b. produces only moderate persuasive effects
   c. can exert powerful persuasive effects
   d. does not show adaptation effects

3. Which of the following places a major emphasis on subjective factors in the perception of thresholds?
   a. Weber's law
   b. Fechner's law
   c. Steven's power factor
   d. signal detection theory

4. The receiving area of a retinal cell is called the:
   a. cone
   b. fovial field
   c. rod
   d. receptive field

5. The fact that we are generally much more aware of the changes in our sensory environments rather than the constants is the general idea behind:
   a. signal detection theory
   b. sensory adaptation
   c. the method of constant stimuli
   d. sensory equalization

6. The major difference between a green light and a blue light is the:
   a. wave frequency
   b. wave purity
   c. wavelength
   d. wave saturation

7. Which theory of color vision best explains why the color of an afterimage is the complement of the original color?
   a. the trichromatic theory
   b. the opponent process theory
   c. both theories explain this phenomenon equally well
   d. neither theory adequately explains this phenomenon

8. When watching a wild car chase scene in a movie we can be thankful for:
   a. chunking
   b. lateral processing
   c. bottom-up processing
   d. the phi phenomenon

9. Which of the following is not one of the pictorial depth cues?
   a. convergence
   b. linear perspective
   c. relative height
   d. texture gradients

10. Which of the following is an example of what is meant by perceptual constancy?
    a. Moths are always attracted to light.
    b. A round pie tin always appears to us as round.
    c. Proximal and distal stimuli are always identical.
    d. Absolute thresholds always remain the same.

11. Gate-control theory is an attempt to explain:
    a. why the perception of pain is so subjective
    b. how subliminal perception works
    c. how receptive fields influence one another
    d. how the optic chiasm directs visual information

12. Research has shown that the perception of pitch depends on:
    a. the area stimulated on the basilar membrane
    b. the frequency at which the basilar membrane vibrates
    c. both the area stimulated and the frequency at which the basilar membrane vibrates
    d. the frequency at which the ossicles vibrate

13. Which of the following is not considered to be one of the four fundamental tastes?
a. sour
b. sweet
c. burnt
d. bitter

14. Our sense of balance depends upon:
a. the semicircular canals
b. the kinesthetic senses
c. visual cues
d. all of the above are involved in our sense of balance

15. Which of the following terms perhaps best describes human perception?
a. accurate
b. objective
c. subjective
d. unknowable

16. When judging the steepness of a hill, human beings:
a. are rather accurate
b. tend to underestimate the steepness
c. tend to overestimate the steepness
d. are better when making visual judgments of steepness than judgments based on touch

17. When politicians point out that their misdeeds are only miniscule when judged against their competitors, they are making use of:
a. the door-in-the-face technique
b. comparitors
c. bottom-up processing
d. top-down processing

Answers: 1. c **2.** b **3.** d **4.** d **5.** b **6.** c **7.** b **8.** d **9.** a **10.** b **11.** a **12.** c **13.** c **14.** d **15.** c **16.** c **17.** b.

Chapter Five

Variations in Consciousness

REVIEW OF KEY IDEAS

ON THE NATURE OF CONSCIOUSNESS

1. **Discuss and evaluate the nature of consciousness.**

    1-1. The personal awareness of internal and external events is how psychologists define _consciousness_. Consciousness is like a moving stream in that it is constantly _changing_.

    1-2. Not only is consciousness constantly changing, but it also exists at different levels. Freud believed that at its deepest level we would find the _unconscious_. Moreover, there is a _continuum_ of levels of awareness from the conscious to the unconscious. There (is/is not) some awareness during sleep and even while under anesthesia.

    1-3. Consciousness must have evolved because it increased the likelihood of survival and reproductive success, perhaps because it allowed for forethought and _planning_. Several other equally plausible explanations have also been offered, but as of now (only one/none) has been supported by empirical evidence.

    Answers: 1-1. consciousness, changing **1-2.** unconscious, continuum, is **1-3.** planning, none.

2. **Discuss the relationship between consciousness and EEG activity.**

    2-1. EEG recordings reveal that there (is/is not) some relationship between brain waves and levels of consciousness. There are four principal bands of brain wave activity, based on the frequency of the wave patterns, these are alpha, beta, delta, and theta. Identify these wave patterns from their descriptions given below.

    beta (a) alert (13-24 cps)   _theta_ (c) deep sleep (4-7 cps) Stage A

    alpha (b) relaxed (8-12 cps)   _delta_ (d) deepest sleep (1-4 cps) (REM SLEEP

2-2. While variations in consciousness are correlated with variations in brain activity, the causal basis of this relationship remains _unknown_.

Answers: **2-1.** is (a) beta (b) alpha (c) theta (d) delta **2-2.** unknown.

BIOLOGICAL RHYTHMS AND SLEEP

3. **Summarize what is known about our biological clocks and their relationship to sleep.**

   3-1. One of the biological rhythms, the daily or 24-hour circadian rhythm, is influential in the regulation of sleep and wakefulness. This is accomplished through the regulation of several bodily processes, including body temperature. Describe below what happens to body temperature when we:

   (a) begin to fall asleep.
   °T begins to drop
   muscles become relax

   (b) continue into deeper sleep.
   °T drops more

   (c) begin to awaken.
   —°T increases

   3-2. There is evidence that exposure to _sunlight_ is responsible for regulating the 24-hour circadian clock. Sunlight affects the suprachiasmatic nucleus in the hypothalamus which in turn signals the _pineal_ gland. The pineal gland then secretes the hormone melatonin which is a major player in adjusting biological clocks. Getting out of sync with the circadian rhythm is more likely to occur when the days are (shortened/lengthened).

   Answers: **3-1.** (a) temperature decreases (b) temperature continues to decrease (c) temperature begins to increase **3-2.** light (or sunlight), pineal, shortened.

4. **Summarize the evidence on the value of melatonin for resetting biological clocks.**

   4-1. Research has shown that low doses of melatonin can (check those that apply):
   a. sometimes alleviate the effects of jet lag
   b. serve as an effective sedative for some people
   c. slow the aging process
   d. enhance sex

   4-2. What are the long-term consequences from taking large doses of melatonin on a daily basis?
   They are unknown

   Answers: **4-1.** Only a and b are correct. **4-2.** They are unknown.

THE SLEEP AND WAKING CYCLE

5. **Describe how sleep research is conducted.**

5-1.   Sleep research is conducted by electronically monitoring various bodily activities such as brain waves, [EEG] muscular activity, [EMG] eye movements, [EOG] and so on, while persons actually ___sleep___ in a specially prepared laboratory setting. Through the use of a television camera or a window, researchers also ___watch___ the subjects during sleep.

Answers: **5-1.** sleep, observe (watch).

6. Describe how the sleep cycle evolves through the night

6-1.   Answer the following questions regarding the sleep cycle.

(a) How many stages are there in one sleep cycle?   4

(b) Which two stages make up slow-wave sleep?   3—4

(c) Which brain waves are prominent during slow-wave sleep.   delta (REM)

Answers: **6-1.** (a) four (or five if you've included REM sleep) (b) 3 and 4 (c) delta.

7. Compare and contrast REM and NREM sleep.

7-1.   What particularly differentiates NREM sleep from rapid eye movement sleep, or ___REM___ sleep, is that during REM sleep the brain wave pattern resembles that of a person who is wide ___awake___. However, REM sleep is actually a fifth stage of sleep in which the muscle tone is extremely relaxed and the sleeper is virtually ___paralyzed___. It is also during REM sleep that vivid ___dreaming___ is most likely to occur.

7-2.   The sleep cycle is repeated approximately ___4___ times during an average night of sleep. NREM sleep dominates the early part of the sleep period, but ___REM___ sleep and dreaming dominate the later stages of sleep. As one progresses though the night the depth of NREM sleep tends to progressively (<u>increase/decrease</u>).

Answers: **7-1.** REM, awake, paralyzed, dreaming **7-2.** four, REM, decrease.

8. Summarize age trends in patterns of sleep.

8-1.   Not only do newborns sleep more frequently and for more total hours during a day than do adults, but they also spend a greater proportion of time in ___REM___ sleep. As they grow older, the children move toward longer but (<u>more/less</u>) frequent sleep periods and the total proportion of REM sleep declines from about 50 percent to the adult level of about ___20___ percent. During adulthood there is a gradual shift towards the (<u>lighter/deeper</u>) stages of sleep.

Answers: **8-1.** REM, less, 20, lighter.

hypothalamus deals wit sleep

9. **Summarize how culture influences sleep patterns.**

   9-1. Answer the following questions regarding sleeping patterns across cultures.

   (a) Which pattern, children sleeping with their parents (co-sleeping) or children sleeping alone, is the most widely practiced?

   (b) Where are the "siesta" cultures generally located?

   Tropical Region

   (c) What is the effect of industrialization on the practice of siestas?

   Practice Declines

   Answers: **9-1.** (a) co-sleeping (b) tropical regions (c) The practice declines.

10. **Discuss the neural and evolutionary basis of sleep.**

    10-1. Sleep and wakefulness is apparently under the control of several neural structures, but one that appears to be particularly essential for both sleep and wakefulness is the reticular _formation_. When a part of this system, called the ascending _reticular_ _activation_ system (ARAS) is severed in cats, the cats remain in continuous _asleep_. When the ARAS is stimulated in normal cats, they act _awake_.

    10-2. However, many other brain structures and at least five neurotransmitters are also involved in the regulation of sleep. There (is/is not) a "sleep center" in the brain nor is there any one neurotransmitter that serves as a _sleep_ chemical.

    10-3. At least three hypotheses attempt to account for the evolutionary (adaptive) basis of sleep: sleep evolved to conserve energy, it reduces exposure to many sources of danger, and it helps to restore body resources. Which hypothesis has the greater empirical support?

    to conserve energy

    Answers: **10-1.** formation, reticular activating, sleep, alert or awake **10-2.** is not, sleep **10-3.** Sleep evolved to conserve energy.

11. **Summarize evidence on the effects of complete and partial sleep deprivation, including the chapter's Featured Study.**

    11-1. Answer the following questions regarding the effects of different kinds of sleep deprivation.

    (a) While both complete and partial sleep deprivation have a negative effect on mood and also on performance on both cognitive and perceptual-motor tasks, what is rather surprising about the degree of these negative effects?

    They are modest

(b) In what way might increased sleepiness be a major problem with respect to the workplace?

increase accidents

11-2. In the Featured Study it was observed that sleep deprived students performed substantially worse on a cognitive task than non-deprived students. How did the sleep deprived students rate their own effort, concentration, and performance?

they were not aware

Answers: 11-1. (a) The effects tend to be modest (b) It can lead to increased accidents. **11-2.** They were unaware of these deficits.

12. Discuss the effects of selective deprivation of REM sleep and slow-wave sleep.

12-1. Studies in which subjects were selectively deprived of REM sleep, leaving NREM sleep undisturbed, found (substantial/little) negative effects from REM deprivation. One curious effect that has been noted from selective REM deprivation is that subjects tend to increase their amount of (NREM/REM) sleep when given the first opportunity to do so. This same rebound effect has also been found with stages 3 and 4 or __slow__-__wave__ sleep.

Answers: 12-1. little, REM, slow-wave.

13. Discuss the prevalence, causes, and treatments of insomnia.

13-1. While practically everybody will suffer from occasional bouts of insomnia, it is estimated that chronic problems with insomnia occur in about ___15___ percent of all adults, and another ___15___ percent complain of occasional insomnia. There are three basic types of insomnia, which are easily remembered because one type occurs at the beginning of sleep, one type during sleep, and the third type at the end of sleep. Thus, one type involves difficulty in initially ___falling___asleep; one type involves difficulty in ___remaining___ asleep; and one type involves persistent ___early___ awakening.

13-2. While there are a number of different causes of insomnia, most of them appear to revolve around the anxiety and emotional reactions that result from the ___stress___ of everyday living. Also health problems and taking certain ___drug___ can also be a factor.

13-3. Since there are many different causes of insomnia, it seems reasonable that there (is/is not) a single form of treatment. However, researchers agree that the most commonly used form of treatment, using sedatives, or ___sleep___ pills, is not the treatment of choice. Evidence shows that while sleeping pills do promote sleep, they also interfere with both the slow-wave and ___REM___ part of the sleep cycle.

Answers: 13-1. 15, 15, falling, remaining, early **13-2.** stress (or problems), drugs **13-3.** is not, sleeping, REM.

14. Describe the symptoms of narcolepsy, sleep apnea, night terrors, nightmares, and somnambulism.

14-1. Described below are five different case histories of persons suffering from five different sleep disorders. Make the appropriate diagnosis for each one.

(a) Throckmorton is a young child who frequently wakes up during the night with a loud piercing cry, but cannot describe what happened to him; he usually returns quickly to sleep. A night spent at the sleep clinic discloses that the episodes generally occur during NREM sleep. Throckmorton is most likely suffering from __night__ __terror__.

(b) Galzelda reports that occasionally, even when typing a term paper or driving a car, she will quickly drop into a deep sleep. The sleep is often accompanied by dreams, which indicates REM sleep. Gazelda is most likely suffering from ~~sleep apnea~~. narcolepsy

(c) Ajax is a young child who frequently wakes up terrified and relates vivid dreams to his parents who rush to comfort him. The family physician tells the parents there is probably nothing to worry about, unless these episodes persist, and that the child will most likely outgrow this problem. The diagnosis here is probably __nightmare__.

(d) Mr. Whistletoe will occasionally get up late at night and walk around the house. Unfortunately, Mr. Whistletoe is completely unaware of this behavior and usually returns to bed without awakening. Upon awakening the next morning he is surprised by a new bruise on his leg and he wonders how the chair in the living room got tipped over. Mr. Whistletoe would be diagnosed as suffering from __somnambulism__, or sleep walking.

(e) Hendrieta complains that during a night's sleep she frequently wakes up grasping for breath. A visit to the sleep clinic discloses that indeed she does stop breathing for brief periods all through the night. Hendrieta undoubtably suffers from __sleep__ __apnea__.

Answers: 14-1. (a) night terrors (b) narcolepsy (c) nightmares (d) somnambulism (e) sleep apnea.

THE WORLD OF DREAMS

15. Discuss the nature of dreams.

15-1. The conventional view of dreams is that they are mental experiences during REM sleep and often have a bizarre storylike quality and vivid imagery. What do many theorists now think of this view?

15-2. In what way do non-REM dreams appear to differ from REM dreams?

Answers: 15-1. They question many aspects of this view. **15-2.** They are less vivid and less storylike.

16. Summarize findings on dream content.

16-1. Calvin Hall, who analyzed the contents of more than 10,000 dreams, concluded that the content of most dreams is (exotic/mundane). Moreover, he found that dreams seldom involve events that are not centered on _____. Hall also found that dreams tend to be like soap operas in that they revolve around such common themes as misfortune, _____, and _____.

16-2. Answer the following questions regarding the differences in dream content between men and women. Which sex is more likely to dream about:

_____ (a) acting aggressively

_____ (b) sex with strangers

_____ (c) children

16-3. What did Freud mean when he stated that our dreams reflect day residue?

16-4. What other factor has an inconsistent effect on our dreams?

Answers: 16-1. mundane, ourselves, sex, aggression **16-2.** (a) men (b) men (c) women **16-3.** They are influenced by what happens to us in our daily lives. **16-4.** external stimuli (dripping water, ringing phones, etc.).

17. Describe some cultural variations in beliefs about the nature and importance of dreams.

17-1. Say which of the following statements about dreams is more characteristic of Western cultures (W) or non-Western cultures (NW).

_____W_____ (a) Little significance paid as to the meaning of dreams.

_____NW_____ (b) Remembering dreams is important.

_____NW_____ (c) Believe that dreams may provide information about the future.

_____U_____ (d) Are likely to report frequent dreams involving food.

Answers: 17-1. (a) W (b) NW (c) NW (d) Persons from any culture who are chronically hungry.

18. Describe the three theories of dreaming covered in the chapter.

18-1. The text mentions three theories as to why we need to dream. Tell what cognitive purpose, if any, each of these theories proposes as to the purpose of dreaming.

(a) This was Sigmund Freud's theory about the need to dream.
    They serve the purpose of wish-fulfilment

(b) This theory proposed by Rosalind Cartwright is cognizant of the fact that dreams are not restricted by logic or reality.
    Dreams allow creative problem solving

(c) The activation-synthesis theory of Hobson and McCarley proposes that dreams occur as side effects of neural activation of the cortex by lower brain centers.

Answers: **18-1.** (a) Dreams serve the purpose of wish fulfillment. (b) Dreams allow for creative problem-solving. (c) Dreams serve no cognitive purpose.

HYPNOSIS: ALTERED CONSCIOUSNESS OR ROLE PLAYING?

19. **Discuss hypnotic susceptibility, list some prominent effects of hypnosis, and explain the role-playing and altered-state theories of hypnosis.**

19-1. While there are many different hypnotic induction techniques, they all lead to a heightened state of _suggeshbility_ Research shows that individuals (do/do not) vary in their susceptibility to hypnotic induction. In fact, approximately _10_ percent of the population does not respond at all, and approximately _10_ percent are highly susceptible to hypnotic induction. People who are highly susceptible tend to have _better_ attitudes about hypnosis.

19-2. The text lists several of the more prominent effects that can be produced by hypnosis. Identify these effects from their descriptions given below.

(a) Reducing awareness of pain. _ane'sthetic_

(b) Engaging in acts one would not ordinarily do. _disinhibition_

(c) Perceiving things that do not exist or failing to perceive things that do exist. _hallucination_

(d) Claiming that sour foods taste sweet. _sensory_ _distortion_

(e) Carrying out suggestions following the hypnotic induction session. _posthypnotic suggestion_

(f) Claiming to forget what occurred during the induction session. _amnesia_

Answers: **19-1.** suggestibility, do, 10, 10, positive (or favorable) **19-2.** (a) anesthetic (b) disinhibition (c) hallucinations (d) sensory distortions (e) posthypnotic suggestions (f) amnesia.

20. **Explain the role-playing and altered-states theories of hypnosis.**

20-1. A theory of hypnosis proposed by Barber and Orne is that hypnosis is really a form of acting or role playing in which the subjects are simply playing as if they are hypnotized. What two lines of evidence support this theory?

20-2. A theory of hypnosis proposed by Hilgard is that hypnosis does in fact result in an altered state of conscious. This theory holds that hypnosis results in a dissociation or _____ of consciousness into two parts. One half of the divided consciousness communicates with the hypnotist while the other half remains _____, even from the hypnotized subject. In this case, pain perceived by the "hidden" part of the consciousness (is/is not) reported to the "aware" part of consciousness. The divided state of consciousness proposed by Hilgard (is/is not) a common experience in everyday life. One such example of this commonly experienced state is appropriately called highway _____.

Answers: **20-1.** Nonhypnotized subjects can duplicate the feats of hypnotized subjects and it has been shown that hypnotized subjects are often merely acting out their expectations of how hypnotized subjects should act. **20-2.** splitting or dividing, hidden, is not, is, hypnosis.

MEDITATION: PURE CONSCIOUSNESS OR RELAXATION?

21. Summarize the evidence on the short-term and long-term effects of meditation.

21-1. Certain short-term physiological changes may occur during meditation. One of the most prominent of these changes is that EEG brain waves change from the rapid beta waves to the slower _alpha_ and theta waves. This change to slower waves is accompanied by (an increase/<u>a decrease</u>) in metabolic activity, such as heart rate, oxygen consumption, etc. All of these physiological changes are characteristic of a normal state of _relaxation_ . This state of relaxation (<u>is</u>/is not) unique to meditation.

21-2. The claims made for the long-term effects of meditation may have some merit in that some studies have shown that subjects have shown improved mood and lessened anxiety and fatigue, as well as better physical health and increased longevity. These changes can (<u>also</u>/not) be induced by other commonly used methods for inducing relaxation. The claim that meditation can produce a unique state of pure consciousness (has/<u>has not</u>) been conclusively proven.

Answers: **21-1.** alpha, a decrease, relaxation, is not **21-2.** also, has not.

ALTERING CONSCIOUSNESS WITH DRUGS

22. List and describe the major types of abused drugs and their effects.

22-1. The text list six different categories of psychoactive drugs; identify these drugs from the descriptions given below.

(a) This drug is the most widely used, and abused, of all psychoactive drugs and produces a relaxed euphoria that temporarily boosts self-esteem. Wine and beer are both examples of the drug _alcohol_ .

(b) While this class of drugs derived from opium is effective at relieving pain, it can also produce a state of euphoria, which is the principal reason that opiates, or _narcotics_, are attractive to recreational users.

(c) The drugs in this class, such as LSD, mescaline and psilocybin, are known for their ability to distort sensory and perceptual experiences, which is why they are given the collective name of _hallucinogens_ .

(d) The drugs in this class include marijuana, hashish and THC. Although they vary in potency, each of them can produce a mild and an easy going state of euphoria along with enhanced sensory awareness and a distorted sense of time. This class of drugs gets its name from the hemp plant _cannabis_ from which they are all derived.

(e) This class of drugs is known for its sleep-inducing (sedation) and behavioral depression effects, resulting in tension reduction and a relaxed state of intoxication. While there are several different drugs in this class, the barbiturates are the most widely abused. Commonly known as "downers", they are more properly called _sedatives_

(f) This class of drugs produces arousal in the central nervous system and ranges from mildly arousing drugs like caffeine and nicotine, to strongly arousing drugs like cocaine and the amphetamines. Known for their ability to produce an energetic euphoria, the drugs in this class go by the name of _stimulants_.

Answers: 22-1. (a) alcohol (b) narcotics (c) hallucinogens (d) cannabis (e) sedatives (f) stimulants.

23. Explain why drug effects vary and how psychoactive drugs exert their effects in the brain.

23-1. Taking a specific drug (will/will not) always have the same effect on the same person. This is because drug effects have _____ causation; individual, environmental, and drug factors can combine in many ways to produce the final effect. For example, one's expectations can strongly affect reactions to a drug. This is known as the _____ effect. Moreover, as one continues to take a specific drug, it requires a greater amount of the drug to achieve the same effect. This phenomenon is called drug _____.

23-2. Psychoactive drugs affect the CNS by selectively influencing _____ systems in a variety of ways. The action takes place at the juncture between neurons, called the _____. Some psychoactive drugs mimic the effects of naturally occurring neurotransmitters, while others act by increasing or decreasing the availability of selective _____. Both sedatives and alcohol exert their key effects at GABA synapses. When these two drugs are taken together their combined depressive effect on the CNS may be greater than the sum of their individual effects. Drugs having this effect are said to be _____.

23-3. It is now believed that virtually all abused drugs gain their reward effect by (increasing/decreasing) activity in the mesolimbic dopamine pathway, which has been characterized as the "_____ pathway".

Answers: 23-1. will not, multifactorial, placebo, tolerance **23-2.** neurotransmitter, synapse, neurotransmitters, synergistic **23-3.** increasing, reward.

24. Summarize which drugs carry the greatest risk of tolerance, physical dependence, and psychological dependence.

24-1. When a person must continue taking a drug to avoid withdrawal illness, addiction, or _____ dependence is said to occur. When a person must continue taking a drug to satisfy intense emotional craving for the drug, then _____ dependence is said to occur.

24-2. As can be seen in Table 5.5 in the text, the three riskiest drugs in terms of tolerance and physical and psychological dependence are:

24-3. What physiological change in the brain appears to facilitate both physical and psychological dependence?

Answers: 24-1. physical, psychological **24-2.** narcotics/opiates, sedatives, stimulants **24-3.** Alterations in synaptic transmission.

25. Summarize evidence on the major physical health risks associated with drug abuse.

25-1. What two physical effects were found in the study in which rats were allowed unlimited access to heroin or cocaine and which drug was the most deadly?

25-2. There are three major ways in which drugs may affect physical health. The most dramatic way is when a person takes too much of a drug, or drugs, and dies of an _____. Another way is when drug usage directly damages bodily tissue; this is referred to as a _____ effect. The third way is when drug usage results in accidents, improper eating and sleeping habits, infections, etc. These effects are collectively called _____ effects.

25-3. Say whether the following statements concerning marijuana are true or false.

____ (a) Pregnant women should not smoke marijuana.

____ (b) Marijuana produces only a slight and insignificant decrease in the immune response.

____ (c) Marijuana can have lasting effects on a male-smoker's sexual functioning.

Answers: 25-1. loss of body weight and death, cocaine **26-2.** overdose, direct, indirect **25-3.** (a) true (b) true (c) false.

26. Discuss how drug abuse is related to psychological health.

26-1. While there is good evidence of a linkage between excessive drug abuse and poor mental health, the data are only correlational. What interpretive problem does this pose?

26-2. Shedler and Block showed in their study of eighteen-year-olds that frequent users of illicit drugs were more likely to have had a prior history of maladjustment in their childhood than less frequent users. One conclusion is that prior maladjustment leads to excessive drug use. What is another possible conclusion?

Answers: 26-1. It's difficult to say which causes which. **26-2.** Ineffective child rearing leads to both maladjustment and excessive drug use.

PUTTING IT IN PERSPECTIVE

27. Explain how the chapter highlighted four of the text's unifying themes.

27-1. Identify which of the underlying themes (psychology evolves in a sociohistorical context, experience is subjective, cultures mold some aspects of behavior, and psychology is theoretically diverse) is illustrated by the following statements.

(a) Psychologists have followed many different approaches and developed many different theories in their attempt to understand consciousness.

(b) The study of consciousness by psychologists followed rather than preceded renewed public interest in this topic.

(c) There are striking individual differences in the way people respond to hypnosis, meditation, and drugs.

(d) The significance given to dreams and sleep patterns can be influenced by this factor.

Answers: 27-1. (a) Psychology is theoretically diverse. (b) Psychology evolves in a sociohistorical context. (c) Experience is subjective. (d) Culture molds some aspects of behavior.

APPLICATION: ADDRESSING PRACTICAL QUESTIONS ABOUT SLEEP AND DREAMS

28. Summarize evidence on common questions about sleep discussed in the Application.

28-1. Answer the following questions about sleep and napping.

(a) How much sleep do we require?

(b) While napping can be refreshing for most people, in what way can it prove inefficient?

(c) Why are drugs such as sedatives and alcohol likely to interfere with refreshing sleep?

(d) What does evidence show about the effectiveness of attempting to learn complex material, such as a foreign language, during deep sleep?

28-2. In addition to developing sensible daytime habits to combat insomnia, there are numerous methods for facilitating actually going to sleep. A common feature in all of them is that they generate a feeling of _____. Some methods generate a feeling of boredom, which is akin to relaxation. The important point here is that one (does/does not) ruminate on the heavy events in life when attempting to go to sleep.

Answers: 28-1. (a) It varies across individuals. (b) Insufficient time is spent in deeper sleep. (c) They interfere with REM and slow-wave sleep. (d) It is very ineffective. **28-2.** relaxation or calmness, does not.

29. **Summarize evidence on the common questions about dreams discussed in the Application.**

29-1. While there are some persons who claim they never dream, what is really happening is that they cannot _____ their dreams. Dreams are best recalled when waking occurs during or immediately following (REM/NREM) sleep. Determination and practice (can/cannot) improve one's ability to recall dreams. A dream whose action takes place over a 20-minute period will actually last for approximately _____ minutes.

29-2. Freud believed that dreams do require interpretation because their true meaning, which he called the _____ content, is symbolically encoded in the obvious plot of the dream, which he called the _____ content. Freud's theory that dreams carry hidden symbolic meaning would mean that dream interpretation (is/is not) a very complicated affair. More recent researchers now believe that dreams are (more/less) complicated than Freud believed. Calvin Hall makes the point that dreams require some interpretation simply because they are mostly (visual/verbal).

29-3. In what way does lucid dreaming differ from regular dreaming?

29-4. Indicate whether the following statements are "true" or "false".

_____ (a) Evidence shows that some control over one's dreams is possible, but it is not easy and results are not always consistent.

_____ (b) There have been several reported cases of persons reporting their own deaths as the result of fatal dreams.

_____ (c) It has been shown that subjects can communicate with researches using prearranged eye signals during lucid dreaming.

Answers: 29-1. remember (or recall), REM, can, 20 **29-2.** latent, manifest, is, less, visual **29-3.** In lucid dreaming one is aware that one is dreaming. **29-4.** (a) true (b) false (c) true.

CRITICAL THINKING APPLICATION

30. **Discuss the influence of definitions and how they are sometimes misused as explanations for the phenomena they describe.**

30-1. Whether alcoholism is a disease or a result of personal failure depends on _____ gets to make up the definition. In fact, there is (only one/no) conclusive way to determine if alcoholism is a disease.

30-2. To say that someone drinks too much because she is alcoholic is an example of _____ reasoning. Definitions can never serve as _____ of the thing they are defining.

Answers: 30-1. who, no **30-2.** circular, explanations.

REVIEW OF KEY TERMS

Alcohol
Ascending reticular activating
   system (ARAS)
Biological rhythms
Cannabis
Circadian rhythms
Dissociation
Electroencephalograph (EEG)
Electromyograph (EMG)
Electrooculograph (EOG)
Hallucinogens

Hypnosis
Insomnia
Latent content
Lucid dreams
Manifest content
Meditation
Narcolepsy
Narcotics or opiates
Nightmares
Night terrors
Non-REM (NREM) sleep

Physical dependence
Psychoactive drugs
Psychological dependence
REM sleep
Sedatives
Sleep apnea
Slow-wave sleep (SWS)
Somnambulism
Stimulants
Tolerance

EEG   **1.** A device that monitors the electrical activity of the brain.

EMG   **2.** A device that records muscle activity and tension.

EOG   **3.** A device that records eye movements.

Biological Rythms   **4.** Periodic fluctuations in physiological functioning.

Circardian rhythms   **5.** The 24-hour biological cycles found in humans and many other species.

REM   **6.** Sleep involving rapid eye movements.

NREM   **7.** Sleep stages 1 through 4, which are marked by an absence of rapid eye movements.

Ascending Recticula-   **8.** Consists of the afferent fibers running through the reticular formation that
Activation System   influence physiological arousal.

opiates   **9.** Drugs that are derived from opium that are capable of relieving pain. These drugs are also called narcotics.

Insomnia   **10.** Involves chronic problems in getting adequate sleep.

narcolepsy   **11.** A disease marked by sudden and irresistible onsets of sleep during normal waking hours.

sleep alnea   **12.** Reflexive grasping for air that awakens a person and disrupts sleep.

nightmare terros   **13.** Abrupt awakenings from NREM sleep accompanied by intense autonomic arousal and feelings of panic.

nightmare   **14.** Anxiety arousing dreams that lead to awakening, usually from REM sleep.

sommambulism   **15.** Occurs when a sleeping person arises and wanders about in deep NREM sleep.

hypnosis   **16.** A systematic procedure that typically produces a heightened state of
medt   suggestibility.

dissosciation   **17.** Involves a splitting off of mental processes into two separate, simultaneous streams of awareness.

meditation   **18.** A family of medical exercises in which a conscious attempt is made to focus
hypnosis   attention in a nonanalytical way.

psychoactive drug   **19.** Chemical substances that modify mental, emotional or behavioral functioning.

slow wave sleep   **20.** Sleep stages 3 and 4 in which low-frequency delta waves become prominent in EEG recordings.

sedative   **21.** Drugs that have sleep-inducing and behavioral depression effects.

stimulant   **22.** Drugs that tend to increase central nervous system activation and behavioral activity.

hallucinogen   **23.** A diverse group of drugs that have powerful effects on mental and emotional functioning, marked most prominently by distortions in sensory and perceptual experience.

cannabis   **24.** The hemp plant from which marijuana, hashish, and THC are derived.

alcohol   **25.** A variety of beverages containing ethyl alcohol.

tolerance   **26.** A progressive decrease in a person's responsiveness to a drug.

Physical dependence   **27.** A condition that exists when a person must continue to take a drug to avoid withdrawal illness.

can psychological dependen   **28.** A condition that exists when a person must continue to take a drug to satisfy mental and emotional craving for the drug.

_____   **29.** Freud's term that refers to the plot of a dream at the surface level.

_m_   **30.** Freud's term that refers to the hidden or disguised meaning of events in a dream.

lucid dream   **31.** Dreams in which persons are aware that they are dreaming.

Answers: 1. electroencephalograph (EEG) **2.** electromyograph (EMG) **3.** electro-oculograph (EOG) **4.** biological rhythms **5.** circadian rhythms **6.** REM sleep **7.** non-REM sleep **8.** ascending reticular activating system (ARAS) **9.** narcotics or opiates **10.** insomnia **11.** narcolepsy **12.** sleep apnea **13.** night terrors **14.** nightmares **15.** somnambulism **16.** hypnosis **17.** dissociation **18.** meditation **19.** psychoactive drugs **20.** slow-wave sleep (SWS) **21.** sedatives **22.** stimulants **23.** hallucinogens **24.** cannabis **25.** alcohol **26.** tolerance **27.** physical dependence **28.** psychological dependence **29.** manifest content **30.** latent content **31.** lucid dreams.

REVIEW OF KEY PEOPLE

Theodore Barber   Sigmund Freud   J. Alan Hobson
Rosalind Cartwright   Calvin Hall   William James
William Dement   Ernest Hilgard

_____   **1.** Originated the term, "the stream of consciousness".

_____   **2.** Argued for the existence of the unconscious and the hidden meaning of dreams.

_____   **3.** As one of the pioneers in early sleep research, he coined the term REM sleep.

_____   **4.** After analyzing thousands of dreams, he concluded that their contents are generally quite mundane.

_____   **5.** Proposes a problem-solving view as a reason for dreaming.

_____   **6.** One of the authors of the role playing theory of hypnosis.

_____   **7.** A proponent of the altered state (divided consciousness) theory of hypnosis.

_____   **8.** His activation-synthesis model proposes that dreams are only side effects of neural activation.

Answers: 1. James **2.** Freud **3.** Dement **4.** Hall **5.** Cartwright **6.** Barber **7.** Hilgard **8.** Hobson.

SELF-QUIZ

1. Which brain wave is probably operating while you are taking this quiz?
   a. alpha
   b. beta
   c. theta
   d. delta

2. What did William James mean by his tern "the stream of consciousness"?
   a. consciousness always remains at the same level
   b. consciousness never stops
   c. consciousness is constantly changing
   d. consciousness is beyond personal control

3. The circadian rhythm operates around a:
   a. 1-year cycle
   b. 28-day cycle
   c. 24-hour cycle
   d. 90-minute cycle

4. The most vivid dreams generally occur during:
   a. REM sleep
   b. NREM sleep
   c. the early hours of sleep
   d. when alpha brain waves are present

5. What appears to be responsible for regulating the circadian rhythm?
   a. amount of time spent sleeping
   b. amount of time spent awake
   c. cultural practices
   d. exposure to light

6. Severing the ascending reticular activating system in cats caused them to:
   a. become very aggressive
   b. become very fearful
   c. remain in continuous wakefulness
   d. remain in continuous sleep

7. The content of most dreams is usually:
   a. mundane
   b. exotic
   c. exciting
   d. erotic

8. Which of the following sleep disorders is most life threatening?
   a. nightmares
   b. narcolepsy
   c. sleep apnea
   d. somnambulism

9. Persons can be made to act as if they are hypnotized even without the use of hypnotic induction. This statement is:
   a. true
   b. false

10. Which of the following physiological changes is unique to meditation?
    a. increased alpha rhythms
    b. decreased heart rate
    c. decreased oxygen consumption
    d. All of these thing are common to many form of relaxation.

11. Psychoactive drugs exert their effect on the brain by:
    a. decreasing blood supply to the brain
    b. altering neurotransmitter activity
    c. breaking down essential brain amino acids
    d. penetrating the nucleus of the neurons

12. The most widely abused drug in the United States is:
    a. alcohol
    b. cocaine
    c. heroin
    d. hallucinogens

13. Which of the following is likely to produce highly subjective events?
    a. hypnosis
    b. meditation
    c. psychoactive drugs
    d. All of the above can produce highly subjective events.

14. Which of the following statements is correct?
    a. Most people do not dream in color.
    b. Practice will not improve the ability to recall dreams.
    c. From birth until death everyone dreams.
    d. Dreams generally last only 1 or 2 minutes.

15. What was found in the Featured Study regarding the effects of sleep deprivation in college students?
    a. sleep deprivation had little effect on their ability to perform cognitive tasks
    b. sleep deprivation had a substantial negative effect on their mood
    c. sleep deprivation had a substantial positive effect on their ability to perform cognitive tasks because the students compensated by increasing their effort
    d. the students were unaware of the actual negative effect of the deprivation

Answers: **1.** b **2.** c **3.** c **4.** a **5.** d **6.** d **7.** a **8.** b **9.** a **10.** d **11.** b **12.** a **13.** d **14.** c **15.** d.

Chapter Six

Learning Through Conditioning

REVIEW OF KEY IDEAS

CLASSICAL CONDITIONING

1. **Describe Pavlov's demonstration of classical conditioning and the key elements in this form of learning.**

   1-1. Classical conditioning is a type of learning that occurs when two stimuli are paired or associated closely in time. In Pavlov's initial demonstration, the two stimuli were a bell and __food__.

   1-2. The response to one of the two stimuli occurs naturally and does not have to be learned or acquired through conditioning. This "unlearned" stimulus, in this case the food, is technically known as the __UC__ stimulus.

   1-3. The other stimulus is said to be neutral in the sense that it does not initially produce a response. When a response to this neutral stimulus is *acquired* or *learned*, the technical name for it is the __CR__ stimulus. In Pavlov's initial study the conditioned stimulus was the sound of a __bell__.

   1-4. The unconditioned stimulus in Pavlov's original study was the _____ and the conditioned stimulus was the _____. Salivation to the meat powder is known as the _____ response; salivation to the bell is termed the _____ response.

   1-5. Label the parts of the classical conditioning sequence. Place the commonly used abbreviations for these terms in the parentheses.

   (a) meat _____ *cB* _____ (   )

   (b) salivation to meat: _____ *c* _____ (   )

   (c) bell: _____ *c S* _____ (   )

   (d) salivation to bell: _____ (   )

2. **Discuss how classical conditioning may shape phobias and physiological processes, including sexual arousal.**

2-1.   The kids in the neighborhood where I (R.S.) grew up used to dig tunnels in a neighbor's backyard. One day someone got stuck in the tunnel and couldn't get out. Eventually he got out, but after that he didn't want to play in tunnels again. To this day that person still has an intense fear not only of tunnels but of closed-in spaces in general. Label the parts of the classical conditioning process involved in the acquisition of the phobia of closed-in spaces. Use the abbreviations CS, CR, UCS, and UCR. (Hint: Even though "getting stuck" certainly involves a behavior or response, it also has stimulus components.)

   UCS   getting stuck

   UCR CER   fear produced by getting stuck

   _CS_   tunnels and closed-in spaces

   _CS_   fear of tunnels and closed-in spaces

2-2.   The individual described above had developed an intense fear or phobia, acquired in part through the process of _classical_ conditioning. Other emotions can be conditioned as well. For example, the smell of smoke and Beemans gum described in your text, the playing of "our song," and the sight of one's home after a long absence could all produce a pleasant emotional response (or perhaps a slightly weepy, sentimental feeling). Such smells, sounds, or sights would be considered _CS_ stimuli.

2-3.   Similarly, certain physiological responses can be conditioned. Label the parts of the conditioning process in the study on immunosuppression in rats described in the text. (Use the abbreviations CS, CR, UCS, and UCR.)

   _____   the immunosuppressive drug

   _____   unusual taste

   _____   decreased antibody production produced by the drug

   _____   decreased antibody production produced by the taste

2-4.   Evidently sexual arousal can be classically conditioned as well. Subjects in the featured study were 29 adult male Japanese _____ . Half of the quail copulated with a female quail in a distinctive, white-painted chamber; this group was the (experimental/control group). For the remaining half, the control group, copulation took place in their home cages.

2-5.   In classical conditioning language, the conditioned stimulus in this study was the (painted chamber/home cage/female quail). The unconditioned stimulus in this study was the (painted chamber/home cage/female quail). The unconditioned response would be arousal to the female quail; the conditioned response would be the additional or enhanced arousal to the painted chamber.

2-6. Results were that during test trials in the distinctive chamber (with the terrycloth, artificial female), quail in the experimental condition released more _____ than did quail in the control group. Release of the additional semen was attributed to classical conditioning. The enhanced arousal produced by the special chamber would be considered the _____ response.

2-7. In quail or in humans, stimuli routinely paired with sex evidently become _____ stimuli for sexual arousal. One implication of this study for evolutionary theory is that the capacity for classical conditioning, in this case of sexual arousal, has _____ value for a species. Conditioned arousal produces more sperm, which enhances the likelihood of fertilization and passing on of one's genes.

Answers: **2-1.** UCS, UCR, CS, CR **2-2.** classical, conditioned **2-3.** UCS, CS, UCR, CR **2-4.** quail, experimental **2-5.** painted chamber, female quail **2-6.** semen (and spermatozoa), conditioned **2-7.** conditioned, survival.

3. Describe the classical conditioning phenomena of acquisition, extinction, and spontaneous recovery.

3-1. *Acquisition* of a conditioned response occurs when the CS and UCS are contiguous, or paired. Not all pairings result in conditioning, however. What characteristics of a CS are more likely to produce acquisition of a CR?

> *beginning stage of learning* [handwritten]
>
> *An intense CS is likely to produce condition* [handwritten]

3-2. Timing is also important for acquisition. In the diagram below, the UCS is shown at the top in bold and three possible arrangements of the CS are shown below it. Label the CS-UCS presentations as *trace*, *simultaneous*, or *short-delayed*.

UCS —— on ... off

CS —— on ... off   (a) _____

CS —— on ... off   (b) _____

CS —— on ... off   (c) _____

3-3. Which of the above arrangements is most effective for establishing a conditioned response?

_____

3-4. Acquisition refers to the formation of a conditioned response. What is the term that refers to the weakening or disappearance of a CR? _____

3-5. Extinction in classical conditioning occurs when the _____ stimulus is presented *alone*, without the _____ stimulus.

3-6. After CRs are extinguished they may reappear, even without further conditioning.

(a) For example, after extinction of a response, a dog may again show the conditioned response (e.g., salivation to a bell) when returned to the apparatus in which it was originally conditioned. What is the name of this type of "reappearance" of the CR? _____ _____

(b) When, or under what circumstance, is spontaneous recovery likely to occur?

(c) If an animal is extinguished in a different environment from the one in which conditioning took place, it is likely to again show a CR when returned to the original environment. What is the name of this effect? _____ _____

Answers: 3-1. A novel or particularly intense CS is more likely to produce conditioning. **3-2.** (a) short-delayed (b) trace (c) simultaneous **3-3.** short-delayed **3-4.** extinction **3-5.** conditioned, unconditioned **3-6.** (a) spontaneous recovery (b) after extinction, following a period of nonexposure to the CS (c) the renewal effect.

4. Describe the processes of generalization and discrimination and summarize the classic study of Little Albert.

4-1. With regard to the case of Little Albert:

(a) What was the CS?

Rat

(b) The UCS?

Hear of rat

4-2. Albert was also afraid of white dogs and white rabbits. What is the name of the process that resulted in his acquisition of these additional fear responses? generalization

4-3. Why would Albert be more likely to develop a fear of a white rabbit, say, than a white car or a dark horse? cuz of the fur

4-4. The more similar stimuli are to the CS, the more likely the organism will generalize from the CS to the other stimuli. The less similar stimuli are to the CS, the more likely the organism is to discrimint them from the CS.

4-5. Casey (R. Ss cat) salivates when she hears the sound of food being dumped into her bowl. The process by which this salivary response was learned is classical. The food is a(an) (CS/UCS/CR/UCR). The sound of the food is a(an) (CS/UCS/CR/UCR). Salivation to the sound is a(an) (CS/UCS/CR/UCR).

4-6. Pets are also likely to salivate when they hear other sounds that are similar to the ones to which they were conditioned. Dishes being pulled from the cupboard, for example, might sound similar to cat food going into a bowl. Salivation to these other sounds represents _____.

4-7. With continued training, in which food is paired only with the sound of food entering the bowl and not with the other sounds, the animal will learn to salivate only to the rattling bowl. The process of learning to respond only to one particular stimulus and not to a range of similar stimuli is termed _discrimination_.

Answers: **4-1.** (a) a white rat (b) a loud noise **4-2.** generalization **4-3.** Because of similarity. The more similar the other stimuli to the CS, the more likely generalization is to occur. **4-4.** generalize, discriminate **4-5.** classical, UCS, CS, CR **4-6.** generalization **4-7.** discrimination.

5. Explain what happens in higher-order conditioning.

5-1. Suppose that a _bell_ and _meat powder_ are paired, as in the original Pavlovian study. At some point a conditioned salivary response will occur to the bell. Suppose that in a new series of trials a _clicking sound_ (a new, neutral stimulus) is paired with the bell. Assuming that the stimuli are potent enough, that the timing is right, and so on, a _____ response will occur to the clicking sound.

5-2. The process described above, in which a stimulus that previously functioned as a _conditioned_ stimulus was used as an _unconditioned_ stimulus, is known as _____ conditioning.

5-3. In our example, in which the clicking sound and bell were paired, which stimulus acted as the UCS?
_____

Answers: **5-1.** conditioned **5-2.** higher-order **5-3.** The bell.

OPERANT CONDITIONING

6. Discuss the nature of operant responding in comparison to the types of responding typically governed by classical conditioning.

6-1. A major feature of Pavlovian or classical conditioning is that conditioned responses occur when two stimuli are paired or associated. For example, when a sound and food are paired together, a conditioned salivary response occurs to the _sound_ .

6-2. In contrast, in operant conditioning, learning or conditioning occurs from stimuli that (precede/follow) the response, the stimuli that are the "payoff" or _reinforce_ of that particular behavior.

6-3. Learning theorists originally supposed that the two types of conditioning controlled different types of responses, that classical conditioning controlled reflexive or (voluntary/involuntary) responses (such as salivation or leg flexion) while operant conditioning controlled voluntary responses. While this distinction holds up (all of the time/much of the time), it is now clear that the only absolute distinction is in terms of procedure.

Answers: **6-1.** sound **6-2.** follow, reinforcers (consequence) **6-3.** involuntary, much of the time.

7. Describe Thorndike's work and explain his law of effect.

7-1. E. L. Thorndike's pioneering work on what he referred to as _instrumental_ learning provided the foundation for Skinner's _operant_ conditioning.

7-2. According to Thorndike's law of _e_ffec_t____, if a response leads to a *satisfying effect* in the presence of a stimulus, the association between the stimulus and response is strengthened. Thorndike's law of effect is similar to Skinner's concept of reinforcement: both emphasize the __consequence_, of behavior.

Answers: **7-1.** instrumental, operant **7-2.** effect, consequences.

8. Describe Skinner's principle of reinforcement and the prototype experimental procedures used in studies of operant conditioning.

8-1. A reinforcer is a stimulus or event that (1) is presented *after* a response and that (2) increases the tendency for the response to be repeated. Apply that definition to this example: Grundoon, a captive monkey, occasionally swings on a bar in his cage. Suppose that at some point Grundoon's trainers decide to give him a spoonful of applesauce whenever he swings. Is the applesauce a reinforcer? In terms of the definition above, how do you know that applesauce is a reinforcer?

8-2. The trainers switch to vinegar. Grundoon, an unusual primate, swings quite frequently when this behavior is followed by vinegar. Is vinegar a reinforcer here? How do you know?

8-3. The trainers try another approach. They present Grundoon with fresh fruit *just before* they think he is likely to jump. It so happens that Grundoon's rate of jumping does increase. Is the fruit a reinforcer here? Why or why not?

8-4. The prototypic apparatus used in operant conditioning studies is the operant chamber, better known as the _Skinner box____. On one wall of the chamber is mounted a manipulandum, a device that makes for an easily discernible response. For rats, the manipulandum is usually a small __bar_____; for pigeons, the device is a ___disc_____ that the bird learns to peck.

8-5. A press of the lever or peck at the disk may produce a reinforcer, generally a small bit of food dispensed into the food cup mounted to one side or below the manipulandum. Each of these responses is recorded on a _cumalative_____ ____record_____, a device that creates a graphic record of the number of responses per unit time.

8-6. The cumulative recorder records the *rate* of the behavior, that is, the number of _+_____ made per unit _____.

8-7. Below is a highly stylized version of a cumulative record. About how many responses were made during the first 40 seconds? _____ Which section of the graph (a, b, c, d, or e) has the steepest slope? _____ Which section of the graph illustrates the fastest rate of responding? _____ About how many responses were made between the 40th and 70th seconds? _____

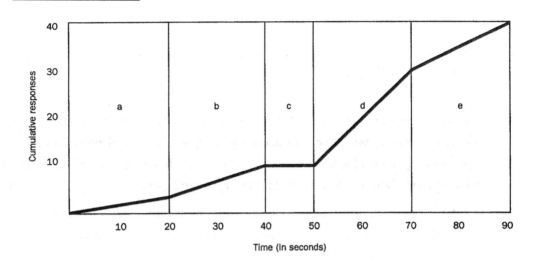

Answers: 8-1. Yes. If the animal's rate of swinging increases when followed by applesauce, then applesauce is a reinforcer. **8-2.** Yes. Because the vinegar is presented *after the response*, and because the *response rate increases*. (Note that this is an imaginary example to illustrate the point that *reinforcement is defined in terms of consequences*, not by subjective judgments about pleasantness and unpleasantness. I don't know of any monkeys that will respond for vinegar.) **8-3.** No. Reinforcing stimuli, by definition, *follow* the response. (Again, this is a contrived example just to illustrate the definition.) **8-4.** Skinner box, lever (or bar), disk **8-5.** cumulative recorder **8-6.** responses, time **8-7.** 10, d, d, 20.

9. Describe the operant conditioning phenomena of acquisition, shaping, and extinction.

9-1. Acquisition refers to the formation of new responses. In classical conditioning, acquisition occurs through a simple pairing of the CS and UCS. In operant conditioning, acquisition involves the procedure known as _____.

9-2. What is shaping? When is it used?

9-3. Extinction in classical conditioning involves removing the UCS while still presenting the CS.

(a) What is the extinction procedure in operant conditioning?

(b) What is the effect of extinction on behavior (response rate)?

(c) What does the term *resistance to extinction* mean?

Answers 9-1. shaping **9-2.** Shaping is the process of reinforcing closer and closer approximations to the desired behavior. It is used in the formation of a new response. **9-3.** (a) No longer presenting the reinforcers after a response. (b) Response rate decreases and may eventually stop. (c) Animals may continue to respond, for a period of time, even when reinforcers are no longer presented. The extent to which they will *continue to respond during extinction* is referred to as *resistance* to extinction.

10. **Explain how stimuli govern operant behavior and how generalization and discrimination occur in operant conditioning.**

   10-1. Suppose that a rat has been shaped so that when it presses a lever it receives a food pellet. With further training, the rat may respond only when a light (or sound, etc.) in the chamber is on and not when it is off. The food pellet (which follows the response) is a _____. The light (which precedes the response) is a _____ stimulus.

   10-2. Reinforcers occur (<u>after/before</u>) the response occurs. Discriminative stimuli occur _____ the response occurs.

   10-3. To create a discriminative stimulus, one reinforces a response only in the presence of a particular stimulus and not in its absence. In time that stimulus will gain control of the response: Animals will tend to emit the response only if the discriminative stimulus is (<u>present/absent</u>) and not if it is _____absent_____.

   10-4. For example, rats can be trained to press a lever when a light comes on and not to press when the light is off. Lever presses that occur when the light is on are followed by a food pellet; those that occur in the dark are not. Label each component of this operant-conditioning process by placing the appropriate letters in the blanks below.

_____ light	a. discriminative stimulus
_____ lever press	b. response
_____ food	c. reinforcer

   10-5. "Heel Fido!" says Ralph. Fido runs to Ralph's side. Fido gets a pat on the head. Label the parts of the operant conditioning sequence by placing the appropriate letters in the blanks. (To avoid confusion, the behavior or response of interest in this example is already labeled.)

_____ Heel Fido!"	a. discriminative stimulus
_____ Fido gets a pat on the head.	b. response
__b__ Fido runs to Ralph's side.	c. reinforcer

   10-6. Phyllis will lend money to Ralph, but only after Ralph promises to pay her back. Ralph is also careful to thank Phyllis for her help. The behavior we are looking at here is Phyllis's lending behavior.

_____ Thank you very much, Phyllis."	a. discriminative stimulus
__b__ Phyllis lends.	b. response
_____ "I promise I'll pay you back."	c. reinforcer

10-7. Generalization occurs in operant as well as classical conditioning. For example, when I put dishes in the sink, our cat would *run to her bowl* looking for food. In technical terms, our cat _____ between the sound of food dropping in her bowl and the *similar* sound of dishes going into the sink. Despite the fact that food does not follow the sound of clattering dishes, our cat did *not* learn to _____ between the sounds in our kitchen.

Answers: 10-1. reinforcer, discriminative **10-2.** after, before **10-3.** present, absent **10-4.** a, b, c **10-5.** a, c, (b) **10-6.** c, (b), a **10-7.** generalizes, discriminate.

11. Discuss the role of delayed reinforcement and conditioned reinforcement in operant conditioning.

11-1. People who smoke like to smoke. Giving up the habit, however, also has its rewards. Given the information about delay of reinforcement, why is the behavior of giving up smoking so difficult to acquire?

11-2. Define the following:

(a) Primary reinforcer:

(b) Secondary or conditioned reinforcer:

Answers: 11-1. Because we, like the rest of the animal kingdom, are more affected by reinforcers that follow our behavior *immediately* than those that follow after a delay. Reinforcement for smoking is immediate; reinforcement for giving up smoking may occur only after a long delay. **11-2.** (a) A primary reinforcer satisfies biological needs, such as needs for food, water, warmth and sex. (b) A secondary, or conditioned, reinforcer is one that is learned or acquired through association with a primary reinforcer. For humans, secondary reinforcers include praise, attention, and money.

12. Identify various types of schedules of reinforcement and discuss their typical effects on responding.

12-1. Schedules of reinforcement are either continuous or intermittent. If reinforcers follow each response, the schedule is referred to as a/an _____-reinforcement schedule, abbreviated CRF. If reinforcers only follow some responses and not others (e.g., FR, VR), or occur as a function of the passage of time (e.g., FI, VI), the schedule is referred to as a/an _____ schedule.

12-2. Identify the following schedules of reinforcement by placing the appropriate abbreviations in the blanks: continuous reinforcement (CRF), fixed ratio (FR), variable ratio (VR), fixed interval (FI), variable interval (VI).

_____ A pigeon is reinforced whenever it has pecked a disk exactly 20 times.

_____ A pigeon is reinforced for pecking a disk, on the average, 20 times.

_____ A rat is always reinforced for the first response that follows a two-minute interval.

_____ A slot machine delivers a payoff, on the average, after every 10th pull of the lever.

_____ Every time the pigeon pecks a disk, it receives a pellet of food.

_____ A rat is reinforced, on the average, for the first response following a two-minute interval.

_____ A pig is reinforced for the first response after 30 seconds, then for the first response after 42 seconds, then for the first response after 5 seconds, and so on.

_____ Every two weeks Ralph picks up his payroll check at the office.

_____ A rat is reinforced after the 73rd response, then after the 22nd response, then after the 51st response, and so on.

12-3. Resistance to extinction refers to the extent to which responses occur during a period of extinction. What is the general effect of the intermittent schedules of reinforcement on resistance to extinction?

12-4. In terms of the effect on _rate_ of responding, what is the general difference between the _ratio_ schedules (FR and VR) and the _interval_ schedules (FI and VI)?

12-5. In terms of the effect on _pattern_ of responding, what is the general difference between _fixed_ schedules and _variable_ schedules?

Answers: **12-1.** continuous, intermittent (or partial) **12-2.** FR, VR, FI, VR, CRF, VI, VI, FI, VR **12-3.** The intermittent schedules increase resistance to extinction. **12-4.** Ratio schedules tend to produce more rapid responding than the interval schedules. **12-5.** Variable schedules tend to produce more regular patterns of responding, without pauses or scalloping, than do their fixed counterparts. They also result in more resistance to extinction.

13. Explain how operant psychologists study choice and summarize what they have learned.

13-1. We make choices. Animals make choices also—for example, whether to seek shelter in a tree or on the ground. In operant theory, choice depends on the payoff or _____ available for a particular behavior.

13-2. To study choice behavior psychologists use two or more reinforcement schedules that operate simultaneously, so-called _____ schedules of reinforcement.

13-3. For example, a pigeon might have the choice between pecking Disk A and Disk B. Suppose the two choices were set up on VI schedules, so that Disk A would reinforce the animal once every minute and Disk B once every two minutes. Which disk would the animal tend to choose more frequently, A or B? _____

13-4. How much more frequently would the animal press disk A? It turns out that the animals will tend to _match_ the rate of responding to the rate of available reinforcement. This is known as the _____ law. For example, if the animal is able to obtain twice as many reinforcers on Disk A as Disk B in a period of time, it will tend to make about twice as many responses on Disk _____. In other words, about two-thirds of the animal's responses will be on Disk A and one-third on Disk B.

13-5. The matching process isn't exact, but it is surprisingly close. Somehow, by using matching, animals are able to make choices that approximate optimal choices. In this way many animals are able to maximize nutrition gained in relation to energy expended, the major principle of _____ theory. Clearly, being able to differentiate reinforcement in this way has _____ value for a species.

Answers: **13-1.** reinforcement (consequences) **13-2.** concurrent **13-3.** A **13-4.** matching, A **13-5.** foraging, survival.

14. Explain the distinction between positive and negative reinforcement.

14-1. Some Skinner boxes may be set up so that a mild electric shock can be delivered to the feet of the animal through the floor of the box. Suppose that whenever the animal presses the bar, the shock is turned *off* for a period of time. Will the lever-pressing behavior be *strengthened* or *weakened*? _____

14-2. By definition, what effect does reinforcement have on behavior? What is the effect of positive reinforcement on behavior? Negative reinforcement?

14-3. With positive reinforcement, a stimulus is *presented* after the response. What is the procedure with negative reinforcement?

Answers: **14-1.** strengthened **14-2.** Reinforcement strengthens (increases the frequency of) behavior. Both positive and negative reinforcement strengthen behavior. **14-3.** The stimulus (an aversive stimulus) is *removed* after the response.

15. Describe and distinguish between escape learning and avoidance learning.

15-1. Review the section on escape and avoidance learning. In escape learning the animal first experiences the aversive stimulus and then makes a response that escapes it. In avoidance learning the animal responds to a cue that permits it to respond *before* the aversive stimulus is delivered, thereby avoiding it altogether. Label the following examples E for escape and A for avoidance.

_____ The weather has changed and Fred is getting cold. He goes inside.

_____ Little Sandra rapidly removes her hand from the hot stove.

_____ A cue light comes on in the dog's shuttle box. It jumps the hurdle to the other side.

_____ Randolph has been told that he will be mugged if he goes outside, so he stays inside.

_____ Sue has learned some new verbal behavior. If she simply says, "No, I don't want that" shortly after a salesman starts his pitch, the salesman will stop bothering her.

_____ Alice sees Ruppert in the distance. If Ruppert sees her he will ask for her course notes, which she doesn't want to lend him. She heads in the other direction.

15-2. What is the major difference between escape learning and avoidance learning?

16. Explain two-process theory and the role of negative reinforcement in avoidance behavior.

16-1. In successful avoidance learning, the organism never experiences the aversive stimulus. For example, when a dog in a shuttle box jumps to the other side it never experiences shock. So, why doesn't the jumping response gradually extinguish? One explanation is that the dog isn't just avoiding the shock, it is also escaping something else as well. It is escaping an *internal* aversive stimulus, namely, conditioned

_____.

16-2. According to two-process theory, fear of the cue stimulus is acquired through (<u>classical/operant</u>) conditioning, through the association of the stimulus and shock. The jumping behavior, on the other hand, is maintained, by (<u>classical/operant</u>) conditioning, by escape from the conditioned fear.

16-3. Escape increases the strength of a response through (<u>negative/positive</u>) reinforcement. The reason that phobic responses are particularly resistant to extinction is because each time an avoidance response is made, the internal _____ stimulus is reduced, which maintains the tendency to avoid.

17. Describe punishment and its effects.

17-1. Punishment involves *weakening* a response by presenting an aversive stimulus after the response has occurred. Review the concepts of reinforcement and punishment by labeling each of the following with one of these terms: *positive reinforcement, negative reinforcement,* or *punishment.*

(a) A stimulus is *presented* after the response; response rate *increases* _____

(b) A stimulus is *presented* after the response; response rate *decreases*: _____

(c) A stimulus is *removed* after the response; response rate *increases*: _____

17-2. Response rate *increases*. Which of the following procedures may have been used?
a. positive reinforcement
b. negative reinforcement
c. punishment
d. either a or b above

17-3. Response rate *decreases*. Which of the following procedures may have been used?
a. positive reinforcement
b. negative reinforcement
c. punishment
d. either *b* or *c* above

17-4. When a rat presses a bar in an operant chamber, the electric shock stops. Bar pressing increases. What procedure has been used?

a. positive reinforcement

b. negative reinforcement

c. punishment

d. extinction

17-5. When the dog ran after the car, his master immediately threw a bucket of water on him. This sequence of events was repeated only twice, and the dog stopped running after the car. What has occurred?

a. positive reinforcement

b. negative reinforcement

c. punishment

d. extinction

17-6. When Randolph stepped out in his new outfit, everyone stared. If Randolph tends *not* to wear this outfit in the future, what has occurred?

a. positive reinforcement

b. negative reinforcement

c. punishment

d. extinction

17-7. In the space below list three negative side effects of punishment.

Answers: 17-1. (a) positive reinforcement (b) punishment (c) negative reinforcement **17-2.** d, because if response rate increases, *either* positive *or* negative reinforcement may be involved **17-3.** c. Not d, because negative reinforcement *increases* response rate. **17-4.** b **17-5.** c **17-6.** c **17-7.** Punishment may (1) suppress responses in general rather than just the response punished, (2) produce unwanted emotional responses, including fear and anger, and (3) increase aggressive behavior.

CHANGING DIRECTIONS IN THE STUDY OF CONDITIONING

18. Discuss the phenomena of instinctive drift, conditioned taste aversion, and preparedness.

18-1. What is instinctive drift?

18-2. Why was the occurrence of instinctive drift surprising to operant psychologists? Discuss this question in terms of the supposed *generality* of the laws of learning.

18-3. What is conditioned taste aversion?

18-4. Why is the occurrence of conditioned taste aversion surprising? Discuss this question in terms of classical conditioning relating to (1) CS-UCS delays and (2) the sense of taste compared with other senses.

18-5. Preparedness is Seligman's idea that there are *species-specific* tendencies to be conditioned in some ways and not in others. Both of the findings discussed above, the phenomena of

_____and _____involve the concept of

_____.

18-6. People are much more likely to die in a car than in an airplane, but phobias related to flying are much more common than phobias about driving. Why is that the case? Try to account for this oddity using Seligman's notion of preparedness.

Answers: 18-1. It is the tendency for instinctive or innate behavior to interfere with the process of conditioning. **18-2.** Before the 1960s, operant psychologists assumed that any response that animals could emit could readily be conditioned. This turned out not to be true. Animals may exhibit instinctive drift, the tendency to respond with certain innate behaviors that actually interfere with the process of conditioning. **18-3.** It refers to the somewhat unusual conditioning involving taste and nausea. If the distinctive taste of a particular food is followed some hours later by sickness (nausea, vomiting, etc.), that taste will become aversive and will itself come to elicit the response of nausea. **18-4.** It is surprising because (1) classical conditioning generally does not occur if there are long CS-UCS delays, and (2) taste is only one of several senses stimulated in this situation. Garcia concluded that animals have an innate tendency to associate taste (rather than sight, sound, etc.) with sickness even though the sickness may occur much later. **18-5.** instinctive drift, conditioned taste aversion, preparedness **18-6.** Seligman's notion of preparedness includes the idea that we are genetically predisposed to develop phobic responses to some stimuli more than to others—to spiders, rodents, and heights more readily than baseballs, lamps, and backyards. Probably because of the heights that are part of flying, flying seems to be more conditionable than driving.

19. Explain the evolutionary perspective on learning.

19-1. Psychologists used to believe that there were highly general "laws" of learning. More recently, studies like those just referred to and the developing field of evolutionary psychology indicate that there probably (are/are not) principles of learning that apply to all species.

19-2. Instead, the new viewpoint emerging among psychologists is that ways of learning have evolved along different paths in different species, so that classical and operant conditioning, for example, are to some extent (universal/specific-specific). Finding food, avoiding predators, and reproducing allow a species to survive, but the ways of learning that accomplish these outcomes depend on the _____ value of these processes.

Answers: 19-1. are not **19-2.** species-specific, adaptive (survival, evolutionary).

20. Describe research on signal relations and response-outcome relations, and explain their theoretical importance.

20-1. In the example of a signal relations study described, the number of conditioning trials in which CS and UCS were paired was the same for two groups, 20 trials. The difference between the two treatment groups was that for one group the (CS/UCS) was presented *alone* for an additional series of 20 trials.

20-2. Theorists originally assumed that classical conditioning is an automatic, reflexive phenomenon that does not depend at all on higher mental processes. If that actually were true, then what should have been the effect of presenting the UCS alone for additional trials? Remember that both groups received exactly the same number of conditioning trials (CS-UCS pairings).

a. Extinction would occur.

b. The UCS-alone trials would weaken conditioning.

c. The UCS-alone trials would have no effect on conditioning.

20-3. In fact, what did occur in the signal relations studies?

a. Extinction.

b. The UCS-alone trials weakened conditioning.

c. The UCS-alone trials had no effect on conditioning.

20-4. These results suggest that the CS *signals* the occurrence of the UCS and that additional trials with the UCS alone weaken the _____ value of the CS. What is surprising about these results? Rather than being an automatic, mechanical process, these studies suggest that classical conditioning involves _____ processes.

20-5. Response-outcome relations refers to the connection between an operant response and its consequences. For example, for a rat in a Skinner box the relationship between the lever press (the response) and the food pellet (the outcome) is this: the rat gets the food *only if* it presses the lever. In other words, the reinforcer is (contingent/not contingent) on the response.

20-6. But does the animal "know" the connection between the response and reinforcer, or is the connection stamped in automatically? That is the crux of the response-outcome relations issue. Evidence suggests that

a. reinforcement and punishment are relatively automatic, mindless processes.

b. cognition is not involved in an organism's responding in an operant chamber

c. humans and other animals actively try to figure out the contingencies, the relationship between response and outcome

20-7. Thus, research on signal relations and response-outcome relations has forced the development of new theories that emphasize a much more _____ explanation of conditioning, an explanation in which organisms actively attempt to detect the *relationship* between their behaviors and environmental events.

20-8. Why are the signal relations studies in classical conditioning and response-outcome relations studies in operant conditioning surprising and of theoretical importance?

Answers: **20-1.** UCS! (If the CS were presented alone, it would be extinction.) **20-2.** c **20-3.** b **20-4.** signaling, cognitive (higher mental) **20-5.** contingent **20-6.** c **20-7.** cognitive **20-8.** These studies indicate that conditioning is not, as assumed earlier, an automatic process but instead depends to a considerable degree on higher mental (cognitive) processes.

OBSERVATIONAL LEARNING

21. Discuss the nature and importance of observational learning.

21-1.   Observational learning occurs when an organism learns by observing others, who are called _____. This type of learning occurs in (humans/animals/both).

21-2.   Why is the concept of observational learning so important? For one thing the idea was surprising to theorists who assumed that all learning could be accounted for by operant and classical conditioning. For another, it extends classical and operant conditioning to include not only *direct* experience but _____ or vicarious experience. We learn not only when we behave but when we _____ the behavior of others.

21-3.   Bandura's theory has helped explain some puzzling aspects of conditioning in human behavior. For example, what happens when parents punish aggressive behavior in their children? While punishment by definition (increases/decreases) the behavior it follows, a parent using punishment also serves as a _____ for aggressiveness. In this way events intended to decrease aggression may, in the longer run, _____ aggression through the process of _____ learning.

Answers: 21-1. models, both **21-2.** indirect, observe **21-3.** decreases, model, increase, observational.

22. List the basic processes in observational learning and discuss Bandura's view on whether reinforcement affects learning or performance.

22-1.   In the space below list and define the four processes that Bandura has identified as crucial components of observational learning. The first letter of each concept is listed at the left.

A_____:

R_____:

R_____:

M_____:

22-2.   Is reinforcement essential for learning? Many learning theorists used to think so, but in Bandura's view reinforcement is essential only for (learning/performance). Bandura asserts that we may learn without being reinforced simply by _____ the behavior of a model, but we are unlikely to perform the response unless we are _____ for doing so.

Answers: 22-1. Attention: Paying attention to a model's behavior and consequences. Retention: Retaining in memory a mental representation of what one has observed. Reproduction: Having the ability to reproduce what one sees, to convert the image to behavior. Motivation: Having the inclination, based on one's assessment of the likely payoff, to reproduce the observed behavior. **22-2.** performance, observing, reinforced.

PUTTING IT IN PERSPECTIVE

23. Explain how the chapter highlighted two of the text's unifying themes.

23-1. Skinner emphasized the importance of *environmental* events (reinforcers, punishers, discriminative stimuli, schedules of reinforcement) as the determinants of behavior. One of our unifying themes, however, is that heredity and environment interact. In support of this theme list the names of three phenomena that show that *biology* has a powerful effect on *conditioning*.

23-2. The second theme well illustrated in this chapter is that psychology evolves in a sociohistorical context. Discuss one concept from operant psychology that appears to have influenced our everyday lives.

Answers: 23-1. instinctive drift, conditioned taste aversion, preparedness **23-2.** Operant psychology has probably influenced the trend in our society toward relying more on the use of positive reinforcement than punishment in child-rearing, in educational settings (e.g., the use of programmed learning), and as a management technique in business.

APPLICATION: ACHIEVING SELF-CONTROL THROUGH BEHAVIOR MODIFICATION

24. Describe how to specify your target behavior and gather baseline data for a self-modification program.

24-1. What behavior do you want to change? The question sounds simple, but the task of defining a _____ behavior is frequently quite tricky.

24-2. The behavior that you select must be defined in terms of observable events so that you will know if and when it changes. For example, for the problem of anger control, which of the following would be the most *directly observable* definition of "anger"?
a. inner turmoil
b. intense hostility
c. loud voice and clenched fists

24-3. Once you specify the target behavior you must gather _____ data on your behavior prior to the intervention. At this time you should also keep track of events that precede the target behavior, the _____ events, and also the positive and negative reinforcers that follow it, the _____ of your behavior.

Answers: 24-1. target (specific) **24-2.** c, although even those behaviors would have to be further described in a behavior modification program. Alternative a is not really observable. Alternative b could be behaviorally defined, but as it stands it is hard to know precisely which behaviors intense hostility refers to. **24-3.** baseline, antecedent, consequences.

25. Discuss your options for increasing or decreasing a response in designing a self-modification program.

25-1. To increase a target behavior you would use _____. The reinforcer (can/can not) be something that you already are receiving. For example, you probably already watch TV, go to movies, or buy things for yourself, so you could make one of these events _____ on an increased frequency of the target behavior.

25-2. You would specify exactly what behavioral goals must be met before you receive the reinforcer; that is, you would arrange the _____. If your goal is to increase studying, you might specify that TV watching for one hour is _____ on having studied for two hours.

25-3. Or, you might specify that for each hour you studied you would earn points that could be "spent" for watching TV, or going to movies, or talking with friends, and so on. This type of arrangement is referred to as a _____ economy.

25-4. A fairly obvious way to decrease a target behavior is to use _____. The problem with this approach is that it is difficult to follow through with self-punishment. So, there are two guidelines to keep in mind when using punishment in a self-control program: (1) Use punishment only in conjunction with _____ reinforcement; and (2) use a relatively _____ punishment that you, or perhaps a third party, will be able to administer.

25-5. It is also possible to use reinforcement to decrease behavior. For example, if you want to gradually reduce the amount that you smoke, you could reinforce yourself whenever you smoke fewer than a particular number of cigarettes per day. Paradoxically, you are using _____ to decrease behavior.

25-6. For some situations you may be able to identify events that reliably precede the behaviors you are trying to stop. For example, for some people smoking is at least under partial control of certain types of social events. So, one strategy for decreasing a behavior is to identify, and then avoid, the (antecedent/consequent) events that may control the behavior.

Answers: **25-1.** reinforcement, can, contingent **25-2.** contingency, contingent **25-3.** token **25-4.** punishment, positive, mild **25-5.** reinforcement **25-6.** antecedent.

26. Discuss how to execute, evaluate, and end a self-modification program.

26-1. Successful execution of the program depends on several factors. To avoid cheating try creating a formal written behavioral _____. Or, make an arrangement so that (only you/someone else) delivers the reinforcers and punishments.

26-2. If your program isn't working, some small revision may turn it around. Try increasing the strength of the reinforcer or else try _____ the delay between the behavior and delivery of the reinforcer.

26-3. It is generally a good idea to specify in advance the conditions under which you would end the program. You may wish to phase it out by having a/an (gradual/immediate) reduction in the frequency or potency of reinforcers, although for some successful programs the new behaviors become self-maintaining on their own.

27. Describe how classical conditioning is used to manipulate emotions.

27-1. It is easy to forget that Pavlovian conditioning involves more than salivating dogs. It involves emotion, and in that respect it is important for a range of reactions—from phobias to sexual arousal to the effects of advertising. For practice with conditioning concepts label each of the following:

(a) A glamorous woman is shown entering an automobile. Label each of the following with CS, UCS, CR, and UCR.

_____ the woman

_____ the car

_____ attraction to the car

_____ attraction to the woman

(b) A politician stands in front of an American flag.

What is the CS? _____

the UCS? _____

(c) A salesman takes you to lunch.

What is the CS? _____

The UCS? _____

The CR? _____

27-2. Of course, there's more going on in these examples than just classical conditioning. When we receive a favor, we are not only being conditioned but may feel obliged to pay back or _____ the person's favor.

27-3. While the examples we've used involve liking or attraction, other emotions may be conditioned as well—such as feelings of masculinity and femininity. Want to be more masculine? Smoke these cigarettes, ads may suggest. Not that we must be conscious of manipulation attempts, for conditioning (does/ does not) seem to require our awareness.

27-4. How do we protect ourselves against attempts to manipulate our emotions? One suggestion from research on persuasion is that merely being _____ of the pervasiveness of conditioning will by itself provide some protections against manipulation strategies.

Answers: **27-1.** (a) UCS, CS, CR, UCR (b) the politician, the flag (c) the salesman (or his product), the lunch, liking for the salesman (or his product) **27-2.** reciprocate **27-3.** does not **27-4.** forewarned (aware).

REVIEW OF KEY TERMS

Acquisition	Fixed-ratio (FR) schedule	Primary reinforcers
Antecedents	Higher-order conditioning	Punishment
Avoidance learning	Instinctive drift	Reinforcement
Behavioral contract	Instrumental learning	Reinforcement contingencies

Behavior modification
Classical conditioning
Concurrent schedules of reinforcement
Conditioned reinforcers
Conditioned response (CR)
Conditioned stimulus (CS)
Continuous reinforcement
Cumulative recorder
Discriminative stimuli
Elicit
Emit
Escape learning
Extinction
Fixed-interval (FI) schedule

Intermittent reinforcement
Law of effect
Learning
Matching law
Negative reinforcement
Observational learning
Operant chamber
Operant conditioning
Optimal foraging theory
Partial reinforcement
Pavlovian conditioning
Phobias
Positive reinforcement
Preparedness

Resistance to extinction
Schedule of reinforcement
Secondary reinforcers
Shaping
Skinner box
Spontaneous recovery
Stimulus discrimination
Stimulus generalization
Token economy
Trial
Unconditioned response (UCR)
Unconditioned stimulus (UCS)
Variable-interval (VI) schedule
Variable-ratio (VR) schedule

learns   **1.** A relatively durable change in behavior or knowledge that is due to experience.

phobias   **2.** Irrational fears of specific objects or situations.

Classical condition   **3.** The most common name of a type of learning in which a neutral stimulus acquires the ability to evoke a response that was originally evoked by another stimulus.

Pavlovian conditon   **4.** Another name for classical conditioning derived from the name of the person who originally discovered the conditioning phenomenon.

   5. Two or more reinforcement schedules simultaneously available for two or more different responses.

UCS   **6.** A stimulus that evokes an unconditioned response.

UCR   **7.** The response to an unconditioned stimulus.

_CS_   **8.** A previously neutral stimulus that has acquired the capacity to evoke a conditioned response.

_CR_   **9.** A learned reaction to a conditioned stimulus that occurs because of previous conditioning.

Elicit   **10.** To draw out or bring forth, as in classical conditioning.

   11. Any presentation of a stimulus or pair of stimuli in classical conditioning.

   12. The formation of a new response tendency.

   13. Under concurrent schedules of reinforcement, rate of responding tends to match the rate of reinforcement available on each alternative response.

   14. The gradual weakening and disappearance of a conditioned response tendency.

   15. The reappearance of an extinguished response after a period of nonexposure to the conditioned stimulus.

   16. Occurs when an organism responds to new stimuli that are similar to the stimulus used in conditioning.

   17. Occurs when an organism learns not to respond to stimuli that are similar to the stimulus used in conditioning.

   18. Occurs when a conditioned stimulus functions as if it were an unconditioned stimulus.

   19. This term, introduced by Skinner, refers to learning in which voluntary responses come to be controlled by their consequences.

_____ 20. Another name for operant conditioning, this term was introduced earlier by Edward L. Thorndike.

_____ 21. Law stating that if a response in the presence of a stimulus leads to satisfying effects, the association between the stimulus and the response is strengthened.

_____ 22. Occurs when an event following a response strengthens the tendency to make that response.

_____ 23. A standard operant chamber in which an animal's responses are controlled and recorded.

_____ 24. Production of voluntary responses in responding in operant conditioning.

_____ 25. The circumstances or rules that determine whether responses lead to presentation of reinforcers; or, the relationship between a response and positive consequences.

_____ 26. Device that creates a graphic record of operant responding as a function of time.

_____ 27. The reinforcement of closer and closer approximations of the desired response.

_____ 28. The food-seeking behaviors of many animals maximize nutrition gained in relation to energy expended to locate and eat the foods.

_____ 29. Occurs when an organism continues to make a response after delivery of the reinforcer for it has been terminated.

_____ 30. Cues that influence operant behavior by indicating the probable consequences (reinforcement or nonreinforcement) of a response.

_____ 31. Stimulus events that are inherently reinforcing because they satisfy biological needs.

_____ 32. Stimulus events that acquire reinforcing qualities by being associated with primary reinforcers.

_____ 33. A specific pattern of presentation of reinforcers over time.

_____ 34. Occurs when every instance of a designated response is reinforced.

_____ 35. The name for all schedules of reinforcement in which a designated response is reinforced only some of the time.

_____ 36. The schedule in which the reinforcer is given after a fixed number of nonreinforced responses.

_____ 37. The schedule in which the reinforcer is given after a variable number of nonreinforced responses.

_____ 38. The schedule in which the reinforcer is given for the first response that occurs after a fixed time interval has elapsed.

_____ 39. The schedule in which the reinforcer is given for the first response that occurs after a variable time interval has elapsed.

_____ 40. Occurs when a response is strengthened because it is followed by the arrival of a rewarding (presumably pleasant) stimulus.

_____ 41. Occurs when a response is strengthened because it is followed by the removal of an aversive (unpleasant) stimulus.

_____ 42. Occurs when an organism engages in a response that brings aversive stimulation to an end.

_____ 43. Occurs when an organism engages in a response that prevents aversive stimulation from occurring.

44. Occurs when an event that follows a response weakens or suppresses the tendency to make that response.

45. Occurs when an animal's innate response tendencies interfere with conditioning processes.

46. Occurs when an organism's responding is influenced by the observation of others, who are called models.

47. A systematic approach to changing behavior through the application of the principles of conditioning.

48. Events that typically precede your target behavior and may play a major role in governing your target response; also, another term for discriminative stimuli.

49. A system for distributing symbolic reinforcers that are exchanged later for a variety of genuine reinforcers.

50. A written agreement outlining a promise to adhere to the contingencies of a behavior-modification program.

51. When a designated response is reinforced only some of the time; another name for intermittent reinforcement.

52. Another name for secondary reinforcers.

53. A species-specific predisposition to be conditioned in certain ways and not in others.

54. A small enclosure in which an animal's responses are recorded and followed by specified consequences; a Skinner box.

Answers: 1. learning **2.** phobias **3.** classical conditioning **4.** Pavlovian conditioning **5.** concurrent schedules of reinforcement **6.** unconditioned stimulus (UCS) **7.** unconditioned response (UCR) **8.** conditioned stimulus (CS) **9.** conditioned response (CR) **10.** elicit **11.** trial **12.** acquisition **13.** matching law **14.** extinction **15.** spontaneous recovery **16.** stimulus generalization **17.** stimulus discrimination **18.** higher-order conditioning **19.** operant conditioning **20.** instrumental learning **21.** law of effect **22.** reinforcement **23.** Skinner box **24.** emit **25.** reinforcement contingencies **26.** cumulative recorder **27.** shaping **28.** optimal foraging strategy **29.** resistance to extinction **30.** discriminative stimuli **31.** primary reinforcers **32.** secondary reinforcers **33.** schedule of reinforcement **34.** continuous reinforcement **35.** intermittent reinforcement **36.** Fixed-ratio (FR) schedule **37.** variable-ratio (VR) schedule **38.** Fixed-interval (FI) schedule **39.** variable-interval (VI) schedule **40.** positive reinforcement **41.** negative reinforcement **42.** escape learning **43.** avoidance learning **44.** punishment **45.** instinctive drift **46.** observational learning **47.** behavior modification **48.** antecedents **49.** token economy **50.** behavioral contract **51.** partial reinforcement **52.** conditioned reinforcers **53.** preparedness **54.** operant chamber.

REVIEW OF KEY PEOPLE

Albert Bandura   Robert Rescorla   E. L. Thorndike
John Garcia   Martin Seligman   John B. Watson
Ivan Pavlov   B. F. Skinner

1. The first to describe the process of classical conditioning.

2. Founded behaviorism; examined the generalization of conditioned fear in a boy known as "Little Albert."

3. Developed a principle known as the law of effect; coined the term *instrumental learning.*

4. Elaborated the learning process known as operant conditioning; investigated schedules of reinforcement; developed programmed learning.

	5.	Asserted that environmental stimuli serve as signals and that some stimuli in classical conditioning are better signals than others.
	6.	Described and extensively investigated the process of observational learning.
	7.	Discovered that taste aversion was conditioned only through taste and nausea pairings and not through other stimulus pairings, such as taste and shock.
	8.	Proposed the theory of preparedness, the notion that there are species-specific predispositions to condition to certain stimuli and not to others.

Answers: 1. Pavlov **2.** Watson **3.** Thorndike **4.** Skinner **5.** Rescorla **6.** Bandura **7.** Garcia **8.** Seligman

SELF-QUIZ

1. In Pavlov's original demonstration of classical conditioning, salivation to the bell was the
   a. conditioned stimulus
   b. conditioned response
   c. unconditioned stimulus
   d. unconditioned response

2. Sally developed a fear of balconies after almost falling from a balcony on a couple of occasions. What was the conditioned response?
   a. the balcony
   b. fear of the balcony
   c. almost falling
   d. fear resulting from almost falling

3. When the UCS is removed and the CS is presented alone for a period of time, what will occur?
   a. classical conditioning
   b. generalization
   c. acquisition
   d. extinction

4. Sally developed a fear of balconies from almost falling. Although she has had no dangerous experiences on bridges, cliffs, and the view from tall buildings, she now fears these stimuli as well. Which of the following is likely to have produced a fear of these other stimuli?
   a. instinctive drift
   b. spontaneous recovery
   c. generalization
   d. discrimination

5. A researcher reinforces closer and closer approximations to a target behavior. What is the name of the procedure she is using?
   a. shaping
   b. classical conditioning
   c. discrimination training
   d. extinction

6. John says, "Please pass the salt." Ralph passes the salt. "Thank you," says John. John's request precedes a behavior (salt passing) that is reinforced ("Thank you"). Thus, the request "Please pass the salt" is a _____ for passing the salt.
   a. discriminative stimulus
   b. response
   c. positive reinforcer
   d. conditioned stimulus (CS)

7. A rat is reinforced for the first lever-pressing response that occurs, *on the average*, after 60 seconds. Which schedule is the rat on?
   a. FR
   b. VR
   c. FI
   d. VI

8. When the rat presses a lever, the mild electric shock on the cage floor is turned off. What procedure is being used?
   a. punishment
   b. escape
   c. discrimination training
   d. avoidance

9. A cue light comes on in the dog's shuttle box. It jumps the hurdle to the other side. What procedure is being used?
   a. punishment
   b. escape
   c. discrimination training
   d. avoidance

10. In the two-process explanation of avoidance, the cue stimulus acquires the capacity to elicit fear through the process of
    a. operant conditioning
    b. classical conditioning
    c. generalization
    d. discrimination

11. The contingencies are as follows: if the response occurs, a stimulus is *presented*; if the response does not occur, the stimulus is not presented. Under this procedure the strength of the response *decreases*. What procedure is being used?
    a. positive reinforcement
    b. negative reinforcement
    c. punishment
    d. avoidance training

12. In terms of the traditional view of conditioning, research on conditioned taste aversion was surprising because
    a. there was a very long delay between CS and UCS
    b. the dislike of a particular taste was operantly conditioned
    c. conditioning occurred to all stimuli present when the food was consumed
    d. the sense of taste seems to be relatively weak

13. Animal trainers (the Brelands) trained pigs to put coins in a piggy bank for a food reward. The animals learned the response but, instead of depositing the coins immediately in the bank, the pigs began to toss them in the air, drop them, push them on the ground, and so on. What had occurred that interfered with conditioning?
    a. conditioned taste aversion
    b. blocking
    c. instinctive drift
    d. S & L scandal

14. Which of the following produces strong resistance to extinction?
    a. a continuous reinforcement schedule
    b. an intermittent reinforcement schedule
    c. optimal foraging behavior
    d. discrimination and differentiation

15. Earlier learning viewpoints considered classical and operant conditioning to be automatic processes involving environmental events that did not depend at all on biological or cognitive factors. Research in which of the following areas cast doubt on this point of view?
    a. blocking and signal relations
    b. instinctive drift and conditioned taste aversion
    c. response-outcome relations
    d. all of the above

Answers: 1. b **2.** b **3.** d **4.** c **5.** a **6.** a **7.** d **8.** b **9.** d **10.** b **11.** c **12.** a **13.** c **14.** b **15.** d.

Chapter Seven

Human Memory

REVIEW OF KEY IDEAS

ENCODING: GETTING INFORMATION INTO MEMORY

1. **List and describe the three basic human memory processes.**

   1-1. The three basic human memory processes are:

   (a) Putting the information in, a process called _encoding_.

   (b) Holding onto the information, a process called _storage_.

   (c) Getting the information back out, a process called _retrieval_.

   Answers: 1-1. (a) encoding (b) storage (c) retrieval.

2. **Discuss the role of attention in memory and contrast the early- and late-selection theories of attention.**

   2-1. If you are being introduced to a new person and you want to remember her name, it is first necessary to give selective _attention_ to this information. This requires _filter_ out irrelevant sensory input. The debate between early and late selection theories of attention is an argument over when this filtering takes place, before or after _____ is given to the arriving material.

   2-2. While there is ample evidence to support both early- and late-selection theories of attention, what conclusion have some theorists been led to?

   Answers: 2-1. attention, filtering, meaning **2-2.** The location of the attention filter may be flexible rather than fixed.

3. **Describe the three levels of information processing proposed by Craik and Lockhart.**

3-1. Craik and Lockhart propose three levels for encoding incoming information, with ever increasing retention as the depth of processing increases. In their order of depth these three levels are:

(a) _structural_   (b) _Phonemic_   (c) _semantic_

3-2. Below are three-word sequences. Tell which level of processing each sequence illustrates and why.

(a) cat   IN   tree   _~~Phon~~ Semantic_

(b) car   BAR   czar   _Phonemic_

(c) CAN   CAP   CAR   _Structual_

3-3. If this theory is correct then we would expect most persons to best remember the sequence in _Sem_ . This is because the words in this sequence have greater _meaning_ than do the other two sequences. It has been found that processing time (is/is not) a reliable index of depth of processing, and thus what constitutes "levels" remains vague.

Answers: 3-1. (a) structural (b) phonemic (c) semantic **3-2.** (a) Semantic because we immediately give meaning to the words. (b) Phonemic because the words sound alike. (c) Structural because the words look alike. **3-3.** (a) cat in tree, meaning, is not.

4. **Describe three techniques for enriching encoding and research on each.**

4-1. Elaboration helps us to better remember the words RUN FAST CAT than the words WORK SLOW TREE. Why is this?

4-2. According to Paivio's dual-coding theory, why is it easier to remember the word APPLE rather than the word PREVAIL?

4-3. What is the general idea behind self-referent encoding?

Apply it to personal experience

Answers: 4-1. Because the words RUN FAST CAT allow us to make richer and more elaborate associations among them than do the other three words (for example you can imagine a cat running fast). **4-2.** Because it is easier to form a visual image of the word APPLE thus allowing for storage of both the word and image. **4-3.** We are more likely to remember information when it is relevant to ourselves.

STORAGE: MAINTAINING INFORMATION IN MEMORY

5. Describe the role of the sensory store in memory.

    5-1. Sensory memory allows for retention of information for a very (brief/long) period of time. The retention time for sensory memory for both vision and audition is about ___1/3 s___. During this brief period the information (remains in/is changed from) its original sensory form.

Answers: **5-1.** brief, 1/4 second, remains in.

6. Discuss the characteristics of short-term memory.

    6-1. Indicate whether the following statements regarding short-term memory are true or false.

        ____F____ (a) Has a virtually unlimited storage capacity.

        ____T____ (b) Has a storage capacity of seven, plus or minus two, items.

        ____T____ (c) Requires continuous rehearsal to maintain information in store for more than 20 or 30 seconds.

        ____F____ (d) Stores information more or less permanently.

        ____T____ (e) Chunking can help to increase the capacity of this system.

Answers: **6-1.** (a) false (b) true (c) true (d) false (e) true.

7. Discuss Baddeley's model of working memory.

    7-1. Say which component of Baddeley's working memory—phonological rehearsal loop, visuospatial sketchpad, or executive control system—is operating in the following situations.

(a) You are mentally weighing the pros and cons of attending a particular university.

        execute

(b) You continue to recite a phone number as you walk towards the phone.

        Phon

(c) You are describing the location of a restaurant to a friend.

        visual

Answers: **7-1.** (a) executive control system (b) phonological rehearsal loop (c) visuospatial sketchpad.

8. Evaluate the hypothesis that all memories are stored permanently in long-term memory (LTM).

    8-1. There are two views regarding the durability of information in LTM. One is that no information is ever lost and the other is that ___never___ information is lost. Those who favor the "no-loss" view explain forgetting as a failure of ___encoding___. The information is still there, we just cannot get it out.

8-2.   How do the some-loss proponents counter the following three lines of evidence cited by the no-loss proponents?

(a) Flashbulb memories of previous events?

(b) The remarkable recall of hypnotized subjects?

(c) Penfield's electrically triggered memories?

Answers: 8-1. some, retrieval **8-2.** (a) They often tend to be inaccurate and less detailed with the passage of time. (b) Their recall of information is often found to be incorrect. (c) The memories were often incorrect and resembled dreams or hallucinations more than real events.

9. **Evaluate the issues in the debate about whether short-term and long-term memory are really separate.**

9-1.   The traditional view is that short-term memory differs from long-term memory in that it depends on phonemic (sound) encoding while long-term memory depends on ___semantic___ (meaning) encoding. These two systems are also said to differ in the manner in which forgetting occurs. The loss of memory in STM is thought to result from time-related decay, while LTM forgetting is attributed to ___interference___

9-2.   What research findings undermine the traditional view?

9-3.   How do theorists who support a unitary ìgenericî memory store explain such phenomena as the constant repeating of a phone number in short-term memory?

Answers: 9-1. semantic, interference **9-2.** Semantic encoding and interference have also been found in short-term memory. **9-3.** This is merely the generic memory store in an elevated state of activation.

10. **Describe conceptual hierarchies, schemas, and semantic networks, and their role in long-term memory (LTM).**

10-1.   Group the following words into two groups or categories:

   rose   dog   grass   cat   tree   rat

You probably grouped the words into plants and animals, which is the general idea behind ___clustering___.
Thus clustering leads to forming categories (concepts) and in turn the categories are organized into
_____ hierarchies. For example, the categories of plants and animals can be placed under the higher
category (hierarchy) of _____ things.

10-2. It also appears that LTM also stores information in an organized clusters of knowledge about particular objects or events called _____. For example, in the study cited by the text, the subjects who falsely recalled seeing books did so because of their schema of what a professor's _____ looks like. A particular kind of schema that organizes what people know about common activities, such as grocery shopping or washing clothes, is called a _____.

10-3. In addition to conceptual categories, it appears that LTM also stores information in terms of semantic networks. If you understand the idea behind semantic networks and its related idea of spreading activation, you should be able to answer the questions below.

Person A attends an urban university and frequently studies while riding a bus to and from school.

Person B attends a university located in a rural area and frequently studies outside in one of the many park-like areas surrounding the school.

(a) When asked to think of words associated with the word STUDY, which of the students is most likely to think of the word GRASS?_____

(b) Which person is most likely to think of the word TRAFFIC?_____

(c) Which person is most likely to think of the word PEACEFUL?_____

Answers: 10-1. clustering, conceptual, living **10-2.** schemas, office, script **10-3.** (a) person B (b) person A (c) person B.

11. Explain how parallel distributed processing (PDP) models view the representation of information in memory.

11-1. PDP models assume that a piece of knowledge is represented by a particular _pattern_ of activation across an entire system of innerconnected neural networks. This approach is called "connectionism" because the information lies in the strengths of the _____.

11-2. The PDP approach has at least two strengths. First, it (<u>agrees</u>/disagrees) with the findings from neurophysiological research. Second, it can account for the (slow/<u>blazing</u>) speed of human's cognitive functioning.

Answers: 11-1. pattern, connections **11-2.** agrees, blazing.

RETRIEVAL: GETTING INFORMATION BACK OUT OF MEMORY

12. Explain how retrieval cues and context cues influence retrieval.

12-1. In the following examples indicate whether retrieval cues or context cues are being used to retrieve information from long-term memory.

(a) In trying to recall the name of a high school classmate, you get the feeling that his first name began with an "L," and begin saying names like Larry, Leroy, Lionel, etc.

(b) Or you may attempt to recall the high school classmate by imagining the history class in which he sat in the row next to you.

Answers: **12-1.** (a) retrieval cues (b) context cues.

13. Discuss Bartlett's work and research on the misinformation effect.

13-1. Bartlett's work with the "The War of the Ghosts," found that the subjects reconstructed the original tale to fit with their already established _____. Since we use schemas to move information in and out of long-term memory, it is not too surprising that retrieved information may be altered by these schemas.

13-2. For example, Elizabeth Loftus found that subjects, when tested at a later date, were much more likely to falsely recall seeing broken glass on a videotaped scene when they were originally asked, "How fast were the cars going when they (hit/smashed) into each other." In this case the word "smashed" resulted in a different _____ than did the word "hit." The distortion of memory by the word "smashed" is an example of how post-event information can result in the _____ of an original memory.

13-3. While research evidence clearly shows that post-event misinformation does cause alterations in memory, it not so clear about the underlying mechanisms. One theory, covered so far, is that the misinformation replaces and wipes out the original memory. What other theory has been proposed to account for this phenomenon?

Answers: **13-1.** schemas **13-2.** smashed, schema, reconstruction **13-3.** The misinformation interferes with retrieving the original information.

14. Discuss the implications of evidence on source monitoring and reality monitoring.

14-1. A third explanation for distorted memory retrieval involves source monitoring. Both source monitoring and its subtype, reality monitoring, require us to make attributions about the _____ of memories. Errors in memory from both kinds of monitoring are (rare/common).

14-2. Say whether the situations below are examples of source monitoring (S) or reality monitoring (R).

_____ (a) You become convinced that you broke your arm when you were five years old, but your mother tells you that it never happened.

_____ (b) You attribute a funny story to your good friend Tom when in fact it was Fred, whom you don't really care for, who told you the story.

_____ (c) You believe that you received an "A" in high school algebra, but your transcript shows a "C".

Answers: **14-1.** origins, common **14-2.** (a) R (b) S (c) R.

FORGETTING: WHEN MEMORY LAPSES

15. Describe Ebbinghaus's forgetting curve and three measures of retention.

15-1. Ebbinghau's forgetting curve, using nonsense syllables and himself as the subject, showed that forgetting was most rapid in the (<u>first/second</u>) 9 hours after learning the material. Latter research has shown that the dramatic decline is (<u>the same/much less</u>) when more meaningful material is involved.

15-2. Which of the three different methods of measuring forgetting is illustrated in each of the following situations?

(a) You are asked to identify a suspect in a police lineup.

(b) You time yourself while learning 20 new French words. After a week you find you have forgotten some of the words, and you again time yourself while learning the list a second time.

(c) You are asked to draw a floor plan of your bedroom from memory.

Answers: 15-1. first, much less **15-2.** (a) recognition (b) relearning (c) recall.

16. Explain how forgetting may be due to ineffective encoding.

16-1. Why are most people unable to recognize the correct penny shown at the beginning of this chapter in the text?

16-2. What is another name for information loss due to ineffective coding of this kind?

16-3. Why is semantic coding better than phonemic coding for enhancing future recall of written material?

Answers: 16-1. They never encoded the correct figure in their memories. **16-2.** pseudoforgetting **16-3.** Semantic coding will lead to deeper processing and more elaborate associations.

17. Compare and contrast decay and interference as potential causes of forgetting.

17-1. Two other theories of forgetting propose additional factors that may be involved in retrieval failure. One theory holds that retrieval failure may be due to the impermanence of the memory storage itself. This is the notion behind the _____ theory of forgetting. Decay theory is best able to explain retrieval failure in _____ memory and to a lesser extent in (short-term/long-term) memory.

17-2. The other theory attributes retrieval failure to other information already in the memory or to information arriving at a later time. This is the notion behind the _____ theory of forgetting. According to interference theory, the failure may be caused by interference from information already in the memory, a phenomenon called _____ interference, or the failure may be caused by interference occurring after the original memory was stored, a phenomenon called _____ interference. Interference is most likely to occur when the materials being stored are very (similar/different).

Answers: 17-1. decay, sensory store, short-term **17-2.** interference, proactive, retroactive, similar.

18. Explain how forgetting may be due to factors in the retrieval process.

18-1. Breakdowns in the retrieval process can occur when the encoding specificity principle is violated. This means there has been a mismatch between the original memory code and the _____ cue being used to retrieve the information. A common instance of this violation is seen when one attempts to retrieve a semantically coded word with (semantic/phonemic) retrieval cues.

18-2. Retrieval failure may also occur when there is a poor fit between initial encoding processing and the processing required by the measure of retention. In other words, the two kinds of processing are not transfer-_____.

18-3. Sigmund Freud felt that some breakdowns in the retrieval process could be attributed to purposeful suppression of information by unconscious forces, a phenomenon called _____ forgetting. Freud called motivated forgetting _____.

Answers: 18-1. retrieval, phonemic **18-2.** appropriate **18-3.** motivated, repression.

19. Summarize evidence for the view that most recovered memories of childhood sexual abuse are genuine.

19-1. Those who argue that most of these recovered memories are genuine assert that the frequency of sexual abuse in childhood is (less/more) widespread than most people realize.

19-2. What did the study find that did a 17-year follow-up of 129 female children who had emergency treatment for sexual abuse?

Answers: 19-1. more **19-2.** 38 percent failed to report the original incident.

20. Summarize evidence for the view that most recovered memories of childhood sexual abuse are inaccurate.

20-1. How do the skeptics of these recovered memories of childhood sexual abuse explain their origin?

20-2. What is the only way to tell for certain if a recovered memory is genuine or a pseudomemory?

Answers: 20-1. Some suggestible people are convinced by persuasive therapists (that these events must have happened). **20-2.** through independent corroborative evidence.

21. Describe the Featured Study on the creation of false memories.

21-1. Answer the following questions regarding the Featured Study.

(a) What kinds of persons made up the two groups in this study.

(b) What three factors increased the probability of the psuedomemory effect?

Answers: 21-1. (a) Persons who scored high or low in hypnotic susceptibility. (b) Being highly susceptible to hypnosis, being hypnotized, and experiencing rapport with the hypnotist.

IN SEARCH OF THE MEMORY TRACE: THE PHYSIOLOGY OF MEMORY

22. Summarize evidence on the biochemistry and neural circuitry underlying memory.

22-1. Which of the following biochemical changes have been implicated in the physiology of memory?

(a) an increase or decrease in the release of neurotransmitters

(b) induced changes in RNA

(c) hormones that can either facilitate or impair memory storage

(d) interference with protein synthesis

22-2. Answer the following questions regarding the neural circuitry of memory.

(a) What caused a rabbit to lose its memory of a conditioned eye blink?

(b) What neural changes were found in rats that learned to run a series of mazes?

(c) What does research with long-term potentiation (LTP) and the demonstration of an increase in neuronal dendritic trees tell us about how memory is stored?

Answers: 22-1. a, c, d **22-2.** (a) Destruction of an area in the cerebellum. (b) Increased growth of neuronal dendritic trees. (c) Specific memories may have specific localized dedicated neural circuits.

23. **Distinguish between two types of amnesia and identify the anatomical structures implicated in memory.**

   23-1.   Amnesia cases due to head injury provide clues about the anatomical basis of memory. There are two basic types of head-injury amnesia. When the memory loss is for events prior to the injury, it is called _____ amnesia. When the memory loss is for events following the injury, it is called _____ amnesia.

   23-2.   What general region of the brain appears to play a major role in the consolidation of memories?

   23-3.   Consolidation is an hypothesized process which involves the gradual conversion of information into durable memory _____ stored in long-term memory. These memories are then stored in the same areas of the _____ that were originally involved in processing the sensory input that led to the memories.

   Answers: 23-1. retrograde, anterograde **23-2.** the entire hippocampul region **23-3.** codes, cortex.

ARE THERE MULTIPLE MEMORY SYSTEMS?

24. **Distinguish between implicit versus explicit memory and their relationship to declarative and procedural memory.**

   24-1.   Label the two following situations as to whether they are examples of implicit or explicit memory.

   (a) After studying for your history test, you were able to easily recall the information during the exam.

   (b) While studying for your history exam, you unexpectedly recall an incident from the previous summer.

   24-2.   Another division of memory systems has been hypothesized for declarative memory and procedural memory. Identify these two divisions from their descriptions given below.

   (a) This system allows you to drive a car or play a piano with minimal attention to the execution of movements that are required.

(b) This system allows you to explain how to drive a car or play a piano to a friend.

24-3. It has been suggested that there is an apparent relationship between implicit memory and _____ memory and between explicit memory and _____ memory.

Answers: **24-1.** (a) explicit (b) implicit **24-2.** (a) procedural (b) declarative **24-3.** (a) procedural (b) declarative.

25. Explain the distinctions between episodic memory versus semantic memory and prospective versus retrospective memory.

25-1. It has also been hypothesized that declarative memory can be further subdivided into semantic and episodic memory. Identify these two kinds of memory from the following descriptions:

(a) This kind of memory acts like an encyclopedia, storing all of the factual information you possess.

(b) This kind of memory acts like an autobiography, storing all of your personal experiences.

25-2. Still another possibility is that we have separate memory systems for prospective and retrospective memory. The distinction here is between our ability to remember events from the past or previously learned information, _____ memory, and our ability to remember or perform actions in the future, _____ memory.

25-3. Which form of prospective memory appears to give us the most trouble when we try and retrieve it, memory of event-based tasks or memory of time-based tasks?

Answers: **25-1.** (a) semantic (b) episodic **25-2.** retrospective, prospective **25-3.** time-based tasks.

PUTTING IT IN PERSPECTIVE

26. Explain how this chapter highlighted three of the text's unifying themes.

26-1. Three unifying themes were especially noteworthy in this chapter: the subjectivity of experience, psychology's theoretical diversity, and multifactorial causation. The text mentions two areas in which subjectivity may influence memory. Identify them below.

(a) We often see only that which gets the focus of our _____.

(b) Every time we tell about a particular experience, details are added or subtracted because of the _____ nature of memory.

26-2. The numerous debates about the nature of memory storage, the causes of forgetting, and the existence of multiple memory systems nicely illustrates psychology's _____ _____.

26-3. Since the memory of a specific event can be influenced by many factors, operating in each of the three memory stores, it is obvious that memory, like most behavior, has _____

_____.

APPLICATION: IMPROVING EVERYDAY MEMORY

27. Discuss the importance of rehearsal, distributed practice, and interference in efforts to improve everyday memory.

27-1. The text lists three general strategies for improving everyday memory. Identify which strategy is being employed in the following examples.

(a) Most persons can remember their phone number because of extensive_____.

(b) Willie Nurd the bookworm always takes breaks between study periods when changing subject matter. Willie must realize the importance of _____ practice.

(c) Ajax never studies any other material besides mathematics on the day of his math exams in order to minimize _____.

27-2. The serial position effect means that words in the middle of a list will need (more/less) of our attention.

28. Discuss the value of deep processing, transfer-appropriate processing, and good organization in efforts to improve everyday memory.

28-1. Answering questions such as these is much better than simply underlining the same material in the text because it forces you to engage in _____.

28-2. The self-quiz at the end of this chapter will help you prepare for a similar multiple-choice test because you are taking advantage of _____-_____ processing. When employing transfer-appropriate processing it is wise to use fact-oriented processing when the test will emphasize remembering factual material and problem-oriented processing when the test will emphasize _____ solving.

28-3. Outlining material from textbooks can enhance retention because it leads to better _____ of the material.

29. Describe some verbal and visual mnemonic devices that can be used to improve everyday memory.

29-1. Specific strategies for enhancing memory are called _____ devices. Examples of strategies which do not employ visual images are listed below. See if you can identify which strategy is being employed in each illustration.

(a) Using the phrase, "My Very Excellent Mother Just Sells Nuts Under Protest", to remember the names and positions of the planets illustrates the use of an _____.

(b) International Business Machines is easily identified by its _____, IBM.

(c) The phrase, "One two three four, I left my keys in the drawer," illustrates the use of

_____.

(d) Since you are going to the store your roommate asks you to bring her a bar of Ivory soap, a box of Kleenex, and a Snickers bar. You then make up a story which begins, "On my way to the Ivory Coast to check on the latest shipment of Kleenex, I ...." Here you're making use of a _____ method as a mnemonic device.

29-2.   Three techniques involving visual imagery can also serve as helpful mnemonic devices: the link method, the method of loci, and the keyword method. Identify them in the examples below.

(a) You want to remember the name of your bus driver, Ray Blocker, who has especially large forearms. You form an image of a man using his large arms to block light rays from his face.

(b) You want to remember to buy bananas, eggs, milk, and bread. You visualize walking in your front door and tripping on a bunch of bananas. Stumbling forward into the hallway you notice broken eggs on the table etc.

(c) You imagine yourself using a banana to break eggs, which you then pour into a bowl of milk and bread.

Answers: 29-1. mnemonic (a) acrostic (b) acronym (c) rhyming (d) narrative 29-2. (a) keyword method (b) method of loci (c) link method.

CRITICAL THINKING APPLICATION

30.   Explain how hindsight bias and overconfidence contribute to the frequent inaccuracy of eye-witness testimony.

30-1.   The frequent inaccuracy of eye-witness testimony is due in part to the reconstructive nature of memory, source monitoring, and the misinformation effect. In addition, the text points out that still another factor is our tendency to mold our interpretation of the past to fit how events actually turned out. This is called the _____ _____.

30-2.   The failure to seek disconfirming evidence can often lead to the _____ effect, which is still another reason for the frequent inaccuracy of eye-witness testimony.

Answers: 30-1. hindsight bias 30-2. overconfidence

REVIEW OF KEY TERMS

Anterograde amnesia	Declarative memory system	Forgetting curve
Attention	Dual-coding theory	Implicit memory
Chunk	Elaboration	Interference theory
Clustering	Encoding	Keyword method
Conceptual hierarchy	Encoding specificity principle	Levels of processing theory
Connectionist models	Episodic memory system	Link method
Consolidation	Explicit memory	Long-term memory (LTM)
Decay theory	Flashbulb memories	Long-term potentiation (LTP)

Method of loci
Mnemonic devices
Nondeclarative memory system
Nonsense syllables
Overlearning
Parallel distributed processing (PDP)
Proactive interference
Procedural memory system
Prospective memory
Reality monitoring
Recall

Recognition
Rehearsal
Relearning
Repression
Retention
Retrieval
Retroactive interference
Retrograde amnesia
Retrospective memory
Schema
Script

Self-referent encoding
Semantic memory system
Semantic networks
Sensory memory
Serial-position effect
Short-term memory
Source-monitoring
Source-monitoring error
Storage
Tip-of-the-tongue phenomenon
Transfer-appropriate processing.

_____ 1. Putting coded information into memory.

_____ 2. Maintaining coded information in memory.

_____ 3. Recovering information from memory stores.

_____ 4. The process of focusing awareness on a narrowed range of stimuli or events.

_____ 5. Involves remembering to perform actions in the future.

_____ 6. Involves remembering events from the past or previously learned information.

_____ 7. The initial processing of information is similar to the type of processing required by the subsequent measure of retention.

_____ 8. Assumes that cognitive processes depend on patterns of activation in highly interconnected computational networks that resemble neural networks.

_____ 9. Memory which involves the intentional recollection of previous experiences.

_____ 10. A theory that proposes that deeper levels of processing result in longer lasting memory codes.

_____ 11. Involves linking a stimulus to other information at the time of encoding.

_____ 12. A theory that memory is enhanced by forming both semantic and visual codes since either can lead to recall.

_____ 13. Preserves information in the original sensory form for a very brief time.

_____ 14. A limited capacity memory store that can maintain unrehearsed information for 20 to 30 seconds.

_____ 15. The process of repetitively verbalizing or thinking about new information.

_____ 16. A group of familiar stimuli stored as a single unit.

_____ 17. An unlimited capacity memory store that can hold information over lengthy periods of time.

_____ 18. Unusually vivid and detailed recollections of momentous events.

_____ 19. Occurs when subjects show better recall of items at the beginning and end of a list than for items in the middle.

_____ 20. Memory for factual information.

_____ 21. Memory for actions, skills, and operations.

_____ 22. Memory made up of chronological, or temporally dated, recollections of personal experiences.

_____ 23. Memory that contains general knowledge that is not tied to the time when the information was learned.

_____ 24. The tendency to remember similar or related items in a group.

_____ 25. These consist of concepts joined together by links that show how the concepts are related.

_____ 26. A long lasting increase in neural excitability at synapses along a specific neural pathway.

_____ 27. An organized cluster of knowledge about a particular object or sequence of events.

_____ 28. A particular kind of schema that organizes what people know about common activities.

_____ 29. A temporary inability to remember something you know accompanied by the feeling that it's just out of reach.

_____ 30. Consonant-vowel-consonant letter combinations that do not correspond to words (NOF, KER, etc.).

_____ 31. A curve graphing retention and forgetting over time.

_____ 32. The proportion of material remembered.

_____ 33. The ability to remember information without any cues.

_____ 34. Requires the selection of previously learned information from an array of options (e.g., multiple-choice tests).

_____ 35. Requires the memorization of information a second time to determine how much time or effort is saved.

_____ 36. Attributes forgetting to the impermanence of memory storage.

_____ 37. Attributes forgetting to competition from other material.

_____ 38. Occurs when new information impairs the retention of previously learned information.

_____ 39. Occurs when previously learned information impairs the retention of new information.

_____ 40. States that the value of a retrieval cue depends on how well it corresponds to the memory code.

_____ 41. Involves purposeful suppression of memories (motivated forgetting).

_____ 42. A theoretical process involving the gradual conversion of information into durable memory codes stored in long-term memory.

_____ 43. The loss of memory for events that occurred prior to a brain injury.

_____ 44. The loss of memory for events that occur after a brain injury.

_____ 45. Strategies for enhancing memory.

_____ 46. The continued rehearsal of material after it has apparently been mastered.

_____ 47. Involves forming a mental image of items to be remembered in a way that connects them together.

_____ 48. A mnemonic device that involves taking an imaginary walk along a familiar path.

_____ 49. Involves associating a concrete word with an abstract word and generating an image to represent the concrete word.

_____ 50. A multi-level classification system based on common properties among items (e.g., cats, animals, living things).

_____ 51. Is apparent when retention is exhibited on a task that does not require intentional remembering.

_____ 52. The process of deciding how or whether information is personally relevant.

_____ 53. The process of making attributions about the origins of memories.

54. The process of deciding whether memories are based on external or internal sources.

55. An error that occurs when a memory derived from one source is attributed to another.

56. Another term for the procedural memory system which houses memory for actions, skills, and operations.

Answers: 1. encoding **2.** storage **3.** retrieval **4.** attention **5.** prospective memory **6.** retrospective memory **7.** transfer-appropriate processing **8.** connectionists models and parallel distributed processing (PDP) **9.** explicit memory **10.** levels of processing theory **11.** elaboration **12.** dual-coding theory **13.** sensory memory **14.** short-term memory (STM) **15.** rehearsal **16.** chunk **17.** long-term memory (LTM) **18.** flashbulb memories **19.** serial position effect **20.** declarative memory system **21.** procedural memory system **22.** episodic memory system **23.** semantic memory system **24.** clustering **25.** semantic networks **26.** long-term potentiation **27.** schema **28.** script **29.** tip-of-the-tongue phenomenon **30.** nonsense syllables **31.** forgetting curve **32.** retention **33.** recall **34.** recognition **35.** relearning **36.** decay theory **37.** interference theory **38.** retroactive interference **39.** proactive interference **40.** encoding specificity principle **41.** repression **42.** consolidation **43.** retrograde amnesia **44.** anterograde amnesia **45.** mnemonic devices **46.** overlearning **47.** link method **48.** method of loci **49.** keyword method **50.** conceptual hierarchy **51.** implicit memory **52.** self-referral encoding **53.** source monitoring **54.** reality monitoring **55.** source-monitoring error **56.** nondeclarative memory.

REVIEW OF KEY PEOPLE

Richard Atkinson & Richard Shiffrin
Fergus Craik and Robert Lockhart
Herman Ebbinghaus

Marcia Johnson
Elizabeth Loftus
George Miller

Brenda Milner
Endel Tulving

1. Proposed three progressively deeper levels for processing incoming information.

2. Influential in the development of the model of three different kinds of memory stores (sensory, STM and LTM).

3. She, and her colleagues, proposed the notions of source and reality monitoring.

4. Demonstrated that the reconstructive nature of memory can distort eyewitness testimony.

5. Used nonsense syllables to become famous for his forgetting curve.

6. One of his many contributions was the encoding specificity principle.

7. Proposed the concept of chunking for storing information in short-term memory.

8. Followed the case of HM, who had his hippocampus removed.

Answers: 1. Craik & Lockhart **2.** Atkinson & Shiffrin **3.** Johnson **4.** Loftus **5.** Ebbinghaus **6.** Tulving **7.** Miller **8.** Milner.

SELF-QUIZ

1. Which of the following is not one of the three basic human memory processes?
   a. storage
   b. retrieval
   c. decoding
   d. encoding

2. Which one of the three levels of processing would probably be employed when attempting to memorize the following three-letter sequences: WAB WAC WAD?
   a. structural
   b. semantic
   c. phonemic
   d. chunking

3. According to Paivio's dual-coding theory
   a. words are easier to encode than images
   b. abstract words are easier to encode than concrete words
   c. visual imagery may hinder the retrieval of words
   d. it should be easier to remember the word banana than the word justice

4. Retrieval from long-term memory is usually best when the information has been stored at which level of processing?
   a. structural
   b. semantic
   c. phonemic
   d. chunking

5. Which of the memory stores can store the least amount of information?
   a. sensory store
   b. short-term memory
   c. long-term memory

6. Which of the following sequences of words would be most subject to a clustering effect?
   a. FAN HEAVEN JUSTICE CHIAR
   b. HOUSE VACATION MOUSE STATISTIC
   c. BLUE DOG CAMEL YELLOW
   d. CONVERSE ICICLE CONCEPT THINKING

7. Which word best describes the speed of human cognitive functioning?
   a. slow
   b. moderate
   c. rapid
   d. blazing

8. When you attempt to recall the name of a high school classmate by imagining yourself back in the English class with her, you are making use of
   a. retrieval cues
   b. context cues
   c. schemas
   d. recognition cues

9. You recall being lost in a shopping mall at the age of five but your parents assure you that it never happened. Errors like this are most likely due to
   a. ineffective encoding
   b. a reality monitoring error
   c. a source monitoring error
   d. the misinformation effect

10. Taking this particular self-test measures your
    a. constructive errors
    b. reconstructive errors
    c. recall
    d. recognition

11. Ineffective encoding of information may result in
    a. the primacy effect
    b. the recency effect
    c. pseudoforgetting
    d. chunking

12. Decay theory is best able to explain the loss of memory in
    a. sensory store
    b. long-term memory
    c. short-term memory
    d. repressed memory

13. When you violate the encoding specificity principle, you are likely to experience an inability to
    a. encode information
    b. store information
    c. retrieve information
    d. form a visual image of the material you want to retrieve

14. Which of the following statements is the most accurate evaluation as to the authenticity of the recall of repressed memories?
    a. Research confirms that they are authentic.
    b. Research confirms that they are not authentic.
    c. Research cannot confirm or deny their authenticity.

15. Which of these appear to be intimately related?
    a. implicit and procedural memory
    b. implicit and semantic memory
    c. explicit and procedural memory
    d. implicit and declarative memory

16. It is very easy to recall the name of your high school because it has been subjected to extensive
    a. deep processing
    b. clustering
    c. chunking
    d. rehearsal

17. The failure to seek out disconfirming evidence can often lead to
    a. the overconfidence effect
    b. the reconstructive bias
    c. the hindsight bias
    d. a source monitoring error

Answers: 1. c **2.** a **3.** d **4.** c **5.** b **6.** c **7.** d **8.** b **9.** b **10.** d **11.** c **12.** a **13.** c **14.** c **15.** a **16.** d **17.** a.

Chapter Eight
Language and Thought

REVIEW OF KEY IDEAS

THE COGNITIVE REVOLUTION IN PSYCHOLOGY

1. Describe the "cognitive revolution" in psychology.

1-1. Answer the following questions regarding the cognitive revolution in psychology.

(a) In what decade did this revolution get underway?

(b) Why were earlier cognitive approaches abandoned?

(c) What theoretical school openly opposed the cognitive approach?

Answers: 1-1. (a) The 1950s (b) They were too subjective (as opposed to being empirical or objective). (c) Behaviorism.

LANGUAGE: TURNING THOUGHTS INTO WORDS

2. Outline the key properties of language.

2-1. Language is characterized by four properties; it is symbolic, semantic, generative, and structured. Identify each of these properties in the following statements.

(a) Applying rules to arrange words into phrases and sentences illustrates the ___structure___ property of language.

(b) Using words, or geometric forms, to represent objects, actions or events illustrates the ___symbolic___ property of language.

(c) Making different words out of the same letters, such as NOW and WON, illustrates the
_____semantic_____ property of language.

(d) Giving the same meaning to different words, such as chat, katz, and cat, illustrates the
_____general_____ aspect of language.

2-2.   Identify the following parts (units) of language.

(a) With around 40 of these basic sounds you can say all of the words in the English language.
_____Phonemes_____

(b) Phonemes are combined into these smallest units of meaning in a language, which may include root words as well as prefixes and suffixes. _____morph_____

(c) The component of language concerned with understanding the meaning of words and word combinations is called _____semantic_____.

(d) These rules specify how words can be combined into phrases and sentences. _____S_____

Answers: 2-1. (a) structured (b) symbolic (c) generative (d) semantic **2-2.** (a) phonemes (b) morphemes (c) semantics d) syntax.

3. Outline the development of human language during the first year.

3-1.   Answer the following question regarding the development of language during the first year of life.

(a) What are a child's three major vocalizations during the first 6 months of life?

(b) What is the range in months for the babbling stage of language development?

(c) What gradually occurs as the babbling stage progresses?

Answers: 3-1. (a) crying, laughing, and cooing (b) 6 to 18 months (c) The babbling increasingly resembles spoken language.

4. Describe children's early use of single words and word combinations.

4-1.   What does the text mean when it states that the receptive vocabulary of toddlers is much larger than their productive vocabulary?

4-2. Identify the following phenomenon observed in children's early use of language.

(a) What phenomenon is illustrated when a child calls all four-legged creatures "doggie"? _over es_

(b) What phenomenon is illustrated when a child correctly communicates her desire to know where the family dog is simply by asking, "doggie"?_____

(c) What phenomenon is illustrated when a child complains to her mother, "doggie eat cookie"?_____

(d) What phenomenon is illustrated when a child says, "doggie runned away"?

(e) What phenomenon is illustrated when a child puns, "I love your "I's"?_____

(f) Solve the following anagram that best describes how children acquire language skills. FWSYLIFT_____

Answers: 4-1. They can understand more spoken words than they can reproduce themselves. **4-2.** (a) overextensions (b) holophrases (c) telegraphic speech (d) overregularization (e) metalinguistic awareness (f) SWIFTLY.

5. Summarize the effect of bilingualism on language and cognitive development and the factors that influence the learning of a second language.

5-1. What does research comparing monolingual and bilingual children show with respect to their language and cognitive development?

5-2. What two factors positively influence the learning of a second language?

Answers: 5-1. They are largely similar in their rate of development (in both areas). **5-2.** starting at an early age and becoming acculturated.

6. Summarize evidence on language acquisition in animals.

6-1. Indicate whether each of the following is true or false.

_____ (a) Researchers have been able to teach chimpanzees to use symbols to communicate.

_____ (b) Chimpanzees find it difficult to catch onto the rules of language.

_____ (c) Language acquisition in chimpanzees appears to be very similar to language acquisition in children.

Answers: 6-1. (a) true (b) true (c) false

7. **Discuss the possible evolutionary basis of language.**

   7-1.   What evolutionary advantage might language have given human populations when compared to the Neanderthals (whom many believe lacked the language capabilities found in human beings)?

   Answers: 7-1. The Neanderthals became extinct (and we're still here).

8. **Compare and contrast the behaviorist, nativist, and interactionist perspectives on the acquisition of language.**

   8-1.   Identify the following perspectives on the acquisition of language.

   (a) This perspective places great emphasis on the role of reinforcement and imitation._____

   (b) This perspective assumes that children make use of a language acquisition device (LAD) to acquire transformational rules which enable them to easily translate between surface structure and deep structure._____

   (c) This interactionist perspective argues that language development is tied to progress in thinking and general cognitive development. _____

   (d) This interactionist perspective argues that language development is directed to some extent by the social benefits children derive from interaction with mature language users._____
   _____

   8-2.   Which perspective places greatest emphasis on:

   (a) nurture _____

   (b) nature _____

   (c) nature interacting with nurture _____

   Answers: 8-1. (a) behaviorist (b) nativist (c) cognitive theories (d) social communication theories **8-2.** (a) behaviorist (b) nativist (c) interactionist.

9. **Discuss culture and language and the status of the linguistic relativity hypothesis.**

   9-1.   What is the major idea behind Benjamin Whorf's linguistic relativity hypothesis?

   9-2.   What did Eleanor Rosch's experiment show when she compared the color recognition ability of English-speaking people and Dani people, who have only two words for color?

   9-3.   While language does not appear to invariably determine thought, it might exert some influence over the way we approach an idea. In other words, one's language may make it either_____or more_____to think along certain lines.

PROBLEM SOLVING: IN SEARCH OF SOLUTIONS

10. **List and describe the three types of problems proposed by Greeno.**

10-1. Greeno has proposed three types of problems (arrangement, inducing structure, and transformation). Identify each of these types categories from descriptions given below.

(a) This type of problem requires the problem solver to discover the relations among the parts of the problem.

(b) This type of problem requires the problem solver to place the parts in a way that satisfies some specific criterion.

(c) This type of problem requires the problem solver to carry out a sequence of changes or rearrangements in order to reach a specific goal.

10-2. Which types of Greeno's problems are represented in the following situations?

(a) What two three-letter English words can be made from the letters TBU?

(b) Fill in the missing word in, grass is to green as snow is to _____".

(c) You need to take your child to a pediatrician, your dog to the veterinarian, and your mother to the hairdresser all within a limited time period. You think to yourself, "I'll take the kid and the dog and pick up Mom. Mom can stay with the kid at the doctor's office while I take the dog to the vet. Then I'll...

10-3. Which type of problems are often solved in a sudden burst of insight?

Answers: **10-1.** (a) arrangement (b) inducing structure (c) transformation **10-2.** (a) inducing structure (b) arrangement (c) transformation **10-3.** arrangement.

11. Explain the difference between well-defined problems and ill-defined problems.

11-1. When your task is to find how many times 13 can be divided in 936 then you are dealing with a _____-_____ problem. When your task is to manage the election campaign for your friend who is running for college president then you are dealing with an _____-_____ problem.

Answers: **11-1**. well-defined, ill-defined.

12. Explain how irrelevant information and functional fixedness can hinder problem solving.

12-1. Which of the barriers to effective problem solving, irrelevant information or functional fixedness, are you overcoming when you:

(a) make a financial decision without first consulting your horoscope?

(b) use a page of newspaper as a wedge to keep a door open?

Answers: **12-1**. (a) irrelevant information (b) functional fixedness.

13. Explain how mental set and unnecessary constraints can hinder problem solving.

13-1. Which of the barriers to effective problem solving, mental set or unnecessary constrains, are you overcoming when you:

(a) color outside the lines to create a more interesting picture?

(b) teach an old dog a new trick?

Answers: **13-1**. (a) unnecessary constraints (b) mental set.

14. Describe a variety of general problem-solving strategies.

14-1. The text describes a variety of different problem-solving techniques, or_____. Which of these heuristics (means/ends analysis, forming subgoals, working backward, searching for analogies, or changing the representation of the problem) would be most applicable in solving the following problems?

(a) While opening your car door you drop the keys. The keys hit your foot and bounce underneath the car, too far to reach. It has stopped raining so you close your umbrella and ponder how to get your keys.

(b) You have accepted the responsibility for chairing the homecoming celebration at your school.

(c) Alone at night in the office you observe that the ribbon is missing from a printer you want to use. After obtaining a new ribbon you can't figure out how to install it correctly. Glancing around you see a similar printer with the ribbon installed.

(d) As an entering freshman in college, you have already chosen a field of study and a specific graduate school you wish to attend. Now all you have to do is accomplish this goal.

(e) You have agreed to become the campaign chairwoman of a friend who wants to run for student body president. Obviously your goal is to make your friend look like a good choice to students, but which heuristic do politicians often employ here?

Answers: 14-1. heuristics (a) search for analogies (the umbrella can be used as a rake) (b) form subgoals (c) work backwards (see how the ribbon comes out) (d) means/ends analysis (e) change the representation of the problem (make the opponents look like a bad choice).

15. **Discuss the distinction between field independence and dependence.**

   15-1.   Answer the following true-false questions regarding the distinctions between field dependent and field independent persons.

   _____ (a)   Field dependent persons are more likely to use internal cues to orient themselves in space.

   _____ (b)   Field independent persons are more likely to recognize the component parts of a problem rather than just seeing it as a whole.

Answers: 15-1. (a) false (b) true.

16. **Discuss cultural variations in cognitive style as they relate to problem solving.**

   16-1.   Answer the following true-false questions regarding cultural variations in cognitive style.

   _____ (a)   Persons living in cultures that depend on hunting and gathering for their subsistence are generally more field dependent than persons living in more sedentary agricultural societies.

   _____ (b)   Persons raised in cultures with lenient child-rearing practices and an emphasis on personal autonomy tend to be more field independent.

DECISION MAKING: CHOICES AND CHANCES

17. Compare the additive and elimination by aspects approaches to selecting an alternative.

17-1.   Indicate which of these two approaches to decision making would be best when:

(a) The task is complex and there are numerous alternatives to choose from.

(b) You want to allow attractive attributes to compensate for unattractive attributes.

Answers: 17-1. (a) elimination by aspects (b) additive.

18. Discuss conflict in decision making and the idea that one can think too much about a decision.

18-1.   What do persons often do when faced with a conflict in which they can't decide between alternative choices?

18-2.   Recent studies have shown that thinking too much about a problem (will/may not) lead to a better solution. One reason suggested for this is that gathering more and more information that is less and less important _____ the picture.

Answers: 18-1. They delay their decision. **18-2.** may not, clutters or confuses.

19. Explain the factors that individuals typically consider in risky decision-making.

19-1.   What differentiates risky decision-making from other kinds of decision making?

19-2.   What is the most you can know when making a risky decision?

19-3.   What two things must be known in order to calculate the expected value of making a risky decision when gambling with money?

19-4.   How does the concept of subjective utility explain why some persons still engage in risky decision-making when the expected value predicts a loss?

Answers: 19-1. The outcome is uncertain. **19-2.** the probability of a particular outcome **19-3.** the average amount of money you could expect to win or lose with each play and the probability of a win or loss **19-4.** The personal worth of the outcome may outweigh the probability of losing.

20. Describe the availability and representativeness heuristics.

20-1. Estimating the probability of an event on the basis of how often one recalls it has been experienced in the past is what Tversky and Kahneman call a (an) _____ heuristic.

20-2. When most people are asked if there are more words that begin with N or words that have N as the third letter, they apply the availibity heuristic and guess incorrectly. Explain why they do this.

20-3. Estimating the probability of an event on the basis of how similar it is to a particular model or stereotype of that event is what Tversky and Kahncman call a _____ heuristic.

20-4. "Steve is very shy. He has a high need for structure and likes detail. Is Steve more likely to be a salesperson or a librarian?" When persons are given this problem, they usually guess that he is a librarian even though there are many more salespersons than there are librarians. Explain why they do this.

Answers: 20-1. availability **20-2.** Because they can immediately recall many more words that begin with N than words having N as the third letter. **20-3.** representativeness **20-4.** Because they employ the representativess heuristic and Steve fits the stereotype of a librarian.

21. Describe base rate neglect and the conjunction fallacy and their causes.

21-1. Identify which example of flawed reasoning, base rate neglect or the conjunction fallacy, is being described below.

(a) Estimating that the odds of two uncertain events happening together are greater than the odds of either event happening alone.

(b) Guessing that "Steve" is a librarian and not a salesperson.

(c) Which one of these two errors in judgment is a misapplication of the representativeness heuristic?

Answers: 21-1. (a) the conjunction fallacy (b) base rate neglect (c) base rate neglect.

22. Summarize the research on the alternative outcomes effect.

    22-1.   Answer the following questions regarding the Featured Study.

        (a) Was the objective probability of obtaining the focal outcome easy or difficult to calculate in these two studies?

        (b) What happened when the objective probability of the focal outcome remained the same but the distribution of alternative outcomes was narrowed (eg., 2/9 versus 2/ **1-1-1-1-1-1-1**)?

        (c) What does this research tell us about the notion of objective probabilities?

Answers: 22-1. (a) easy (b) Subjective estimates of its likelihood decline. (c) They are ultimately very subjective.

23. Explain evolutionary theorists' evaluation of cognitive research on flaws in human decision strategies.

    23-1.   According to evolutionary theorists, is the human mind better wired to deal with:

        (a) base rates and probabilities or raw frequencies?

        (b) whole actions or parts of actions?

    23-2.   What happens when problems are reformulated in ways that resemble problems ancient humans had to face?

Answers: 23-1. raw frequencies (b) whole actions **23-2.** the irrationality decreases.

PUTTING IT IN PERSPECTIVE

24. Explain how this chapter highlighted four of the text's themes.

    24-1.   Indicate which one of the four unifying themes (the interaction of heredity and the environment, behavior is shaped by cultural heritage, the empirical nature of psychology, and the subjectivity of experience) are best represented by the following statements.

        (a) Psychologists developed objective measures for higher mental processes thus bringing about the cognitive revolution.

(b) The manner in which questions are framed can influence cognitive appraisal of the questions.

(c) Neither pure nativist theories nor pure nurture theories appear to adequately explain the development of language.

(d) The ecological demands of one's environment appear to somewhat affect one's cognitive style.

Answers: 24-1. (a) the empirical nature of psychology (b) the subjectivity of experience (c) the interaction of heredity and the environment (d) Behavior is shaped by cultural heritage.

UNDERSTANDING PITFALLS IN DECISION MAKING

25. Explain what is meant by the gambler's fallacy and the law of small numbers.

    25-1. Identify which example of the flawed reasoning, the gambler's fallacy or the law of small numbers, is being described below.

        (a) The belief that a small sampling of cases can be as valid as a large sampling of cases.

        (b) The belief that the odds of a chance event increases if the event hasn't occurred recently.

Answers: 25-1. (a) the law of small numbers (b) the gambler's fallacy.

26. Describe the propensity to overestimate the improbable and seek confirming evidence.

    26-1. What flaw in reasoning often results from intense media coverage of dramatic, vivid, but infrequent events.

    26-2. What omission leads to the confirmation bias when making decisions?

    26-3. How is the confirmation bias related to belief perseverance?

27. Discuss the overconfidence effect and the effects of framing on decisions.

27-1. Answer the following true/false questions regarding the overconfidence effect.

_____ (a) We are much less subject to this effect when making decisions about ourselves as opposed to more worldly matters.

_____ (b) Scientists are not generally prone to this effect when making decisions about information in their own fields.

_____ (c) In the study of college students cited by the text it was observed that the gap between personal confidence and actual accuracy of decisions increased as the confidence level increased.

27-2. Asking persons if they would prefer their glass of wine to be half-full or half-empty illustrates the general idea behind the_____ of questions.

27-3. Are persons more likely to take risky options when the problem is framed so as to obtain gains, or when it is framed so as to cut losses?

Answers: **27-1.** (a) false (b) false (c) true **27-2.** framing **27-3.** when it is framed so as to cut losses.

28. Describe some language manipulation strategies that people use to shape others' thoughts.

28-1. State which language manipulation strategy is being used in each of the following situations.

(a) A politician says that his opponent "has an IQ somewhat below room temperature."

(b) Pet owners have their pets "put to sleep" when they become terminally ill.

(c) Only someone unbelievably stupid would be against more gun control legislation.

(d) Insurance companies sell "life insurance" policies rather than "death benefits" policies.

28-2. Research examining semantic slanting shows that an organization is best advised to slant its objectives so as to be (for/against) something when attempting to accomplish its goal.

Answers: **28-1.** (a) name calling (b) semantic slanting (c) anticipatory name calling (d) semantic slanting **28-2.** for.

REVIEW OF KEY TERMS

Acculturation
Algorithm
Alternative outcomes effect
Availability heuristic
Belief perseverance
Bilingualism
Cognition
Compensatory decision models
Confirmation bias
Conjunction fallacy
Decision making
Fast mapping
Field dependence-independence
Framing

Functional fixedness
Gambler's fallacy
Heuristic
Ill-defined problems
Insight
Language
Language acquisition device (LAD)
Linguistic relativity
Mean length of utterance (MLU)
Mental set
Metalinguistic awareness
Morphemes
Noncompensatory decision models
Overextension

Overregularization
Phonemes
Problem solving
Problem space
Representativeness heuristic
Risky decision making
Semantics
Syntax
Telegraphic speech
Theory of bounded rationality
Trial and error
Underextension
Well-defined problems

_____ 1. The component of language concerned with understanding the meaning of words and word combinations.

_____ 2. A collection of symbols, and rules for combining those symbols, that can be used to create an infinite variety of messages.

_____ 3. The smallest units of sound in a spoken language.

_____ 4. The smallest units of meaning in a language.

_____ 5. The rules that specify how words can be combined into phrases and sentences.

_____ 6. Using a word incorrectly to describe a wider set of objects or actions than it is meant to.

_____ 7. Using a word to describe a narrower set of objects that it is meant to.

_____ 8. Single-word utterances that represent the meaning of several words.

_____ 9. The ability to reflect on the use of language.

_____ 10. Consists of the acquisition of two languages that employ different speech sounds, vocabulary, and grammatical rules.

_____ 11. The degree to which a person is socially and psychologically integrated into a new culture.

_____ 12. Basing the estimated probability of an event on the ease with which relevant instances come to mind.

_____ 13. Basing the estimated probability of an event on how similar it is to the typical prototype of that event.

_____ 14. The mental processes involved in acquiring knowledge.

_____ 15. The tendency to perceive an item only in terms of its most common use.

_____ 16. The sudden discovery of a correct solution to a problem following incorrect attempts.

_____ 17. A strategy for solving problems.

_____ 18. The process by which children map a word on an underlying concept after only one exposure to the word.

_____ 19. The average of youngsters' spoken statements (measured in morphemes).

_____ 20. Generalizing grammatical rules to irregular cases where they do not apply.

_____ 21. Decision making models which allow for attractive attributes to compensate for unattractive attributes.

_____ 22. Decision making models that do not allow for some attributes to compensate for others.

_____ 23. Making decisions under conditions of uncertainty.

_____ 24. A hypothetical innate mechanism or process that facilitates the learning of language.

_____ 25. Persisting in using problem-solving strategies that have worked in the past.

_____ 26. The theory that one's language determines one's thoughts.

_____ 27. The active efforts to discover what must be done to achieve a goal that is not readily attainable.

_____ 28. Trying possible solutions sequentially and discarding those that are in error until one works.

_____ 29. Evaluating alternatives and making choices among them.

_____ 30. How issues are posed or how choices are structured.

_____ 31. Occurs when peoples' belief about whether an outcome will occur changes depending on how alternative outcomes are distributed, even though the summed probability of the alternative outcomes is held constant.

_____ 32. A methodical, step-by-step procedure for trying all possible alternatives in searching for a solution to a problem.

_____ 33. The tendency to hang onto beliefs in the face of contradictory evidence.

_____ 34. The tendency to seek information that supports one's decisions and beliefs while ignoring disconfirming evidence.

_____ 35. Occurs when people estimate that the odds of two uncertain events happening are greater than the odds of either event happening alone.

_____ 36. Refers to individuals' tendency to rely primarily on either external or internal frames of reference when orienting themselves in space.

_____ 37. The belief that the odds of a chance event increase if the event hasn't occurred recently.

_____ 38. Problems in which one or more elements among the initial state, the goal state, and the constraints are incompletely or unclearly specified.

_____ 39. Problems in which the initial state, the goal state, and the constraints are clearly specified.

_____ 40. Refers to the set of possible pathways to a solution considered by the problem solver.

_____ 41. Asserts that people tend to use simple strategies in decision making that focus only on a few facets of available options and often result in "irrational" decisions that less than optimal.

Answers: 1. semantics **2.** language **3.** phonemes **4.** morphemes **5.** syntax **6.** overextensions **7.** underextensions
8. telegraphic speech **9.** metalinguistic awareness **10.** bilingualism **11.** acculturation **12.** availability heuristic
13. representativeness heuristic **14.** cognition **15.** functional fixedness **16.** insight **17.** heuristic **18.** fast mapping
19. mean length of utterances (MLU) **20.** overregularization **21.** compensatory decision models **22.** noncompensatory
decision models **23.** risky decision-making **24.** language acquisition device (LAD) **25.** mental set **26.** linguistic
relativity **27.** problem solving **28.** trial and error **29.** decision making **30.** framing **31.** alternative outcomes effect
32. algorithm **33.** belief perseverance **34.** confirmation bias **35.** conjunction fallacy **36.** field dependence-independence
37. gambler's fallacy **38.** ill-defined problems **39.** well-defined problems **40.** problem space **41.** theory of bounded
rationality.

REVIEW OF KEY PEOPLE

Noam Chomsky
Leda Cosmides & John Tooby
Daniel Kahneman

Steven Pinker
Sue Savage-Rumbaugh
Herbert Simon

B. F. Skinner
Amos Tversky

_____ 1. Won the Nobel Prize for his research on decision making and artificial intelligence.

_____ 2. Proposed that children learn language through the established principles of learning.

_____ 3. Proposed that children learn language through a biologically built-in language acquisition device.

_____ 4. One of the co-researchers who showed people base probability estimates on heuristics that do not always yield reasonable estimates of success.

_____ 5. Along with her colleagues she taught the chimp, Kanzi, to communicate in a way that made use of all the basic properties of language.

_____ 6. Argues that human language ability is a species-specific trait that is the product of natural selection.

_____ 7. Argue that the human mind has evolved to solve specific adaptive problems.

Answers: 1. Simon **2.** Skinner **3.** Chomsky **4.** Kahneman & Tversky **5.** Savage-Rumbaugh **6.** Pinker **7.** Cosmides & Tooby.

SELF-QUIZ

1. Which of the following explanations best explains the success of the cognitive revolution in psychology?
   a. the refining of introspection as a research method
   b. the development of empirical methods
   c. the use of psychotherapy to explore the unconscious
   d. the success in teaching chimps to use language

2. Which of the following is not one of the basic properties of language?
   a. generative
   b. symbolic
   c. structured
   d. alphabetical

3. The word SLOWLY would be an example of a
   a. metalinguistic
   b. phoneme
   c. syntactical unit
   d. morpheme

4. When a child says that TUB and BUT are constructed of the same three letters, she is showing an awareness of
   a. morphemes
   b. phonemes
   c. metalinguistics
   d. syntax

5. Which of the following statements is incorrect?
   a. A chimp has learned to sign (ASL) more than 150 words.
   b. Children and chimps appear to learn language in a similar manner.
   c. A chimp has shown comprehension for both words and their relation to one another.
   d. The ability to use language may not be unique to humans.

6. The fact that children appear to learn rules, rather than specific word combinations, when acquiring language skills argues most strongly against which theory of language development?
   a. cognitive
   b. behaviorist
   c. nativist
   d. social communication

7. Which one of Greeno's problems is exemplified by the anagram?
   a. arrangement
   b. inducing structure
   c. transformation
   d. chunking

8. Which barrier to problem solving are you overcoming when you use a piece of paperclip as a temporary replacement for the screw that fell out of your glasses?
   a. irrelevant information
   b. functional fixedness
   c. mental set
   d. unnecessary constraints

9. Which of the following heuristics would you probably employ if assigned the task of carrying out a school election?
   a. work backwards
   b. representativeness
   c. search for analogies
   d. form subgoals

10. Field independent persons are most likely to come from cultures that
    a. encourage strict child-rearing practices
    b. have a stable agricultural base
    c. encourage lenient child-rearing practices
    d. stress conformity

11. When faced with having to choose among numerous alternatives, most persons will opt for
    a. an elimination by aspects approach
    b. an additive approach
    c. a means/end analysis
    d. a subjective-utility model

12. Most persons mistakenly believe that more people die from tornadoes than from asthma. This is because they mistakenly apply
    a. a means/end analysis
    b. a compensatory decision model
    c. an availability heuristic
    d. a representativeness heuristic

13. Failure to actively seek out contrary evidence may lead to
    a. overestimating the improbable
    b. the conjunction fallacy
    c. the gambler's fallacy
    d. the confirmation bias

14. People generally prefer a choice that provides an 80 percent chance of success over one that provides a. 20 percent chance of failure. This illustrates the effect of
    a. the availability heuristic
    b. the representativeness heuristic
    c. framing
    d. mental set

15. Owners of automobile junkyards prefer to use the term automobile recycling centers. This is an example of the use of
    a. framing
    b. semantic slanting
    c. anticipatory name calling
    d. subjective utility

Answers: 1. b **2.** d **3.** d **4.** c **5.** b **6.** b **7.** a **8.** b **9.** d **10.** c **11.** a **12.** c **13.** d **14.** c **15.** b

Chapter Nine

Intelligence and Psychological Testing

REVIEW OF KEY IDEAS

KEY CONCEPTS IN PSYCHOLOGICAL TESTING

1. **List and describe the principle categories of psychological tests.**

   1-1.   Most psychological tests can be placed into one of two very broad categories. These two categories are: _____ tests and _____ tests.

   1-2.   There are three categories of mental abilities tests. Below are examples of each of these categories. Identify them.

       (a) The ACT and SAT tests you may have taken before entering college are examples of _____ tests.

       (b) The exams you frequently take in your introductory psychology class are examples of _____ tests.

       (c) Tests used to demonstrate general intellectual giftedness are examples of _____ tests.

   1-3.   Personality tests allow an individual to compare himself or herself to other persons with respect to particular personality _____. Personality tests generally (do/do not) have right and wrong answers.

   Answers: 1-1. mental ability, personality (in either order) **1-2.** (a) aptitude (b) achievement (c) intelligence
   1-3. characteristics or traits, do not.

2. **Explain the concepts of standardization and test norms.**

   2-1.   Developing test norms and uniform procedures for use in the administration and scoring of a test is the general idea behind test _____.

2-2. In order to interpret a particular score on a test it is necessary to know how other persons score on this test. This is the purpose of test _____. An easy method for providing comparisons of test scores is to convert the raw scores into _____ scores.

Answers: **2-1.** standardization **2-2.** norms, percentile.

3. Explain the meaning of test reliability and how it is estimated.

3-1. The ability of a test to produce consistent results across subsequent measurements of the same persons is known as its _____. Psychological tests (are/are not) perfectly reliable.

3-2. Readministering the same test to the same group of persons a week or two following the original testing (test-retest) allows one to estimate the _____ of a test. If a test is highly reliable, then a person's scores on the two different administrations will be very similar. The amount of similarity can be assessed by means of the _____ coefficient. The closer the correlation comes to 1.0 the (more/less) reliable the test is.

3-3. Another method for assessing reliability to break the test into two equal halves and derive a correlation for the two halves. This method is called _____-_____ reliability.

Answers: **3-1.** reliability, are not **3-2.** reliability, correlation, more **3-3.** split-half.

4. Explain the three types of validity and how they are assessed.

4-1. The ability of a test to actually measure what it claims to measure is known as its _____. The term validity is also used to refer to the accuracy or usefulness of the _____ based on a test.

4-2. There are three general kinds of validity. Identify each of these kinds from the descriptions given below.

(a) This kind of validity will tend to be high when, for example, scores on the ACT and SAT actually predict success in college. _____

(b) This kind of validity will be of particular importance to you when taking your exams for this class. It will be high if the exam sticks closely to the explicitly assigned material. _____

(c) This kind of validity is more vague than the other two kinds and refers to the ability of a test to measure abstract qualities, such as intelligence. _____.

4-3. As with the estimation of reliability, the estimation of validity makes use of the _____ _____.

Answers: **4-1.** validity, inferences or decisions **4-2.** (a) criterion-related validity, (b) content validity, (c) construct validity **4-3.** correlation coefficient.

THE EVOLUTION OF INTELLIGENCE TESTING

5. Summarize the contributions of Galton and Binet to the evolution of intelligence testing.

5-1. Identify each of the above men from the descriptions of their contributions given on the next page.

(a) This man developed the first useful intelligence test. His tests were used to predict success in school, and scores were expressed in terms of mental age. _____

(b) This man began the quest to measure intelligence. He assumed that intelligence was mainly inherited and could be measured by assessing sensory acuity. He also invented correlation and percentile test scores._____

Answers: 5-1. (a) Binet (b) Galton.

6. Summarize the contributions of Terman and Wechsler to the evolution of intelligence testing.

6-1. Identify each of the above men from the descriptions of their contributions given below.

(a) This man revised Binet's tests to produce the Stanford-Binet Intelligence Scale, the standard for all future intelligence tests. He also introduced the intelligence quotient (IQ).

_____

(b) This man developed the first successful test of adult intelligence, the WAIS. He also developed new intelligence tests for children.

_____

(c) In developing his new intelligence tests, this man added many non-verbal items which allowed for the separate assessment of both verbal and non-verbal abilities. He also replaced the IQ score with one based on the normal distribution. _____

Answers: 6-1. (a) Terman (b) Wechsler (c) Wechsler.

BASIC QUESTIONS ABOUT INTELLIGENCE TESTING

7. Explain the meaning of an individual's score on a modern intelligence test.

7-1. Answer the following questions regarding intelligence test scores.

(a) In what manner is human intelligence assumed to be distributed?

(b) What percentage of people have an IQ score below 100?

(c) What percentage of persons would score two or more standard deviations above the mean? (see Fig. 9.7 in the text)

Answers: 7-1. (a) It forms a normal distribution. (b) 50% (c) 2 percent.

8. **Describe the reliability, validity, and stability of modern intelligence tests.**

   8-1. Answer the following questions about the reliability of modern intelligence tests.

   (a) What are reliability estimates (correlation coefficients) are found for most modern intelligence tests?

   (b) What might be a problem here with respect to an individual's test score?

   8-2. Answer the following questions with respect to the validity and stability of modern intelligence tests.

   (a) What is the correlation between IQ tests and grades in school?

   (b) What is the correlation between IQ tests and the number of years of schooling that people complete?

   (c) What might be a general problem with assuming intelligence tests are a valid measure of general mental ability?

   Answers: 8-1. (a) They are in the low .90's. (b) Temporary conditions could lower the score. **8-2.** (a) .40's and 50's (b) .60 to .80 (c) They principally focus on academic/verbal intelligence and ignore other kinds of intelligence.

9. **Discuss how well intelligence tests predict vocational success.**

   9-1. Is the ability of intelligence tests to predict vocational success much higher or much lower than their ability to predict academic success?

   9-2. What do current court rulings and laws now require when using tests for purposes of hiring or promoting?

   Answers: 9-1. much lower **9-2.** The tests must measure specific abilities that are related to job performance.

10. **Discuss the use of IQ tests in non-Western cultures.**

    10-1. Which of the following statements best summarizes the history of IQ testing in non-Western cultures?

    (a) Most Western and non-Western cultures have successfully adapted the IQ tests to their own cultures.

    (b) Many non-Western cultures have different conceptions of what intelligence is and do not necessarily accept Western notions as to how it can be measured.

10-2. What did Cole and his colleagues conclude regarding the ingredients of intelligence across cultures?

Answers: 10-1. b **10-2.** They are culture-specific.

EXTREMES OF INTELLIGENCE

11. Describe how mental retardation is defined and divided into various levels.

11-1. In addition to having subnormal mental abilities (IQ scores of less than 70 to 75), what else is included in the definition of mental retardation?

11-2. There are four levels of mental retardation; mild, moderate, severe, and profound. Identify each of these levels from the descriptions given below:

(a) These persons have IQ scores below 20 and require total care.

(b) These persons have IQ scores between 50 and 75 and may become self-supporting citizens after leaving school and becoming adults.

(c) These persons have IQ scores between 35 and 50 and can be semi-independent in a sheltered environment.

(d) These persons have IQ scores between 20 and 35 and can help to contribute to their self-support under total supervision.

Answers: 11-1. The individual must show deficiencies in adaptive (everyday living) skills originating before age 18. **11-2.** (a) profound (b) mild (c) moderate (d) severe.

12. Discuss what is known about the causes of mental retardation.

12-1. Although there are over 350 organic syndromes associated with retardation, including Down's syndrome, Phenylketonuria, and hydrocephaly, organic causes only account for about _____ percent of retardation cases.

12-2. There are two general hypotheses as to the causes of the remaining 75 percent of retardation cases, most of which are diagnosed as mild. One theory is that retardation results from subtle _____ defects that are difficult to detect. The other theory suggests that retardation is caused by a variety of unfavorable _____ conditions.

Answers: 12-1. 25 **12-2.** (a) physiological, environmental.

13. Discuss the role of IQ tests in the identification of gifted children.

13-1. Answer the following questions regarding gifted children:

(a) Although it is contrary to federal law, what method is used almost exclusively to identify gifted children?

(b) What is the lowest IQ score that is generally needed to qualify children as gifted?

Answers: 13-1. (a) scores on IQ tests (b) 130.

14. Describe the personal characteristics of the gifted and the adult achievements of the gifted.

14-1. Answer the following questions regarding the personal characteristics of the gifted.

(a) What did Terman's long-term study of gifted children show with respect to the physical, social, and emotional development of these children?

(b) Ellen Winner took a special look at profoundly (IQ above 180) gifted children. What did she estimate to be the incidence of interpersonal and emotional problems in these children when compared to other children?

(c) What three factors must interact and be present to an exceptional degree in order to produce the rarest form of giftedness according to Renzulli?

Answers: 14-1. (a) They were above average in all three areas. (b) It's about twice as high in the profoundly gifted children. (c) intelligence, motivation, creativity (in any order).

HEREDITY AND ENVIRONMENT AS DETERMINANTS OF INTELLIGENCE

15. Summarize the empirical evidence that heredity affects intelligence.

15-1. Below are the mean correlations for the intelligence of four different groups of children: *siblings reared together, fraternal twins reared together, identical twins reared apart*, and *identical twins reared together*. Match the group with the appropriate correlation.

.86 _____   .60 _____

.72 _____   .44 _____

15-2. What do the above correlations tell us about the role of heredity on intelligence?

Answers: 15-1. (.86) identical twins reared together (.72) identical twins reared apart (.60) fraternal twins reared together (.44) siblings reared together **15-2.** That heredity plays a significant role in intelligence.

16. Discuss the Burt affair and estimates of the heritability of intelligence.

16-1. Answer the following questions regarding the Cyril Burt affair.

(a) While Burt's data may have been flawed, how do they stack up with the data from other similar studies?

(b) What does the Burt affair tell us regarding the debate about the influence of heredity and environment on intelligence?

16-2. What relationship has been found between the intelligence of children adopted out at birth and their biological parents?

16-3. The consensus estimate of experts is that the heritability ratio for human intelligence hovers around 60 percent. What does this mean?

16-4. Why can you not use a heritability ratio to explain a particular individual's intelligence?

Answers: 16-1. (a) They are in fairly close agreement. (b) The debate has important sociopolitical implications. **16-2.** There is a significant correlation in intelligence. **16-3.** The variation in intelligence in a particular group is estimated to be 60% due to heredity (leaving 40% for environmental factors). **16-4.** It is a group statistic and may give misleading results when applied to particular individuals.

17. **Describe various lines of research that indicate that environment affects intelligence.**

    17-1. What cumulative effects on intelligence have been found among children reared in deprived environments?

    17-2. What effects on intelligence have been found among children moved from deprived environments to more enriched environments?

    17-3. What relationship has been found between the intellectual quality of home environment and the intelligence of children?

    17-4. Answer the following questions regarding the "Flynn effect."

        (a) What did Flynn's research show with respect to generational changes in IQ scores since 1930 in the industrialized world?

        (b) Can these generational changes be attributed to heredity?

Answers: **17-1.** There is a gradual decrease in intelligence (across time). **17-2.** There is a gradual increase in intelligence (across time). **17-3.** They are significantly correlated. **17-4.** (a) Scores have been steadily rising. (b) no.

18. **Using the concept of reaction range, explain how heredity and the environment interact to affect intelligence.**

    18-1. The notion behind the concept of reaction range is that heredity places an upper and lower _____ on how much an individual can vary with respect to a characteristic such as intelligence. The reaction range for human intelligence is said to be around _____ IQ points.

    18-2. This means that a child with an average IQ of 100 can vary between 88 and 112 IQ points, depending on the kind of _____ he or she experiences.

    18-3. The major point here is that the limits for intelligence are determined by _____ factors and the movement within these limits is determined by _____ factors.

Answers: **18-1.** limit, 20-25 **18-2.** environment **18-3.** genetic or hereditary, environmental.

19. **Discuss heritability and socioeconomic disadvantage as alternative explanations for cultural differences in IQ.**

    19-1. Two explanations for the cultural differences in IQ scores are listed below. Tell what each of these explanations means.

        (a) Jensen's heritability explanation.

        (b) Socioeconomic disadvantage.

    19-2. Which of these two explanations is best supported by research evidence?

Answers: 19-1. (a) The cultural differences are due to heredity. (b) The cultural differences are due to environmental factors. **19-2.** socioeconomic disadvantage.

20. **Discuss the possible contributions of stereotype vulnerability and cultural bias to ethnic differences in average IQ.**

    20-1. Steele's theory of stereotype vulnerability holds that a widely held stereotype that certain racial groups are mentally inferior acts on the members of these groups so as to make them (more/less) vulnerable (they tend to under perform) when confronted with tests assessing intellectual ability. Steele believes that this same vulnerability (does/does not) exist for women entering domains dominated by men. Research so far (does/does not) support the theory of stereotype vulnerability.

    20-2. What did the text conclude about the possible effects of cultural bias with respect to ethnic differences in IQ scores?

Answers: 20-1. more, does, does **20-2.** It produces only weak and inconsistent effects.

NEW DIRECTIONS IN THE ASSESSMENT AND STUDY OF INTELLIGENCE

21. **Describe new trends in the assessment study of intelligence.**

    21-1. The notion that intelligence is a function of general mental abilities, (Spearman's "g"), dominated the early thinking in test development. However. Cattell and Horn believe that intelligence should be divided into intelligence which involves reasoning ability , memory capacity, and speed of information processing, which they call _____ intelligence, and intelligence that involves ability to apply acquired knowledge and skills in problem solving, which they call _____ intelligence.

    21-2. As test-developers have began to turn away from tests designed to measure general intelligence, what kinds of tests are replacing them?

21-3. Which biologically oriented approach to measuring intelligence, reaction time or inspection time, appears to be the more promising?

Answers: 21-1. fluid, crystallized **21-2.** tests of specific mental abilities **21-3.** inspection time.

22 . Describe Sternberg's and Gardner's theories of intelligence.

22-1. Sternberg's triarchic theory proposes that intelligence is composed of three basic parts. Match these parts with their individual functions:

_____ Contextual subtheory

_____ Experiential subtheory

_____ Componential subtheory

(a) Emphasizes the role played by society.

(b) Emphasizes the cognitive processes underlying intelligence.

(c) Emphasizes the interplay between intelligence and experience.

22-2. Gardner has proposed seven relatively distinct human intelligences. What does his research show with respect to a "g" factor among these separate intelligences?

Answers: 22-1. Contextual (a), Experiential (c), Componential (b) **22-2.** There does not appear to be a "g" factor. (people display a mix of strong, weak, and intermediate abilities.)

PUTTING IT IN PERSPECTIVE

23. Discuss how the chapter highlighted three of the text's unifying themes.

23-1. Answer the following questions about the three unifying themes.

(a) What theme is exemplified by the Cyril Burt affair?

(b) What theme is exemplified by the different views about the nature of intelligence held by Western and non-Western cultures

(c) What theme is exemplified by the extensive research using twin studies, adoption studies, and family studies?

Answers: **23-1.** (a) Psychology evolves in a sociohistorical context. (b) Cultural factors shape behavior. (c) Heredity and environment jointly influence behavior.

APPLICATION: MEASURING AND UNDERSTANDING CREATIVITY

24. Discuss popular ideas about the nature of creativity.

24-1. Popular notions about creativity would have us believe that creative ideas arise from nowhere, occur in a burst of insight, are not related to hard work, and are unrelated to intelligence. What does the text say about these notions?

Answers: **24-1.** They are all false.

25. Describe creativity tests and summarize how well they predict creative achievement.

25-1. Most tests of creativity attempt to assess (conventional/divergent) thinking, such as: List as many uses as you can for a book. Creativity scores are based on the _____ of alternatives generated and the originality and _____ of the suggested alternatives.

25-2. Creativity tests are rather (good/mediocre) predictors of creativity in the real world. One reason for this is that they attempt to treat creativity as a (specific/general) trait while research evidence seems to show it is related to quite _____ particular domains.

Answers: **25-1.** divergent, number, usefulness (utility) **25-2.** mediocre, general, specific.

26. Discuss associations between creativity and personality, intelligence, and mental illness.

26-1. What two traits appear to be at the core of the personality characteristics common to creative people?

26-2. What is the intelligence level of most highly creative people?

26-3. What form of mental illness appears to be associated with creative achievement?

Answers: **26-1.** independence and nonconformity **26-2.** average to above average. **26-3.** mood disorders

CRITICAL THINKING APPLICATION

27. Explain how appeals to ignorance and reification have cropped up in numerous debates about intelligence.

27-1. Tell whether the following statements represent examples of appeals to ignorance or to reification.

(a) He doesn't do very well in college because he's lacking in intelligence.

(b) If only 25% of the cases of mental can be attributed to biological causes, the remaining 75% must be due to environmental factors.

(c) The down side to creativity is that it can lead to mood disorders.

(d) More money should be spent on research to find the accurate heritability coefficient of intelligence.

Answers: 27-1. (a) reification (b) appeals to ignorance (c) appeals to ignorance (d) reification.

REVIEW OF KEY TERMS

Achievement tests
Aptitude tests
Construct validity
Content validity
Convergent thinking
Correlation coefficient
Creativity
Criterion-related validity
Crystallized intelligence
Deviation IQ scores

Divergent thinking
Factor analysis
Fluid intelligence
Heritability ratio
Intelligence quotient (IQ)
Intelligence tests
Mental age
Mental retardation
Normal distribution

Percentile score
Personality tests
Psychological test
Reaction range
Reification
Reliability
Standardization
Test norms
Validity

_____ 1. A standardized measure of a sample of a person's behavior.

_____ 2. Tests that measure general mental ability.

_____ 3. Tests that measure various personality traits.

_____ 4. Tests that assess talent for specific kinds of learning.

_____ 5. Tests that gauge the mastery and knowledge of various subject areas.

_____ 6. The development of uniform procedures for administering and scoring tests, including the development of test norms.

_____ 7. Data that provides information about the relative standing of a particular test score.

_____ 8. Number indicating the percentage of people who score above or below a particular test score.

_____ 9. The measurement consistency of a test.

_____ 10. The ability of a test to measure what it was designed to measure.

_____ 11. The degree to which the content of a test is representative of the domain it is supposed to measure.

_____ 12. The degree to which the scores on a particular test correlate with scores on an independent criterion (test).

_____ 13. The degree to which there is evidence that a test measures a hypothetical construct.

_____ 14. A score indicating the mental ability typical of a chronological age group.

_____ 15. Mental age divided by chronological age and multiplied by 100.

_____ 16. A symmetrical, bell-shaped curve that describes the distribution of many physical and psychological attributes.

_____ 17. Scores that translate raw scores into a precise location in the normal distribution.

_____ 18. Subnormal general mental ability accompanied by deficiencies in everyday living skills originating prior to age 18.

_____ 19. An estimate of the percentage of variation in a trait determined by genetic inheritance.

_____ 20. Genetically determined limits on intelligence.

_____ 21. Method that uses the correlation among many variables to identify closely related clusters.

_____ 22. The ability to apply acquired knowledge and skills to problem solving.

_____ 23. Includes reasoning ability, memory capacity, and speed of information processing.

_____ 24. The generation of ideas that are original, novel, and useful.

_____ 25. Thinking that attempts to narrow down a list of alternatives to a single best solution.

_____ 26. Thinking that attempts to expand the range of alternatives by generating many possible solutions.

_____ 27. A numerical index of the degree of relationship between two variables.

_____ 28. Occurs when a hypothetical abstract concept is given a name and then treated as though it were a concrete, tangible object.

Answers: **1.** psychological test **2.** intelligence tests **3.** personality tests **4.** aptitude tests **5.** achievement tests **6.** standardization **7.** test norms **8.** percentile score **9.** reliability **10.** validity **11.** content validity **12.** criterion-related validity **13.** construct validity **14.** mental age **15.** intelligence quotient **16.** normal distribution **17.** deviation IQ scores **18.** mental retardation **19.** heritability ratio **20.** reaction range **21.** factor analysis **22.** crystallized thinking **23.** fluid thinking **24.** creativity **25.** convergent thinking **26.** divergent thinking **27.** correlation coefficient **28.** reification.

REVIEW OF KEY PEOPLE

Alfred Binet   Arthur Jensen   Robert Sternberg
Sir Francis Galton   Sandra Scarr   Lewis Terman
Howard Gardner   Claude Steele   David Wechsler

_____ 1. Developed the Standford-Binet Intelligence Scale.

_____ 2. Developed the first successful test of adult intelligence.

_____ 3. Postulated a cognitive triarchic theory of intelligence.

_____ 4. Proposed a reaction range model for human intelligence.

_____ 5. Developed the first useful intelligence test.

_____ 6. Postulated a heritability explanation for cultural differences in intelligence.

_____ 7. Began the quest to measure intelligence.

_____ 8. Proposed a stereotype vulnerability theory as an explanation for racial differences on IQ test scores.

_____ 9. Has suggested the existence of a number of relatively autonomous human intelligences.

Answers: **1.** Terman **2.** Wechsler **3.** Sternberg **4.** Scarr **5.** Binet **6.** Jensen **7.** Galton **8.** Steele **9.** Gardner.

1. This self-test you are now taking is an example of:
   a. an aptitude test
   b. an achievement test
   c. an intelligence test
   d. a criterion-related test

2. Which of the following statistics is generally used to estimate reliability and validity?
   a. the correlation coefficient
   b. the standard deviation
   c. the percentile score
   d. the median

3. What kind of validity do test such as the SAT and ACT particularly strive for?
   a. content validity
   b. construct validty
   c. absolute validity
   d. criterion-related validity

4. With respect to modern intelligence tests:
   a. validity is generally higher than reliability
   b. reliability and validity are about the same
   c. reliability is generally higher than validity
   d. I have no idea what you're talking about.

5. Which of the following retarded groups can often pass for normal as adults?
   a. mild
   b. moderate
   c. profound
   d. both mild and moderate

6. What percentage of mental retardation cases have been definitely linked to organic causes?
   a. approximately 25%
   b. approximately 50%
   c. approximately 75%
   d. approximately 90%

7. Terman's long-term study of gifted children found that they tended to excel in:
   a. physical development
   b. social development
   c. emotional development
   d. they excelled in all three areas

8. Which of the following groups shows the lowest correlation with respect to intelligence?
   a. fraternal twins reared together
   b. fraternal twins reared apart
   c. identical twins reared apart
   d. siblings reared together

9. If the heritability ratio for intelligence is 80%, this means that for you as an individual 80% of your intelligence is determined by heredity and 20% is determined by your environment. This statement is:
   a. true
   b. false

10. The "Flynn effect" arises from the observation that the general intelligence in industrialized societies:
   a. has been rising across time
   b. has been declining across time
   c. has remained steady across time
   d. is primarily effected by heredity and not environment

11. If the reaction range concept of human intelligence is correct, then a child with exactly normal intelligence will probably not get much higher than an IQ of:
   a. 107
   b. 112
   c. 122
   d. 130

12. Which of the following explanations for racial differences in intelligence is best supported by research evidence.
   a. Jensen's heritability theory
   b. cultural bias in IQ tests
   c. cultural disadvantage
   d. Watson's differential conditioning theory

13. Steele's theory of stereotype vulnerability is an attempt to explain:
   a. why Asian-Americans score higher than average on IQ tests
   b. why African-Americans score lower than average on IQ tests
   c. why cultural bias must necessarily be inherent in all intelligence tests
   d. why the general intelligence in a population declines across time

14. Spearman's "g" infers that:
   a. most kinds of intelligence are highly related
   b. most kinds of intelligence are not highly related
   c. intelligence is highly correlated with personality characteristics
   d. intelligence is primarily genetic in origin

15. Most tests of creativity emphasize:
   a. convergent thinking
   b. divergent thinking
   c. bursts of insight
   d. getting at unconscious thought processes

16. Which of the following statements is an example of reification?
   a. Birds of a feather flock together.
   b. Creative people are born not raised.
   c. She gets good grades in school because she is intelligent.
   d. Intelligence tests are only moderate predictors of vocational success.

Answers: 1. b 2. a 3. d 4. c 5. a 6. a 7. d 8. d 9. b 10. a 11. b 12. c 13. b 14. a 15. b 16. c.

Chapter Ten

Motivation and Emotion

REVIEW OF KEY IDEAS

THE DIVERSITY OF HUMAN MOTIVES

1. **Distinguish between the two major categories of motives found in humans.**

   1-1. Most theories of motivation distinguish between ___biological___ motives (e.g., for food, water, sex, warmth) and ___social___ motives. Biological needs are generally essential for the ___survival___ of the group or individual.

   1-2. Social motives (e.g., for achievement, autonomy, affiliation) are acquired as a result of people's experiences. While there are relatively few biological needs, people theoretically may acquire an unlimited number of ___social___ needs.

   1-3. While the distinction between biological and social needs is useful, the differences (<u>are/are not</u>) always clear cut. For example, aggression, listed in Figure 10.1 as a biological need, is considered by some theorists to be more a function of learning than of biology.

   1-4. In the following sections we will focus on two ___biological___ needs, hunger and sexual motivation, and two ___social___ needs, affiliation and achievement.

   Answers: 1-1. biological, social, survival **1-2.** social **1-3.** are not **1-4.** biological, social.

THE MOTIVATION OF HUNGER AND EATING

2. **Summarize evidence on the areas of the brain implicated in the regulation of hunger.**

   2-1. Within the brain the major structure implicated in eating behavior is the ___hypothalamus___.

   2-2. Researchers used to think that eating was controlled by "on" and "off" centers in the hypothalamus.

When the lateral hypothalamus was stimulated, animals began to eat; when the ventromedial hypothalamus was stimulated animals stopped eating. While these structures are still considered important in hunger regulation, researchers now believe that eating is controlled to a greater extent by complex (neural circuits/brain centers).

2-3. In addition, researchers have changed their conclusions about the relative importance of various structures. According to current thinking, which of the following areas of the hypothalamus plays the most important role in hunger?

a. lateral hypothalamus (LH)

b. ventromedial hypothalamus (VMH)

c. paraventricular nucleus (PVN)

Answers: 2-1. hypothalamus **2-2.** neural circuits **2-3.** c.

3. Summarize evidence on how fluctuations in blood glucose and hormones affect hunger.

3-1. Much of the food we consume is converted into ___glucose___, a simple sugar that is an important source of energy.

3-2. Based on research findings about glucose, Mayer proposed that the theory that there are there are specialized neurons, which he called ___glucostats___, that function to monitor glucose levels in the blood. Lower levels of glucose are associated with a/an (increase/decrease) in hunger. (While glucostats were originally thought to be in the brain, their location and exact nature remain obscure.)

3-3. For cells to extract glucose from the blood, the hormone ___insulin___ must be present. Insulin will produce a (an) (increase/decrease) in the level of sugar in the blood, with the result that the person experiences a (an) (increase/decrease) in the sensation of hunger. Thus, insulin is another factor contributing to hunger.

3-4. More recently a hormone called leptin has been discovered which, circulated to the brain in the bloodstream, provides information about the fat in the body. Leptin is produced by fat cells. Higher levels of fat result in higher levels of ___leptin___, which tend to (increase/decrease) the sensation of hunger.

Answers: 3-1. glucose **3-2.** glucostats, increase **3-3.** insulin, decrease, increase **3-4.** leptin, decrease.

4. Summarize evidence how culture, learning, food cues, and stress influence hunger.

4-1. Although we have some innate taste preferences (e.g., for fat), it is also clear that ___learning___ affects some of our food choices and even influences the amounts that we eat. For example, taste preferences and aversions may be learned by pairing a taste with pleasant or unpleasant experiences, the process of ___classical___ conditioning.

4-2. In addition, we are more likely to eat food that we see others eating, especially if the others are parents or friends. Thus, food preferences are acquired indirectly through the process of ___observational___ learning as well as directly through conditioning.

4-3. Most people also experience hunger based on the appearance, taste, and smell of food and the effort involved in securing food. These and other food-related ___*cues*___ in our environments clearly affect when and what we eat.

4-4. Besides affecting eating habits and providing cues to eating, the environment may also provide unpleasant or frustrating events that produce emotional ___*stress*___, a factor that may also trigger eating in many people. Although stress and increased eating are linked, recent evidence suggests that the important factor may be heightened physiological ___*arousal*___ accompanying stress rather than the stress itself.

Answers: **4-1.** learning (environment, culture), classical **4-2.** observational **4-3.** cues **4-4.** stress, arousal.

5. Discuss the contribution of genetic predisposition, dietary restraint, and set point to obesity.

5-1. It is by now clear that many factors affect body weight and that some of the most important are genetic. For example, Stunkard et al. (1986) found that adopted children were much more similar in BMI to their (biological/adoptive) parents than to their (biological/adoptive) parents, even though they were brought up by the latter.

5-2. The most striking finding of the Stunkard et al. (1990) study with twins was that (identical/fraternal) twins reared apart were more similar in BMI than (identical/fraternal twins reared in the same family environment. These results support the belief that (genetics/environment) plays an important role in body weight.

5-3. The concept of set point may help explain why body weight remains so stable. The theory proposes that each individual has a "natural" body weight determined in large part by the number of ___*fat cells*___ that an individual happens to have. Although the number of fat cells in the body may increase through persistent overeating, the number is usually (very stable/highly variable) throughout one's lifetime.

5-4. The larger the (number/size) of fat cells, the higher the set point. Dieting or weight gain produces a change in the ___*size*___ of the fat cells but not, in most cases, the ___*#*___ of fat cells. The mechanism for monitoring set point, and the condition of the fat cells, may involve the hormone ___*leptin*___.

5-5. According to the dietary restraint concept, the world is divided into two types of people: unrestrained eaters, who eat as much as they want when they want; and ___*restrain*___ eaters, who closely monitor their food intake and frequently go hungry.

5-6. While restrained eaters are constantly on guard to control their eating, at times they may lose control and eat to excess. In other words, restraint may be disrupted or ___*disinhibt*___, with the result that people overeat. Paradoxically, then, restraint in eating may contribute to obesity.

Answers: **5-1.** biological, adoptive **5-2.** identical , fraternal, genetics **5-3.** fat cells, very stable **5-4.** number, size, number, leptin **5-5.** restrained. **5-6.** disinhibited.

SEXUAL MOTIVATION AND BEHAVIOR

6. **Describe the impact of hormones and pheromones in regulating animal and human sexual behavior.**

    6-1. Hormones are clearly linked to sexual behavior. For example, castrated rats have no sexual interest, but if they are injected with the hormone _testrone_ their sexual motivation revives. In humans, the effect of hormones on sexual behavior is considerably (greater/less) than is the case with lower animals.

    6-2. The major female sex hormones are called _estrogen_ and the major male sex hormones
           androgens
           ~~testrone~~_____. Both of these gonadal hormones occur in both sexes, however. Higher levels of the hormone _testerones_, a key androgen, are related to higher levels of sexual activity in (males only/females only/both sexes).

    6-3. A pheromone is a _chemical_ secreted by one animal that affects the _behaviol_ of other animals. Prominent among behaviors affected are sexual behaviors, but for human beings there is (only preliminary/strongly supported) evidence about possible pheromones and sexual responding.

    6-4. Nonetheless, pheromones do seem to affect human behavior. For example, women living together tend to have _sychronize_ cycles that occur at the same time, an effect attributed to _phremones_.

    6-5. Describe the study involving sweat and menstrual synchronization.

    Answers: 6-1. testosterone, less **6-2.** estrogens, androgens, testosterone, both sexes **6-3.** chemical, behavior, only preliminary **6-4.** menstrual, pheromones **6-5.** One study found that a solution of alcohol and sweat taken from some women and rubbed on the lips of other women tended to produce synchronized menstrual cycles.

7. **Summarize evidence on the impact of erotic materials, including aggressive pornography, on human sexual behavior.**

    7-1. How do men and women react to erotic materials? Answer this questions in terms of:

          (a) reported dislike of the materials
               women

          (b) physiological responses

          (c) sexual activity after viewing

    7-2. In the Zillman and Bryant studies described, male and female undergraduate subjects were exposed to relatively heavy doses of pornography over a period of weeks. What effect did this have on:

          (a) attitudes about sexual practices

(b) satisfaction with their sexual partners

7-3. Aggressive pornography usually depicts violence against women.

(a) What laboratory evidence indicates that viewing aggressive pornography affects aggression against women?

(b) What is the effect of viewing aggressive pornography on attitudes toward rape?

Answers: 7-1. (a) Women are more likely than men to report disliking erotic materials. (b) Women and men are both physiologically responsive to erotic materials. (As your author notes, differences between reported liking and physiological response may be due to the less sexist nature of the erotica used in laboratory settings.) (c). For a few hours immediately after exposure, the likelihood of sexual activity occurring is somewhat increased (although data on this issue are inconsistent). **7-2.** (a) Attitudes about sexual practices became more liberal; for example, both males and females came to view premarital and extramarital sex as more acceptable. (b) Subjects became less satisfied with their partners in terms of physical appearance and sexual performance. **7-3.** (a) Some studies have found that pornography depicting violence against women increases male subjects' aggressive behavior toward women. In these laboratory studies, aggression is defined as willingness to deliver electric shock to other subjects. (b) Exposure to aggressive pornography appears to make sexual coercion or rape seem less offensive.

8. Discuss parental investment theory and findings on human gender differences in sexual activity.

8-1. Triver's parental investment theory is the idea that a species' mating patterns are determined by the investment each sex must make to produce and nurture offspring. Since human females are the ones who are pregnant for nine months and subsequently breast feed the offspring, their _investment_ in the child is, by this analysis, greater than that of human males.

8-2. Parental investment theory is that idea that the sex that makes the smaller investment will compete in order to have mating opportunities with the sex that makes the larger investment, and that the sex that makes the larger investment will be more selective of partners. Thus, males of many mammalian species, including human beings, seek to maximize their reproductive potential by mating with (<u>as many</u>/as few) females as possible. Females, on the other hand, optimize their reproductive potential by being (<u>selective</u>/ unrestricted) in mating.

8-3. In line with predictions from parental investment theory and evolutionary theory in general, several studies have found that in comparison to women, men will show (1) (<u>more</u>/less) interest in sexual activity in general, (2) desire for a greater _variety_ of sexual partners, and (3) more willingness to engage in sex without being _committed_ to the partner.

Answers: 8-1. investment **8-2.** as many, selective **8-3.** more, variety, committed.

9. **Describe the Featured Study on culture and mating preferences and evolutionary analyses of jealousy.**

9-1.   According to evolutionary theories, what characteristics do human females look for in a male partner? What do males look for in a female partner?

9-2.   More than 10,000 people participated in Buss's study. The people surveyed were from (the United States/ 37 different cultures).

9-3.   In one or two sentences, summarize the results of Buss's study.

9-4.   What conclusions can reasonably be drawn from Buss's study? Place a T or F in the blanks.

_____   Some of the differences in mating preferences were universal across cultures.

_____   The data are consistent with evolutionary theories of sexual motivation.

_____   The data may be explained by alternative interpretations that do not derive from evolutionary theory.

_____   One possible alternative explanation of the data is that women value men's economic resources because their own potential has been restricted.

9-5.   Evolutionary psychologists explain gender differences in jealousy in a similar manner. Paternity (who the father is) is not always certain. Maternity is certain. Thus, if males want to make sure that they pass on their genes, they must be concerned with paternity, and their jealousy relates to (sexual/emotional) infidelity. For females, on the other hand, certain that the child is theirs, the male partner's resources and, hence, his (sexual/emotional) commitment is the more important factor.

Answers: 9-1. According to the evolutionary theories, women want men who will be able to acquire resources that can be invested in children–men with education, money, status, and ambition. Men, on the other hand, want women who have good breeding potential, women who are beautiful, youthful, and in good health. **9-2.** 37 different cultures **9-3.** Results supported predictions from the evolutionary theories: women placed more value than men on finding a partner with good financial prospects; men placed more value than women on the characteristics of youth and physical attractiveness (as summed up in the song Summertime from Gerschwin's Porgy and Bess, "Oh, your daddy's rich, and your mama's good looking.") **9-4.** All of these statements are true or represent reasonable inferences. Some differences were universal, and the data are consistent with evolutionary theories. At the same time there are alternative explanations involving the fact of discrimination against women in virtually all societies. **9-5.** sexual, emotional.

10. **Summarize evidence on the nature of sexual orientation and on how common homosexuality is.**

10-1.   Sexual orientation refers to a person's preference for emotional and sexual relationships with individuals of the other sex, the same sex, or either sex. Those who prefer relationships with the other sex are termed heterosexual with the same sex homo , and with either sex bi .

10-2. Because people may have experienced homosexuality in varying degrees, it seems reasonable to consider sexual orientation as a/an (<u>continuum</u>/~~all-or-none distinction~~). In part because of this definitional problem and in part due to prejudice against homosexuals, it is difficult to determine precisely the proportion of homosexuals in the population. A frequently cited statistics is 10%, but recent survey place the proportion at about _____.

Answers: **10-1.** heterosexuals (straights), homosexuals (gays or lesbians), bisexuals **10-2.** continuum, 5-8%. See Figure 10.16 in your text for more detailed information.

11. Summarize evidence on the determinants of sexual orientation.

11-1. What factors determine sexual orientation? Psychoanalysts thought the answer involved some aspect of the parent-child relationship. Behaviorists assumed that it was due to the association of same-sex stimuli with sexual arousal. Thus, both psychoanalytic and behavioral theorists proposed (<u>environmental</u>/~~biological~~) explanations of homosexuality.

11-2. Extensive research on the upbringing of homosexuals has (~~supported~~/<u>not supported</u>) the idea that homosexuality is largely explainable in terms of environmental factors.

11-3. Recent studies have produced evidence that homosexuality is in part genetic. Which of the following types of studies have supported this conclusion? (Place Y for yes or N for no in the blanks.)

N___ Studies of hormonal differences between heterosexuals and homosexuals.

Y___ Studies of twins and adopted children.

Y___ Autopsy studies of the hypothalamus.

X___ Differences in genetic material on the X chromosome.

11-4. Subjects in one of the studies described were gay men who had either an identical twin brother, a fraternal twin brother, or an adopted brother. For each of the categories, what percent of the brothers of the subjects were also gay? Place the appropriate percentages in the blanks.

_____ Identical twins   22 percent

_____ Fraternal twins   11 percent

_____ Adopted brothers   52 percent

11-5. LeVay (1991) has reported that a cluster of neurons in the anterior __hypothalamus__ is (<u>smaller</u>/~~larger~~) in gay men than in straight men. Since all of the gay men in this study had died of AIDS, which itself may produce changes in brain structure, these findings should be interpreted with caution. Nonetheless, these data support the idea that there are (~~environmental~~/<u>biological</u>) factors that are related to sexual orientation.

11-6. The fact that identical twins, who are genetically the same, turn out to share sexual orientation only half of the time suggests that __biology__ factors are involved in some way. In an attempt to account for the role of the environment, Daryl Bem has developed an interactionist view which contends that genes determine (~~sexual orientation~~/<u>temperament</u>), and it is the environment's response to temperament that accounts for differences in sexual orientation.

11-7. For example, if some boys by temperament don't enjoy aggressive play typical of their sex, then they may experience discomfort, perhaps resulting from teasing and taunting. Discomfort leads to emotional _arousal_ associated with their same-sex peers which, in some unspecified way, becomes transformed into sexual attraction.

Answers: 11-1. environmental **11-2.** not supported **11-3.** N, Y, Y, Y **11-4.** 52%, 22%, 11%. Note that a companion study for lesbians found similar results. **11-5.** hypothalamus, smaller, biological **11-6.** environmental, temperament **11-7.** arousal.

12. Outline the four phases of the human sexual response.

12-1. Write the names of the four phases of the human sexual response in the order in which they occur. (Hint: I made up a mnemonic device that's hard to forget. The first letter of each phase name produces EPOR, which happens to be ROPE spelled backward.)

(a) _Excitement_

(b) _Plateau_

(c) _Orgasm_

(d) _Resolution_

12-2. In the blanks below write the first letter of each phase name that correctly labels the descriptions below.

_E_   Rapid increase in arousal (respiration, heart rate, blood pressure, etc.)

_E_   Vasocongestion of blood vessels in sexual organs; lubrication in female

_P_   Continued arousal, but at a slower place

_O_   Tightening of the vaginal entrance

_O_   Pulsating muscular contractions and ejaculation

_R_   Physiological changes produced by arousal subside.

_R_   Includes a refractory period for men
         ↳ pi when man feels no sexual feeling

Answers: 12-1. (a) excitement (b) plateau (c) orgasm (d) resolution **12-2.** E, E, P, P, O, R, R.

AFFILIATION: IN SEARCH OF BELONGINGNESS

13. Describe the affiliation motive and how it is measured.

13-1. Most human beings seek the company of others, a need referred to as the _affiliation_ motive.

13-2. In a recent theoretical review of research on affiliation, Baumeister and Leary assert that the need to affiliate has a strong basis in (<u>learning/evolution</u>). For human beings, as for many other animals, bonding with others permits more effective hunting, defense, and care of offspring. Affiliation, in other words, appears to have to have _survival_ value

13-3. Need for affiliation may be measured by a test known as the Thematic Apperception Test, or _T A T_ for short. This test involves asking subjects to write or tell _____ in response to pictures of people in various scenes.

13-4. Certain themes emerge from the TAT stories that reflect the strengths of various needs or motives. How well does the TAT measure affiliation? Validity studies have shown that people who devote more time to seeking and maintaining friendships do, in fact, tend to score higher on the need for _____ on the TAT.

Answers: 13-1. affiliation **13-2.** evolution, survival (adaptive) **13-3.** TAT, stories **13-4.** affiliation.

ACHIEVEMENT: IN SEARCH OF EXCELLENCE

14. Describe the achievement motive and discuss how individual differences in the need for achievement influence behavior.

14-1. People with high achievement motivation have a need to:

a. master difficult challenges

b. outperform others

c. excel and compete

(d) all of the above

14-2. What is the relationship between estimates of achievement motive in a country and the economic growth of that county?

↑economic growth ∝ ↑achievement

14-3. The procedure used for measuring need for achievement is the same as that used to measure need for affiliation: subjects tell stories about pictures shown in the _TAT_ .

14-4. How do people who score high on need for affiliation differ from those who score low?

There are more hard & working

Answers: 14-1. d **14-2.** Countries with estimated high achievement motivation have higher economic growth (and greater productivity in general). **14-3.** TAT **14-4.** They tend to work hard, compete, be persistent, be successful in their careers, etc.

15. Explain how situational factors and fear of failure affect achievement strivings.

15-1. According to Atkinson's elaboration of McClelland's views, achievement-oriented behavior is determined not only by (1) achievement motivation but by (2) the _probability_ that success will occur and (3) the _incentive_ value of success.

15-2. As the difficulty of a task increases, the ___probability___ of success at the task decreases. At the same time, success at harder tasks may be more satisfying, so the ___incentive___ value of the task is likely to increase. When both the incentive value and probability of success are weighed together, people with a high need for achievement would tend to select tasks of (~~extreme~~/moderate) difficulty.

15-3. In addition to success, Atkinson has included fear of failure in the equation. Thus, Atkinson proposes that there are six factors that affect pursuit of achievement: a motivation to achieve (to be successful) and a motivation to avoid ___failure___; perceived probability of ___success___ and the perceived probability of ___failure___; and the incentive values of both ___success___ and ___failure___.

15-4. The motivation to avoid failure may either stimulate achievement or inhibit achievement. Explain.

Answers: 15-1. probability, incentive **15-2.** probability, incentive, moderate **15-3.** failure; success, failure; success, failure **15-4.** One may achieve in order to avoid failure on a task; thus, fear of failure may lead to achievement. On the other hand, one may avoid failure by not pursuing the task at all; thus, fear of failure could also lead to lack of achievement.

THE ELEMENTS OF EMOTIONAL EXPERIENCE

16. Describe the cognitive component of emotion.

16-1. The word cognition refers to thoughts, beliefs, or conscious experience. When faced with an ugly-looking insect (or, for some people, the edge of a cliff or making a speech in public), you might say to yourself, "This is terrifying (or maybe disgusting)." This thought or cognition has an evaluative aspect: we assess our emotions as pleasant or unpleasant. Thus, one component of emotion is the thinking or ___cognitive___ component, which includes ___evaluations___ in terms of pleasantness-unpleasantness.

Answers: 16-1. cognitive, evaluation.

17. Describe the physiological underpinnings of emotion.

17-1. The second component of emotion is the ___physiological___ component, primarily actions of the ___autonomic___ nervous system. Your encounter with the insect might be accompanied by changes in heart rate, breathing, or blood pressure—or by increased electrical conductivity of the skin, known as the ___Galvanic___ skin response (GSR).

17-2. Lie detectors don't actually detect lies, they detect ___emotion___ reflected by changes in heart rate, respiration, and GSR. Emotion does not necessarily reflect lying, however. Because of (relatively high/~~very low~~) error rates, polygraph results (~~can~~/cannot) be used as evidence in most courtrooms.

17-3. Recent evidence suggests that the brain structure known as the ~~hypothalamus~~ _amygdala_ plays a central role in emotion. For example, research has found that animals who have their amygdalas destroyed cannot learn classically conditioned ___fear___ responses.

17-4. The amygdala doesn't process emotion by itself but is at the core of a complex set of neural circuits. Sensory information relating to fear arrives at the thalamus and from there is relayed along two pathways, to the nearby _____ and also to areas in the _____.

17-5. The amygdala processes information extremely rapidly, which has clear _____ value for the organism in threatening situations. The cortex responds more slowly but in greater detail and relays potentially moderating information to the amydala. While the hub of this vigilance system seems to be the _____, both pathways are useful in assessing threat.

Answers: **17-1.** physiological, autonomic, galvanic **17-2.** emotion (autonomic arousal), relatively high, cannot **17-3.** amygdala, fear **17-4.** amygdala, cortex **17-5.** survival (adaptive), amygdala.

18. Discuss the body language of emotions and the facial feedback hypothesis.

18-1. We communicate emotions not only verbally but _____, through our postures, gestures, and, especially, in our facial _____.

18-2. Ekman and Friesen found that there are _____ fundamental facial expressions of emotion: happiness, sadness, anger, fear, surprise, and disgust. Children who have been blind since birth frown and smile just like sighted children, which supports the idea that basic facial expressions are largely (learned/ innate).

18-3. According to some researchers facial expressions not only reflect emotions but help create them. This viewpoint, known as the _____ hypothesis, asserts that facial muscles send signals to the brain that help produce the subjective experience of emotion. For example, turning up the corners of your mouth will tend to make you feel _____.

Answers: **18-1.** nonverbally (through body language), expressions **18-2.** six, innate **18-3.** facial-feedback, happy.

19. Discuss cross-cultural similarities and variations in emotional experience.

19-1. Ekman and Friesen asked people in different cultures to label the emotion shown on photographs of faces. What did they find?

19-2. Different cultures show striking similarities in other aspects of emotional experience as well. For example, regardless of culture, meeting with friends tends to trigger one emotion and encountering failure another. Thus, certain types of _____ trigger the same emotions across cultures.

19-3. Similarly, the characteristics of _____ arousal that accompany emotion also appear to be largely invariant across cultures.

19-4. While there are similarities in emotional expression across cultures, there are also striking differences. For example, certain word labels for emotion (e.g., sadness, anxiety, remorse) that exist in some cultures (also occur/do not occur) in others.

19-5. Although people in different cultures tend to show the same basic expressions of emotion, when they do so is governed by different cultural norms. What emotions are you "supposed" to show at a funeral, or when watching a sporting event? The unwritten rules that regulate our display of emotion, known as _____ rules, vary considerably across cultures.

Answers: 19-1. People from very different cultures, including cultures that have had virtually no contact with the West, show considerable agreement in labeling photographs of facial expressions with approximately six basic emotions. These data support the idea that emotional expression is largely universal. **19-2.** events (experiences, situations) **19-3.** physiological **19-4.** do not occur **19-5.** display.

THEORIES OF EMOTION

20. **Compare and contrast the James-Lange and Cannon-Bard theories of emotion and explain how Schachter reconciled these conflicting views in his two-factor theory.**

   20-1. For each of the following statements indicate the theory being described.

   (a) _____ The subjective experience of emotion is caused by different patterns of autonomic arousal.

   (b) _____ Emotions can not be distinguished on the basis of a autonomic arousal; general autonomic arousal causes one to look for an explanation or label.

   (c) _____ Love is accompanied by a different autonomic pattern from hate.

   (d) _____ The subjective experience of emotion is caused by two factors, by arousal and by cognition.

   (e) _____ Emotions originate in subcortical brain structures; different emotions produce almost identical patterns of autonomic arousal.

   (f) _____ Ralph observes that his heart pounds and that he becomes a little out of breath at times. He also notices that these signs of arousal occur whenever Mary is around, so he figures that he must be in love.

   20-2. In what sense does Schachter's theory reconcile the James-Lange and Cannon-Bard theories?

   Answers: 20-1. (a) James-Lange (b) Schachter's two-factor (c) Schachter's two-factor (d) James-Lange (e) Cannon-Bard (f) Schachter's two-factor **20-2.** Schachter's view is similar to the James-Lange theory in that arousal is thought to precede the conscious experience of emotion; it is similar to the Cannon-Bard theory in that there is assumed to be just one general physiological arousal response rather than a different visceral response for each emotion. Since arousal is in large part the same regardless of the emotion, Schachter proposed that we feel different emotions as a result of inferences we make from events in the environment.

21. **Summarize the evolutionary perspective on emotion.**

   21-1. By preparing an organism for aggression and defense, the emotion of anger helps an organism survive. The emotions of fear, surprise, and interest have similar functions. From an evolutionary perspective, all emotions developed because of the _____ value they have for a species.

21-2. Evolutionary theorists view emotions primarily as a group of (<u>innate</u>/learned) reactions that have been passed on because of their survival value. They also believe that emotions originate in subcortical areas, parts of the brain that evolved before the cortical structures associated with higher mental processes. In the view of evolutionary theorists, emotion evolved before thought and is largely (dependent on/ <u>independent of</u>) thought.

21-3. How many basic, inherited emotions are there? The evolutionary writers assume that the wide range of emotions we experience are blends or variations in intensity of approximately _____ innate or prewired primary emotions.

Answers: **21-1.** survival (adaptive) **21-2.** innate, independent of **21-3.** eight (between six and ten).

PUTTING IT IN PERSPECTIVE

22. Explain how this chapter highlighted five of the text's unifying themes.

22-1. Five of the text's organizing themes were prominent in this chapter. Indicate which themes fit the following examples by writing the appropriate abbreviations in the blanks below: CC for cultural contexts, SH for sociohistorical context, TD for theoretical diversity, HE for heredity and environment, and MC for multiple causation.

(a) Achievement behavior is affected by achievement motivation, the likelihood of success, the likelihood of failure, and so on. _____

(b) Display rules in a culture tell us when and where to express an emotion. _____

(c) Changing attitudes about homosexuality have produced more research on sexual orientation; in turn, data from the research has affected societal attitudes. _____

(d) Body weight seems to be influenced by set point, blood glucose, and inherited metabolism. It is also affected by eating habits and acquired tastes, which vary across cultures. _____, _____, and _____

(e) The James-Lange theory proposed that different emotions reflected different patterns of physiological arousal; Cannon-Bard theory assumed that emotions originate in subcortical structures; Schachter viewed emotion as a combination of physiological arousal and cognition _____.

Answers: **22-1.** (a) MC (b) CC (c) SH (d) HE, MC, CC (e) TD.

PERSONAL APPLICATION: EXPLORING THE INGREDIENTS OF HAPPINESS

23. Summarize information on factors that do not predict happiness.

23-1. Indicate whether each of the following statements is true or false.

_____ There is very little correlation between income and happiness.

_____ Younger people tend to be happier than older people.

_____ People who have children tend to be happier than those without children.

_____ People with high IQ scores tend to be happier than those with low IQ scores.

_____ There is a negligible correlation between physical attractiveness and happiness.

23-2. List five factors discussed in your text that have little or no relationship to happiness.

Answers: 23-1. T, F, F, F, T **23-2.** money (income), age, parenthood (either having or not having children), intelligence, physical attractiveness.

24. Summarize information on factors that are moderately or strongly correlated with happiness.

24-1. Indicate whether each of the following statements is true or false.

_____ One of the strongest predictors of happiness is good health. .

_____ Social support and friendship groups are moderately related to happiness.

_____ Religious people tend to be somewhat happier than nonreligious people.

_____ People in collectivist societies tend to be somewhat happier than those in individualistic societies.

_____ Marital status is strongly related to happiness; married people tend to be happier than single people.

_____ Job satisfaction tends to be strongly related to general happiness; people who like their jobs tend to be happy.

_____ Differences in personality have a negligible relationship to happiness; introverts, on the average, are just as happy as extraverts.

24-2. List four factors that are moderately correlated with happiness and three that are strongly correlated.

Answers: 24-1. F (Because people adapt, there is only a moderate relationship between health and happiness.), T, T, F (People in individualistic societies tend to be happier. Of course, whether it's the collectivism-individualism dimension that causes the difference is hard to know because the societies compared differ in many other respects as well.) T, T, F (People who are extraverted, optimistic, and have high self-esteem tend to be happier.) **24-2.** Moderately related: health, social activity (friendship), religion, and culture (individualistic vs. collectivistic). Strongly related: marriage, work (job satisfaction), and personality.

25. Explain four conclusions that can be drawn about the dynamics of happiness.

25-1. One conclusion about happiness is that how we feel about our health, wealth, job, and age are more important than the facts of our situation. In other words, the objective realities are less important than our _____ reactions.

25-2. In addition, the extent of our happiness depends on the comparison group. Generally, people compare themselves to others who are similar in some dimension, such as friends or neighbors. In the final analysis, our happiness is relative to the _____ to which we compare ourselves.

25-3. A third conclusion is that our baseline for judging pleasantness and unpleasantness constantly changes. When good things happen, we shift our baselines (what we feel we "need" or want) upward; when bad things happen, we shift down. In other words, people _____ to changing circumstances.

25-4. Finally, many people find happiness despite seemingly insurmountable problems. Because we are so adaptable, the quest for happiness is never completely _____.

Answers: 25-1. subjective **25-2.** group (people) **25-3.** adapt (adjust) **25-4.** hopeless.

CRITICAL THINKING APPLICATION
ANALYZING ARGUMENTS: MAKING SENSE OUT OF CONTROVERSY

26. Describe the key elements in arguments.

26-1. In logic, an argument is a series of statements which claims to prove something (whether it does or not). Arguments are comprised of two major parts, a conclusion and one or more premises. The _____ are statements intended to present evidence or proof. The _____ supposedly derives from or is proved by the premises.

26-2. Consider this logical argument: "Any field of study that uses the scientific method is a science. Psychology uses the scientific method. Thus, psychology is a science." Label the parts of the argument below (C for conclusion and P for premise).

_____ Any field of study that uses the scientific method is a science.

_____ Psychology uses the scientific method.

_____ Thus, psychology is a science.

Answers: 26-1. premises, conclusion **26-2.** P, P, C. Note that this is an example of a valid argument. One may or may not agree with the premises (e.g., they may define science differently), but the conclusion logically follows from the premises.

27. Explain some common fallacies that often show up in arguments.

27-1. Read over the section on common logical fallacies described in your text. Then match the examples with the appropriate terms. (Suggestion: Use the abbreviations IR, CR, SS, WA, and FD for matching. Note that there are five fallacies and seven examples; two fallacies are used twice.)

irrelevant reasons   slippery slope

circular reasoning   weak analogies

false dichotomy

(a) _____ Trouble sleeping causes great difficulty in our lives because insomnia is a major problem for people.

(b) _____ People with insomnia should use the herb melatonin because insomnia is an enormous problem in our country.

(c) _____ Vitamin C is extremely effective in slowing the aging process. I know it is effective because I have taken it for many years. Obviously, the reason I take Vitamin C is that it works to reduce aging.

(d) ____ If we don't stop communism in Viet Nam now, it will spread next to Laos, then to Cambodia, and then to the entire Southeast Asian Peninsula.

(e) ____ We saw what happened when Chamberlain gave in to Hitler. The same thing will happen again unless we stand up to the tyranny in the Middle East.

(f) ____ We can fight in the Balkans now, or we can prepare for World War III.

(g) ____ Ralph bought a blender on a Tuesday in Peoria and it lasted a long time. If I buy a blender on a Tuesday in Peoria, it should also last a long time.

Answers: 27-1. (a) CR. The premise and conclusion are the same. (b) IR. Insomnia may be a problem but that does not lead to the conclusion that the herb melatonin should be taken. (c) CR. The conclusion, the first statement, is simply a restatement of the premise, which is the last statement. (d) SS. The argument is that if you allow one thing to happen, then a series of other things will inevitably happen. In fact, there may be no necessary connection between the events. (e) WA. While the two situations may have a degree of similarity, they are also likely to be sufficiently dissimilar to make the argument invalid. (f) FD. The choice seems to be between the two options, but, logically, these are not the only choices. We may also do both, or neither. (g) WA. While the situations share some elements in common, this does not mean that they share all elements or that some elements cause others.

REVIEW OF KEY TERMS

Achievement motive
Affiliation motive
Androgens
Aphrodisiac
Argument
Assumptions
Bisexuals
Body Mass Index (BMI)
Display rules
Emotion
Estrogens

Galvanic skin response (GSR)
Glucose
Glucostats
Hedonic Adaptation
Heterosexuals
Homeostasis
Homosexuals
Individualism
Lie detector
Motivation

Obesity
Orgasm
Pheromone
Polygraph
Premisis
Refractory period
Set point
Sexual orientation
Subjective well-being
Vasocongestion

motivation 1. Goal-directed behavior that may be affected by needs, wants, interests, desires, and incentives.

display rules 2. Cultural norms that regulate the expression of emotions.

argument 3. One or more premises that are used to provide support for a conclusion.

premisis 4. The reasons presented in an argument to persuade someone that a conclusion is true.

assumptions 5. Premises in an argument which are assumed but for which no proof or evidence is offered.

BMI 6. A measure of weight that controls for variations in height; weight in kilograms divided by height in meters, squared.

7. Refers to cultures that put group goals ahead of personal goals and defines a person's identity in terms of the groups to which a person belongs.

Glucose 8. Blood sugar.

Glucostat 9. Neurons that are sensitive to glucose.

hedonic adaptation	**10.**	A hormone secreted by the pancreas needed for extracting glucose from the blood.
individualism	**11.**	Refers to cultures that put personal goals ahead of group goals and defines a person's identity in terms of the personal attributes.
set pt	**12.**	The theoretical natural point of stability in body weight.
obesity	**13.**	The condition of being overweight.
estrogen	**14.**	The principal class of female sex hormones.
androgen	**15.**	The principal class of male sex hormones.
pheromones	**16.**	A chemical secreted by one animal that affects the behavior of another animal.
aphrodisiac	**17.**	Substance purported to increase sexual desire.
vasocongestion	**18.**	Engorgement of the blood vessels.
orgasm	**19.**	Sexual climax.
refractory period	**20.**	A time following orgasm during which males are unresponsive to sexual stimulation.
sexual orientation bi-sex	**21.**	Whether a person prefers emotional-sexual relationships with members of the same sex, the other sex, or either sex.
hetero-	**22.**	People who seek emotional-sexual relationships with members of the same sex.
homo	**23.**	People who seek emotional-sexual relationships with members of the other sex.
bi-	**24.**	People who seek emotional-sexual relationships with members of either sex.
affiliation	**25.**	The motive to associate with others.
subjective well	**26.**	Individuals' personal perceptions of their overall happiness and life satisfaction.
achievement motive	**27.**	The need to master difficult challenges and to excel in competition with others.
GSR	**28.**	An increase in the electrical conductivity of the skin related to an increase in sweat gland activity.
emotion	**29.**	A reaction that includes cognitive, physiological, and behavioral components.
Polygraph	**30.**	The technical name for the "lie detector."
Lie detector	**31.**	The informal name for polygraph, an apparatus that monitors physiological aspects of arousal (e.g., heart rate, GSR).

Answers: 1. motivation **2.** display rules **3.** argument **4.** premises **5.** assumptions **6.** body mass index (BMI) **7.** collectivism **8.** glucose **9.** glucostats **10.** hedonic adaptation **11.** individualism **12.** set point **13.** obesity **14.** estrogens **15.** androgens **16.** pheromone **17.** aphrodisiac **18.** vasocongestion **19.** orgasm **20.** refractory period **21.** sexual orientation **22.** homosexuals **23.** heterosexuals **24.** bisexuals **25.** affiliation motive **26.** subjective well-being **27.** achievement motive **28.** galvanic skin response (gsr) **29.** emotion **30.** polygraph **31.** lie detector

---

REVIEW OF KEY PEOPLE

John Atkinson	Paul Ekman & Wallace Friesen	William Masters & Virginia Johnson
David Buss	William James	Henry Murray
Walter Cannon	David McClelland	Stanley Schachter

_____	**1.** Proposed that emotions arise in subcortical areas of the brain.
_____	**2.** Compiled an influential catalogue of common social needs; also devised the TAT.
_____	**3.** Prominent evolutionary theorist who explored, among many other topics, gender differences in human mate preferences.
_____	**4.** Proposed that eating on the part of obese people is controlled by external cues; devised the two-factor theory of emotion.
_____	**5.** Stressed the importance of the amygdala as the core of a set of interacting neural circuits that process emotion.
_____	**6.** Did the ground-breaking work on the physiology of the human sexual response.
_____	**7.** Is responsible for most of the early research on achievement motivation.
_____	**8.** Emphasized additional factors in an elaboration of McClelland's theory of achievement motivation.
_____	**9.** In a series of cross-cultural studies found that people can identify six or so basic emotions from facial expressions.
_____	**10.** Thought that emotion arose from oneís perception of variations in autonomic arousal.

Answers: 1. Cannon **2.** Murray **3.** Buss **4.** Schachter **5.** LeDoux **6.** Masters & Johnson **7.** McClelland **8.** Atkinson **9.** Ekman & Friesen **10.** James.

SELF-QUIZ

1. What happens when a rat's ventromedial hypothalamus (VMH) is lesioned?
   a. The rat starts eating.
   b. The rat looks for a sexual partner.
   c. The rat becomes aggressive.
   d. The rat loses bladder and bowel control.

2. The presence of the hormone Leptin in the bloodstream tends to:
   a. decrease hunger
   b. accompany stress
   c. contribute to general arousal level
   d. signal sexual activity

3. What is the effect of insulin on blood glucose?
   a. Glucose level increases.
   b. Glucose level decreases.
   c. Glucose changes to free fatty acids.
   d. CCK increases.

4. Which data from twin studies provide the most convincing evidence of the influence of heredity on body weight?
   a. Identical twins reared together are more similar than fraternal twins reared together.
   b. Identical twins reared together are more similar than fraternal twins reared apart.
   c. Identical twins reared apart are more similar than fraternal twins reared apart.
   d. Identical twins reared apart are more similar than fraternal twins reared together.

5. Which of the following is thought to be a major determinant of set point?
a. number of fat cells
b. size of fat cells
c. calories expended in exercise
d. sucrose in the bloodstream

6. The presence of testosterone is related to higher levels of sexual activity in:
a. males
b. females
c. both males and females
d. androids

7. A chemical secreted by one animal that affects the behavior of another animal is known as a (an):
a. androgen
b. affiliatrogen
c. hormone
d. pheromone

8. According to this theory, the sex that makes the larger investment in offspring (bearing, nursing, etc.) will be more selective of partners than the sex that makes the smaller investment.
a. adaptation level theory
b. parental investment theory
c. investment differentiation theory
d. social learning theory

9. According to the evolutionary theories, men seek as partners women who:
a. are similar to them in important attitudes
b. have a good sense of humor
c. are beautiful, youthful, and in good health.
d. have good financial prospects

10. What test is generally used to measure need for achievement?
a. the TAT
b. the GSR
c. the Rorschach
d. the MMPI

11. Evidence regarding facial expression in different cultures and observation of the blind suggests that:
a. Schachter's two-factor theory is correct
b. facial expression of emotion is to a large extent innate
c. emotions originate in the cortex
d. learning is the major factor in explaining basic facial expressions

12. Which of the following proposed that emotion arises from one's perception or interpretation of autonomic arousal?
a. Schachter
b. Cannon-Bard
c. LeDoux
d. McClelland

13. Which of the following theories assert that thinking or cognition plays a relatively small role in emotion?
a. two factory theory
b. James-Lange theory
c. achievement theory
d. evolutionary theory

14. Of the following, which has been found to be most strongly associated with happiness?
    a. physical attractiveness
    b. health
    c. job satisfaction
    d. general intelligence

15. Someone exhorts people to take action against company policy, as follows: "We can oppose this changes, or we can live out our lives in poverty." While the intent of the argument may be appropriate and persuasive, logically it would be which of the following fallacies?
    a. slippery slope
    b. weak analogy
    c. false dichotomy
    d. circular reasoning

Answers: 1. a **2.** a **3.** b **4.** d **5.** a **6.** c **7.** d **8.** b **9.** c **10.** a **11.** b **12.** a **13.** d **14.** c **15.** c.

Chapter Eleven

Human Development Across the Life Span

REVIEW OF KEY IDEAS

PROGRESS BEFORE BIRTH: PRENATAL DEVELOPMENT

1. **Outline the major events of the three phases of prenatal development.**

   1-1. Each box below represents one month in the typical pregnancy; each short line at the top of the boxes represents one week. Indicate the beginning and end of each phase of prenatal development by placing the appropriate capital letters from the diagram in the blanks after the descriptions below.

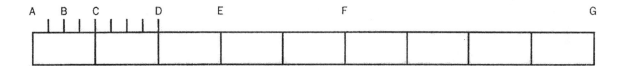

   a) The germinal stage begins at conception, represented by point ____A____ in the diagram, and ends at point __B____.

   (b) The embryonic stage begins at point __B____ and ends at point __D____.

   (c) The fetal stage begins at point __D____ and ends at point ____G____.

   1-2. List the names of the three phases of prenatal development in the order in which they occur. In the parentheses at the right indicate the age ranges encompassed by each stage.

   (a) __Germinal__   (0 - 2 wks)

   (b) __Embryonic__   (2- end 2mth)

   (c) __Fetal__   (2 -   9mth)

1-3. Match the letter identifying each stage in the previous question with the descriptions below.

_B E_ The placenta begins to form.

_B_ At the end of this stage the organism begins to have a human appearance; it is about an inch in length.

_A_ The zygote begins to implant in the uterine wall; about one in five are rejected.

_E_ Muscles and bones develop and physical movements occur.

_B_ Most major birth defects probably have their origins in this stage.

_C_ The age of viability (about 22 to 26 weeks after conception) occurs during this stage.

Answers: 1-1. (a) A, B (b) B, D (c) D, G **1-2.** (a) germinal (birth to two weeks) (b) embryonic (two weeks to two months) (c) fetal (two months to nine months) **1-3.** a, b, a, c, b, c.

2. Summarize the impact of environmental factors on prenatal development.

2-1. Indicate whether the following statements concerning environmental factors and fetal development are true (T) or false (F).

_T_ Severe malnutrition increases the risk of birth complications and neurological deficits.

_F_ Studies consistently indicate that moderate malnutrition does not have a harmful effect on infant development.

_F_ Few if any drugs consumed by a pregnant woman are able to pass through the placental barrier.

_T_ Relative to its affluence the U. S. has a high infant mortality rate.

_F_ Recent studies indicate that moderate drinking during pregnancy produces no risk for the developing fetus.

_T_ Heavy drinking of alcohol by a pregnant woman may produce microencephaly, heart defects, and retardation in her child.

_T_ Smoking during pregnancy is related to increased risk of miscarriage and other birth complications.

_T_ The placenta screens out many but not all infectious diseases.

_T_ Genital herpes is usually transmitted during the birth process, when newborns come into contact with their mothers' lesions.

_T_ AIDS is transmitted primarily during the birth process, when newborns come into contact with their mothers' blood cells.

_T_ Good quality prenatal care is associated with fewer premature births and higher infant survival rates.

Answers: 2-1. T, F, F, T, F, T, T, T, T, T, T.

3. **Describe general trends and principles and cultural variations in motor development**

3-1. In the space below, list and describe the two basic trends in motor development described in the text.

Cephalocaudal trend:

Proximodistal trend:

3-2. The average ages at which children display various behaviors and abilities are referred to as developmental _norm_. While these averages provide useful information they don't reflect variability, and the age at which children display certain behaviors or abilities varies (enormously/~~very little~~) across children.

3-3. Thus, with regard to the behavior of walking up steps, for example, (Figure 11.6), which of the following is true?

a. children walk up steps at approximately the same age.   F

b. many normal children walk up steps well after or well before the average age indicated.   T

3-4. The process that underlies the developmental norms is *maturation*. What is maturation? (Be specific with regard to the factors of heredity and environment.)

Reaching the level that show

3-5. Cross-cultural research has revealed a considerable degree of consistency between cultures in terms of when and in what order motor skills appear. In general, early motor development is much more dependent on (~~maturation~~/culture) than is later motor development. As children in a culture grow older, however, the motor skills that they acquire depend to a greater extent on (~~maturation~~/culture).

Answers: **3-1.** Head to foot: children tend to gain motor control of the upper body before the lower body. Center outward: the tendency to gain control of the torso before the limbs. **3-2.** norms, enormously **3-3.** b **3-4.** Maturation refers to developmental changes that occur in an organism as a result of *genetic*, as opposed to environmental, factors. **3-5.** maturation, culture.

4. **Summarize the findings of Thomas and Chess's longitudinal study of infant temperament.**

4-1. Identify the following designs by indicating whether they are longitudinal or cross-sectional.

(a) _____   In this experimental design researchers compare groups of subjects of differing ages at a single point in time.

(b) _____   This design measures a single group of subjects over a period of time.

4-2.   Using a longitudinal design Thomas and Chess identified three basic temperaments, described below. Place the names of these temperamental styles in the appropriate blanks.

(a) _secure easy_   Happy, regular in sleep and eating, adaptable.

(b) _slow_   Less cheery, less regular in sleep and eating, more wary of new experiences.

(c) _hard to warm up_   Glum, erratic in sleep and eating, irritable.

4-3.   The largest group of children (about 40%) were of the _____ temperament, another 15% were _____, and 10% were in the _____ category. The remaining 35% showed mixtures of these three temperaments.

4-4.   What is the major result and conclusion from the Thomas and Chess study?

Answers: 4-1. (a) cross-sectional (b) longitudinal **4-2.** (a) easy (b) slow-to-warm-up (c) difficult **4-3.** (a) easy (b) slow-to-warm-up (c) difficult (d) 35 % **4-4.** Temperament seems to be very stable across time; a child's temperament at 3 months tended to be a fair predictor of temperament at 10 years. These and more recent data suggest that temperament has a strong basis in one's genetic inheritance.

5. Summarize theories of attachment and research on patterns of attachment and their effects.

5-1.   Newborn babies do not form attachments to their mothers immediately. They begin to show a strong preference for their mothers, often crying when they are separated, beginning at about _6-8 mth_ months of age.

5-2.   The emotional distress that occurs when some infants are separated from their caregivers is called _separation_ anxiety. This distress peaks at about _14-18_ months of age and then begins to decline.

5-3.   Research by Ainsworth and her colleagues indicates that attachments between mothers and their infants tend to fall into three categories. Label each of the following with the pattern of attachment described: *secure*, *anxious-ambivalent*, or *avoidant*.

(a) _anxious ambivalent_   The infant is anxious even when the mother is near, becomes very agitated when she leaves, and is not comforted when the mother returns.

(b) _avoidant_   The infant seeks little contact with the mother and is not distressed when she leaves.

(c) _secure_   The infant plays comfortably when the mother is present, is upset when the mother leaves, but is quickly calmed by her when she returns.

5-4. Although one cannot assume a causal relationship, attachment in infancy has been found to be related to behavior in later childhood. Which of the following tend to describe children who have had secure attachments in infancy? Place a Y (yes) or N (no) in the blanks.

_Y_ high self-esteem

_N_ low in leadership ability

_Y_ better social skills, more close friends

_Y_ persistence, curiosity, and self-reliance

_Y_ better cognitive development

Answers: 5-1. 6 to 8 **5-2.** separation, 14 to 18 **5-3.** (a) anxious-ambivalent (b) avoidant (c) secure **5-4.** Y, N, Y, Y, Y.

6. Discuss bonding at birth, day care, and culture in relation to attachment.

6-1. Is infant-mother "bonding" during the first few hours after birth important? Research thus far indicates that skin-to-skin contact between mothers and infants

a. tends to produce stronger attachments later

b. results in clear short-term benefits

c. is of no established benefit, either short- or long-term

6-2. Does day care affect infant-mother attachment? Belsky has found that day care for more than 20 hours per week increases the likelihood that a/an (insecure/secure) attachment will form between mother and infant

6-3. Belsky's findings must be put in perspective, however. Which of the following statements are/is true (T) or false (F)?

_____ The proportion of insecure attachments found in the Belsky studies is only slightly higher than the US norm.

_____ The preponderance of other studies suggests that day care is not harmful to children's attachment relationships.

_____ Considering the deprived childrearing conditions in many homes, day care can have beneficial effects on some children's social development.

6-4. Separation anxiety occurs at roughly the same ages across different cultures. There are cross-cultural differences, however, in the proportion of infants who fall into the three attachment categories (see Table 11.1 in your text).

(a) Which cultural sample (USA, Germany, or Japan) showed the highest proportion of *avoidant* attachments? _____

(b) Which cultural sample evidenced virtually *no avoidant attachments* at all?

_____

(c) Which sample showed the highest levels of *anxious/ambivalent* attachments?

_____

(d) Which two countries had the highest proportion of *secure* attachments?

_____ and _____

Answers: 6-1. c (As appealing as the practice may be, research so far has failed to find convincing evidence that it has either short- or long-term benefits.) **6-2.** insecure **6-3.** T, T, T **6-4.** (a) Germany (b) Japan (c) Japan (d) Japan, USA.

7. **Explain Belsky's evolutionary perspective on attachment.**

7-1. Belsky proposed that in our evolutionary past the relative harshness of the environment affected parent-child attachment style, which in turn affected the later __reproductive__ strategy of the sexually mature offspring.

7-2. For example, a harsh, unsafe environment with scarce resources would cause parents to have little time for the child, which would produce a/an (~~secure~~/insecure) attachment. When the child reached sexual maturity, the earlier attachment style would yield a sexually (opportunistic/~~enduring~~) mating strategy. Such a strategy would maximize reproductive potential in environments where long-term survival is (~~ensured~~/precarious).

7-3. In contrast, a safe environment rich in resources would allow parents the time and energy to be responsive to an infant's needs, which would produce a/an __secure__ attachment. Belsky asserts that such an attachment is associated with (quality/~~quantity~~) in later mating relationships with relatively (few/~~many~~) sexual partners and a strong romantic bond.

7-4. In short, Belsky proposed that the local __day__ _____ affected parent-child _____ which influenced the child's later _____ strategy, which in turn had _____ value for the environment in which it occurred.

Answers: 7-1. reproductive **7-2.** insecure, opportunistic, precarious **7-3.** secure, quality, few **7-4.** environment, attachment, reproductive, adaptive (survival, reproductive fitness).

8. **Outline the basic tenets of Erikson's theory and describe his stages of childhood personality development.**

8-1. Erikson's theory is clearly derived from Freudian psychoanalytic theory. Freud asserted that there are five childhood stages that determine the adult's personality. In contrast, Erikson proposed that there are _____ stages that influence personality across an individual's (childhood/entire lifespan).

8-2. Erikson described four childhood stages and four adult stages. In the spaces below write the names of the crises that mark the four *childhood* stages, and indicate in the parentheses the approximate ages at which the crises are supposed to occur.

(a) __trust__ vs. __mistrust__   (0 - 1   )

(b) __autonomy__ vs. __shame / doubt__   (2 - .3   )

(c) _Initiative_ vs. _guilt_ (3 - c)

(d) _idustry_ vs. _inferns(_ (6. -adole)

8-3. Below are descriptions of several individuals. In what childhood stage would they have acquired these characteristics, according to Erikson? Use the letters from the question above to indicate the stages.

_d_ Jack has trouble functioning effectively in the world outside his family; he is unproductive, and he lacks a sense of competence.

_a_ Kristi is insecure and suspicious of everyone.

_c_ Larry was torn between being independent of his family and avoiding conflict; as an adult he feels guilty and lacks self-esteem.

_b_ From an early age Maureen's parents never seemed satisfied with what she did. Maureen is plagued by a sense of shame and self-doubt.

8-4. As you may have noted in responding to the previous item, a weakness of Erikson's theory is that it attempts to account for very (few/many) aspects of personality. Thus, the theory cannot explain the enormous individual _differences_ between people.

Answers: **8-1.** 8, entire lifespan **8-2.** (a) trust vs. mistrust (first year) (b) autonomy vs. shame and doubt (second year) (c) initiative vs. guilt (ages 3 to 6) (d) industry vs. inferiority (age 6 through puberty) **8-3.** d, a, c, b **8-4.** few, differences (variation).

9. Outline Piaget's stages of cognitive development and discuss the strengths and weaknesses of Piaget's theory.

9-1. The diagram below represents Piaget's four main stages of development. Write the names of the stages in the appropriate blanks.

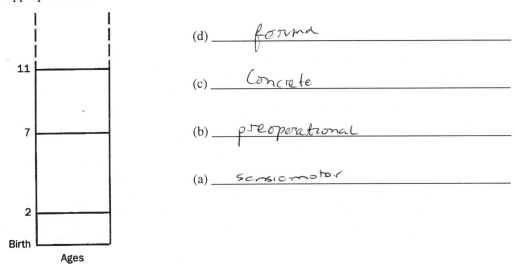

(d) _formal_

(c) _Concrete_

(b) _preoperational_

(a) _sensiomotor_

9-2. Following is a list of characteristics of children's thinking during various stages. Identify the stage by placing the correct letter (from the diagram above) in the blanks.

_c_ At the end of this stage the child is beginning to develop the capacity for symbolic thought (to think terms of mental images).

_a_ At the beginning of this stage the child's behavior is dominated by reflexes and the ability to coordinate sensory input and movement.

_c_ The child understands conservation and can handle hierarchical classification but tends not to use abstractions.

_d_ The child's thought processes are abstract and systematic.

_a_ Object permanence occurs toward the end of this stage.

_a_ During the first part of this stage, "out of sight, out of mind" might describe the child's reaction to hidden objects.

_b_ When water is poured from a wide beaker into a taller beaker, children say there is now more water in the taller beaker.

_b_ The child demonstrates a lack of understanding of conservation.

_b_ The child shows the shortcomings of centration, irreversibility, egocentrism, and animism.

_c_ For the first time the child in this stage is mentally able to undo an action and also is able focus on more than one feature of a problem at the same time.

9-3. When my (R. S.) daughter Vanessa was about 5, I placed two rows of stones on the grass, as illustrated below. Each row contained the same number of stones.

Row A: • • • • • • • •

Row B: • • • • • • • •

I then spread out one row so that it took up more space:

Row A: • • • • • • • •

Row B: • • • • • • • •

(a) I then asked Vanessa to point to the row that now had more stones. If Vanessa behaved like other preoperational children, which row would she point to? _____A_____

(b) The preoperational child has not yet mastered the principle that physical quantities remain constant in spite of changes in their shape or, in this case, arrangement. What is the name of this principle? _____Centration_____

9-4. Some research has demonstrated that certain aspects of Piaget's theory may be incorrect in detail. For example, there is some evidence that object permanence and some aspects of conservation may develop (earlier/~~later~~) than Piaget had thought.

9-5. Piaget also had little to say about individual _____ in development or about so-called _____ of stages in which elements of an earlier stage may appear in a later one.

9-6. Piaget thought that people of all cultures would pass through the stages at the same time; subsequent research has found that this (is/is not) the case. While the *sequence* of stages appears to be relatively invariant across cultures, the _____ that children follow in passing through these stages varies considerably across cultures. Nonetheless, Piaget's brilliance, the novelty of his approach, and the wealth of research that his theory inspired assure his place in history.

Answers: 9-1. (a) sensorimotor (b) preoperational (c) concrete operations (d) formal operations **9-2.** a, a, c, d, a, a, b, b, b, c **9-3.** (a) Row A (at which point Samantha, then 8 and in the stage of concrete operations, was astonished by her sister's choice and informed her that there were the same number in both!) (b) conservation **9-4.** earlier **9-5.** differences, mixing **9-6.** is not, timetable (age, time).

10. Summarize evidence which suggests that some cognitive abilities could be innate and describe how children's understanding of mental states progresses.

10-1. When infants look at a stimulus that is presented repeatedly, the strength of their responses gradually decreases. They spend less and less time looking at the stimulus, and their heart and respiration rates decrease. This reduction in response strength is known as _____. When a new stimulus is presented, response strength increases, a process known as _____.

10-2. By using the habituation-dishabituation technique, researchers can tell when a child is able to discriminate between different events. For example, at 3 to 4 months of age, infants understand that (write T or F for each of the following):

_____ Objects on slopes roll down rather than up.

_____ One solid object cannot pass through another.

_____ Objects move in continuous paths.

10-3. Similarly, 5-month-old infants exhibit surprise, indicated by the response of (habituation/dishabituation), when an object is added or removed from behind a screen and the expected number of objects is not there. This result suggests that infants (are/are not) able to add and subtract small numbers.

10-4. Because these cognitive abilities occur at such an early age, before infants would have much chance to learn them, some theorists have concluded that these capacities are (acquired/innate).

10-5. But why would we be pre-wired to understand addition and subtraction? The (nativists/evolutionary theorists) assume that basic addition and subtraction abilities had survival value for our ancestors.

10-6. Further, evolutionary theorists assert that the mind is _____, that it has compartments designed by natural selection to solve specific problems. For example, the domain-specific ability to understand that objects may be added to (and subtracted from) would have clear _____ value in a hunting, foraging, and social bargaining society.

10-7. Another current line of research examines children's understanding of mental states. Consider this example. An experimenter shows a child a candy box and asked what it contains. The child responds, "Candy." In fact, when the box is opened, he sees that it contains crayons. The child is then asked what he would expect another child to say when the other child is shown the closed box.

(a) Suppose the first child is five years old. What does he say that the second child will say when shown the closed box, "candy" or "crayons?" _____

(b) Suppose a three-year-old child is asked the same question. He says that candy is in the box, and when the box is opened he sees it is crayons. What does he say the second child will say is in the closed box? _____

(c) Once shown that the box contains crayons, the three-year-old is also asked what he originally said. What does he say he said, candy or crayons? _____

10-8. Why does the three-year-old child respond this way? Because most children under four years do not understand than there can be a difference between *beliefs* and *external reality*; they can not yet appreciate the possibility that people can hold _____ beliefs that do not accurately reflect reality.

10-9. After age 4, children's reasoning about mental states gradually improves. Several theories have been proposed to explain these developmental sequences. Some view children as similar to _____, constantly testing and revising theories to explain the world around them. Others propose an evolutionary interpretation, asserting that children's thinking about mind is yet another domain-specific _____ adapted by evolution to solve the problem of understanding other people.

Answers: 10-1. habituation, dishabituation 10-2. T, T, T 10-3. dishabituation, are 10-4. innate 10-5. evolutionary theorists 10-6. modularized, survival (adaptive) 10-7. (a) candy (b) crayons (c) crayons 10-8. false 10-9. scientists, module.

11. Describe children's progress in attention and memory.

11-1. Information-processing theories compare the mind to a _____. This approach has been especially useful in accounting for aspects of _____ developmental involving attention and memory.

11-2. While children's attention span increases during the preschool years, most four-year-olds still can't attend to a task for very long. Attention span continues to increase during the school years, and children also gradually improve in their ability to filter out irrelevant input (like background noise) and focus their attention _____.

11-3. With regard to memory, infants do remember things for days or perhaps months, but for some reason childhood memories are not very enduring. Most adults cannot remember experiences that occur before age 3 or 4, a condition referred to as _____.

11-4. After children acquire language their memory ability gradually improves throughout the remainder of their childhood. They adopt *strategies* that enhance the storage and retrieval of information, as in the following examples. Label each strategy and indicate the age at which each tends to appear.

(a) I repeatedly misspelled friend on spelling tests in the third grade, and my teacher said to practice, practice, practice. She told me to repeat the spelling over and over in my mind, and I did. This technique is called _____, and most children start using it *routinely* at around age _____.

(b) Sue is trying to remember the names of various types of trees. She organizes them into three groups: those with leaves, those with needles, and those with flowers. She is using the technique of _____. Individuals start using this technique at around age _____.

(c) Suppose you want to commit to memory the names of Piaget's stages. You come up with this mnemonic: Some Psychologists Can't Forget (S, P, C, F). Even better, you think of the meaning of the stage names and create new examples that illustrate each one. You are using _____, which tends to occur only after age _____.

Answers: **11-1.** computer, cognitive **11-2.** selectively **11-3.** infantile amnesia **11-4.** (a) rehearsal, 8 (b) organization, 9 (c) elaboration, 11.

12. **Outline Kohlberg's stages of moral development and summarize the strengths and weaknesses of Kohlberg's theory.**

12-1. Kohlberg's theory includes three moral levels, each with two stages for a total of six stages. Indicate which of the three moral levels is described in each of the following statements.

(a) Acts are considered wrong because they are punished or right because they lead to positive consequences. _____

(b) Individuals at this level conform very strictly to society's rules, which they accept as absolute and inviolable. _____

(c) This level is characterized by situational or conditional morality, such that stealing might be considered wrong in one circumstance but permissible in another. _____

12-2. The central ideas of Kohlberg's theory have received a fair amount of support. Research has found that children (do/do not) tend to progress through Kohlberg's stages in the order that he indicated. As children get older, stages 1 and 2 reasoning tend to decrease while stages 3 and 4 reasoning tend to _____.

12-3. There have also been several criticisms of Kohlberg's theory. First, individuals may show characteristics of several different stages at the same time. In other words, as was true of other stage theories, there tends to be a "_____" of stages.

12-4. Second, researchers have focused too heavily on (Kohlberg's/newly created) dilemmas, which tends to narrow the scope of research on moral reasoning.

12-5. It may also be the case that Kohlberg's theory is much more (value-free/culture-specific) than he had supposed. For example, subjects from small, technologically unsophisticated village societies (usually/rarely) show reasoning beyond stage 3.

Answers: **12-1.** (a) preconventional (b) conventional (c) postconventional **12-2.** do, increase **12-3.** mixing **12-4.** Kohlberg's **12-5.** culture-specific, rarely.

13. **Describe the major events of puberty and the Featured Study on the timing of sexual maturation.**

    13-1. Read over the section on <u>Puberty and the Growth Spurt</u> in your text. Then fill in the blanks below with the appropriate terms.

        (a) _____ The approximately two-year span preceding puberty that is marked by rapid growth in height and weight.

        (b) _____ The period of time during which secondary sex characteristics appear.

        (c) _____ Physical features that distinguish one sex from another but that are not essential for reproduction (e.g., facial hair in males, breasts in females).

        (d) _____ The stage during which sexual functions essential for reproduction reach maturity.

        (e) _____ The stage that includes menarche in females and the production of sperm in males.

        (f) _____ The first occurrence of menstruation.

        (g) _____ The transitional period between childhood and adulthood that includes early physical changes (puberty) and later cognitive and social changes.

        (h) _____ In our society this stage begins at around age 13 and ends at about age 22.

    13-2. The featured study refers to Belsky's analysis of attachment in terms of _____ theory, discussed earlier. Belsky proposed that the harshness of the current environment affects parent-child attachment style, which affects the later reproductive strategy of the offspring. Thus, stress in early family relations might cause (<u>earlier/later</u>) sexual maturation.

    13-3. Participants in the featured study were more than 200 mothers and daughters. The daughters were _____ years old when the study began and 12-13 when it terminated.

    13-4. At the beginning of the study the mothers were interviewed about the quality of their family relationships (discipline, conflict, parental support, etc.) After eight years the daughters were interviewed. Results showed (<u>strong/modest</u>) correlations between family stress and earlier sexual maturation. Lower scores on parental supportiveness and parental affection, for example, tended to be associated with (<u>earlier/later</u>) sexual maturation.

Answers: 13-1. (a) pubescence (b) pubescence (c) secondary sex characteristics (d) puberty (e) puberty (f) menarche (g) adolescence (h) adolescence **13-2.** evolutionary, earlier **13-3.** 3-4 **13-4.** modest, earlier.

14. Evaluate the assertion that adolescence is a time of turmoil.

14-1. How tumultuous is adolescence? With regard to suicide and other indicants of stress, current data indicate that: (Mark T or F for each of the following statements.)

_____ Suicide among adolescents is higher than for any other age group.

_____ The ratio of attempted to completed suicides is higher for adolescents than for any other age group.

_____ Adolescence does bring an increase in conflicts between parents and their children.

_____ In general, adolescents encounter more storm and stress than do people in other periods of life.

Answers: **14-1.** F, T, T, T.

15. Discuss some common patterns of identity formation in adolescence.

15-1. Adolescence is a period of change, so it is readily understandable that adolescents tend to focus on the struggle for _____, the question of "Who am I?"

15-2. Recall that Erik Erikson described four crises that mark childhood. What is the crisis that marks adolescence, according to Erikson? _____ vs. _____

15-3. Marcia (1966, 1980) has described four orientations that people may adopt in attempting to resolve the identity crisis. These are not stages that people pass through in an orderly manner but statuses that they may adopt on either a relatively permanent or temporary basis. One possible status is simply to take on the values and roles prescribed by one's parents; this is termed _____. While this may temporarily resolve the crisis, in the long run the individual may not be comfortable with the adopted identity. A second orientation involves a period of experimentation with various ideologies and careers and a delay in commitment to any one; this is termed _____. If the experimentation and lack of commitment become permanent, the individual is said to be in a status of _____ _____. On the other hand, if the consideration of alternatives leads to conviction about a sense of self, one takes on the status referred to as _____ _____.

Answers: **15-1.** identity **15-2.** identity, confusion **15-3.** foreclosure, moratorium, identity diffusion, identity achievement.

THE EXPANSE OF ADULTHOOD

16. Summarize evidence on the stability of personality and the prevalence of the midlife crisis.

16-1. Do people change throughout their lifetimes, or does personality tend to remain the same? Research evidence supports the conclusion that:

a. personality is stable across one's lifetime

b. personality changes across one's lifetime

c. both of the above

d. neither of the above

16-2. Explain how it is possible that personality appears both to stay the same and to change dramatically over time.

16-3. Two influential studies conducted in the 1970s asserted that people experience a period of emotional turmoil some time between ages 35 and 45, a transitional phase known as the _____ _____.

16-4. The mid-life crisis, described as a period of reappraisal and assessment of time left, was thought by Gould and Levinson to be a transitional phase that affected (<u>a minority/most</u>) adults. More recently, a large number of other investigators, using more objective methods, have found that (<u>very few/most</u>) people go through a midlife crisis.

Answers: 16-1. c **16-2.** Some personality traits (e.g., extroversion-introversion) appear to be quite stable; others (e.g., masculinity-femininity) tend to change as people grow older. **16-3.** midlife crisis **16-4.** most, very few.

17. Outline Erikson's stages of development in adulthood.

17-1. In the spaces below write the names of the crises that mark Erikson's three stages of adulthood. In the parentheses indicate the approximate period of adulthood during which the crises are supposed to occur.

(a)_____ vs. _____   (   )

(b)_____ vs. _____   (   )

(c)_____ vs. _____   (   )

17-2. Following are descriptions of the crises occurring in each of the above stages. Indicate the stages by placing the appropriate letters (a, b, or c from the previous question) in the blanks.

_____ Concern for helping future generations versus a self-indulgent concern for meeting one's own desires.

_____ Concern to find meaning in the remainder of one's life versus a preoccupation with earlier failures and eventual death.

_____ Concern for developing a capacity for intimacy with others versus a strategy in which others are manipulated as a means to an end.

Answers: 17-1. (a) intimacy vs. isolation (early adulthood) (b) generativity vs. self-absorption (middle adulthood) (c) integrity vs. despair (aging years) **17-2.** b, c, a.

18. Describe typical transitions in family relations during the adult years.

18-1. In contemporary American society there are many living arrangements other than the traditional family consisting of never-divorced parents, a breadwinner father and homemaker mother, and two or more kids. In fact, only _____ percent of American families fits this image.

18-2. In part as a result of economic factors and in part due to an increased emphasis on personal autonomy, remaining single or postponing marriage is a much more acceptable option today than it was a few decades ago. Nonetheless, people emerge from families and most ultimately form new families. Over _____ % of adults eventually marry.

18-3. While the first few years of married life tend to be quite happy, the current era of changing gender roles is likely to cause tension for the newly married. According to a recent survey, men and women have different views about the meaning of the term *equality*. What do *men* mean by equality in marriage? How do *women* define this concept? What is the evidence about task sharing?

18-4. What event in the family cycle tends to cause the first drop in marital satisfaction? When does marital satisfaction tend to start climbing back?

Answers: 18-1. 7 **18-2.** 90 **18-3.** In one recent survey, half the men were unable to define equality in marriage at all; the other half defined it in psychological terms. Women defined it more concretely—in terms of sharing tasks and responsibilities. The evidence indicates that women are still doing the bulk of the housework in America even when employed outside the home. **18-4.** Although most couples rate parenthood as a very positive experience, marital satisfaction tends to drop at the birth of the first child. Marital satisfaction tends to increase when children leave home. The "empty nest" seems to have little lasting negative impact.

19. Discuss patterns of career development in both men and women.

19-1. Donald Super breaks career development into five major stages. List these stages in the spaces below next to the approximate ages at which they occur. (See Table 11.2.)

_____ (birth to adolescence)

_____ (adolescence to mid 20s)

_____ (mid 20s to mid 40s)

_____ (mid 40s to mid 60s)

_____ (mid 60s on)

19-2. Following are descriptions of events that may occur during the five stages. Place the names of the stages described in the appropriate blanks. (Refer to your text and Table 11.2.)

_____ This stage ranges from no thought about vocation to thought based on fantasy, then likes and dislikes, then ability.

_____ The individual finishes school, may try out various work experiences, shifts jobs if the first are not gratifying.

_____ The person is likely to receive support and guidance from a mentor.

_____ Future job moves almost always take place within the same occupational area.

_____ The concern is with retaining achieved status rather than improving it.

_____ Energy may shift from work to the family or leisure activities.

_____ Involves preparation to leave the work place.

19-3. Most of the research findings on career development summarized above are based on (men/women). Although it was originally believed that these findings would apply equally well to women, evidence has indicated that this (is/is not) the case. The pattern for men frequently reveals a clear, consistent path toward vocational success; the pattern for women is much less predictable and may be characterized as nearly _____.

19-4. Which of the following are factors that contribute to the less direct career paths of women? Place a T next to statements that are likely factors, an F next to those that are not.

_____ Women are more likely than men to interrupt their careers for child rearing or other family reasons.

_____ Women place as much priority on their own career goals as those of their husbands.

_____ Women are less likely than men to enjoy the benefits of mentoring (e.g., "old boy" network).

_____ Women face discrimination, especially at upper management levels (the "glass ceiling").

Answers: 19-1. growth, exploration, establishment, maintenance, decline **19-2.** growth, exploration, establishment, establishment, maintenance, maintenance, decline **19-3.** men, is not, random **19-4.** T, F, T, T.

20. **Describe the physical changes associated with aging.**

20-1. As we age, our physical and cognitive characteristics change. Indicate which of the following physical traits increase and which decrease by placing checkmarks in the appropriate blanks.

	INCREASES	DECREASES
Physical changes		
Proportion of body fat:	_____	_____
Overall weight:	_____	_____
Number of neurons in the brain :	_____	_____
Visual acuity:	_____	_____
Ability to see close:	_____	_____
Hearing:	_____	_____

20-2. An abnormal condition marked my loss of memory and several other cognitive abilities is termed a _____. Dementia occurs in approximately _____ % of individuals over age 65.

20-3. Women's reaction to menopause varies a great deal, but the evidence in general is that menopause is accompanied by (intense/little) emotional distress.

Answers: 20-1. Body fat and overall weight increase (except that overall weight may decrease somewhat after the mid-50s); the rest decrease. **20-2.** dementia, 15 **20-3.** little.

21. Describe the cognitive changes associated with aging.

21-1. With regard to changes in cognitive ability that may accompany aging, which of the following is/are true? (Mark T or F.)

_____ Average test scores in cognitive ability show some decline after age 60.

_____ For the majority of people the decline in general intelligence that occurs in later years is relatively slight.

_____ Crystallized intelligence is more likely to decline with aging than fluid intelligence.

_____ The memory loss that accompanies aging is relatively severe for the majority of people.

_____ The type of general cognitive loss that occurs with aging is thought to involve processing speed.

_____ Problem solving ability generally remains unimpaired as people age if older people are given additional time to compensate for reduced speed.

Answers: 21-1. T, T, F, F, T, T.

PUTTING IT IN PERSPECTIVE

22. Explain how this chapter highlighted the interaction of heredity and environment.

22-1. The behavior of a child is the result of the child's genetic inheritance and its environment, which includes the behavior of the child's parents. In turn, the behavior of the parents toward the child is affected both by their inherited characteristics and by the behavior of the child. Thus, behavior is the result not of heredity or environment operating separately but of an _____ between the two factors.

22-2. To understand the concept of *interaction* consider this problem: There is a form of mental retardation that results from phenylketonuria, an inherited inability to metabolize a common amino acid in milk. When fed milk, children born with phenylketonuria become mentally retarded. Is this type of retardation an inherited disorder?

a. Yes, it's genetic.

b. No, it's caused by the environment.

c. A certain proportion of the causal factors are hereditary and the remainder are due to the environment.

d. The disorder results from heredity and environment operating jointly.

22-3. This chapter has been concerned with changes in human behavior across the life span. The theme being stressed here is that these changes result from an *interaction* of heredity and environment. In your own words, explain how the interaction operates.

Answers: 22-1. interaction **22-2.** d. (This disorder might at first seem to be inherited, since there is a genetic trait involved. But the retardation does not occur if the infant is not fed milk products, which involves the environment. The point is that this disorder, like behavior in general, cannot be attributed solely to nature or to nurture or even to relative weights of each; it is a function of an *interaction* between the two. **22-3.** The interaction of heredity and environment refers to the fact that we are a product of both factors. It means more than that, however. Heredity and environment don't operate separately. Interaction means that the genetic factors affect the operation of the environment and that environmental factors affect genetic predispositions. The influence of one factor *depends on* the effects of the other.

APPLICATION: UNDERSTANDING GENDER DIFFERENCES

23. Summarize evidence on gender differences in behavior and discuss the significance of these differences.

23-1. Which gender tends to show more of (or score higher on tests of) the following abilities or traits? Circle the correct answer at the right.

Cognitive

verbal skills	MALES	FEMALES	NEITHER
mathematical skills	MALES	FEMALES	NEITHER
visual-spatial skills	MALES	FEMALES	NEITHER

Social

aggression	MALES	FEMALES	NEITHER
sensitivity to nonverbal cues	MALES	FEMALES	NEITHER
risk-taking	MALES	FEMALES	NEITHER
sexually permissive attitudes	MALES	FEMALES	NEITHER
assertiveness	MALES	FEMALES	NEITHER
anxiety	MALES	FEMALES	NEITHER
nurturance	MALES	FEMALES	NEITHER

23-2. There is an enormous overlap between the genders with regard to these traits. There are, of course, many females who are more aggressive than the average male and many males who are more sensitive to nonverbal cues than the average female. Thus, it is important to note that the differences referred to in this section are differences between group _____ and that the size of the differences is relatively _____.

24. Explain how biological factors are thought to contribute to gender differences.

24-1. For evolutionary theorists, the relative invariance of gender differences found across cultures reflects natural selection. From this perspective males are more sexually active and permissive than females because reproductive success for males is maximized by seeking (few/many) sexual partners. Greater aggressiveness has survival value for males because it enhances their ability to acquire material _____ sought by females selecting a mate.

24-2. Evolutionary theorists also assert that ability differences between the genders reflect the division of labor in our ancestral past. Males were primarily the hunters and females the gatherers, and the adaptive demands of hunting may have produced males' superiority at most _____ tasks.

24-3. The evolutionary view of gender is certainly an interesting and plausible explanation of the remarkable similarity in gender differences across cultures. The viewpoint has its critics, however. For one thing, there are reasonable _____ theories of gender differences; for another, the evolutionary explanation is relatively (easy/difficult) to test empirically.

24-4. Concerning other biological factors, several studies indicate that hormones are a major factor in shaping gender differences. For example, females exposed prenatally to high levels of an _____-like drug given their mothers during pregnancy tend to show more male-typical behavior than do other females.

24-5. Recent studies have also found that normal aging men given testosterone to enhance their sexual function tend to show increases in _____ perception. While these correlational studies involving hormones support the role of biology in gender development, it is important to note that they are based on (small/large) samples of people who have (normal/abnormal) conditions.

24-6. Other biological evidence suggests that males depend more heavily on the left hemisphere for verbal processing and the right for spatial processing than is the case with females. In other words, males may tend to exhibit more cerebral _____ than females. Results on this topic have been mixed, however. In addition, it would be difficult to see how gender differences in *specialization* could account for gender differences in *ability*, that is, the superiority of males on spatial tasks and the superiority of females on _____ tasks.

25. Explain how environmental factors are thought to contribute to gender differences.

25-1. Many researchers remain convinced that gender differences are largely shaped by the environment. One of the ways that children learn gender roles is from the consequences for their behavior, the rewards and punishments that they receive in the process known as _____ conditioning.

25-2. Children also acquire information by seeing what others do, the process of _____ learning. While children imitate both males and females, they are more likely to imitate the behavior of (<u>same-sex/opposite-sex</u>) models.

25-3. In addition to operant conditioning and observational learning, children are active participants in their own gender-role socialization, the process referred to as _____-socialization. First, once they discover (at age 5 or 6) that being a boy or girl is a permanent condition, they will then _____ themselves as boys or girls. Second, following classification in terms of gender children will _____ characteristics and behaviors associated with their gender. Third, they will bring their _____ in line with their values by engaging in "sex-appropriate" behaviors.

25-4. Whether through operant conditioning, observational learning, or self-socialization, the major forces for gender-role socialization occur in three main areas of the child's environment: in their _____, in _____, and in the _____.

Answers: **25-1.** operant **25-2.** observational (modeling), same-sex **25-3.** self, classify (categorize), value, behavior **25-4.** families, schools, media.

CRITICAL THINKING APPLICATION

26. Explain the argument that fathers are essential for healthy development and some criticism of this line of reasoning.

26-1. Over the past several decades the percentage of children brought up without fathers in the home has steadily increased, from about 17% in 1960 to more than 35% today. During the same period there has also been a dramatic (<u>decrease/increase</u>) in teen pregnancy, juvenile delinquency, violent crime, drug abuse, eating disorders, and family dysfunction in general.

26-2. Further, fatherless children are _____ times more likely than fathered children to do one or more of the following: drop out of high school, become a teenage parent, become a juvenile delinquent. In other words, father absence (<u>appears to cause/is correlated with</u>) a host of unfortunate cultural trends.

26-3. The writers referred to in your text assert that the presence of a father is essential for a child's well-being. As you are aware, however, one cannot infer causation on the basis of _____ data alone.

26-4. Among the reasonable alternative explanations for the correlational relationship found are the following. Father absence frequently occurs when the parents _____, so it is possible that this factor, rather than father absence, may cause the negative effects referred to. In addition, father absence is much more frequent in (<u>low-income/high-income</u>) families, so it is possible that poverty, rather than father absence, may cause some (or all) of the negative effects.

26-5. In your continued critical thinking about the assertions discussed, recall also the fallacies in reasoning introduced in Chapter 10: irrelevant reasons, circular reasoning, slippery slope, weak analogies, and false dichotomy. Which of these apply to the following assertions? Use the abbreviations IR, CR, SS, WA, or FD.

(a) ____ "To tolerate the trend of fatherlessness is to accept the inevitability of continued societal recession."

(b) _____ "If present trends continue, our society could be on the verge of social suicide."

Answers: 26-1. increase **26-2.** 2 to 3, is correlated with **26-3.** correlational **26-4.** divorce, low-income **26-5.** (a) FD. The quote may have elements of more than one fallacy, but the author really is posing a dichotomy: Either we reduce father absence, or else we will face social decline. Of course, we could do both (reduce father absence and face social decline) or neither. (b) SS. The argument is that if we allow one event to happen, then other events will inevitably follow on this slippery slope that will lead to disaster.

REVIEW OF KEY TERMS

Age of viability	Fetal stage	Object permanence
Animism	Gender	Placenta
Attachment	Gender differences	Prenatal period
Centration	Gender roles	Primary sex characteristics
Cephalocaudal trend	Gender stereotypes	Proximodistal trend
Cognitive development	Germinal stage	Puberty
Conservation	Habituation	Pubescence
Cross-sectional design	Infantile amnesia	Secondary sex characteristics
Dementia	Irreversibility	Separation anxiety
Development	Longitudinal design	Sex
Developmental norms	Maturation	Social clock
Dishabituation	Menarche	Socialization
Egocentrism	Mentor	Stage
Embryonic stage	Meta-analysis	Temperament
Family life cycle	Mid-life crisis	Zygote
Fetal alcohol syndrome	Motor development	

Development _____

1. The sequence of age-related changes that occurs as a person progresses from conception to death.

_____ 2. The period of pregnancy, extending from conception to birth.

_____ 3. The first two weeks after conception.

_____ 4. The structure that connects the circulation of the fetus and the mother but that blocks passage of blood cells.

_____ 5. The second stage of prenatal development, lasting from two weeks after conception until the end of the second month.

_____ 6. The third stage of prenatal development, lasting from two months after conception through birth.

_____ 7. The age at which the baby can first survive in the event of a premature birth.

_____ 8. A collection of congenital problems associated with a mother's excessive use of alcohol during pregnancy.

_____ 9. Adults' inability to remember events from early childhood.

_____ 10. Developmental changes in muscular coordination required for physical movement.

_____ 11. The head-to-foot direction of motor development.

_____ 12. The center-outward direction of motor development.

_____ 13. The average ages at which people display certain behaviors and abilities.

_____ 14. Characteristic mood, energy level, and reactivity.

_____ 15. One group of subjects is observed over a long period of time.

_____ 16. Investigators compare groups of subjects of differing ages at a single point in time.

_____ 17. A difficult, turbulent period of doubt and reappraisal of one's life that may occur at midlife.

_____ 18. Emotional distress displayed by an infant when separated from a person with whom it has formed an attachment.

_____ 19. Culturally constructed distinctions between femininity and masculinity.

_____ 20. Widely held beliefs about females' and males' abilities, personality traits, and social behavior.

_____ 21. Development of thinking, reasoning, remembering, and problem solving.

_____ 22. The gradual reduction in response strength that occurs when people are repeatedly exposed to some event.

_____ 23. The increase in response strength that occurs when people are exposed to a new stimulus event.

_____ 24. A mental capacity that involves recognizing that objects continue to exist even when they are no longer visible.

_____ 25. Piaget's term for the awareness that physical quantities remain constant in spite of changes in their shape or appearance.

_____ 26. The Piagetian term for the tendency to focus on just one feature of a problem and neglect other important features.

_____ 27. The inability to cognitively visualize reversing an action.

_____ 28. Thinking characterized by a limited ability to share another person's viewpoint.

_____ 29. A sequence of stages that families tend to progress through.

_____ 30. Someone with a senior position in an organization who serves as a role model, tutor, and advisor to a younger worker.

_____ 31. The attribution of lifelike qualities to inanimate objects.

_____ 32. A developmental period during which certain behaviors and capacities occur.

_____ 33. The biologically based categories of male and female.

_____ 34. A close, emotional bond of affection between an infant and its caregiver.

_____ 35. Physical features associated with gender that are not directly needed for reproduction.

_____ 36. The physical structures necessary for reproduction.

_____ 37. The two-year span preceding puberty marked by the appearance of secondary sex characteristics and by rapid growth.

_____ 38. The first occurrence of menstruation.

_____ 39. The stage during which reproductive functions reach maturity.

_____ 40. A person's notion of a developmental schedule that specifies what he or she should have accomplished by certain points in life.

_____ 41. Developmental changes that reflect one's genetic blueprint rather than environment.

_____ 42. A one-celled organism created by the process of fertilization, the union of sperm and egg.

_____ 43. Behavioral differences between females and males.

_____ 44. A statistical procedure for combining data from different studies to estimate the size of a particular variable's effects.

_____ **45.** The acquisition of norms, roles, and behaviors expected of people in a particular group.

_____ **46.** Expectations concerning what is the appropriate behavior for each sex.

_____ **47.** An abnormal condition marked by multiple cognitive deficits; more prevalent in older adults but not a product of normal aging

Answers: 1. development **2.** prenatal period **3.** germinal stage **4.** placenta **5.** embryonic stage **6.** fetal stage **7.** age of viability **8.** fetal alcohol syndrome **9.** infantile amnesia **10.** motor development **11.** cephalocaudal trend **12.** proximodistal trend **13.** developmental norms **14.** temperament **15.** longitudinal design **16.** cross-sectional design **17.** mid-life crisis **18.** separation anxiety **19.** gender **20.** gender stereotypes **21.** cognitive development **22.** habituation **23.** dishabituation **24.** object permanence **25.** conservation **26.** centration **27** irreversibility **28.** egocentrism **29.** family life cycle **30.** mentor **31.** animism **32.** stage **33.** sex **34.** attachment **35.** secondary sex characteristics **36.** primary sex characteristics **37.** pubescence **38.** menarche **39.** puberty **40.** social clock **41.** maturation **42.** zygote **43.** gender differences **44.** meta-analysis **45.** socialization **46.** gender roles **47.** dementia.

REVIEW OF KEY PEOPLE

Mary Ainsworth   Erik Erikson   Lawrence Kohlberg
Jay Belsky   Jean Piaget   Alexander Thomas & Stella Chess
John Bowlby

_____ **1.** Conducted a major longitudinal study in which they identified three basic styles of children's temperament.

_____ **2.** Research on daycare; also, proposed the evolutionary view that early attachment is a determinant of later reproductive strategy.

_____ **3.** Theorized that there are critical periods in human infants' lives during which attachments must occur for normal development to take place.

_____ **4.** Partitioned the life span into eight stages, each accompanied by a psychosocial crisis.

_____ **5.** Pioneered the study of children's cognitive development.

_____ **6.** Developed a stage theory of moral development.

_____ **7.** Described three categories of infant-mother attachment.

Answers: 1. Thomas & Chess **2.** Belsky **3.** Bowlby **4.** Erikson **5.** Piaget **6.** Kohlberg **7.** Ainsworth.

SELF-QUIZ

1. Which prenatal period begins at the second week and ends at the second month of pregnancy?
a. germinal stage
b. embryonic stage
c. fetal stage
d. seminal stage

2. In which prenatal stage do most major birth defects probably have their origins?
a. germinal stage
b. embryonic stage
c. fetal stage
d. seminal stage

3. A child is shown a candy box. When asked what he thinks is in it, he says, "Candy." He is then shown that the candy box actually contains crayons. He is then asked what he thinks another child will say when shown the same closed box. He says that he thinks the next child will say, "Crayons." What would be the best guess about the age of the child?
   a. 3 years
   b. 5 years
   c. 6 years
   d. 7 years

4. According to Belsky's evolutionary viewpoint, the current harshness of an environment affects parent-child attachment, which in turn affects the offspring's later:
   a. accommodation and assimilation
   b. adaptation to traumatic events
   c. reproductive strategy
   d. decision to give birth

5. What is the major conclusion from Thomas and Chess's longitudinal study of temperament?
   a. Children's temperaments tend to go through predictable stages.
   b. The temperament of the child is not a good predictor of the temperament of the adult.
   c. Opposites attract.
   d. Children's temperaments tend to be consistent over the years.

6. The crisis occurring in the first year, according to Erikson, is one involving:
   a. trust versus mistrust
   b. initiative versus guilt
   c. industry versus inferiority
   d. identity versus conformity

7. During which stage in Piaget's system is the child first able to handle conservation problems and hierarchical classification problems?
   a. sensorimotor
   b. preoperational
   c. concrete operations
   d. formal operations

8. A child in the early sensorimotor period is shown a ball, which she watches intensely. The ball is then hidden under a pillow. What will the child do?
   a. ask, "Where is the pillow?"
   b. stare at the pillow but not pick it up
   c. move the pillow and pick up the ball
   d. ignore the pillow, as if the ball didn't exist

9. Who developed a stage theory of moral development?
   a. Piaget
   b. Kohlberg
   c. Gould
   d. Bowlby

10. Which of the following cognitive capacities is most likely to decline as a function of aging?
    a. speed of processing
    b. crystallized intelligence
    c. problem-solving ability
    d. specialized intelligence

11. Some research have found that very young children (e.g., 5 months old) appear to be aware of the addition or subtraction of objects from behind a screen. The technique used in these studies was:
    a. sensory preconditioning
    b. self-socialization
    c. classical conditioning
    d. habituation-dishabituation

12. Which of the following factors tends to be accompanied by a drop in ratings of marital satisfaction?
    a. childlessness during early married life
    b. the birth of the first child
    c. the first child's departure for college
    d. when the last child leaves home

13. Females tend to score slightly higher than males on tests of:
    a. verbal ability
    b. mathematical ability
    c. visual-spatial ability
    d. cerebral specialization

14. Females exposed to high levels of androgen during prenatal development tend to show:
    a. more male-typical behavior than other females
    b. more stereotypic female behavior than other females
    c. less cerebral specialization than other females
    d. a larger corpus collosum than other females

15. Once children discover that their gender is permanent, they are likely to want to engage in behavior that is "sex appropriate" as defined by their culture. This process is referred to as:
    a. operant conditioning
    b. observational learning
    c. self-socialization
    d. classical conditioning

Answers: 1. b **2.** b **3.** a **4.** c **5.** d **6.** a **7.** c **8.** d **9.** b **10.** a **11.** d **12.** b **13.** a **14.** a **15.** c.

Chapter Twelve

Personality: Theory, Research, and Assessment

REVIEW OF KEY IDEAS

THE NATURE OF PERSONALITY

1. **Define the construct of personality in terms of consistency and distinctiveness.**

   1-1. I can always tell when my colleague across the hall has finished for the day because I hear squeaking as he carefully moves his computer table under his bookcase. And I know what follows: He closes and reshelves his books, sorts the papers on his desk into two piles, and slides the pens and pencils into his desk drawer bin. The fact that my colleague engages in the *same behaviors* almost every day illustrates the feature of personality termed _____.

   1-2. When I'm done, on the other hand, I usually just stand up and walk out, leaving my generally messy desk behind. The fact that my colleague and I *differ* with respect to office neatness illustrates the feature of personality termed _____.

   Answers: 1-1. consistency (stability) **1-2.** distinctiveness (behavioral differences).

2. **Explain what is meant by a personality trait and describe the five factor model.**

   2-1. A consistent or durable disposition to behave in a particular way is referred to as a personality _____. Personality trait descriptions frequently consist of a series of _____, such as anxious, excitable, shy, aggressive, and so on.

   2-2. There are an enormous number of trait words that could be used to describe people. Gordon Allport, for example, listed several thousand. Raymond Cattell reduced Allport's list to just _____ traits, and more recently McCrae and Costa have described yet a simpler model involving only _____ traits.

   2-3. Some researchers maintain that more than five factors are needed to describe personality. Others contend that fewer than five factors are needed. Of the various models, however, the dominant conception of personality structure is currently the _____-factor model.

2-4. Below are listed some of the adjectives that describe each of the five factors. List the name of each of the factors next to the appropriate adjectives. (The five factors are relatively easy to remember if one thinks of NEO, which may mean "new," and adds AC: NEOAC.)

_____: outgoing, sociable

_____: imaginative, nonconforming

_____: anxious, insecure

_____: dependable, disciplined

_____: sympathetic, trusting

Answers: 2-1. trait, adjectives **2-2.** 16, five **2-3.** five **2-4.** extraversion, openness to experience, neuroticism, conscientiousness, agreeableness.

PSYCHODYNAMIC PERSPECTIVES

3. List and describe the three components into which Freud divided the personality and indicate how these are distributed across three levels of awareness.

3-1. Below is a schematic illustration of the three Freudian structures of personality. Label each.

(b) _____   (c) _____

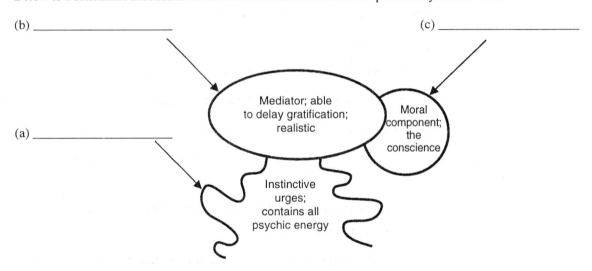

(a) _____

3-2. Freud superimposed levels of consciousness on the psychic structures. The following illustration makes clear that two of the structures exist at all three levels while one is entirely unconscious. Label the levels.

(a) _____

(b) _____

(c) _____

4. Explain the preeminence of sexual and aggressive conflicts in Freud's theory and describe the operation of defense mechanisms.

4-1. Freud believed that most of our conflicts arise from _____ and _____ urges. Conflicts relating to these areas were preeminent in his mind because (1) they are subject to subtle social _____ and, for that reason, are a source of confusion; and (2) they are less likely to be immediately gratified and more apt to be _____ than other urges.

4-2. Following is a list of the defense mechanisms. Match each with the correct description by placing the appropriate letters in the blanks.

A. rationalization   D. displacement   F. regression

B. repression   E. reaction formation   G. identification

C. projection

_____ A return to an earlier, less mature stage of development.

_____ Forming an imaginary or real alliance with a person or group; becoming like them.

_____ Creating false but reasonable-sounding excuses.

_____ Pushing distressing thoughts into the unconscious.

_____ Attributing ones own thoughts, feelings, or conflicts to another.

_____ Expressing an emotion that is the exact opposite of the way one really, but unconsciously, feels.

_____ Diverting emotional feelings from their original source to a substitute target.

4-3. Using the letters from the previous question, match the defense mechanisms with the following examples.

_____ After John and Marsha break up, John says he hates Marsha; this statement helps him defend against his real feelings of affection.

_____ "Society is filled with perverts," says the preacher; but later evidence suggests that he is the one with the sexual conflicts.

_____ In reaction to the stress of entering college, Alice starts acting like a grade-school kid.

_____ Bruce acts like John Wayne, and he owns tapes of all the Duke's movies.

_____ Mary is angry at her mother, so she kicks her baby brother.

5. **Outline Freud's psychosexual stages of development and their theorized relations to adult personality.**

5-1. List Freud's stages of psychosexual development, in the order in which they are supposed to occur, in the blanks below. Place the ages in the parentheses.

(a) _____ ( )

(b) _____ ( )

(c) _____ ( )

(d) _____ ( )

(e) _____ ( )

5-2. The following behaviors or personality characteristics are supposed to result from fixation at a particular psychosexual stage. Place the names of the correct stages in the blanks.

(a) She has problems with anger control, is hostile toward people in authority, and defies any attempt at regulation of her behavior. _____

(b) He eats too much, drinks too much, and smokes. _____

(c) He has occasional outbursts of hostility toward his father that he can't understand. In family arguments he sides with his mother. _____

5-3. The Oedipus complex occurs during the _____ stage, between the ages of _____ and _____. This complex theoretically involves an erotically tinged attraction toward the (same-sex/opposite-sex) parent and a strong hostility toward the (same-sex/opposite-sex) parent. Resolution of the Oedipus complex involves (increasing/stopping) both the child's erotic attraction and the child's hostility.

Answers: 5-1. (a) oral (first year) (b) anal (second year) (c) phallic (ages 3 through 5) (d) latency (age 5 to puberty) (e) genital (puberty on) **5-2.** (a) anal (b) oral (c) phallic **5-3.** phallic, 3, 5, opposite-sex, same-sex, stopping.

6. **Summarize the revisions of Freud's theory proposed by Jung and Adler.**

6-1. Freud devised the theory and method of treatment termed *psychoanalysis*. To differentiate his approach from Freud's, Jung called his theory _____ _____. Like Freud, Jung emphasized the unconscious determinants of personality. Unlike Freud, he proposed that the unconscious consists of two layers, a _____ unconscious and a _____ unconscious. The personal unconscious is similar to Freud's unconscious, but it has less emphasis on sexuality. The collective unconscious is a repository of inherited, ancestral memories that Jung termed

_____.

6-2. Jung's major contribution to psychology is considered by many to be his description of two major personality types: _____, reserved, contemplative people who tend to be concerned with their own internal world of thoughts; and _____, outgoing people who are more interested in the external world of others.

6-3. For Freud, the driving energy behind the human personality was sexuality; for Jung it may have been the collective unconscious. For Adler, it was striving for _____ and the attempt to overcome childhood feelings of inferiority. Efforts to overcome imagined or real inferiorities involve _____ through development of one's abilities. While Adler considered compensation to be a normal mechanism, he saw _____ as an abnormal attempt to conceal feelings of inferiority.

6-4. Adler is associated with the term _____ _____, an exaggerated feeling of inadequacy supposedly caused by parental pampering or neglect in early childhood. To a greater extent than either Freud or Jung, Adler emphasized the effects of the social context on personality development. For example, he thought that _____ _____ (that is, whether one is an only child, first-born, second-born, etc.) had a major effect on personality. Although the concept created considerable interest, birth order has turned out to be a (weaker/ stronger) and (more/less) consistent factor than he had supposed.

Answers: 6-1. analytical psychology, personal, collective, archetypes **6-2.** introverts, extraverts **6-3.** superiority, compensation, overcompensation **6-4.** inferiority complex, birth order, weaker, less.

7. Summarize the strengths and weaknesses of the psychodynamic approach to personality.

7-1. Psychoanalytic formulations have had a major impact on the field of psychology. List the three contributions discussed in your text.

7-2. Psychoanalytic formulations have also been extensively criticized. After each of the following statements list the particular criticism, from the discussion in your text, that the statement invites.

(a) Freud proposed that females develop weaker superegos and that they have a chronic sense of inferiority caused by penis envy. _____

(b) Although he discussed some characteristics associated with the psychosexual stages, Freud didn't really specify which events, occurring during which childhood stages, produce which sets of personality traits. _____

(c) Support for the theories has been provided solely by clinical case studies and by clinical intuition. _____

Answers: 7-1. the discovery that *unconscious forces* can influence behavior, that *internal conflict* may generate psychological distress, and that *early childhood experiences* influence the adult personality **7-2.** (a) sexism (b) vague (untestable ideas) (c) inadequate or weak evidence.

BEHAVIORAL PERSPECTIVES

8. **Discuss how Skinner's principles of operant conditioning can be applied to the structure and development of personality.**

   8-1. Which of the following processes plays an important part in Skinner's ideas about human behavior?

   a. mental conflict

   b. the mind

   c. free will

   d. none of the above

   8-2. According to Skinner, much of our behavior is affected by reinforcement, punishment, or extinction—in other words, by the environmental _____ that follow our behavior. For example, if some individuals behave in a consistently aggressive manner (i.e., have aggressive personality traits), they do so because they have been _____ for behaving aggressively in the past.

   8-3. Skinner recognized that there are differences between people and that people behave relatively consistently over time. Distinctiveness and consistency occur, however, not because of what's going on in an individual's *mind* but because of what has occurred previously in their _____.

   8-4. Thus, for Skinner, personality is not mental, but environmental. People's minds don't change, their environment changes. Skinner makes a strong case for the point of view that our behavior is caused or _____ rather than free, and that the determinants are largely _____ rather than genetic.

   Answers: **8-1.** d **8-2.** consequences (stimuli, events), reinforced **8-3.** environment **8-4.** determined, environmental.

9. **Describe Bandura's social learning theory and compare it to Skinner's viewpoint.**

   9-1. In what respect is Bandura's point of view similar to Skinner's?

   9-2. Three of the major differences between Bandura's and Skinner's viewpoints involve the concepts listed below. Carefully define and explain these concepts and indicate how they represent a difference from Skinner's position.

   (a) reciprocal determinism:

   (b) observational learning:

   (c) self-efficacy:

9-3. According to Bandura whom do we imitate, and in what circumstances?

Answers: 9-1. It is similar in that Bandura believes that personality is largely shaped through learning.
9-2. (a) *Reciprocal determinism* refers to the point of view that not only does environment determine behavior, as Skinner asserted, but that behavior determines environment, and, further, that behavior, environment, and mental processes all mutually affect one another. (b) *Observational learning* is the process through which we learn behaviors by observing the consequences of someone else's (i.e., a model's) behavior. For example, we learn not only by being reinforced, as Skinner proposed, but by observing someone else being reinforced. (c) *Self-efficacy* is a belief in our ability to perform certain behaviors. This belief affects whether we undertake those behaviors and how well we perform them. Skinner makes no allowance for mentalistic concepts such as self-efficacy. **9-3.** We tend to imitate models whom we like, consider attractive and powerful, view as similar to ourselves, and whom we observe being reinforced.

10. Identify Mischel's major contribution to personality theory and indicate why his ideas have generated so much controversy.

10-1. Mischel's major contribution to personality theory is his contention that human behavior is determined to a much greater extent by the _____ than by _____

10-2. Why is this such a controversial idea for personality theory?

Answers: 10-1. situation (situational factors), personality (personality traits) **10-2.** The notion is controversial because the very definition of personality involves the word *consistency*. Mischel's findings suggest that behavior is not as consistent as personality theorists may have thought, that it is strongly affected by an ever-changing situation.

11. Summarize the strengths and weaknesses of the behavioral approach to personality.

11-1. The major strengths of the behavioral approach have been its commitment to empirical _____. Empirical means observable, and for the behaviorists the subject matter of the science of human behavior must be, at some level, _____.

11-2. The major weaknesses of the behavioral approach, according to its critics, have been its overdependence on research involving _____ subjects, the _____ nature of its objection to the concepts of free will and cognition, and its _____ view of personality as nothing more than a series of stimulus-response associations.

Answers: 11-1. research, observable **11-2.** animal, dehumanizing, fragmented.

HUMANISTIC PERSPECTIVES

12. Explain how humanism was a reaction against both the behavioral and psychodynamic approaches and discuss the assumptions of the humanistic view.

12-1. The humanistic movement reacted against the behavioral approach because of its mechanistic view of personality and its emphasis on _____ research, and against the psychoanalytic approach because of its emphasis on _____ drives.

12-2. The humanistic viewpoint found fault with both movements because they stressed
_____, or absolute causation. The humanists also thought that the behaviorists and the
Freudians failed to recognize the (<u>unique/common</u>) qualities of human behavior.

12-3. Humanistic psychology emphasizes the (<u>similarities/differences</u>) between human beings and the other
animal species; believes we (<u>are controlled by/can rise above</u>) our biological heritage; asserts that we are
largely (<u>rational/irrational</u>) creatures; and maintains that a person's (<u>subjective/objective</u>) view of the
world is more important than _____ reality.

Answers: **12-1.** animal, primitive (animalistic) **12-2.** determinism, unique **12-3.** differences, can rise above, rational,
subjective, objective.

13. Identify the single structural construct in Rogers's person-centered theory and summarize his view of personality development.

13-1. Who are you? What are you like? What are your unique qualities? What is your typical behavior? Your
answers to these questions are likely to reflect what Rogers called the _____.

13-2. Although Ralph tends to be a submissive and somewhat lazy person (and that is the way his friends,
family, and co-workers describe him), he views himself as hard-working and dynamic, a leader both on
the job and at home.

(a) What is Ralph 's self-concept?

(b) Is his self-concept congruent or incongruent?

(c) According to Rogers, what parental behavior may have led to this incongruence?

(d) According to Rogers, what parental behavior would have resulted in Ralph's achieving congruence
rather than incongruence?

13-3. Define the following Rogerian concepts.

(a) conditional love:

(b) unconditional love:

13-4. What is defensiveness for Rogers?

Answers: 13-1. self or self-concept **13-2.** (a) that he is hard-working, dynamic, and a leader (b) incongruent (c) conditional love or acceptance (d) unconditional love or acceptance **13-3.** (a) affection given conditionally, the condition being that the child or adult must live up to another's expectations (b) affection given without conditions, full acceptance of the person not dependent on what he or she is or does. **13-4.** As with Freud, people defend against anxiety by distorting or denying reality. For Rogers, people's defensiveness arises when people defend their self-concepts against inconsistent experiences. Thus, defensiveness is related to incongruence.

14. Explain Maslow's hierarchy of needs and summarize his findings on the characteristics of self-actualizing people.

14-1. Maslow proposed that human needs are arranged in a hierarchy, usually depicted as a pyramid, with the most basic, physiological needs at the _____ and higher-level needs closer to the _____.

14-2. The lower level needs would include needs for food, water, and factors related to survival and security. Next in the hierarchy would be a need for acceptance by others. Higher level needs, called _____ needs, would include the need for knowledge and aesthetic beauty. At the top of the pyramid is the need for _____, the need to express one's full potential.

14-3. A higher level need would be activated only after a lower level need is satisfied. For example, a need for knowledge would be activated (<u>before/after</u>) needs for esteem, belongingness, and several lower level needs had been reasonably well satisfied.

14-4. In a few words, what did Maslow mean by self-actualization?

14-5. Suppose a woman had the talent and ambition to be a mathematician but followed the urging of others and became a nurse instead. How does her behavior relate to self-actualization and mental health, according to Maslow?

14-6. Which of the following, according to Maslow, are characteristic of self-actualized people? Place Y in the blank if the description applies, N if it does not.

_____ spontaneous

_____ has more profound emotional experiences than others

_____ uncomfortable being alone

_____ not dependent on others for approval

_____ thrive on their work

_____ extreme in personality (e.g., either conforming or rebellious)

15.   Summarize the strengths and weaknesses of the humanistic approach to personality.

15-1.   To its credit, the humanistic movement called attention to the possibility that a person's

_____ views may be more important than objective reality. The movement also

emphasized the importance of the _____ or self-concept and stressed the study of the

(normal/abnormal) personality.

15-2.   Critics have also identified several weaknesses of the humanistic formulations. Match the weaknesses

listed below with the statements by placing the appropriate letters in the blanks.

a. poor testability

b. unrealistic view of human nature

c. inadequate evidence

_____   Humanistic psychologists tend to scorn research, so little experimental support for their views has

emerged.

_____   Even without research, some of the descriptions, such as of self-actualized personalities, have an

idealized, perfectionistic ring.

_____   Humanistic ideas are frequently difficult to define, so research on some concepts is difficult or

impossible.

BIOLOGICAL PERSPECTIVES

16.   Describe Eysenck's theory of personality.

16-1.   According to Eysenck, individual differences in personality can be understood in terms of a hierarchy of

traits. At the top of the hierarchy are three fundamental higher-order traits from which all other traits

derive: _____, _____, and _____.

16-2.   Eysenck asserted that a major factor in personality involves the ease with which people can be

_____. Eysenck believed that differences in conditionability, like personality differ-

ences in general, are to a large extent (environmentally/genetically) determined.

16-3.   Conditionability, in turn, is related to extraversion-introversion. According to Eysenck (extraverts/

introverts) have higher levels of physiological arousal, a characteristic that makes them (more/less)

readily conditioned.

16-4.   Why would conditionability be related to introversion? Because easily conditioned people could be

readily conditioned to fear social situations. People who fear social situations may be classified as

_____.

16-5. Research evidence examining Eysenck's idea about introversion and physiological arousal is (<u>mixed/</u><u>clearcut</u>). While there does seem to be a physiological basis for introversion, it has been hard to establish the role of arousal.

Answers: 16-1. extraversion, neuroticism, psychoticism **16-2.** conditioned, genetically **16-3.** introverts, more **16-4.** introverts **16-5.** mixed.

17. Summarize behavioral genetics research on personality and its conclusions.

17-1. The most important and conclusive result from the various twin studies is the finding that the personalities of (<u>identical/fraternal</u>) twins reared (<u>together/apart</u>) were more similar than those of (<u>identical/</u><u>fraternal</u>) twins reared (<u>together/apart</u>). This outcome has been found with several dependent measures, including the factors of the Big Five personality inventory as well as peer ratings.

17-2. Approximately what percentage of the variance in personality is assumed to be caused by genetic factors?

a. 10 to 20 percent

b. 20 to 40 percent

c. 40 to 60 percent

d. 60 to 80 percent

17-3. How important a determinant of personality is family environment, according to the results of these studies?

a. of very little importance

b. of about the same importance as heredity

c. more important than heredity

17-4. The twin studies have had a major impact on the way psychologists think about the causes of human behavior. Why are the results so important and so surprising?

17-5. Since twin studies conclude that heredity has a major impact on personality, then at some point personality should be linked to specific genetic structures. In fact this has occurred for the characteristic of _____ seeking. Although the result has been replicated, the findings have been (<u>inconsistent/</u><u>consistent</u>), which suggests that the relationship between the gene and the trait may be somewhat weak.

Answers: 17-1. identical, apart, fraternal, together. This is the most important comparison because, even though the fraternal twins shared the same environment, their common environment did not make them nearly as similar as twins who did not have a common environment *but who shared the same heredity.* **17-2.** c **17-3.** a **17-4.** Theories of development and personality have tended to stress the importance of the environment, especially the family environment; the recent twin studies find heredity to be very important and family environment to be of little importance. Thus, the results are contrary to the expectations of most of us and of much of the theorizing in the field of personality. **17-5.** novelty, inconsistent.

18. **Outline Buss's explanation for why the Big Five traits are important.**

18-1. As group animals, we gain an advantage by being able to predict the behavior of other human beings. That is, the ability to recognize the "Big Five" characteristics in others has _____ value for our species.

18-2. For example, it is desirable to know who in our group will fulfill their commitments, the trait of _____ ; who will fall apart under stress, the trait of _____; who will be a good problem solver, the trait of _____ , and so on.

18-3. The fact that these traits appear as dimensions across a variety of cultures attests to their importance. For Buss, our ability to _____ these traits in others also has adaptive significance.

Answers: **8-1.** adaptive (survival, evolutionary) **18-2.** conscientiousness, neuroticism, openness to experience **18-3.** recognize.

19. **Summarize the strengths and weaknesses of the biological approach to personality.**

19-1. People frequently blame parents for kids' personalities. I recently asked a friend of mine why she thought a mutual acquaintance of ours was so obnoxious. She said, "Well, raised with such crazy parents, what would you expect?" I asked, "Is that an argument for environment or heredity?" That is one of the benefits of the twin studies: They put data in place of speculation. But what are some of the weaknesses of the biological approach? One is that heritability ratios should be regarded only as _____ that will vary depending on sampling and other procedures. Another is that the attempt to apportion variance into heredity and environment is artificial since heredity and environment always _____. Finally, there is no truly comprehensive biological _____ of personality.

Answers: **19-1.** estimates, interact, theory.

CONTEMPORARY EMPIRICAL APPROACHES TO PERSONALITY

20. **Discuss the meaning of sensation seeking and identify the characteristics of high sensation seekers.**

20-1. Sensation seeking refers to the degree to which people tend to seek or avoid high levels of sensory stimulation, a tendency that is to a large extent genetically inherited, according to Zuckerman. Indicate which of the following characteristics describe high-sensation seekers and which describe low, by placing an H or L in the blanks.

_____ Risk taking

_____ Easily bored

_____ Takes comfort in the routine

_____ More likely to drink heavily

_____ More likely to engage in recreational drug use

_____ Tends to ignore middle class rules and conventions

_____ Relishes extensive travel, finding new and unusual friends

_____ Tends toward sexual experimentation

_____ Tends to like mountain climbing, skydiving, scuba diving

_____ Relatively tolerant of stress

_____ More likely to have difficulty in school, exhibit poor health habits

20-2. Sensation seeking seems to be a fairly potent personality characteristic that may influence the course of romantic relationships. Do people tend to prefer partners who are similar to themselves in sensation seeking, or do opposites attract with regard to this characteristic?

Answers: 20-1. H, H, L, H, H, H, H, H, H, H, H **20-2.** As is the case with personality traits in general, people prefer partners who are similar to themselves in sensation seeking.

21. Explain what is meant by self-monitoring and discuss the effects of self-monitoring on interpersonal relationships.

21-1. Describe the characteristics of people who are high in self-monitoring with regard to the following situations:

(a) impression management: They are relatively (<u>good at/poor at</u>) creating the desired impression.

(b) control of facial expressions: They are (<u>able/not able</u>) to feign emotion by controlling their facial expressions.

(c) spotting deception: They are (<u>good at/poor at</u>) spotting deception in others.

(d) dating and sexual relationships: They tend to have (<u>more/fewer</u>) partners and (<u>stronger/weaker</u>) emotional commitments.

21-2. The two personality traits discussed in this and the previous learning objective overlap to some extent. To review these concepts, match the specific trait with the behavioral descriptions by placing the appropriate abbreviations in the blanks.

Hi-SS   high sensation seeking

Lo-SS   low sensation seeking

Hi-SM   high self-monitoring

Lo-SM   low self-monitoring.

(a) _____   Last summer Ralph decided on the spur of the moment to sell his car and spend two months traveling by foot in India. Ralph's hobbies include sky-diving and gambling.

(b) _____   Margie figures she knows what people want and she successfully adjusts her personality to fit the occasion or person she is with. She is good at feigning emotion and also good at detecting deception in others. She changes sexual partners frequently and avoids emotional commitments.

(c) ____ Alice usually doesn't try to hide her feelings and isn't very good at it when she does try. She prefers close relationships with the opposite sex to playing the field. She isn't especially gullible, but she also isn't really good at figuring out when people are trying to deceive her.

(d) ____ Jan hates it when her boyfriend drives too fast, and she refuses to go skiing with him because she thinks it's too dangerous.

Answers: 21-1. (a) good at (b) able (c) good at (d) more, weaker **21-2.** (a) Hi-SS (b) Hi-SM (c) Lo-SM (d) Lo-SS.

CULTURE AND PERSONALITY

22. Summarize research on the cross-cultural validity of the five-factor model and on cultural variations in conceptions of self.

22-1. For a decade or so after World War II, researchers using the Freudian model attempted to find a modal personality type representative of each culture. This attempt was (<u>successful/not successful</u>).

22-2. With the current increased attention to cultural factors, interest in the relationship between personality and culture has again surfaced, and the new data have revealed both cross-cultural similarities and differences. With regard to similarity, precisely the same "_____" personality factors tend to emerge in different cultures.

22-3. With regard to differences, research by Markus and Kitayama clearly indicates that the individualistic orientation characteristic of the West is not universal across cultures. While Americans tend to value (<u>independence/connectedness</u>), Asians value (<u>interdependence/uniqueness</u>) among people. Similarly, while American parents encourage their children to (<u>stand out/blend in</u>), Asian parents emphasize taking pride in the accomplishments of (<u>each individual/the group</u>).

22-4. Even though the Big Five traits appear to emerge in widely different cultures, this does not mean that these and other traits have the same meaning in different cultures. For example, Eastern cultures emphasize (<u>self-enhancement/self-criticism</u>), which tends to correlate with lower self-esteem. Somewhat surprisingly, however, self-esteem in these cultures (<u>does/does not</u>) correlate with subjective well-being.

Answers: 22-1. not successful **22-2.** Big Five **22-3.** independence, interdependence, stand out, the group **22-4.** self-criticism, does not.

PUTTING IT IN PERSPECTIVE

23. Explain how the chapter highlighted three of the text's unifying themes.

23-1. We've just discussed one of the three themes emphasized in this chapter, that our behavior is influenced by our cultural heritage. Two other themes prominently demonstrated in the area of personality are that the field is theoretically _____ and that psychology evolves in a _____ context.

23-2. Freudian, behavioral, and biological perspectives of personality assume that behavior is determined; the _____ perspective does not. The biological perspective stresses genetic inheritance; the behavioral perspective stresses (heredity/environment). As these examples illustrate, the study of personality has produced an enormous amount of theoretical _____.

23-3. Concerning sociohistorical context, it is clear that theories of personality have strongly affected our culture. For example, the surrealist art movement, begun in the 1920s, derives directly from _____ psychology, as do other movements in literature and the arts. And the current debate on the effects of media violence is to a large extent a product of research in social _____ theory.

23-4. In turn, culture has affected psychology. For example, it seems quite likely that the sexually repressive climate of Victorian Vienna caused Freud to emphasize the _____ aspects of human behavior; and it is clear, from Freud's own description, that World War I influenced his development of the second Freudian instinct, the _____ instinct. Thus, psychology evolves in a _____ context.

Answers: **23-1.** diverse, sociohistorical **23-2.** humanistic, environment, diversity **23-3.** psychoanalytic (Freudian), learning **23-4.** sexual, aggression, sociohistorical.

APPLICATION: UNDERSTANDING PERSONALITY ASSESSMENT

24. Outline the four principal uses of personality tests.

24-1. List the four principal uses of personality tests in the blanks next to the correct descriptions.

(a) Psychological _____: Measuring personality traits in empirical studies.

(b) _____: Advising people on career plans and decisions.

(c) _____ selection: Choosing employees in business and government.

(d) Clinical _____: Assessing psychological disorders.

Answers: **24-1.** (a) research (b) Counseling (c) Personnel (d) diagnosis.

25. Describe the MMPI, 16PF, and NEO Personality Inventory and summarize the strengths and weaknesses of self-report inventories.

25-1. The MMPI, 16PF, and NEO Personality Inventories are (projective/self-report) tests. All three tests are also used to measure (single/multiple) traits.

25-2. Identify which tests (MMPI, 16PF, or NEO) are described by each of the following.

(a) _____ Originally designed to diagnose psychological disorders.

(b) _____, _____ Originally designed to assess the normal personality.

(c) _____ Contains 187 items.

(d) _____ Contains 567 items.

(e) _____ Measures the "big five" personality traits.

(f) _____ Includes four validity scales to help detect deception.

25-3. The major strength of self-report inventories, in comparison with simply asking a person what they are like, is that they provide a more precise and more (<u>objective/personal</u>) measure of personality.

25-4. The major weakness of self-report inventories is that they are subject to several sources of error, including the following: (1) Test-takers may intentionally fake responses, that is, may engage in deliberate _____. (2) While not realizing it, people may answer questions in ways to make themselves "look good," the _____ _____ bias. (3) In addition, some people tend either to agree or to disagree with nearly every statement on a test, a source of error involving _____ sets.

Answers: 25-1. self-report, multiple **25-2.** (a) MMPI (b) 16PF, NEO (c) 16PF (d) MMPI (e) NEO (f) MMPI **25-3.** objective **25-4.** deception, social desirability, response.

26. Describe the projective hypothesis and summarize the strengths and weaknesses of projective tests.

26-1. If you have ever looked at clouds and described the images you've seen, you've done something similar to taking a projective test. If you thought that the images you saw reflected something about your personality, then you also accepted the *projective hypothesis*. The projective hypothesis is the idea that people will tend to _____ their characteristics onto ambiguous stimuli, so that what they see reveals something about their personalities and problems.

26-2. Two major projective tests are the Rorschach, a series of _____, and the TAT, a series of simple _____.

26-3. The advantages of projective tests are that (1) since the way the tests are interpreted is not at all obvious, it is difficult for people to engage in intentional _____; and (2) projective tests may help tap problems or aspects of personality of which people are _____.

26-4. The major weakness of projective tests concerns inadequate evidence that they are either _____ (consistent) or _____ (measure what they are intended to measure). Nonetheless, the tests are still valued and used by many clinicians. It should also be noted that when users agree on a systematic scoring procedure, some projective tests have shown adequate reliability and validity. Thus, as discussed in Chapter 10, the _____ has proven to be a particularly useful test in research on achievement motivation.

Answers: 26-1. project **26-2.** inkblots, pictures (scenes) **26-3.** deception, unconscious (unaware) **26-4.** reliable, valid, TAT.

27. Discuss how hindsight bias affects everyday analyses of personality, as well as some theoretical analyses of personality.

27-1. I am writing this sentence on the weekend after an enormous drop in the stock market, the largest point loss (not percentage loss) in Dow history. I know what faces me Monday morning: the pundits and my colleagues will say they saw it coming. If everyone saw it coming, why didn't everyone sell last week? Because we didn't see it coming. Rather, once exposed to information, we are inclined to believe that we already knew it, the cognitive tendency known as the _____.

27-2. Recall from Chapter 11 the experiment with the three-year-old and the candy box. The child first guesses that candy is in the candy box. After the child sees that crayons are in the candy box, the three-year-old will usually insist that he always thought that there were crayons in the box. The five-year-old doesn't make this mistake, but these data suggest that the _____ begins early, that from a young age we reconstruct past events in terms of _____ information.

27-3. Suppose you meet someone who is achievement motivated and fiercely independent. You learn that this person was brought up by adoptive parents who were somewhat distant and undemonstrative. Would you connect the events, thinking that the parent's child-rearing style accounted for their child's independence? Or, suppose that the person brought up by these parents is depressed and chronically unemployed. Would you connect the parenting and personality in this case, too? You might, because people tend to interpret _____ events in terms of _____ , which is a definition of the hindsight bias.

27-4. What is the hindsight bias? Write a definition in the space below.

27-5. In what way might psychoanalytic interpretations involve the hindsight bias?

27-6. How might evolutionary theory's account of the emergence of the Big Five traits reflect the hindsight bias?

Answers: 27-1. hindsight bias (By the way, it is now Monday morning and the market is up. I knew it!)
27-2. hindsight bias, present (current, outcome, recent) **27-3.** past (previous), present information (outcomes, current information) **27-4.** Once we know something, we tend to reinterpret past events in terms of that information. Or, once exposed to information, we tend to think we knew it all along. Or, knowing the outcome of events tends to bias our recall and interpretation of those events. **27-5.** Once exposed to the fact that the Big Five traits appear world-wide, a theorist can fairly easily explain why that might be the case. If a dozen entirely different traits had emerged, one could imagine that there could be an evolutionary explanation for that occurrence as well. **27-6.** Once the analyst is exposed to an individual's personality, he or she can easily explain how the person's childhood experiences could account for the present behavior.

REVIEW OF KEY TERMS

Archetypes
Behaviorism
Collective unconscious
Compensation
Conscious
Defense mechanisms
Displacement
Ego
Extraverts
Factor analysis
Fixation
Hierarchy of needs
Hindsight bias
Humanism
Id
Identification

Incongruence
Introverts
Model
Need for self-actualization
Observational learning
Oedipal complex
Personal unconscious
Personality
Personality trait
Phenomenological approach
Pleasure principle
Preconscious
Projection
Projective tests
Psychodynamic theories
Psychosexual stages

Rationalization
Reaction formation
Reality principle
Reciprocal determinism
Regression
Repression
Self-actualizing persons
Self-concept
Self-efficacy
Self-monitoring
Self-report inventories
Sensation seeking
Striving for superiority
Superego
Unconscious

Personality

personality trait

hierarchy of needs

1. An individual's unique constellation of consistent behavioral traits.

2. A characteristic that represents a durable disposition to behave in a particular way in a variety of situations.

3. A systematic arrangement of needs, according to priority, in which basic, physiological needs must be met before social or growth needs are aroused.

4. All the diverse theories, descended from the work of Sigmund Freud, that focus on unconscious mental forces.

5. The primitive, instinctive component of personality that operates according to the pleasure principle.

6. The id's demands for immediate gratification of its urges.

7. The decision-making component of personality that operates according to the reality principle.

8. The ego's delay of gratification of the id's urges until appropriate outlets and situations can be found.

9. The moral component of personality that incorporates social standards about what represents right and wrong.

10. Consists of whatever you are aware of at a particular point in time.

11. Contains material just beneath the surface of awareness that can be easily retrieved.

12. Contains thoughts, memories, and desires that are well below the surface of conscious awareness.

13. The series of largely unconscious Freudian reactions that protect a person from unpleasant emotions such as anxiety or guilt.

14. The defense mechanism that pushes distressing thoughts and feelings into the unconscious or keeps them from emerging into consciousness.

15. Attributing your own thoughts, feelings, or motives to another.

16. Creating false but plausible excuses to justify unacceptable behavior.

17. Diverting emotional feelings (usually anger) from their original source to a substitute target.

_____ 18. Behaving in a way that is exactly the opposite of one's true (but unconscious) feelings.

_____ 19. Reverting to immature patterns of behavior.

_____ 20. Bolstering self-esteem by forming an imaginary or real alliance with some person or group.

_____ 21. Developmental periods with a characteristic sexual focus that leave their mark on adult personality

_____ 22. A failure to move forward from one stage to another as expected.

_____ 23. Characterized by erotically tinged desires for one's opposite-sex parent and hostility toward one's same-sex parent.

_____ 24. Jungian concept referring to the structure holding material that is not in one's awareness because it has been repressed or forgotten.

_____ 25. A storehouse of latent memory traces inherited from our ancestral past.

_____ 26. Emotionally charged images and thought forms that have universal meaning.

_____ 27. People who tend to be preoccupied with the internal world of their own thoughts, feelings, and experiences.

_____ 28. People who tend to be interested in the external world of people and things.

_____ 29. An Adlerian concept referring to a universal drive to adapt, to improve oneself, and to master life's challenges.

_____ 30. Efforts to overcome imagined or real inferiorities by developing one's abilities.

_____ 31. Personality tests that ask people a series of questions about their characteristic behavior.

_____ 32. A statistical procedure that identifies clusters of variables that are highly correlated with one another.

_____ 33. A theoretical orientation based on the premise that scientific psychology should study only observable behavior.

_____ 34. The assumption that internal mental events, external environmental events, and overt behavior all influence one another.

_____ 35. Learning that occurs when an organism's responding is influenced by the observation of others.

_____ 36. A person whose behavior is observed by another.

_____ 37. Our belief about our ability to perform behaviors that should lead to expected outcomes.

_____ 38. A theoretical orientation that emphasizes the unique qualities of humans, especially their freedom and potential for personal growth.

_____ 39. Approach that assumes we have to appreciate individuals' personal, subjective experiences to truly understand their behavior.

_____ 40. A collection of beliefs about one's own nature, unique qualities, and typical behavior.

_____ 41. A Rogerian concept referring to the degree of disparity between one's self-concept and one's actual experience.

_____ 42. The need to fulfill one's potential.

_____ 43. People with exceptionally healthy personalities, marked by continued personal growth.

_____ 44. The biased interpretation of past events in terms of present information.

_____ 45. A generalized preference for high or low levels of sensory stimulation.

_____ 46. The degree to which people attend to and control the impression they make on others in social interactions.

_____ 47. A person's overall assessment of her or his personal adequacy or worth.

Answers: 1. personality **2.** personality trait **3.** hierarchy of needs **4.** psychodynamic theories **5.** id **6.** pleasure principle **7.** ego **8.** reality principle **9.** superego **10.** conscious **11.** preconscious **12.** unconscious **13.** defense mechanisms **14.** repression **15.** projection **16.** rationalization **17.** displacement **18.** reaction formation **19.** regression **20.** identification **21.** psychosexual stages **22.** fixation **23.** Oedipal complex **24.** personal unconscious **25.** collective unconscious **26.** archetypes **27.** introverts **28.** extraverts **29.** striving for superiority **30.** compensation **31.** self-report inventories **32.** factor analysis **33.** behaviorism **34.** reciprocal determinism **35.** observational learning **36.** model **37.** self-efficacy **38.** humanism **39.** phenomenological approach **40.** self-concept **41.** incongruence **42.** need for self-actualization **43.** self-actualizing persons **44.** hindsight bias **45.** sensation seeking **46.** self-monitoring **47.** self-esteem.

REVIEW OF KEY PEOPLE

Alfred Adler   Sigmund Freud   Walter Mischel
Albert Bandura   Carl Jung   Carl Rogers
Raymond Cattell   Abraham Maslow   B. F. Skinner
Hans Eysenck

_____ 1. The founder of psychoanalysis.

_____ 2. Developed the theory called analytical psychology; anticipated the humanists' emphasis on personal growth and self-actualization.

_____ 3. Founder of an approach to personality named individual psychology.

_____ 4. Modern behaviorism's most prominent theorist, recognized for his theories of operant conditioning.

_____ 5. A contemporary behavioral theorist who elaborated the concept of observational learning.

_____ 6. His chief contribution to personality theory has been to focus attention on the extent to which situational factors govern behavior.

_____ 7. One of the fathers of the human potential movement, he called his approach a person-centered theory.

_____ 8. The humanist who developed a theory of self-actualization.

_____ 9. Theorist who proposed that there are 16 basic personality factors.

_____ 10. He went against the spirit of the times by proposing a biologically oriented theory of personality.

Answers: 1. Freud **2.** Jung **3.** Adler **4.** Skinner **5.** Bandura **6.** Mischel **7.** Rogers **8.** Maslow **9.** Cattell **10.** Eysenck

SELF-QUIZ

1. Personality traits are characterized by
   a. consistency and distinctiveness
   b. charm and wit
   c. change as a function of the situation
   d. lack of individual differences

2. Someone attributes his thoughts or feelings or conflicts to someone else. For example, although he chronically interrupts people, he thinks that other people interrupt him. What Freudian defense mechanism is illustrated?
   a. rationalization
   b. reaction formation
   c. regression
   d. projection

3. Which of the following is entirely unconscious, according to Freud?
   a. the id
   b. the ego
   c. the superego
   d. the archetype

4. Although Osmo at an unconscious level has great hatred for Cosmo, he believes that he likes Cosmo and, to the outside world, gives all the appearance of liking him. Which defense mechanism is Osmo using?
   a. regression
   b. reaction formation
   c. projection
   d. rationalization

5. The Oedipal complex occurs during the
   a. oral stage
   b. anal stage
   c. phallic stage
   d. genital stage

6. Which of the following concepts did Carl Jung originate?
   a. id
   b. superego
   c. inferiority complex
   d. introversion-extraversion

7. Which of the following did Adler emphasize in his theory of personality?
   a. striving for superiority
   b. castration anxiety
   c. introversion-extraversion
   d. the collective unconscious

8. Much of the behavior that we call personality results from reinforcement and observational learning, according to
   a. Jung
   b. Skinner
   c. Bandura
   d. Adler

9. Which of the following tends to emphasize freedom and personal growth in its view of human behavior?
   a. the psychoanalytic approach
   b. the biological approach
   c. the behavioral approach
   d. the humanistic approach

10. According to Rogers, what causes incongruence?
   a. an inherited sense of irony
   b. conditional acceptance or affection
   c. unconditional acceptance or affection
   d. unconditioned stimuli

11. Herb had the desire and potential to be a violinist but became, instead, a trader in hog futures. He decided never to touch the violin again. What is wrong with Herb, according to Maslow?
    a. He suffers from incongruence.
    b. He suffers from castration anxiety.
    c. He has not achieved self-actualization.
    d. He has an inferiority complex.
12. Which of the following views personality in terms of the adaptive significance to the Big Five traits?
    a. Abraham Maslow
    b. William James
    c. the behavioral approach
    d. the evolutionary approach

13. Your friend spends money like water. When you learn that he is from a poverty-stricken background, you attribute his spending patterns to his earlier deprivation. According to the critical thinking analysis, you are likely to do this because of
    a. the hindsight bias
    b. a self-serving attribution
    c. the consistency and distinctiveness of personality
    d. circular reasoning

14. According to Mischel, what is the major factor that predicts human behavior?
    a. childhood experience
    b. specifics of the situation
    c. extraversion and introversion
    d. central and peripheral traits

15. You are asked to tell stories about a series of pictures. Which test is being administered to you?
    a. Rorschach
    b. MMPI
    c. TAT
    d. 16PF

Answers: 1. a **2.** d **3.** a **4.** b **5.** c **6.** d **7.** a **8.** c **9.** d **10.** b **11.** c **12.** d **13.** a **14.** b **15.** c.

Chapter Thirteen

Stress, Coping, and Health

REVIEW OF KEY IDEAS

THE NATURE OF STRESS

1. Discuss the impact of minor stressors.

    1-1. While some forms of stress arise from unusual, traumatic crises, most stress arises from (<u>infrequent/ everyday</u>) problems. These minor hassles appear to be detrimental to mental health because of the _____ nature of stress.

    Answers: **1-1.** everyday, cumulative.

2. Describe the nature of stress.

    2-1. The text defines stress as any circumstances that threaten or are perceived to threaten one's well being, and thereby they tax one's coping abilities. This definition would indicate that the sources of stress are quite (<u>subjective/objective</u>). Or to put it another way, stress lies in the mind of the _____.

    Answers: **2-1.** subjective, beholder or individual.

MAJOR TYPES OF STRESS

3. Describe frustration as a form of stress.

    3-1. Which of the following three situations best illustrates what is meant by frustration?

        (a) Your family moves from a large city to a rather small, rural community.

        (b) You are late for an appointment and stuck in a traffic jam.

(c) You are forced to choose between two good movies on television.

3-2. If you picked choice (b) then you have caught on that frustration always involves the _____ of the pursuit of some goal.

Answers: 3-1. b **3-2.** thwarting or blocking.

4. Identify the three basic types of conflict and discuss which types are most troublesome.

4-1. Many persons do not want to pay their income taxes, but, on the other hand, they don't want to go to jail either. These persons are faced with an _____-_____ conflict.

4-2. Getting married has both positive and negative aspects that make it an excellent example of an_____-_____conflict.

4-3. Consider the problem of the student who has to choose between scholarships for two different universities. Since he cannot accept both, he's faced with an _____-_____ conflict.

4-4. Now that you have correctly identified the three basic types of conflict, list them below in their order of troublesomeness, beginning with the least troublesome.

(a) _____

(b) _____

(c) _____

Answers: 4-1. avoidance-avoidance **4-2.** approach-avoidance **4-3.** approach-approach **4-4.** (a) approach-approach (b) approach-avoidance (c) avoidance-avoidance.

5. Summarize evidence on life change and pressure as forms of stress.

5-1. The Social Readjustment Rating Scale (SRRS) measures the stress induced by _____ in daily living routines. The developers of this scale theorized that all kinds of life changes, both pleasant and unpleasant, would induce stress. Early research showed that high scores on the SRRS were correlated with psychological disturbances and many kinds of physical _____.

5-2. Later research began to indicate that high scores on the SRRS were primarily the result of (<u>pleasant/</u> <u>unpleasant</u>) events. At the present time research seems to indicate that change by itself (<u>is/is not</u>) inevitably stressful.

5-3. There are two kinds of pressure. One is the pressure to get things accomplished, or the pressure to _____. The other is the pressure to abide by rules, or the pressure to _____.

5-4. Which appears to have the strongest influence on mental health, life changes or pressure?

Answers: 5-1. changes, illness **5-2.** unpleasant, is not **5-3.** perform, conform **5-4.** pressure.

RESPONDING TO STRESS

6. **Identify some common emotional responses to stress and discuss the effects of emotional arousal.**

    6-1.   The text describes three different dimensions of emotions that are particularly likely to be triggered by stress. Identify which of these dimensions is most likely to be present in the following situations.

        (a) The emotions in this dimension are likely to be found as a person begins to feel more and more helpless and unable to cope (e.g., you detect signs that your lover is going to leave you).

        (b) The emotions in this dimension are likely to be found as a person begins to feel increasingly put upon and treated unfairly (e.g., you are being falsely accused of a deed you didn't commit).

        (c) The emotions in this dimension are likely to be found as a person faces increasing degrees of conflict or uncertainty (e.g., you're driving on a highway and the fog is gradually becoming thicker).

    6-2.   What does the inverted U hypothesis say about what happens to the optimal arousal level as tasks become more complex?

Answers: 6-1. (a) dejection, sadness, and grief (b) annoyance, anger, and rage (c) apprehension, anxiety, and fear
6-2. The optimal arousal level decreases.

7. **Describe the fight-or-flight response and the three stages of the General Adaptation Syndrome.**

    7-1.   What division of the autonomic nervous system mediates the fight-or-flight response?

    7-2.   Although the body's fight-or-flight response appears to be an evolutionary carry-over from our past, why is it perhaps of more harm than help to modern human beings?

    7-3.   Indicate which of the three stages of the General Adaptation Syndrome is being described in each of the following.

        (a) This is the initial stage in which the body prepares for the fight-or-flight response.

(b) This is the second stage in which the body stabilizes its physiological changes as it begins to effectively cope with the stress.

(c) This is the third stage in which the body's coping resources are becoming depleted and the resistance to many diseases declines.

Answers: 7-1. sympathetic nervous system **7-2.** Because most stressful situations generally require a more complex response than simple fight or flight. **7-3.** (a) stage of alarm (b) stage of resistance (c) stage of exhaustion.

8. **Discuss the two major pathways along which the brain sends signals to the endocrine system in response to stress.**

    8-1. Fill in the missing parts in the diagram below detailing the two major pathways along which the brain sends signals to the endocrine system.

CEREBRAL CORTEX

(a) _____

SYMPATHETIC NS	PITUITARY GLAND
	ACTH
(b) _____ (GLAND)	(c) _____ (GLAND)
CATECHOLAMINES	CORTICOSTEROIDS
Increases heart rate & respiration, etc.	Increases energy, inhibits tissue inflammation, etc.

Answers: 8-1. (a) hypothalamus (b) adrenal medulla (c) adrenal cortex.

9. **Describe and evaluate aggression and self-indulgence as behavioral responses to stress.**

    9-1. Answer the following questions regarding aggression and self-indulgence as responses to stress.

    (a) Which of these responses is illustrated by the saying: "When the going gets tough, the tough go shopping"? _____

    (b) Which of these responses is frequently, but not always, triggered by frustration?
    _____

    (c) Which of these responses is linked to internet addiction? _____

    9-2. What is a common fault with both of these behavioral responses to stress?

Answers: 9-1. (a) self indulgence (b) aggression (c) self-indulgence **9-2.** They divert effort away from solutions to problems.

10. **Discuss the adaptive value of defensive coping and positive illusions.**

   10-1.   Indicate whether each of the following statements regarding defensive coping is true or false.

   _____ (a) Although they are largely unconscious, defense mechanisms can operate at any level of consciousness.

   _____ (b) Only neurotic persons use defensive mechanisms.

   _____ (c) Defense mechanisms are used to shield against emotional discomfort that often occurs with stress, particularly anxiety.

   10-2.   One shortcoming of defensive coping is that it avoids the real problem. What other consequence might arise here?

   10-3.   What conclusion does the text draw regarding small and extreme positive illusions?

Answers: 10-1. (a) true (b) false (c) true **10-2.** poor health **10-3.** Small positive illusions may be beneficial while extreme illusions may be harmful.

THE EFFECTS OF STRESS ON PSYCHOLOGICAL FUNCTIONING

11. **Discuss the effects of stress on task performance and the burnout syndrome.**

   11-1.   Baumeister's theory as to why stress affects task performance is that pressure to perform makes us self-conscious and this elevated self-consciousness disrupts our _____. The term we commonly use for this is _____ under pressure. Research shows that this phenomenon is quite (<u>rare/common</u>) among normal persons.

   11-2.   Indicate whether each of the following statements regarding the burnout syndrome is true or false.

   _____ (a) Burnout appears to result from events that undermine the belief that one's life is meaningful and important.

   _____ (b) The onset of burnout is usually sudden.

Answers: 11-1. attention, choking, common **11-2.** (a) true (b) false.

12. **Discuss posttraumatic stress disorder and other psychological problems and disorders that may result from stress.**

   12-1.   Answer the following questions regarding post-traumatic stress syndrome.

   (a) What is unique about post-traumatic stress disorder?

(b) What are some of the common causes of this syndrome besides combat experience?

12-2. In addition to alcohol abuse and unhappiness, what four other psychological problems appear to be related to chronic stress? (One of them has to do with school, two have to do with sleep, and one involves intimate relationships.)

12-3. Stress has also been implicated in the onset of serious psychological disorders. In addition to schizophrenia, what three other disorders are mentioned?

Answers: 12-1. (a) It is caused by a single episode of extreme stress (b) rape, robbery, assault, seeing someone die, serious automobile accidents, major natural disasters **12-2.** poor academic performance, insomnia, nightmares, sexual difficulties **12-3.** anxiety disorders, depression, eating disorders.

THE EFFECTS OF STRESS ON PHYSICAL HEALTH

13. Describe the Type A behavior pattern and summarize the evidence linking it to coronary heart disease.

13-1. Tell whether the following characteristics are found in Type A or Type B persons.

_____ (a) easygoing

_____ (b) competitive

_____ (c) impatient

_____ (d) amicable

_____ (e) hostile

13-2. Which aspect of the Type A behavior seems to be most highly related to coronary heart disorder.

13-3. What is the increased coronary risk for Type A's when compared to Type B's?

Answers: 13-1. (a) Type B (b) Type A (c) Type A (d) Type B (e) Type A **13-2.** cynical hostility **13-3.** double (or twice as likely).

14. Describe evidence linking emotional reactions and depression to heart disease.

14-1. Research has shown that negative emotions can trigger acute symptoms of heart disease. What other line of evidence, having to do with preventing a second heart attack, supports this relationship between emotions and heart disease?

14-2. Which of the following statements appears to best reflect the relationship between depression and heart disease?

(a) Heart disease can lead to depression.

(b) Depression can lead to heart disease.

Answers: 14-1. Engaging in stress management training reduces the risk. **14-2.** Depression can lead to heart disease.

15. Discuss and evaluate other evidence linking stress to immunosuppression and a variety of physical illnesses.

15-1. Research has found stress to be related to numerous diseases and disorders. What effect on the lymphocytes (the specialized white blood cells that are important in initiating the immune response) appears to be the link between stress and so many disorders?

Answers: 15-1. Stress appears to suppress the proliferation of the lymphocytes (thus suppressing the immune system in general).

16. Describe the Featured Study on stress and the common cold.

16-1. Answer the following questions about the Featured Study.

(a) What two groups were the subjects divided into on the basis of their answers to stress inventories?

(b) Which group showed a significantly higher incidence of colds, after controlling for the roommate effect?

(c) What is rather unique about this particular study?

16-2. While many studies have shown a relationship between stress and numerous physical illness, we can still not state definitely that stress leads to physical illness. Why is this?

FACTORS MODERATING THE IMPACT OF STRESS

17. Discuss how social support and hardiness moderate the impact of stress.

    17-1. What two areas of our health appear to benefit from having strong social support groups?

    17-2. What role does social support apparently play during times of high stress?

18. Discuss how personality and physiological factors are related to stress tolerance.

    18-1. What difference was found between optimists and pessimists with respect to good physical health?

    18-2. What personality characteristic was found to be related to longevity in a recent study from a sample of Terman's gifted children?

    18-3. What condition triggered by autonomic reactivity may also contribute to heart disease?

HEALTH-IMPAIRING BEHAVIOR

19. Discuss the negative impact of smoking, poor nutrition, and lack of exercise on physical health.

    19-1. Answer the following questions regarding the negative impact of smoking on physical health.

        (a) How many fewer years can a 25-year-old male smoker expect to live than a 25-year-old nonsmoker?

(b) What are the two most frequent diseases that kill smokers?

(c) What appears to happen with respect to readiness to give up as smokers cycle through periods of abstinence and relapse?

19-2. Answer the following true-false questions.

_____ (a) Among Americans most deficiencies in diet are because of inability to afford appropriate food.

_____ (b) Regular exercise appears to increase longevity.

_____ (c) Alcohol is the most health-impairing of all the recreational drugs.

Answers: 19-1. (a) 8 years (or 8.3 years) (b) lung cancer and heart disease (c) Readiness to give up smoking builds gradually. **19-2.** (a) false (b) true (c) true.

20. Discuss the relationship between behavioral styles and AIDS.

20-1. What two bodily fluids are most likely to transmit AIDS?

20-2. What two general groups have the highest incidence of AIDS in the United States?

20-3. In the world as a whole, which form of transmission, gay and bisexual or heterosexual, is most common?

20-4. How can one virtually guarantee that he or she will not contact AIDS?

Answers: 20-1. blood and semen **20-2.** Gay & bisexual males and intravenous drug users. **20-3.** heterosexual transmission **20-4.** Stay with only one sexual partner (known to prefer this same lifestyle) and don't use intravenous drugs.

21. Explain how health-impairing lifestyles develop.

21-1. The text list four complementary explanations as to why health-impairing lifestyles develop. Given the hints below, list these four reasons.

(a) slowly

(b) immediate

(c) delayed

(d) "not me"

Answers: 21-1. (a) They develop slowly. (b) The pleasure they provide is immediate. (c) The health-impairing consequences are delayed. (d) The consequences are likely to happen to others (but "not me").

REACTIONS TO ILLNESS

22. **Discuss individual differences in willingness to seek medical treatment.**

    22-1. Indicate whether the following statements regarding individual differences in willingness to seek medical treatment are true or false.

    _____ (a) Delay in seeking treatment is perhaps the biggest problem here.

    _____ (b) The perception of pain and illness is very subjective.

    Answers: 22-1. (a) true (b) true.

23. **Discuss some barriers to effective patient-provider communication and ways to overcome these barriers.**

    23-1. Which of the following factors appears to be a barrier to effective patient-provider communication?

    (a) economic realities   (d) evasiveness

    (b) medical jargon   (e) passivity

    (c) forgetfulness

    23-2. What does the text recommend as the best way to improve patient-provider communication?

    Answers: 23-1. All of these factors. **23-2.** Don't be a passive consumer of medical advice.

24. **Discuss the extent to which people tend to adhere to medical advice.**

    24-1. The text lists three reasons for failure to comply with medical advice. One is that patients often fail to completely _____ treatment instructions. A second is that the treatment may prove to be quite _____. The third reason is not directly related to either instructions or treatment, but rather to the attitude towards the _____. A negative attitude makes compliance (<u>more/less</u>) likely.

Answers: **24-1.** understand, unpleasant (or aversive), physician or doctor, less.

PUTTING IT IN PERSPECTIVE

25. Explain how this chapter highlighted two of the text's unifying themes.

25-1. The fact that the amount of stress in any given situation primarily lies in the eyes of the beholder nicely illustrates the theme that experience is _____.

25-2. The fact that stress interacts with numerous other factors that affect health illustrates the theme of multifactorial _____.

Answers: **25-1.** subjective **25-2.** causation.

APPLICATION: IMPROVING COPING AND STRESS MANAGEMENT

26. Summarize Albert Ellis's ideas about controlling one's emotions.

26-1. The main idea behind Albert Ellis's rational-emotive therapy is that stress is largely caused by _____ thinking. Therefore, by changing one's catastrophic thinking and taking a more rational approach, one can then reduce the amount of _____ being experienced.

26-2. Ellis illustrates this theory by postulating an A-B-C series of events. Describe below what is going on during each of these events.

(A) activating event:

(B) belief:

(C) consequence:

26-3. Since the emotional turmoil in the A-B-C sequence is caused by the B (Belief) sequence, effort must be directed towards changing irrational beliefs. Ellis proposed two techniques for doing this. One must first learn to _____ instances of irrational beliefs. Then one must learn to actively _____ these irrational beliefs.

Answers: **26-1.** catastrophic, stress **26-2.** (A) the activating event that precedes the stress (B) one's belief about the event (C) the emotional consequences that result from the belief **26-3.** detect, dispute.

27. Discuss the adaptive value of humor and releasing pent-up emotions.

27-1. What dual role does humor appear to play in easing stress from difficult situations.

27-2. Why might talking or writing about a problem with a sympathetic friend prove useful when experiencing stress?

Answers: 27-1. It allows for both redefining the problem in a less threatening way and the releasing of tension. **27-2.** It may help to release pent-up tension.

28. Discuss the adaptive value of relaxation and exercise.

28-1. Complete the following statements regarding the adaptive value of relaxation and exercise.

(a) A quiet environment, a mental device, a passive attitude, and a comfortable position are conditions that facilitate:

(b) Eating a balanced diet, getting adequate sleep and exercise, and staying away from overeating and harmful drugs can help to minimize:

Answers: 28-1. (a) learning to relax (b) physical vulnerability.

CRITICAL THINKING APPLICATION

29. Describe some important considerations in evaluating health statistics and making health decisions.

29-1. Which kind of faulty statistical reasoning (correlation is no assurance of causation, statistical significance is not equivalent to practical significance, and failure to consider base rates) is illustrated by the following statements?

(a) Using cell phones may cause brain cancer.

(b) Since heart disease and depression are correlated, heart disease must cause depression.

(c) In a large sample population it was observed that the prevalence of hypertension was statistically significantly higher in higher sodium intake individuals. Therefore, everyone should reduce their sodium intake.

29-2. In addition to seeking information to reduce uncertainty, what other two basic principles of quantitative reasoning does the text suggest?

29-3. What should one do after reaching a decision and initiating action?

Answers: 29-1. (a) failure to consider base rates (and also forgetting that correlation is no assurance of causations) (b) correlation is no assurance of causation (c) statistical significance is not equivalent to practical significance **29-2.** Make risk-benefit assessments and list alternative courses of action **29-3.** Continue to reevaluate the decision (in light of treatment progress, new options, etc.).

REVIEW OF KEY TERMS

Acquired Immune Deficiency
  Syndrome (AIDS)
Aggression
Approach-approach conflict
Approach-avoidance conflict
Avoidance-avoidance conflict
Biopsychosocial model
Burnout
Catastrophic thinking
Catharsis
Conflict

Constructive coping
Coping
Defense mechanisms
Fight-or-flight response
Frustration
General adaptation syndrome
Health psychology
Immune response
Internet addiction
Life changes
Optimism

Posttraumatic stress disorder (PTSD)
Pressure
Primary appraisal
Psychosomatic diseases
Rational-emotive therapy
Secondary appraisal
Social support
Stress
Type A personality
Type B personality

_____ 1. Holds that physical illness is caused by a complex interaction of biological, psychological, and sociocultural factors.

_____ 2. Concerned with how psychosocial forces relate to the promotion and maintenance of health, and the causation, prevention and treatment of illness.

_____ 3. Any circumstances that threaten or are perceived to threaten our well-being and thereby tax our coping abilities.

_____ 4. An initial evaluation of whether an event is irrelevant, relevant but not threatening, or stressful.

_____ 5. An evaluation of oneís coping resources and options for dealing with a particular stress.

_____ 6. Occurs in any situation in which the pursuit of some goal is thwarted.

_____ 7. Occurs when two or more incompatible motivations or behavioral impulses compete for expression.

_____ 8. Occurs when a choice must be made between two attractive goals.

_____ 9. Occurs when a choice must be made between two unattractive goals.

_____ 10. Occurs when a choice must be made whether to pursue a single goal that has both attractive and unattractive aspects.

_____ 11. Any noticeable alterations in oneís living circumstances that require readjustment.

_____ 12. Expectations or demands that one behave in a certain way.

_____ 13. A physiological reaction to threat in which the autonomic nervous system mobilizes an organism for either attacking or fleeing an enemy.

_____ 14. A model of the body's stress response consisting of three stages: alarm, resistance and exhaustion.

_____ 15. An active effort to master, reduce or tolerate the demands created by stress.

_____ 16. Involves any behavior that is intended to hurt someone, either physically or verbally.

_____ 17. Consists of spending an inordinate amount of time on the internet and the inability to control online use.

_____ 18. Largely unconscious reactions that protect a person from unpleasant emotions such as anxiety and guilt.

_____ 19. Relatively healthy efforts to deal with stressful events.

_____ 20. Involves physical, mental and emotional exhaustion that is attributable to work-related stress.

_____ 21. Disturbed behavior that emerges after a major stressful event is over.

_____ 22. A behavior pattern marked by competitive, aggressive, impatient, hostile behavior.

_____ 23. A behavior pattern marked by relaxed, patient, easy-going, amicable behavior.

_____ 24. The body's defensive reaction to invasion by bacteria, viral agents, or other foreign substances.

_____ 25. Various types of aid and succor provided by members of one's social network.

_____ 26. A general tendency to expect good outcomes.

_____ 27. An approach to therapy that focuses on altering clients' patterns of irrational thinking to reduce maladaptive emotions and behavior.

_____ 28. The release of emotional tension.

_____ 29. Unrealistic and pessimistic appraisal of stress that exaggerates the magnitude of a problem.

_____ 30. Physical ailments caused in part by psychological factors, especially emotional distress.

_____ 31. A disorder in which the immune system is gradually weakened and eventually disabled by the human immunodeficiency virus (HIV).

Answers: **1.** biopsychosocial model **2.** health psychology **3.** stress **4.** primary appraisal **5.** secondary appraisal **6.** frustration **7.** conflict **8.** approach-approach conflict **9.** avoidance-avoidance conflict **10.** approach-avoidance conflict **11.** life changes **12.** pressure **13.** fight-or-flight response **14.** general adaptation syndrome **15.** coping **16.** aggression **17.** internet addiction **18.** defense mechanisms **19.** constructive coping **20.** burnout **21.** posttraumatic stress disorder **22.** Type A pattern **23.** Type B pattern **24.** immune response **25.** social support **26.** optimism **27.** rational-emotive therapy **28.** catharsis **29.** catastrophic thinking **30.** psychosomatic diseases **31.** Acquired Immune Deficiency Syndrome (AIDS).

REVIEW OF KEY PEOPLE

Walter Cannon
Robin DiMatteo
Albert Ellis
Meyer Friedman & Ray Rosenman

Thomas Holmes & Richard Rahe
Richard Lazarus
Neal Miller

Michael Scheier & Charles Carver
Hans Selye
Shelley Taylor

_____ 1. Observed that minor hassles were more closely related to mental health than were major stressful events.

_____ 2. Noted for his extensive investigations of the three types of conflict.

_____ 3. These researchers developed the Social Readjustment Rating Scale.

_____ 4. One of the first theorists to describe the "fight-or-flight" response.

_____ 5. Coined the word "stress" and described the General Adaptation Syndrome.

_____ 6. These researchers found a connection between coronary risk and what they called Type A behavior.

_____ 7. Researched the notion that some persons may be hardier than others in resisting stress.

_____ 8. The developer of Rational-Emotive Therapy.

_____ 9. These researchers observed a correlation between optimism and good health in a sample of college students.

_____ 10. A leading expert on patient behavior.

Answers: 1. Lazarus **2.** Miller **3.** Holmes & Rahe **4.** Cannon **5.** Selye **6.** Friedman & Rosenman **7.** Ellis **8.** Scheier & Carver **9.** DiMatteo **10.** Taylor.

SELF-QUIZ

1. Which of the following statements regarding stress is incorrect?
   a. Stress is a subjective experience.
   b. The effects of stress are cumulative.
   c. Minor hassles may prove more stressful than major ones.
   d. One should seek to avoid all stress.

2. You've been invited to dinner at a nice restaurant on the final night of a TV mini series you've been watching and thus find yourself confronted with
   a. pressure
   b. frustration
   c. an approach-avoidance conflict
   d. an approach-approach conflict

3. The week of final exams subjects most students to what kind of stress?
   a. pressure
   b. change
   c. frustration
   d. conflict

4. High scores on the Social Readjustment Rating Scale were found to be correlated with psychological disturbances and
   a. type A behavior patterns
   b. physical illness
   c. pessimistic attitudes
   d. all of the above

5. According to optimal-arousal theories, which of the following situations would be least affected by a high optimal-arousal level?
   a. taking a psychology exam
   b. typing a term paper
   c. buttoning a shirt
   d. learning to drive a car

6. The General Adaptation Syndrome shows that the body
   a. gradually adapts to a particular stress
   b. gradually adapts to all form of stress
   c. may gradually weaken and die from continued stress
   d. can react rapidly to all forms of stress

7. Which of the following organs is involved in both of the body's two major stress pathways?
   a. the adrenal gland
   b. the sympathetic nervous system
   c. the pituitary gland
   d. the pineal gland

8. Aggression is frequently triggered by
   a. helplessness
   b. frustration
   c. loneliness
   d. change

9. Which of the following behavioral responses to stress may result in internet addiction?
   a. defensive coping
   b. self-indulgence
   c. positive illusions
   d. giving up

10. Rape and seeing someone die are two of the principal causes of
    a. post-traumatic stress disorder
    b. burnout
    c. learned helplessness
    d. coronary heart disorder

11. Smoking is to lung cancer as Type A behavior is to
    a. coronary disease
    b. AIDS
    c. defensive coping
    d. mental disorders

12. One of the key links between stress and physical illness may be that the body's response to stress
    a. increases the optimal-arousal level
    b. suppresses the immune system
    c. decreases the optimal-arousal level
    d. suppresses the adrenal gland

13. Health-impairing life styles appear to develop
    a. rapidly
    b. unconsciously
    c. slowly
    d. as a defense against stress

14. A major idea behind Rational-Emotive Therapy is that stress is caused by
   a. conflict
   b. frustration
   c. pressure
   d. catastrophic thinking

15. Analyzing the possible gains and losses before undertaking a health-treatment program is an example of
   a. seeking information to reduce uncertainty
   b. listing alternative courses of action
   c. making a risk-benefit analysis
   d. analyzing base rates

Answers: 1. d **2.** d **3.** a **4.** b **5.** c **6.** c **7.** a **8.** b **9.** b **10.** a **11.** a **12.** b **13.** c **14.** d **15.** c.

Chapter Fourteen

Psychological Disorders

REVIEW OF KEY IDEAS

ABNORMAL BEHAVIOR: MYTHS, REALITIES, AND CONTROVERSIES

1. **Describe the medical model of abnormal behavior.**

   1-1. A model is a metaphor or theory that is useful in describing some phenomenon. For example, the computer is frequently used as a model of thinking. The *medical model* uses physical illness as a model of psychological disorders. Under the medical model, maladaptive behavior is referred to as mental

   _____.

   1-2. The term "mental illness" is so familiar to all of us that we rarely think about the meaning of the concept and whether or not the analogy with disease is a good one. Among the model's critics, Thomas Szasz asserts that words such as *sickness*, *illness*, and *disease* are correctly used only in reference to the

   _____, and that it is more appropriate to view abnormal behavior as a deviation from accepted social _____ than as an illness.

   1-3. The text takes an intermediate position. The medical concepts of diagnosis, etiology, and prognosis have proven useful in treatment and study of psychological disorders, so while there are problems with the medical model, it may be of value as long as one understands that it is just a/an _____ and not a true explanation.

   Answers: 1-1. illness (disease, sickness) **1-2.** body, norms (behavior, standards) **1-3.** analogy (model).

2. **Explain the most commonly used criteria of abnormality.**

   2-1. What does abnormal mean? The three criteria most frequently used are *deviance*, *maladaptive behavior*, and *personal distress*.

   (a) _____: Does not *conform* to cultural norms or standards.

(b) _____: Behavior that *interferes with* the individual's social or occupational functioning.

(c) _____: Intense *discomfort* produced by depression or anxiety.

2-2. Following are three statements that describe a person with a particular type of disorder. Which criterion of abnormal behavior is illustrated by each statement? Place the letters from the list above in the appropriate blanks.

____ Ralph washes his hands several dozen times a day. His handwashing interferes with his work and prevents him from establishing normal friendships.

____ Even if Ralph's handwashing compulsion did not interfere with his work and social life, his behavior still would be considered strange. That is, most people do not do what he does.

____ It is also the case that Ralph's skin is very raw, and he becomes extremely anxious when he does not have immediate access to a sink.

2-3. In some cultures, hearing voices or speaking with gods may be valued. In our culture, however, such behavior is likely to be considered abnormal. While the major categories of disorder may transcend culture, our assessments of abnormality are nonetheless value judgments that are strongly influenced by our _____. Thus, one of the problems involved in defining abnormality is that there are no criteria for psychological disorders that are entirely _____ -free.

2-4. Evolutionary psychologists have recently proposed that abnormality be considered simply an evolved mechanism that is not functioning effectively. For example, as a mechanism for alerting the organism to danger, anxiety has _____ value; as a persistent emotion in the absence of danger it interferes with functioning. While this approach is an attempt to make the criteria of mental illness less _____ -laden, critics question whether or not the viewpoint will in fact yield more objective criteria.

Answers: 2-1. (a) deviance (b) maladaptive behavior (c) personal distress **2-2.** b, a, c **2-3.** culture (society), value (culture) **2-4.** adaptive (survival, evolutionary), value.

3. List three stereotypes of people with psychological disorders.

3-1. In the space below list three stereotypes of people with psychological disorders:

(a) The disorders are _____.

(b) People with the disorders are _____ and dangerous.

(c) People with the disorders behave in a bizarre manner and are very _____ from normal people.

Answers: 3-1. (a) incurable (b) violent (c) different.

4. **Summarize the Featured Study on the admission of pseudopatients to mental hospitals.**

   4-1. What type of people did Rosenhan seek to have admitted to mental hospitals?

   4-2. Once they were admitted, did the pseudopatients continue to complain of hearing voices, or did they behave normally?

   4-3. What proportion of the pseudopatients were admitted to the hospital?

   4-4. Indicate *true* of *false* for each of the following statements.

   _____ (a) Once the patients no longer claimed to hear voices, the professional staff rapidly recognized that they were not abnormal.

   _____ b) Most of the pseudopatients were dismissed within a couple of days.

   _____ (c) The diagnosis for most of the pseudopatients was that they suffered from a relatively mild form of mental disorder.

   4-5. What is the major implication to be drawn from Rosenhan's study?

Answers: 4-1. normal individuals **4-2.** behaved normally **4-3.** all of them (Eight people sought admission to mental hospitals in five states, and all of them were admitted.) **4-4.** (a) false (b) false (The shortest stay was 7 days, the longest 52 days, and the average 19 days.) (c) false (Most were diagnosed with schizophrenia, a severe form of mental illness.) **4-5.** The major implication is that it is difficult, even for mental health professionals, to distinguish normal from abnormal behavior. (The study may also be interpreted to mean that there is a bias toward seeing abnormality where it may not exist or that abnormality is easily feigned.)

5. **List the five diagnostic axes of DSM-IV.**

   5-1. Below are descriptions of the five axes of the DSM-IV classification system. Label each with the correct axis number (I through V).

   _____ Listing of physical disorders

   _____ Diagnosis of long-running personality disorders or mental retardation

   _____ Diagnosis of most of the disorders

   _____ Estimates of the individual's current level of adaptive functioning (social and occupational)

   _____ Notes concerning the severity of stress experienced by the individual in the past year

5-2. The new DSM system has produced praise but some criticism as well. While the consistency it brought to diagnosis is a critically important step, it is important only to the extent that the categories accurately describe real conditions. Some critics have argued that consistency came at the price of sacrificing interest in the _____ of the diagnostic categories.

5-3. Second, decisions about revision of the DSM are made by committees, committees that, it is argued, may be more persuaded by the rhetorical skills of a few committee members than the available _____ evidence.

5-4. Third, the recent DSMs include everyday problems that are not traditionally thought of as mental illnesses (such as nicotine-dependence disorder and gambling disorder). Although it may seem odd to include these in the DSM, what is the advantage of doing so?

Answers: **5-1.** III, II, I, V, IV **5-2.** validity **5-3.** empirical **5-4.** Since many health insurance policies reimburse only for treatment of disorders listed in the DSM, including these "everyday" problems may permit people to bill their insurance companies for treatment.

6. Discuss estimates of the prevalence of psychological disorders.

6-1. Epidemiological studies assess the prevalence of various disorders across a specific period of time. Prevalence refers to the _____ of a population that exhibits a disorder during a specified period of time. For mental disorders, the time period is usually (<u>one year/the entire lifespan</u>).

6-2. According to our best (if still approximate) estimates, what is the prevalence of mental illness in the United States? _____

Answers: **6-1.** percentage (proportion), the entire lifespan **6-2.** Approximately one-third of our population suffers from some form of mental illness at some point in their lives.

ANXIETY DISORDERS

7. List four types of anxiety disorders and describe the symptoms associated with each.

7-1. List the names of the four anxiety syndromes in the space below. As hints, the initial letters of some key words are listed at the left.

GAD: _____

PhD: _____

OCD: _____

PDA: _____ and _____

7-2. Match the anxiety disorders with the symptoms that follow by placing the appropriate letters (from the previous question) in the blanks.

(a) _____   Sudden, unexpected, and paralyzing attacks of anxiety

(b) _____   Not tied to a specific object or event

(c) _____   Senseless, repetitive rituals

(d) _____ Brooding over decisions

(e) _____ Fear of specific objects or situations

(f) _____ Persistent intrusion of distressing and unwanted thoughts

(g) _____ Free-floating anxiety

(h) _____ Frequently includes fear of going out in public

Answers: 7-1. generalized anxiety disorder, phobic disorder, obsessive-compulsive disorder, panic disorder and agoraphobia **7-2.** (a) PDA (in this example, panic attacks) (b) GAD (c) OCD (d) GAD (e) PhD (f) OCD (g) GAD (h) PDA (in this case, agoraphobia).

8. **Discuss the contribution of biological, cognitive, and personality factors, conditioning, and stress to the etiology of anxiety disorders.**

8-1.   Several types of studies suggest there are inherited differences between people in the extent to which they are predisposed to anxiety disorders. For example, twin studies find higher concordance rates for anxiety among _____ twins than _____ twins.

8-2.   Other biological evidence implicates disturbances at synapses using GABA for some types of anxiety disorders and of serotonin for panic attacks and obsessive-compulsive disorder. Thus, the body chemicals known as _____ appear to play an important role in anxiety.

8-3.   Conditioning or learning clearly plays a role as well. For example, if an individual is bitten by a dog, he or she may develop a fear of dogs through the process of _____ conditioning. The individual may then avoid dogs in the future, a response maintained by _____ conditioning.

8-4.   People are more likely to be afraid of snakes than of hot irons. Using Seligman's notion of preparedness, explain why.

8-5.   Two types of anecdotal evidence do not support the conditioning point of view. For example, people with phobias (always can/frequently cannot) recall a traumatic incident, and people who have experienced extreme traumas (always/frequently do not) develop phobias.

8-6.   As discussed in Chapter 6, the conditioning models are being extended to include a larger role for cognitive factors. For example, children probably acquire fears by _____ the behavior of anxious parents.

8-7.   In addition, cognitive theorists indicate that certain *thinking styles* contribute to anxiety. For example, as indicated in your text, the sentence "The doctor examined little Emma's growth" could refer either to height or to a tumor. People who are high in anxiety will tend to perceive the (tumor/height) interpretation. People's readiness to perceive threat, in other words, appears to be related to their tendency to experience _____ .

8-8. Personality also plays a role. Not surprisingly, people who score high on the _____ trait of the "big five" personality factors have an elevated prevalence of anxiety disorders and a poorer prognosis for recovery.

8-9. Finally, *stress* is related to the anxiety disorders. Studies described in your text indicate that stress is related both to _____ disorder and to the development of social _____.

Answers: **8-1.** identical, fraternal **8-2.** neurotransmitters **8-3.** classical, operant **8-4.** Preparedness is Seligman's notion that human beings have evolved to be more prepared or more ready to be conditioned to some stimuli than to others. We have evolved to be more afraid of snakes than of hot irons, the latter having appeared only relatively recently in our evolutionary history. (As a whole, research has provided only modest support for the idea of preparedness in acquisition of phobias.) **8-5.** frequently cannot, frequently do not **8-6.** observing **8-7.** tumor, anxiety **8-8.** neuroticism **8-9.** panic, phobia.

SOMATOFORM DISORDERS

9. Compare and contrast the three somatoform disorders and discuss their etiology.

9-1. For each of the following symptoms, indicate which disorder is described by placing the appropriate letters in the blanks: S for somatization, C for conversion, and H for hypochondriasis.

_____ Serious disability that may include paralysis, loss of vision or hearing, loss of feeling, and so on.

_____ Many different minor physical ailments accompanied by a long history of medical treatment.

_____ Cannot believe the doctor's report that the person is not really ill.

_____ Symptoms that appear to be organic in origin but don't match underlying anatomical organization.

_____ Diverse complaints that implicate many different organ systems.

_____ Usually does not involve disability so much as overinterpreting slight possible signs of illness.

_____ "Glove anesthesia"; seizures without loss of bladder control.

9-2. In the film *Hannah and Her Sisters* Woody Allen is convinced that certain minor physical changes are a sign of cancer. When tests eventually find no evidence of cancer, he is sure the tests have been done incorrectly. Which of the somatoform disorders does this seem to represent? _____

9-3. The somatoform disorders are associated with certain personality types, with particular cognitive styles, and with learning. Among personality types, the self-centered, excitable, and overly dramatic _____ personalities are more at risk for developing these disorders. As with the anxiety disorders, the trait of _____ also appears to be related to somatoform disorders.

9-4. With regard to cognitive factors, focusing excessive attention on internal _____ factors, or believing that good health should involve a complete lack of discomfort, may also contribute to somatoform disorders.

9-5. With regard to learning, the sick role may be positively reinforced through, for example, _____ from others or negatively reinforced by _____ certain of life's problems or unpleasant aspects.

DISSOCIATIVE DISORDERS

10.   Describe three dissociative disorders and discuss their etiology.

10-1.   The three dissociative disorders involve memory and identity. Two of the disorders involve fairly massive amounts of forgetting, dissociative _____ and dissociative _____.

10-2.   People who have been in serious accidents frequently can't remember the accident or events surrounding the accident. This type of memory loss, which involves specific traumatic events, is known as dissociative _____.

10-3.   An even greater memory loss, in which people lose their memories for their entire lives along with their sense of identity, is termed dissociative _____.

10-4.   You may have seen media characterizations of individuals who can't remember who they are—what their names are, where they live, who their family is, and so on. While popularly referred to as amnesia, this type of dissociative disorder is more correctly called dissociative _____.

10-5.   A few years ago there was a spate of appearances on talk shows by guests who claimed to have more than one identity or personality. This disorder is still widely known as _____-_____ disorder (MPD), but the formal name in the DSM-IV is _____ _____ disorder (DID). The disorder is also often (<u>correctly/mistakenly</u>) called schizophrenia.

10-6.   What causes dissociative disorders? Dissociative amnesia and dissociative fugue are related to excessive _____, but little else is known about why these extreme reactions occur in a tiny minority of people.

10-7.   With regard to multiple-personality disorder, the diagnosis is controversial. Although many clinicians believe that the disorder is authentic, Spanos argues that it is the product of media attention and the misguided probings of a small minority of psychotherapists. In other words, Spanos believes that MPD (<u>is/is not</u>) a genuine disorder.

10-8.   While the majority of people with multiple-personality disorders report having been emotionally and sexually _____ in childhood, little is known about the causes of this controversial diagnosis. In fact, in a recent survey of American psychiatrists only _____ of those polled believed that there was enough scientific evidence to warrant including DID as a valid diagnostic category.

MOOD DISORDERS

11. Describe the two major mood disorders.

11-1. While the terms *manic* and *depressive* describe mood, they refer to a number of other characteristics as well, listed below. With one or two words for each characteristic describe the manic and depressive episodes. (Before you make the lists, it may be a good idea to review Table 14.1 and the sections on depressive and bipolar mood disorders.)

	Manic	*Depressive*
mood:	_____	_____
sleep:	_____	_____
activity:	_____	_____
speech:	_____	_____
sex drive:	_____	_____

11-2. Be sure to note that mania and depression are not the names of the two affective disorders. What is the name of the disorder accompanied only by depression? _____ By both manic and depressive states? _____

11-3. The DSM refers to persistent but relatively mild symptoms of depressive disorder as _____ disorder, and to persistent but mild symptoms of bipolar disorder as _____ disorder.

Answers: 11-1. mood: euphoric (elated, extremely happy, etc.) vs. depressed (blue, extremely sad); sleep: goes without or doesn't want to vs. can't (insomnia); activity: very active vs. sluggish, slow, inactive; speech: very fast vs. very slow; sex drive: increased vs. decreased **11-2.** unipolar disorder (major depressive disorder), bipolar disorder **11-3.** dysthymic, cyclothymic.

12. Explain how genetic and neurochemical factors may be related to the development of mood disorders.

12-1. Twin studies implicate genetic factors in the development of mood disorders. In a sentence, summarize the results of these studies.

12-2. While the exact mechanism is not known, correlations have been found between mood disorders and the activities of such _____ as norepinephrine and serotonin. Of these two, recent research suggests that _____ may be the more important, although imbalances among several neurotransmitters appear to be involved.

Answers: 12-1. For mood disorders, the concordance rate for identical twins is much higher than that for fraternal twins (about 67% for the former compared to 15% for the latter). **12-2.** neurotransmitters (neurochemicals), serotonin.

13. **Explain how cognitive factors, interpersonal factors, and stress may be related to the development of mood disorders.**

13-1.   Martin Seligman's model of depression is referred to as the _____ model. While he originally based his theory of depression on an animal conditioning model involving exposure to unavoidable aversive stimuli, he has more recently emphasized (<u>cognitive/behavioral</u>) factors.

13-2.   According to the revised version of learned helplessness, people with a _____ explanatory style are particularly prone to depression. For example, people who attribute obstacles to (<u>situational factors/personal flaws</u>) are more likely to experience depression.

13-3.   Building on learned helplessness theory, _____ theory maintains that a pessimistic explanatory style is just one of several factors—stress and low self-esteem are others—that contribute to depression. For example, people who repetitively focus or _____ about their depression are more likely to remain depressed.

13-4.   With regard to interpersonal factors, depressed people tend to lack _____ skills. How does this characteristic affect the ability to obtain reinforcers?

13-5.   Why do we tend to reject depressed people?

13-6.   What is the relationship between stress and the onset of mood disorders?

Answers: 13-1. learned helplessness, cognitive **13-2.** pessimistic (negative), personal flaws **13-3.** hopelessness, ruminate **13-4.** social (interpersonal). Lack of social skills makes it difficult to obtain certain reinforcers, such as good friends and desirable jobs. **13-5.** Because they are not pleasant to be around. Depressed people complain a lot, are irritable, and tend to pass their mood along to others. **13-6.** There is a moderately strong link between stress and the onset of mood disorders.

SCHIZOPHRENIC DISORDERS

14. **Describe the general characteristics (symptoms) of schizophrenia.**

14-1.   Before we review the different types of schizophrenia, consider some general characteristics of the schizophrenic disorders, as follows.

(a) Delusions and irrational thought: Delusions are false (<u>beliefs/perceptions</u>) (e.g., the idea that one is a world-famous political figure who is being pursued by terrorists when this is not in fact true).

(b) Deterioration of adaptive behavior: The deterioration usually involves social relationships, work, and neglect of personal _____.

(c) Hallucinations: Hallucinations are _____ that occur in the absence of a real stimulus. The most common hallucinations are (<u>auditory/visual</u>).

(d) Disturbed emotion: Emotional responsiveness may be disturbed in a variety of ways. The person may have little or no responsiveness, referred to as _____ affect, or they may show _____ emotional responses, such as laughing at news of a tragic death.

Answers: 14-1. (a) beliefs (b) hygiene (cleanliness) (c) sensory perceptions (perceptions, sensory experiences, perceptual distortions), auditory (d) flat (flattened, blunted), inappropriate (bizarre).

15. **Describe two classification systems for schizophrenic subtypes and discuss the course of schizophrenia.**

15-1. Write the names of the four recognized subcategories of schizophrenia next to the descriptions that follow.

(a) _____ type: Particularly severe deterioration, incoherence, complete social withdrawal, aimless babbling and giggling, delusions centering on bodily functions.

(b) _____ type: Muscular rigidity and stupor at one extreme or random motor activity, hyperactivity, and incoherence at the other; now quite rare.

(c) _____ type: Delusions of persecution and grandeur.

(d) _____ type: Clearly schizophrenic but doesn't fit other three categories.

15-2. Several critics have asserted that there are no meaningful differences among the categories listed above and have proposed an alternative classification system. Nancy Andreasen and others have described a classification system consisting of only two categories, one that consists of _____ symptoms and the other of _____ symptoms.

15-3. In Andreasen's system, "positive" and "negative" do not mean pleasant and unpleasant. Positive symptoms *add* something to behavior (like chaotic speech), and negative symptoms *subtract* something (like social withdrawal). Indicate which of the following are positive and which negative by placing a P or an N in the appropriate blanks.

_____ flattened emotions

_____ hallucinations

_____ bizarre behavior

_____ social withdrawal

_____ apathy

_____ nonstop babbling

_____ doesn't speak

15-4. Theorists hoped that classification of schizophrenia into positive and negative symptoms would provide more meaningful categories in terms of etiology and prognosis. Some differentiation between the two types of symptoms has been found; for example, *positive* symptoms seem to be associated with (better/worse) adjustment prior to the onset of schizophrenia and a (better/worse) prognosis. All in all, however, this system (has/has not) produced a classification that can replace the traditional subtypes.

15-5.   When does schizophrenia tend to emerge?

15-6.   Mark the following T (true) or F (false).

_____   Schizophrenia may have either a sudden or gradual onset.

_____   A schizophrenic can never truly recover from the disorder.

_____   About half of schizophrenic patients experience a significant degree of recovery.

_____   Males tend to have an earlier onset of schizophrenia than females.

_____   Males tend to have more hospitalizations and higher relapse rates than females.

Answers: 15-1. (a) disorganized (b) catatonic (c) paranoid (d) undifferentiated **15-2.** positive, negative **15-3.** N, P, P, N, N, P, N **15-4.** better, better, has not **15-5.** generally during adolescence and early adulthood, rarely after age 45 **15-6.** T, F, T, T, T.

16.   Explain how genetic vulnerability, neurochemical factors, and structural abnormalities in the brain may contribute to the etiology of schizophrenia.

16-1.   As with mood disorders, twin studies implicate genetic factors in the development of schizophrenia. In a sentence, summarize the general results of these studies.

16-2.   As with mood disorders, neurotransmitter substances in the brain are implicated in the etiology of schizophrenia. Although the evidence is somewhat clouded, what is the name of the neurotransmitter thought to be involved? _____

16-3.   In addition to possible neurochemical factors, certain differences in brain structure may be associated with schizophrenia. One of these differences involves enlarged brain _____, which are hollow fluid-filled cavities in the brain. Current thinking, however, is that this brain abnormality is an _____ rather than a cause of schizophrenia.

16-4.   Current research points to the thalamus as a possible structural factor in schizophrenia. The thalamus in schizophrenics tends to be (smaller/larger) and show less metabolic activity than is the case for nonschizophrenics.

Answers: 16-1. For schizophrenia, the concordance rate is higher for identical than for fraternal twins (about 48% for identical compared with about 17% for fraternal twins). (For comparison, recall that the respective percentages found for mood disorders were about 67% and 15%.) **16-2.** dopamine (thought to be a factor because most drugs useful in treating schizophrenia decrease dopamine activity in the brain) **16-3.** ventricles, effect **16-4.** smaller.

17.   Summarize evidence on how neurodevelopmental processes, family dynamics, and stress may be related to the development of schizophrenia.

17-1.   The _____ hypothesis of schizophrenia maintains that schizophrenia is caused in part by early neurological damage that occurs either prenatally or during the birth process.

17-2. Among the causes of neurological damage are _____ infections; _____ which may occur, for example, during famine; and complications that occur during _____.

17-3. Expressed emotion refers to the extent to which a patient's relatives are overly critical or protective or are in other ways overly emotionally involved with the patient. Patients returning to families that are high in expressed emotion have a relapse rate that is much (higher/lower) than that of families low in expressed emotion.

17-4. What role does stress play in the etiology of schizophrenia? Stress is a fact of life, and it is obvious that not everyone who experiences stress develops schizophrenia. Current thinking is that stress may be a precipitating factor for people who are biologically or for other reasons already _____ to schizophrenia.

Answers: **17-1.** neurodevelopmental **17-2.** viral (flu), malnutrition (starvation), delivery (birth, the birth process) **17-3.** higher **17-3.** vulnerable (predisposed).

PERSONALITY DISORDERS

18. Discuss the nature of personality disorders and describe the three broad clusters of such disorders.

18-1. The personality disorders, recorded on Axis II, are frequently (less/more) severe versions of disorders on Axis I. These disorders consist of relatively extreme and (flexible/inflexible) sets of personality traits that cause subjective distress or impaired functioning.

18-2. DSM-IV lists ten disorders, classified into three clusters, as follows:

(a) _____-fearful cluster

(b) _____-eccentric cluster

(c) _____-impulsive cluster

18-3. Match the clusters listed in the previous question with the following descriptions by placing the appropriate letters in the blanks.

_____ Distrustful, aloof, unable to connect emotionally with others

_____ Maladaptive efforts to control fear of social rejection

_____ Overly dramatic or impulsive

18-4. A major problem with the classification of personality disorders is that there is an enormous _____ between the disorders and Axis I, and among the disorders themselves. For example, one study found that the majority of patients diagnosed with a histrionic personality disorder (one of the dramatic-impulsive clusters) also qualified for two or more other personality disorders.

18-5. In hopes of remedying these problems, some theorists have suggested that rather than using nonoverlapping categories, personality disorders should be described in terms of continuous scores on a set of personality _____. While this approach has many advocates, psychologists are not in agreement about which personality dimensions to use or even whether or not this approach has clinical utility.

Answers: 18-1. less, inflexible **18-2.** anxious, odd, dramatic **18-3.** b, a, c **18-4.** overlap **18-5.** dimensions (factors, traits).

19. Describe the antisocial personality disorder and discuss its etiology.

19-1. The *antisocial* personality disorder is more extensively researched than are the other personality disorders and is described in more detail in your text. Check the concepts from the following list that are likely to correctly describe this disorder.

_____ sexually promiscuous   _____ genuinely affectionate

_____ manipulative   _____ impulsive

_____ feels guilty   _____ lacks an adequate conscience

_____ much more likely to occur in males than females   _____ may appear charming

_____ may be a con artist, thug, or unprincipled business executive

19-2. What types of studies support the idea that biological factors are involved in the etiology of the antisocial personality?

19-3. What environmental factors seem to be related to development of an antisocial personality?

Answers: 19-1. All the terms describe the antisocial personality except for *feels guilty* and *genuinely affectionate*. **19-2.** Twin and adoption studies. (There also has been mixed support for Eysenck's idea that antisocial personalities are chronically lower in autonomic arousal and therefore less likely to develop conditioned inhibitions.) **19-3.** Studies suggest that inconsistent, ineffective, or abusive parental discipline may be involved. Since one or both parents may also exhibit antisocial characteristics, observational learning may also be a factor.

PSYCHOLOGICAL DISORDERS AND THE LAW

20. Explain the legal concept of insanity and discuss the grounds for involuntary commitment.

20-1. While the words *insane* and *schizophrenic* may in some cases apply to the same person, the terms do not mean the same thing. The term _____ is a legal term, while _____ is a descriptive term used in psychological diagnosis. For example, an individual troubled by hallucinations and delusions probably fits the category of _____. An individual who is judged by a court not to be responsible for his or her actions would be classified (under the M'naghten rule) as _____.

20-2. The following items concern the insanity defense. Mark True or False.

_____ The insanity defense is used in fewer than 1% of homicide cases.

_____ Available evidence suggests that in by far the majority of cases in which is it used, the insanity defense is a successful defense (i.e., wins the case).

20-3. Roughly, how is insanity defined under the M'naghten rule?

20-4. More frequent than judgments of insanity are proceedings related to involuntary commitment to a psychiatric facility. Answer the following questions about involuntary commitment.

(a) What three criteria are used to determine whether an individual should be committed?

(b) What is required to temporarily commit an individual for one to three days?

(c) What is required for longer-term commitment?

20-5. What American ethical-cultural tradition is ignored in involuntary commitment?

Answers: 20-1. insane, schizophrenic, schizophrenic, insane **20-2.** true, false **20-3.** The M'naghten rule says that insanity exists when a person cannot distinguish right from wrong. **20-4.** (a) In general, for people to be involuntarily committed, mental health and legal authorities must judge them to be (1) dangerous to themselves or (2) dangerous to others, or (3) in extreme need of treatment. (b) Temporary commitment (usually 24 to 72 hours) may be done in emergencies by a psychologist or psychiatrist. (c) Longer-term commitments are issued by a court and require a formal hearing. **20-5.** The principle that people are innocent until proven guilty in a court. Involuntary commitment involves detention (in a mental health facility) without having been proven guilty.

CULTURE AND PATHOLOGY

21. Discuss the evidence on three issues related to culture and pathology.

21-1. Your text divides viewpoints about culture and pathology into *relativists* and *panculturalists*. The

_____ believe that there are basic standards of mental health that are *universal* across

cultures. The _____ believe that psychological disorders *vary as a function of culture*.

21-2. Several questions reflect on this issue. First, are the *same disorders* found in different cultures? To some extent, yes. The three most severe disorders, listed below, are identifiable throughout the world:

_____

_____

_____

21-3. On the other hand, disorders such as hypochondriasis, narcissistic personality, generalized anxiety disorder, and other forms of (milder/more severe) disturbance are not recognized as disorders in some cultures.

21-4. In addition, there are (no disorders/some disorders) that are unique to particular cultures. For example, the obsessive fear about one's penis withdrawing into one's abdomen is found only among Chinese males in Malaya, and _____ nervosa is found only in affluent Western societies.

21-5. The second question concerns whether or not *patterns of symptoms* are similar across cultures. In general, they are. But while delusions are characteristic of schizophrenia in (only Western/all) cultures, the specific delusions reported (vary/are invariant) across cultures. For example, satellites or microwave ovens would not be a part of the delusional systems of people in less technologically advanced countries.

21-6. The third question concerns prevalence rates. For two of the major disorders, _____ and _____ disorder, prevalence rates are quite similar across cultures, about 1 percent, which may be attributable to the strong biological component of these disorders. For most of the other disorders prevalence rates (vary considerably/are fairly constant) across cultures.

21-7. In summary, are psychological disorders universal, or do they vary across cultures?

a. There are some universal standards of normality and abnormality.

b. There are some disorders that are specific to particular cultures.

c. Both of the above: some aspects of psychopathology are universal, some vary as a function of culture.

Answers: **21-1.** panculturalists, relativists **21-2.** schizophrenia, depression, bipolar disorder **21-3.** milder **21-4.** some disorders, anorexia **21-5.** all, vary **21-6.** schizophrenia, bipolar, vary considerably **21-7.** c.

PUTTING IT IN PERSPECTIVE

22. Explain how this chapter highlighted four of the text's organizing themes.

22-1. Below are examples of the highlighted themes. Indicate which theme fits each example by writing the appropriate abbreviations in the blanks: MC for multifactorial causation, HE for the interplay of heredity and environment, SH for sociohistorical context, and C for the influence of culture.

(a) Mood and schizophrenic disorders will occur if one has a genetic vulnerability to the disorder *and* if one experiences a considerable amount of stress. ____

(b) Psychological disorders are caused by neurochemical factors, brain abnormalities, styles of child rearing, life stress, and so on. ____

(c) Anorexia nervosa occurs almost exclusively in affluent Western societies. ____

(d) Decades ago homosexuality was classified as a disorder; in recent DSMs it is not. ____ and ____

Answers: 22-1. (a) HE (b) MC (c) C (d) SH, C.

PERSONAL APPLICATION: UNDERSTANDING EATING DISORDERS

23. **Describe the symptoms and medical complications of anorexia nervosa and bulimia nervosa .**

23-1. What are the names of the two major categories of eating disorder? _____ and

_____

23-2. The most obvious feature of anorexia nervosa is the drastic weight loss that accompanies the disorder. Other characteristics include an intense _____ of gaining weight, a disturbed _____ (they think they are fat, no matter how emaciated they become), and (struggling/refusal) to maintain normal weight.

23-3. The two major subtypes of anorexia have in common a dangerous weight loss. In one case this is accompanied by _____ (severely limiting food eaten) and in the other by bingeing and then _____ (vomiting, using laxatives and diuretics) as well as engagin in excessive exercise.

23-4. The weight loss that accompanies anorexia nervosa is substantial, typically 25-30% below normal weight. A critical diagnostic criterion for anorexia nervosa in women is amenorrhea, the loss of the _____ cycle.

23-5. There are other consequences as well, including serious gastrointestinal difficulties, heart and circulatory problems, and osteoporosis, all of which may lead to death in approximately ____% of cases. Anorexia nervosa patients (usually/rarely) seek treatment on their own.

23-6. Bulimia nervosa shares many of the characteristics of the binge-eating/purging type of anorexia. Its main differentiating feature is the fact that people with bulimia maintain a (relatively normal/drastically decreased) body weight. They are also somewhat more likely to recognize that there is a problem and to cooperate with treatment.

Answers: 23-1. anorexia nervosa, bulimia nervosa **23-2.** fear, body image, refusal **23-3.** restricting, purging **23-4.** menstrual **23-5.** 2-10%, rarely **23-6.** relatively normal.

24. **Discuss the history, prevalence, and gender distribution of eating disorders.**

24-1. Anorexia nervosa was extremely (common/rare) and bulimia nervosa (omnipresent/nonexistent) prior to the middle of the 20th century. Obviously, culture has a great deal to do with this disorder; the combination of abundant food and the desire for thinness that seem to have been a major impetus for the problem. Thus, eating disorders are in large part a product of (Western/developing) cultures.

24-2. Probably as a result of the greater pressure on women to fit the current fashion of thinness, about ____% of individuals with eating disorders are female. Studies suggest that about 1-1.5% of young women develop _____ nervosa and about 2-3% _____ nervosa. The typical age of onset of the disorders is (before/after) age 21. Therapeutic interventions claim some success, but it is estimated that only about ____% of patients experience a full recovery.

Answers: **24-1.** rare, nonexistent, Western **24-2.** 90-95%, anorexia, bulimia, before, 40-50%.

25. Explain how genetic factors, personality, and culture may contribute to eating disorders.

25-1. Data from _____ studies and studies of relatives of people with eating disorders suggest that there is some degree of genetic predisposition for the disorders.

25-2. There are also personality correlates of the disorders that may reflect an underlying vulnerability. For example, people who are impulsive, overly sensitive, and low in self-esteem are more likely to suffer from (bulimia/anorexia) nervosa. People characterized as neurotic, obsessive, and rigid are more likely to have (bulimia/anorexia) nervosa.

25-3. As mentioned previously, cultural values are clearly implicated as well. Over the last half of the 20th century eating disorders (increased/decreased) in prevalence as the ideal body weight (increased/decreased). Although one cannot make causal conclusions it seems likely that the cultural milieu is a major factor in eating disorders.

Answers: **25-1.** twin **25-2.** bulimia, anorexia **25-3.** increased, decreased

26. Explain how family dynamics and disturbed thinking may contribute to eating disorders.

26-1. It is very difficult to sort out cause and effect in case and informal studies, but some theorists contend that parents who are (underinvolved/overly involved) in their children's lives unintentionally push their adolescent children to exert autonomy through pathological eating patterns. Other theorists contend that mothers pass along the thinness message by _____ unhealthy dieting practices.

26-2. Disturbed thinking seems to accompany eating disorders, but whether it is a cause or a result of the disorders is hard to say. (For example, studies of food deprivation in volunteer subjects also find disturbed thinking processes.) In any case, the type of thinking may be characterized as _____ thinking (e.g., If I am not thin, I am nothing; if I eat, I am not in control of my life.).

Answers: **26-1.** overly involved, modeling (endorsing, agreeing with, passing on) **26-2.** rigid (all or none, dichotomous).

CRITICAL THINKING APPLICATION

27. Discuss how mental heuristics can distort estimates of cumulative and conjunctive probabilities.

27-1. Basing an estimate of probability on the extent to which an event is similar to a prototype (or mental representation) is a distortion in thinking referred to as the _____ heuristic.

27-2. Over a lifetime, what is the probability that someone will be afflicted with mental illness? Higher than most people think, about one chance in three. People underestimate this probability in part because when they think of mental illness, they think of severe disturbances, such as schizophrenia. When a _____ such as this comes to mind, people tend to ignore information about _____. This bias in our thinking is called the _____.

27-3. In fact, the lifetime mental illness referred to could be schizophrenia, or obsessive-compulsive disorder, or phobia, or substance abuse disorder, or any of an enormous number of other disorders. Each "or" in this instance should involve (<u>adding/subtracting</u>) estimates of the appropriate probabilities, an example of (<u>conjunctive/cumulative</u>) probabilities. The representativeness heuristic, however, results in our estimating probabilities based on similarity to a _____.

27-4. Here is another probability question: Which of the following is more likely (a or b)?

a. having a phobia

b. having a phobia and being obsessive-compulsive

You don't have to know anything about these disorders or their actual probabilities to know that the answer is _____. In this example, you implicitly know that the likelihood of two events occurring together is less than that of either of these events occurring alone. This example illustrates "and" relationships or _____ probabilities.

27-5. Sometimes the answer is not so apparent. Consider this question:

John was reported to have been brain damaged at birth. At age 14, John's IQ was measured as 70. Of the following, which is most likely? _____

a. John wins a Nobel prize at age 40.

b. John is given an experimental treatment for retardation; John wins a Nobel prize at age 40.

c. John was mixed up with another baby; John's IQ test was scored incorrectly; John wins a Nobel prize at age 40.

27-6. The answer to the previous question is another example of _____ probabilities. If you, like most people that I have shown this problem, picked some answer other than "a," you made the error known as the _____ fallacy.

27-7. Why do we make the conjunction fallacy? In part the mistake results, again, from our tendency to be influenced by prototypes, the _____ heuristic. Even though we know that, logically, the likelihood of two events occurring together is less than the probability of either occurring alone, the additional "explanation" makes the combined result seem more reasonable. In fact, it is just another example of _____ probabilities.

27-8. When you first read about mood disorders, or obsessive-compulsive disorder, or generalized anxiety disorder, or hypochondriasis, did you tend to think that each description might fit you or one of your friends? If so, you were probably influenced by the _____ heuristic.

27-9. The availability heuristic involves the ease with which we can bring something to

_____. The more readily we can think of some event, the more likely it is to influence our judgment about its frequency or _____.

27-10. Review. If one estimates probability based on a mental image or prototype, one is using the _____. If a probability estimate involves several different events occurring together, then one is dealing in _____ probabilities. If any of several events may occur, then _____ probabilities are involved. If we think that two events occurring together are more likely than either occurring alone, we have made the error known as the _____. If we base our estimate of probability on the ease with which something comes to mind, we are using the _____.

Answers: 27-1. representativeness **27-2.** prototype (mental representation), probability, representativeness heuristic **27-3.** adding, cumulative, prototype **27-4.** a, conjunctive **27-5.** a **27-6.** conjunctive, conjunction **27-7.** representativeness, conjunctive **27-8.** availability **27-9.** mind, probability **27-10.** representativeness heuristic, conjunctive, cumulative, conjunction fallacy, availability heuristic.

REVIEW OF KEY TERMS

Agoraphobia
Anorexia nervosa
Antisocial personality disorder
Anxiety disorders
Availability heuristic
Bipolar disorders
Bulimia nervosa
Catatonic schizophrenia
Comorbidity
Concordance rate
Conjunction fallacy
Conversion disorder
Culture-bound disorders
Cyclothymic disorder
Delusions
Diagnosis
Disorganized schizophrenia

Dissociative amnesia
Dissociative disorders
Dissociative fugue
Dissociative identity disorder
Dysthymic disorder
Eating disorders
Epidemiology
Etiology
Generalized anxiety disorder
Hallucinations
Hypochondriasis
Insanity
Involuntary commitment
Major depressive disorder
Medical model
Mood disorders

Multiple-personality disorder
Negative symptoms
Obsessive-compulsive disorder (OCD)
Panic disorder
Paranoid schizophrenia
Personality disorders
Phobic disorder
Positive symptoms
Prevalence
Prognosis
Psychosomatic diseases
Representativeness heuristic
Schizophrenic disorders
Somatization disorder
Somatoform disorders
Undifferentiated schizophrenia

_____ 1. Proposes that it is useful to think of abnormal behavior as a disease.

_____ 2. Involves distinguishing one illness from another.

_____ 3. Refers to the apparent causation and developmental history of an illness.

_____ 4. A forecast about the possible course of an illness.

_____ 5. An eating disorder characterized by fear of gaining weight, disturbed body image, refusal to maintain normal weight, and dangerous measures to lose weight.

_____ 6. The study of the distribution of mental or physical disorders in a population.

_____ 7. Refers to the percentage of a population that exhibits a disorder during a specified time period.

_____ **8.** A class of disorders marked by feelings of excessive apprehension and anxiety.

_____ **9.** Disorder marked by a chronic high level of anxiety that is not tied to any specific threat.

_____ **10.** Disorder marked by a persistent and irrational fear of an object or situation that presents no realistic danger.

_____ **11.** Disorder that involves recurrent attacks of overwhelming anxiety that usually occur suddenly and unexpectedly.

_____ **12.** Disorder marked by persistent uncontrollable intrusions of unwanted thoughts and urges to engage in senseless rituals.

_____ **13.** A fear of going out in public places.

_____ **14.** Physical ailments with a genuine organic basis that are caused in part by psychological factors.

_____ **15.** A class of disorders involving physical ailments that have no authentic organic basis and are due to psychological factors.

_____ **16.** Disorder marked by a history of diverse physical complaints that appear to be psychological in origin.

_____ **17.** Disorder that involves a significant loss of physical function (with no apparent organic basis), usually in a single-organ system.

_____ **18.** Disorder that involves excessive preoccupation with health concerns and incessant worrying about developing physical illnesses.

_____ **19.** A class of disorders in which people lose contact with portions of their consciousness or memory, resulting in disruptions in their sense of identity.

_____ **20.** A sudden loss of memory for important personal information that is too extensive to be due to normal forgetting.

_____ **21.** People's loss of memory for their entire lives along with their sense of personal identity.

_____ **22.** Older term, still widely used, that describes the coexistence in one person of two or more personalities.

_____ **23.** The new term that replaced multiple-personality disorder in the DSM-IV.

_____ **24.** A class of disorders marked by depressed or elevated mood disturbances that may spill over to disrupt physical, perceptual, social, and thought processes.

_____ **25.** Severe disturbances in eating behavior characterized by preoccupation with weight concerns and unhealthy efforts to control weight; includes the syndromes anorexia nervosa and bulimia nervosa.

_____ **26.** A disorder marked by persistent feelings of sadness and despair and a loss of interest in previous sources of pleasure.

_____ **27.** Disorders marked by the experience of both depressive and manic periods.

_____ **28.** Statistic indicating the percentage of twin pairs or other pairs of relatives who exhibit the same disorder.

_____ **29.** Estimating the probably of an event based on the ease with which relevant instances come to mind.

_____ **30.** A class of disorders marked by disturbances in thought that spill over to affect perceptual, social, and emotional processes.

_____ **31.** False beliefs that are maintained even though they clearly are out of touch with reality.

_____ **32.** Sensory perceptions that occur in the absence of a real, external stimulus, or gross distortions of perceptual input.

_____ **33.** Type of schizophrenia dominated by delusions of persecution, along with delusions of grandeur.

_____ **34.** Type of schizophrenia marked by striking motor disturbances, ranging from muscular rigidity to random motor activity.

_____ **35.** Type of schizophrenia marked by a particularly severe deterioration of adaptive behavior.

_____ **36.** Type of schizophrenia marked by idiosyncratic mixtures of schizophrenic symptoms.

_____ **37.** A class of disorders marked by extreme, inflexible personality traits that cause subjective distress or impaired social and occupational functioning.

_____ **38.** Disorder marked by impulsive, callous, manipulative, aggressive, and irresponsible behavior; reflects a failure to accept social norms.

_____ **39.** A legal status indicating that a person cannot be held responsible for his or her actions because of mental illness.

_____ **40.** One part of a classification system of schizophrenia that includes behavioral deficits, such as flattened emotions, social withdrawal, and apathy.

_____ **41.** Legal situation in which people are hospitalized in psychiatric facilities against their will.

_____ **42.** Chronic but relatively mild symptoms of bipolar disturbance.

_____ **43.** Abnormal syndromes found only in a few cultural groups.

_____ **44.** Chronic depression that is insufficient in severity to merit diagnosis of a major depressive episode.

_____ **45.** Estimating the probability of an event based on how similar the event is to a prototype.

_____ **46.** An error in thinking that involves estimating that the odds of two uncertain events happening together are greater than the odds of either event happening alone.

_____ **47.** An eating disorder that involves binge eating followed by unhealthy compensatory efforts such as vomiting, fasting, abuse of laxatives and diuretics, and excessive exercise.

_____ **48.** The coexistence of two or more disorders in the same individual.

_____ **49.** One part of a classification system of schizophrenia that includes behavioral excesses such as hallucinations, delusions, and bizarre behavior.

Answers: 1. medical model **2.** diagnosis **3.** etiology **4.** prognosis **5.** anorexia nervosa **6.** epidemiology **7.** prevalence **8.** anxiety disorders **9.** generalized anxiety disorder **10.** phobic disorder **11.** panic disorder **12.** obsessive-compulsive disorder **13.** agoraphobia **14.** psychosomatic diseases **15.** somatoform disorders **16.** somatization disorder **17.** conversion disorder **18.** hypochondriasis **19.** dissociative disorders **20.** dissociative amnesia **21.** dissociative fugue **22.** multiple-personality disorder **23.** dissociative identity disorder **24.** mood disorders **25.** eating disorders **26.** major depressive disorder **27.** bipolar disorders **28.** concordance rate **29.** availability heuristic **30.** schizophrenic disorders **31.** delusions **32.** hallucinations **33.** paranoid schizophrenia **34.** catatonic schizophrenia **35.** disorganized schizophrenia **36.** undifferentiated schizophrenia **37.** personality disorders **38.** antisocial personality disorder **39.** insanity **40.** negative symptoms **41.** involuntary commitment **42.** cyclothymia **43.** culture-bound disorders **44.** dysthymia. **45.** representativeness heuristic **46.** conjunction fallacy **47.** bulimia nervosa **48.** comorbidity **49.** positive symptoms

REVIEW OF KEY PEOPLE

Nancy Andreasen   Nicholas Spanos   Martin Seligman
David Rosenhan   Thomas Szasz

_____   **1.**   Critic of the medical model; argues that abnormal behavior usually involves a deviation from social norms rather than an illness.

_____   **2.**   Did a study on admission of pseudopatients to a mental hospital; concluded that our mental health system is biased toward seeing pathology where it doesn't exist.

_____   **3.**   Developed the concept of "preparedness"; believes that classical conditioning creates most phobic responses.

_____   **4.**   Proposed an alternative approach to subtyping that divides schizophrenic disorders into just two categories based on the presence of negative versus positive symptoms.

_____   **5.**   Asserts that dissociative identity disorder (multiple-personality disorder) is not a genuine disorder but is the product of media attention and the probings of psychotherapists.

Answers: 1. Szasz **2.** Rosenhan **3.** Seligman **4.** Andreasen **5.** Spanos.

SELF-QUIZ

1. Which of the following concepts or people asserts that abnormal behavior is best thought of as an illness?
   a. the behavioral model
   b. the medical model
   c. Thomas Szasz
   d. Arthur Staats

2. The concordance rate for mood disorders has been found to be about 67% among identical twins and 17% among fraternal twins. These data suggest that the mood disorders
   a. are caused primarily by stress
   b. have an onset at an early age
   c. are due primarily to family environment
   d. are caused in part by genetic factors

3. In Rosenhan's study involving admission of pseudopatients to psychiatric facilities, most of the "patients" were
   a. diagnosed as seriously disturbed
   b. diagnosed as suffering from a mild neurosis
   c. dismissed within two days
   d. misdiagnosed by the ward attendants but correctly diagnosed by the professional staff

4. An individual gets sudden, paralyzing attacks of anxiety and also fears going out in public away from her house. Which anxiety disorder does this describe?
   a. generalized anxiety disorder
   b. phobic disorder
   c. obsessive-compulsive disorder
   d. panic attack and agoraphobia

5. Ralph cleans and scrubs the cupboards in his house seven times each day. Which anxiety disorder does this describe?
   a. generalized anxiety disorder
   b. phobic disorder
   c. obsessive-compulsive disorder
   d. panic disorder

6. Human beings may have evolved to be more easily conditioned to fear some stimuli than others. This is Seligman's notion of
   a. preparedness
   b. anxiety differentiation
   c. somatization
   d. learned helplessness

7. Delusions and hallucinations are likely to characterize
   a. major depressive disorder
   b. hypochondriasis
   c. phobias
   d. schizophrenia

8. Paralysis or loss of feeling that does not match underlying anatomical organization may be a symptom of
   a. somatization disorder
   b. conversion disorder
   c. hypochondriasis
   d. malingering

9. A disorder that was extremely rare prior to the last half of the 20th century is the syndrome
   a. manic-depressive disorder
   b. schizophrenia
   c. obsessive-compulsive disorder
   d. anorexia nervosa

10. The disorder marked by striking motor disturbances ranging from rigidity to random motor activity and incoherence is termed
    a. catatonic schizophrenia
    b. multiple personality
    c. dissociative disorder
    d. paranoid schizophrenia

11. Which of the following are disorders that occur cross-culturally?
    a. generalized anxiety disorder and panic disorder
    b. hypochondriasis and somatization disorder
    c. schizophrenia and bipolar mood disorder
    d. bulimia and anorexia nervosa

12. A disorder characterized by amenorrhea (loss of the menstrual cycle) in women is the syndrome termed
    a. generalized anxiety disorder
    b. bipolar mood disorder
    c. anorexia nervosa
    d. bulimia nervosa

13. An individual thinks he is Jesus Christ. He also believes that, because he is Christ, people are trying to kill him. Assume that this individual is not correct—he is not Christ, and people are not trying to kill him. Which of the following would be the most likely diagnosis?
a. multiple personality
b. paranoid schizophrenia
c. obsessive-compulsive disorder
d. catatonic schizophrenia

14. A court declares that, because of a mental illness, an individual is not responsible for his criminal actions (did not know right from wrong). The individual is
a. insane
b. psychopathic
c. psychotic
d. schizophrenic

15. Being careful not to make the conjunction fallacy, indicate which of the following is more probable
a. Ralph is an alcoholic; Ralph wins a major world tennis tournament.
b. Ralph is an alcoholic; Ralph enters a treatment program; Ralph wins a major world tennis tournament.
c. Ralph is an alcoholic; Ralph enters a treatment program; Ralph has been sober for a year; Ralph wins a major world tennis tournament.
d. Ralph is an alcoholic; Ralph enters a treatment program; Ralph has been sober for a year; Ralph practices tennis 50 hours a week; Ralph wins a major world tennis tournament.

Answers: 1. b **2.** d **3.** a **4.** d **5.** c **6.** a **7.** d **8.** b **9.** d **10.** a **11.** c **12.** c **13.** b **14.** a **15.** a.

Chapter Fifteen

Psychotherapy

REVIEW OF KEY IDEAS

THE ELEMENTS OF THE TREATMENT PROCESS

1. **Identify the three major categories of therapy and discuss how various demographic variables relate to the likelihood of treatment.**

   1-1. Even though she already owns more than a thousand pairs of shoes, Imelba cannot resist the urge to buy more. She checks the Yellow Pages and calls three different psychotherapists regarding possible treatment for her compulsion.

   (a) One therapist tells her that treatment will require her to talk with the therapist so as to develop a better understanding of her inner feelings. This therapist probably belongs to the ~~psychiatrist~~ *insight* school of psychotherapy.

   (b) Another therapist suggests that some form of medication may help alleviate her compulsion. This therapist probably pursues the ~~conseling~~ *clinical / psychology* approach to psychotherapy.

   (c) The third therapist is of the opinion that her urge to buy shoes results from learning, and correcting it requires that she unlearn this compulsion. This therapist probably pursues the ~~psychotric~~ *behavioral* approach to psychotherapy.

   1-2. Indicate whether the following statements about people who seek and choose not to seek psychotherapy are true or false.

   _____F_____ Men are more likely than women to seek psychotherapy.

   _____T_____ The two most common presenting symptoms are excessive anxiety and depression.

   _____ Persons seeking psychotherapy always have identifiable disorders.

   _____ Only a minority of persons needing psychotherapy actually receive treatment.

   _____ Many people feel that seeking psychotherapy is an admission of personal weakness.

2. **Describe the various types of mental health professionals involved in the provision of psychotherapy.**

   2-1. Identify the following kinds of mental health professionals:

   (a) Medically trained persons (physicians) who generally use biomedical and insight approaches to psychotherapy. *psychatrist*

   (b) Persons with doctoral degrees who emphasize behavioral and insight approaches to psychotherapy in treating a full range of psychological problems (two types). *clinical & conselling ps.*

   (c) Nurses who usually work as part of the treatment team in a hospital setting.

   (d) These persons often work with both the patient and family to reintegrate the patient back into society. *psychairic nurse*

   (e) Persons who usually specialize in particular types of problems; such as, vocational, drug, or marital counseling.

INSIGHT THERAPIES

3. **Explain the logic of psychoanalysis and describe the techniques by which analysts probe the unconscious.**

   3-1. Freud believed that psychological disturbances originate from unresolved conflicts deep in the unconscious levels of the mind. His theory of personality, which he called *psychoanalysis*, would be classified as an __*insight*__ approach to psychotherapy. The psychoanalyst plays the role of psychological detective, seeking out problems thought to originate from conflicts left over from early __*childhood*__.

   3-2. The psychoanalyst employs two techniques to probe the unconscious. One technique requires the patient to tell whatever comes to mind no matter how trivial. This technique is called __*free*__ __*assosciation*__. The other technique requires the patient to learn to remember his or her dreams which are then probed for their hidden meaning by the psychoanalyst. This technique is called __*dream*__ __*analyses*__.

4. **Discuss resistance and transference in psychoanalysis.**

4-1.   Freud believed most people (do/do not) want to know the true nature of their inner conflicts and will employ various strategies so as to offer _resistance_ to the progress of therapy. As therapy progresses, the patient often begins to relate to the therapist as though he or she was actually one of the significant persons (mother, father, spouse, etc.) in the patient's life. This phenomenon is called _transference_.

5. **Identify the elements of therapeutic climate and discuss therapeutic process in Rogers's client-centered therapy.**

5-1.   Client-centered therapy, as developed by Carl Rogers, holds that there are three important aspects necessary for a good therapeutic climate. These are genuineness, unconditional positive regard, and empathy. Match these terms with their correct definitions as given below.

  (a) The ability to truly see the world from the client's point of view and communicate this understanding to the client.

  empathy

  (b) The therapist's openness and honesty with the client.

  genuiness

  (c) The complete and nonjudgmental acceptance of the client as a person without necessarily agreeing with what the client has to say. _unconditional positive regards_

5-2.   The major emphasis for client centered therapy is to provide feedback and _clarification_ as the client expresses his or her thoughts and feelings. The idea here is that the client (does/does not) need direct advice. What is needed is help in sorting through personal confusion in order to gain greater _insight_ into true inner feelings.

6. **Discuss the logic, goals, and techniques of cognitive therapy.**

6-1.   Answer the following questions regarding the logic, goals, and techniques of cognitive therapy.

  (a) What is the basic logic behind cognitive therapy? Or to put it another way, what is the origin of many psychological problems according to cognitive therapy?

(b) What is the primary goal of cognitive therapy?

(c) How do cognitive therapists go about trying to change a client's negative illogical thinking?

(d) Cognitive therapy is actually a blend of insight therapy and behavior therapy. What technique from behavior therapy do cognitive therapists frequently employ?

Answers: 6-1. (a) negative illogical thinking (b) to change the client's negative illogical thinking (c) through argument and persuasion (d) homework assignments.

7. **Describe how group therapy is generally conducted and identify some advantages of this approach.**

   7-1. When conducting group therapy, the therapist generally plays a (an) (<u>active/subtle</u>) role, one that is primarily aimed at promoting _group_ cohesiveness. Participants essentially function as _therapist_ for each other, providing acceptance and emotional support.

   7-2. Besides being less expensive, group therapy also has three other advantages: (1) the realization by the participants that their problems (<u>are/are not</u>) unique, (2) the opportunity to work in a safe environment to build _social_ skills, and (3) the fact that group therapy is particularly appropriate for (<u>all/certain</u>) kinds of problems.

   Answers: 7-1. subtle, group, therapists **7-2.** are not, social, certain.

8. **Discuss Eysenck's critique of insight therapy and more recent evidence on the efficacy of insight therapies.**

   8-1. In his review of therapeutic outcome studies with neurotic patients, Eysenck found that about _2/3_ of all treated patients recovered within 2 years. The rate of recovery for untreated patients during this same time period was (<u>lower than/the same as</u>) untreated patients. Eysenck concluded that _spontaneous_ remission accounted for most of the cures ascribed to insight therapies.

   8-2. After reexamining Eysenck's data, Bergin concluded that spontaneous remission accounts for approximately _30-40_ percent of the "recoveries" from neurotic disorders. Recent studies have also concluded that when compared to untreated controls, insight therapies appear to be _superior_ to no treatment or placebo treatment.

   Answers: 8-1. two-thirds, the same as, spontaneous **8-2.** 30-40, superior.

BEHAVIOR THERAPIES

9. Summarize the general principles underlying behavioral approaches to therapy.

9-1. In contrast to insight therapists who believe that pathological symptoms are signs of an underlying problem, behavior therapists believe that the _symptoms_ are the problem. Thus, behavior therapists focus on employing the principles of learning to directly change maladaptive _behavior_. The two general principles underlying this approach are (1) one's behavior is a product of _learning_, and (2) what has been learned can be _unlearned_

Answers: **9-1.** symptoms, behavior, learning, unlearned.

10. Describe the goals and procedures of systematic desensitization and aversion therapy.

10-1. State whether the following situations would be most applicable to systematic desensitization or to aversion therapy.

(a) The treatment goal is to lessen the attractiveness of particular stimuli and behaviors that are personally or socially harmful. ~~desensitization~~

aversion

(b) The treatment goal is to reduce irrational fears such as found in phobias and other anxiety disorders.

desensitization   aversion

(c) The three-step treatment involves pairing an imagined anxiety hierarchy with deep muscle relaxation.

desentization

(d) Treatment involves presenting an unpleasant stimulus, such as electric shock, while a person is engaged in performing a self-destructive, but personally appealing, acts.

aversion

(e) This would be the treatment of choice for students who are unduly anxious about public speaking.

Answers: **10-1.** (a) aversion therapy (b) systematic desensitization (c) systematic desensitization (d) aversion therapy (e) systematic desensitization.

11. Describe the goals and techniques of social skills training and biofeedback.

11-1. As the name implies, social skills training is a behavior therapy designed to improve a clients social or _stronger_ skills. Three different behavioral techniques are employed. First, one is required to closely watch the behavior of socially skilled persons, a technique called _____. Next the client is expected to imitate and practice the behavior he or she has just witnessed, a technique called behavior _____. Finally, the client is expected to perform in social situations requiring increasingly more difficult social skills, a technique called _____.

11-2. Biofeedback works by providing the client with immediate _feedback_ about some bodily function, such as blood pressure or muscle tension, thus leading to better control of these functions. For example, it has been found that clients can lessen the intensity and frequency of both tension and migraine headaches by learning to _reduce_ the muscle tension in their neck and facial muscles.

Answers: 11-1. interpersonal, modeling, rehearsal, shaping **11-2.** feedback, reduce.

12. Discuss evidence on the effectiveness of behavior therapies.

12-1. Compared to the evidence in support of insight therapies, the evidence in favor of behavior therapy is somewhat (weaker/<u>stronger</u>). It is important to remember, however, that behavior therapies are best suited for treating (<u>specific</u>/general) psychological disorders, and that all of the various behavioral techniques (are/<u>are not</u>) equally effective.

Answers: 12-1. stronger, specific, are not.

BIOMEDICAL THERAPIES

13. Describe the principal categories of drugs used in the treatment of psychological disorders.

13-1. Valium and Xanax, popularly called tranquilizers, are used to treat psychological disorders in which anxiety is a major feature. Thus, they are collectively called _antianxiety_ drugs.

13-2. Another class of drugs is used to treat severe psychotic symptoms, such as hallucinations and confusion. These drugs are collectively called _antipsychotic_ drugs.

13-3. Three classes of drugs — tricyclics, MAO inhibitors, and selective serotonin reuptake inhibitors — have been found to be useful in alleviating depression. These drugs are collectively called _____ drugs.

13-4. A rather unique drug can function as both an antidepressant and antimanic agent and thus is effective in treating bipolar mood disorders. This drug is _lithium_.

Answers: 13-1. antianxiety **13-2.** antipsychotic **13-3.** antidepressant **13-4.** lithium.

14. Discuss evidence on the effects and problems of drug treatments for psychological disorders.

14-1. Drug therapies have proven useful in the treatment of many psychological disorders. However, they remain controversial for at least three reasons. Use the hints below to describe these three reasons.

(a) resolve problems

(b) two areas having to do with excess

(c) cure is worse than the disease

Answers: 14-1. (a) They alleviate rather than solve psychological problems. (b) They are over-prescribed and patients are over-medicated. (c) The side effects may be worse than the disease.

15. Describe ECT and discuss its therapeutic effects and its risks.

15-1. Answer the following questions about the nature, therapeutic effects, and risks of ECT.

(a) What is the physical effect of the electric shock on the patient?

Produces convulsion seizures

(b) What general class of disorders warrant conservative use of ECT as a treatment technique?

mood desorder

(c) Why does ECT work?

don't

(d) What are some short-term side effects of ECT?

loss of memory, intellectual impairm

Answers: 15-1. (a) It produces convulsive seizures. (b) severe mood disorders (depression and mania) (c) It is unknown at this time. (d) It can produce intellectual impairment.

6. Summarize the concerns that have been expressed about the impact of managed care on the treatment of psychological disorders.

16-1. Why might the impact on mental health care be more negative with managed health care than for other treatment specialties in carrying out medically necessary treatment programs?

16-2. What cost-cutting strategies, in addition to denial of treatment and prescribing older rather than newer drugs, are often employed by HMO's?

Answers: 16-1. The question of what is medically necessary is more subjective (in the case of mental health treatment). **16-2.** under-diagnosing conditions, failing to make needed referrals, limiting treatment times, rerouting patients to less highly trained professionals (in any order).

17. Discuss the pros and cons of empirically validated treatments.

17-1. What benefits can be gained from the new emphasis on documenting the efficacy of treatments for "specific" problems?

17-2. What concerns have been raised about the emphasis on "specific" empirically documented treatments?

17-3. What might be a problem with identifying a limited number of validated therapies with respect to the bureaucrats who administer HMO's?

Answers: 17-1. Treatment interventions will become more scientific and more reliable. **17-2.** Patients often have a mixture of problems rather than specific problems. **17-3.** It will give them even more control over how therapy is conducted.

CURRENT TRENDS AND ISSUES IN TREATMENT

18. Discuss the merits of blending or combining different approaches to therapy.

18-1. A significant trend in modern psychotherapy is to blend or combine many different treatment approaches. Psychologists who advocate and use this approach are said to be _eclectic_. One outcome study cited by the text suggests there may be merit to this approach. In this study, three different groups of depressed patients were treated by either insight therapy, drug therapy, or both. The greatest improvement was found in patients treated by _both_.

Answers: 18-1. eclectic, both.

19. Discuss the barriers that lead to underutilization of mental health services by ethnic minorities and possible solutions to the problem.

19-1. The text lists four general barriers (cultural, language, access, and institutional) to mental health services for ethnic minorities. Indicate which of these barriers is represented in the following statements.

access (a) Many of the ethnic minorities are in low-paying jobs and without health insurance.

institutio (b) Very few mental health facilities are equipped to provide culturally responsive services.

language (c) There is a limited number of bilingual therapists.

cultural (d) Psychotherapy was developed by whites in the Western world to treat whites in the Western world.

19-2. What would be an optimal, but perhaps impractical, solution to the problems of language and cultural differences between therapists and clients?

19-3. What kind of training was recommended for therapists?

19-4. What suggestion was made with respect to traditional therapies?

Answers. 19-1. (a) access (b) institutional (c) language (d) cultural **19-2.** Ethnically match therapists and clients.
19-3. cultural sensitivity training **19-4.** That they be modified to be more compatible with specific ethnic groups.

INSTITUTIONAL TREATMENT IN TRANSITION

20. Explain why people grew disenchanted with mental hospitals and describe the community mental health movement.

    20-1. After more than a century of reliance on state mental hospitals, the evidence began to grow that these institutions were not helping the patients; rather, in many instances, they were worsening their condition. What condition, unrelated to funding, was said to be responsible for this state of affairs?

    20-2. In order to correct for these shortcomings, the community mental health movement arose as an alternative treatment option. These community based facilities emphasize (<u>short-term/long-term</u>) therapy and getting patients stabilized and back into the community _____.

Answers: 20-1. The removal of patients from their communities separated them from essential support groups.
20-2. short-term, swiftly.

21. Describe the deinstitutionalization trend and evaluate its effects.

    21-1. The transferring of mental health care from large state institutions to community based facilities is what is meant by the term _____. As a result of deinstitutionalization, the number of mental patients in large institutional hospitals has _____ remarkably. The length of stay by patients in mental hospitals has also _____.

    21-2. While deinstitutionalization has resulted in a decrease in the number of patients, as well as their length of stay, the number of admissions to psychiatric hospitals has actually _____. This is because of a large number of readmissions for short-term care, which the text calls "the _____ _____ problem." Another problem brought about by deinstitutionalization is that a large number of discharged patients who have meager job skills and no close support groups make up a substantial portion of the nation's _____ persons.

Answers: 21-1. deinstitutionalization, declined, declined **21-2.** increased, revolving door, homeless.

PUTTING IT IN PERSPECTIVE

22. Explain how this chapter highlighted two of the text's unifying themes.

22-1. What point does the text make about how theoretical diversity influenced the treatment techniques employed by psychotherapy?

22-2. The approaches to psychotherapy discussed in this chapter are not universally accepted or used and some are actually counterproductive in many cultures. Why is this?

Answers: 22-1. It has resulted in better treatment techniques (because of the many diverse approaches). **22-2.** Cultural factors influence psychological processes.

APPLICATION: LOOKING FOR A THERAPIST

23. Discuss where to seek therapy, and the potential importance of a therapist's sex, professional background, and cost.

23-1. Most therapists (are/are not) in private practice. In addition to talking to friends and acquaintances, the text lists many places (Table 15.2) where one might seek psychotherapy. The general idea here is to _____ around when looking for a therapist.

23-2. The text concludes that the kind of degree held by the psychotherapist (is/is not) crucial, although a verifiable degree indicating some kind of professional training is important. The sex of the therapist should be chosen according to the feelings of the _____; it is unwise to engage a therapist whose sex makes the client feel uncomfortable.

23-3. Answer the following questions regarding the cost of psychotherapy.

(a) How does the cost of therapists involved in private practice compare with the fees charged by similar professional groups?

(b) Many community agencies use a sliding scale to assess therapy costs. What does this mean?

Answers: 23-1. are not, shop **23-2.** is not, client **23-3.** (a) The costs are similar. (b) Fees are assessed acording to the ability to pay.

24. Discuss the importance of a therapist's theoretical approach.

24-1. Studies of the effectiveness of various theoretical approaches to therapy show they are (unequal/equal) in overall success. This equality of results among all theoretical approaches (does/does not) apply to all types of problems. The theoretical approach may make a difference for specific types of problems.

25. **Summarize what one should look for in a prospective therapist and what one should expect out of therapy.**

   25-1. The text lists three areas to evaluate when looking for a therapist. Complete the following statements describing these areas.

   (a) Can you talk to the therapist _____?

   (b) Does the therapist appear to have empathy and _____?

   (c) Does the therapist appear to be self-assured and _____?

   25-2. What should one consider before terminating therapy because of lack of progress?

   25-3. What did the Ehrenbergs say about what to expect from psychotherapy?

CRITICAL THINKING APPLICATIONS

26. **Explain how placebo effects and regression toward the mean can complicate the evaluation of therapy.**

   26-1. In addition to therapy itself, what other two factors can influence the outcome of a treatment program?

   26-2. Which of these two factors is least effected by having only a small sample?

   26-3. Which of these factors leads us to predict that persons who score the healthiest on a mental health questionnaire will actually score lower on this questionnaire following a brief therapy intervention?

REVIEW OF KEY TERMS

Antianxiety drugs ✓
Antidepressant drugs ✓
Antipsychotic drugs
Aversion therapy ✓
Behavior therapies ✓
Biofeedback ✓
Biomedical therapies
Client-centered therapy ✓
~~Clinical & counseling psychologists~~
Cognitive therapy ✓
Deinstitutionalization

Dream analysis ✓
Eclecticism
Electroconvulsive therapy (ECT)
~~Free association~~
Group therapy
Insight therapies ✓
Interpretation ✓
Lithium
Mental hospitals
Placebo effects

Psychiatrists ✓
Psychoanalysis
Psychopharmacotherapy
Regression toward the mean
Resistance ✓
Social skills training
Spontaneous remission ✓
Systematic desensitization
Tardive dyskinesia
Transference

clinical & _conseling psychi._   **1.** Two groups of professionals that specialize in the diagnosis and treatment of psychological disorders and everyday behavioral problems.

psychiatrist   **2.** Physicians who specialize in the treatment of psychological disorders.

Insight ther   **3.** Therapies that involve verbal interactions intended to enhance client's self-knowledge and thus produce healthful changes in personality and behavior.

psychoanalysis   **4.** An insight therapy that emphasizes the recovery of unconscious conflicts, motives and defenses through techniques such as free association and transference.

Free assosciation   **5.** A technique in which clients are urged to spontaneously express their thoughts and feelings with as little personal censorship as possible.

Interpretation
Interpretation
Dream analysis
~~_Interpretation_~~   **6.** A technique for interpreting the symbolic meaning of dreams.

7. A therapist's attempts to explain the inner significance of a client's thoughts, feelings, memories and behavior.

Resistance   **8.** A client's largely unconscious defensive maneuvers intended to hinder the progress of therapy.

Transference
Client centered
~~_client_~~ _therapy_   **9.** A process that occurs when clients start relating to their therapist in ways that mimic critical relationships in their lives.

10. An insight therapy that emphasizes providing a supportive emotional climate for clients who play a major role in determining the pace and direction of their therapy.

Cognitie therap   **11.** An insight therapy that emphasizes recognizing and changing negative thoughts and maladaptive beliefs.

12. The simultaneous treatment of several clients.

Behavio   **13.** Therapies that involve the application of learning principles to change a client's maladaptive behaviors.

Desentizan   **14.** A behavior therapy used to reduce anxiety responses through counterconditioning.

aversion therapy   **15.** A behavior therapy in which an aversive stimulus is paired with a stimulus that elicits an undesirable response.

Spontaneous remission   **16.** Recovery from a disorder that occurs without formal treatment.

Social skill Training   **17.** A behavior therapy designed to improve interpersonal skills that emphasizes shaping, modeling, and behavioral rehearsal.

Biofeedback _____ 18. A behavioral technique in which a bodily function is monitored and information about it is fed back to a person to facilitate control of the physiological process.

~~Biomedical therapies~~ 19. Therapies that use physiological interventions intended to reduce symptoms associated with psychological disorders.

psychopramaco therapy
Biomedic 20. The treatment of mental disorders with drug therapy.

antianxiety 21. Drugs that relieve tension, apprehension, and nervousness.

antipsychotic 22. Drugs that gradually reduce psychotic symptoms.

~~ECT~~
Tardive dyskensca 23. A neurological disorder marked by chronic tremors and involuntary spastic movements.

antidepressant 24. Drugs that gradually elevate mood and help bring people out of a depression.

Lithium 25. A chemical used to control mood swings in patients with bipolar mood disorder.

ECT 26. A treatment in which electric shock is used to produce cortical seizure accompanied by convulsions.

Mental hospital 27. A medical institution specializing in the provision of inpatient care for psychological disorders.

Ecletic 28. Involves drawing ideas from two or more systems of therapy, instead of just committing to one system.

deinstitulization 29. Transferring the treatment of mental illness from inpatient institutions to community-based facilities that emphasize outpatient care.

Placebo Effect 30. Occur when people's expectations lead them to experience some change even though they receive a fake treatment.

regression 31. Occurs when people who score extremely high or low on some trait are measured a second time and their new scores fall closer to the mean.

Answers: 1. clinical and counseling psychologists **2.** psychiatrists **3.** insight therapies **4.** psychoanalysis **5.** free association **6.** dream analysis **7.** interpretation **8.** resistance **9.** transference **10.** client-centered therapy **11.** cognitive therapy **12.** group therapy **13.** behavior therapies **14.** systematic desensitization **15.** aversion therapy **16.** spontaneous remission **17.** social skills training **18.** biofeedback **19.** biomedical therapies **20.** psychopharmacotherapy **21.** antianxiety drugs **22.** antipsychotic drugs **23.** tardive dyskinesa **24.** antidepressant drugs **25.** lithium **26.** electroconvulsive therapy (ECT) **27.** mental hospitals **28.** eclecticism **29.** deinstitutionalization **30.** placebo effects **31.** regression toward the mean.

REVIEW OF KEY PEOPLE

Aaron Beck   Hans Eysenck   Carl Rogers
Dorthea Dix   Sigmund Freud   Joseph Wolpe

_____ 1. Developed a systematic treatment procedure that he called psychoanalysis.

_____ 2. The developer of client-centered therapy.

_____ 3. Noted for his work in the development of cognitive therapy.

_____ 4. His early research showed that insight therapies were ineffective.

_____ 5. The developer of systematic desensitization.

_____ 6. One of the early reformers who helped to establish state-funded mental hospitals.

Answers: 1. Freud **2.** Rogers **3.** Beck **4.** Eysenck **5.** Wolpe **6.** Dix.

SELF-QUIZ

1. Which of the following is not a true statement?
   a. Women seek psychotherapy more than men.
   b. The two most common problems that lead to psychotherapy are sexual problems and depression.
   c. Persons seeking psychotherapy don't always have identifiable problems.
   d. Many people feel that seeking psychotherapy is an admission of personal weakness.

2. Which of the following mental health professionals must have medical degrees?
   a. psychiatric social workers
   b. clinical psychologists
   c. psychiatric nurses
   d. psychiatrists

3. Psychoanalysis is an example of what kind of approach to psychotherapy?
   a. insight
   b. learning
   c. biomedical
   d. a combination of learning and biomedical

4. When a client begins relating to his psychoanalyst as though she were his mother, we have an example of
   a. transference
   b. free association
   c. catharsis
   d. restructuring

5. The major emphasis in client-centered therapy is to provide the client with
   a. interpretation of unconscious thinking
   b. cognitive restructuring
   c. feedback and clarification
   d. good advice

6. Which of the following is likely to be found in cognitive therapy?
   a. searching for negative illogical thinking
   b. dream interpretation
   c. free association
   d. an emphasis on childhood conflicts

7. Which kind of therapists are likely to play the least active (most subtle) role in conducting therapy?
   a. behavior therapists
   b. cognitive therapists
   c. group therapists
   d. pychoanalytic therapists

8. Eysenck's study of outcome studies with neurotic patients found that the recovery rate
   a. was best for treated patients
   b. was best for untreated patients
   c. was the same for treated and untreated patients

9. Which of the following therapies is most likely to see the symptom as the problem?
   a. psychoanalysis
   b. client-centered therapy
   c. cognitive therapy
   d. behavior therapy

10. Which of the following therapies would be most likely to employ aversive conditioning?
    a. psychoanalysis
    b. behavior therapy
    c. biomedical therapies
    d. client-centered therapy

11. Which of the following behavior therapy techniques would most likely be used to treat a fear of flying?
    a. systematic desensitization
    b. aversive conditioning
    c. modeling
    d. biofeedback

12. Electroconvulsive therapy (ECT) is now primarily used to treat patients suffering from
    a. anxiety
    b. phobias
    c. severe mood disorders
    d. psychosis

13. Which of the following might be a negative aspect of the emphasis on "specific" empirically validated treatments?
    a. Many clients have a mixture of problems.
    b. These treatments cannot control for placebo effects.
    c. These treatments cannot control for regression toward the mean.
    d. These treatments cannot control for unconscious processes.

14. Psychotherapists who combine several different approaches in their approach to therapy are said to be
    a. enigmatic
    b. eclectic
    c. unspecific
    d. imaginative

15. The trend toward deinstitutionalization mainly came about because large state mental institutions:
    a. were becoming too expensive
    b. were actually worsening the condition of many patients
    c. were overstaffed
    d. were becoming too political

16. Which of the following factors can affect the outcome of a treatment program?
    a. the efficacy of the treatment itself
    b. regression toward the mean
    c. placebo effects
    d. all of these above

Answers: 1. b 2. d 3. a 4. a 5. c 6. a 7. c 8. c 9. d 10. b 11. a 12. c 13. a 14. b 15. b 16. d.

Chapter Sixteen

Social Behavior

REVIEW OF KEY IDEAS

PERSON PERCEPTION: FORMING IMPRESSIONS OF OTHERS

1. **Describe how various aspects of physical appearance may influence our impressions of others**.

   1-1. In general, we attribute _____ characteristics to good-looking people. We tend to view attractive people as warmer, friendlier, better-adjusted, and more poised. Although the influence of looks on judgments of competence is not as great, we are also inclined to see attractive people as (<u>less/more</u>) intelligent and successful than less attractive people.

   1-2. Attractiveness has relatively little impact on judgments of honesty, but people do tend to view baby-faced individuals (large eyes, rounded chin) as more _____ than others and also as more helpless and submissive. (Hey, what about the notorious criminal Babyface Nelson? Well, it's a general guideline, not an absolute principle.) Recent evidence suggests that there (<u>is/is not</u>) an actual association between baby-faced features and these traits.

   1-3. In addition, we make inferences about people based on their nonverbal behavior—how they move, talk, and gesture. For example, based on a 10-second videotape, participants in a recent study guessed others' sexual orientation with a relatively high degree of (<u>accuracy/inaccuracy</u>).

   1-4. In another study involving nonverbal behavior, subjects exposed to a confederate for 10 minutes unintentionally _____ the confederate's behavior. When the confederate either shook his foot or rubbed his face, the subjects tended to do the same thing. This tendency is referred to as the _____ effect.

   Answers: 1-1. positive (desirable, favorable), more **1-2.** honest, is not **1-3.** accuracy (about 70%) **1-4.** mimicked (imitated), chameleon.

2. **Explain how schemas, stereotypes, and other factors contribute to subjectivity in person perception.**

    2-1.   Briefly define the following:

        (a) schemas:

        (b) stereotypes:

    2-2.   Men are competitive, women are sensitive: these are stereotypes. Stereotypes are broad generalizations that tend to ignore the _____ within a group. People who hold stereotypes do not necessarily assume that all members of a particular group have the same characteristics but merely that there is an increased _____ that they do.

    2-3.   Whether probable or absolute, schemas in general and stereotypes in particular direct our perception, so that we tend to see the things we expect to see. Such selective perception results in an overestimation of the degree to which our expectations match actual events, a phenomenon referred to as _____ correlation.

    2-4.   In one study discussed in the text subjects watched a videotape of a woman engaged in various activities (including drinking beer and listening to classical music). For one set of subjects she was described as a librarian and for another as a waitress. What effect did the occupational labels have on subjects' recall of the woman's *activities*? Which of the following is(are) true?

        _____ Subjects in the "librarian" condition tended to recall her listening to classical music.

        _____ Subjects in the "waitress" condition tended to recall her drinking beer.

    2-5.   The study just described illustrates subjectivity in person perception. Our schemas, in this case the _____, that we have about categories of people, affect how we perceive and what we remember.

    Answers: 2-1. (a) clusters of ideas about people and events. (b) a type of schema; widely held beliefs about people based on group membership **2-2.** diversity (variability), probability **2-3.** illusory **2-4.** both are true **2-5.** stereotypes.

3. **Explain the evolutionary perspective on bias in person perception.**

    3-1.   How does one explain bias or prejudice in terms of evolution? To explain anything in terms of evolution one assumes that the particular characteristic or trait had _____ value in our evolutionary past. For example, the bias in favor of physical attractiveness might have signaled health, associated with _____ potential in women and the ability to acquire _____ in men. The stereotype of _____ individuals as submissive and honest may simply be fallout from our adaptive reaction to infants.

3-2. Evolutionary theorists also assert that we needed a quick way to categorize people as friend or enemy or, in more technical terms, as members of our _____ or members of the

_____.

3-3. The question still remains: how could prejudice and bias be adaptive? It must be clear that what was adaptive in our evolutionary past (is also/may not be) adaptive now. Nonetheless, from the point of view of evolutionary theory, cognitive mechanisms involving bias have been shaped by natural

_____.

Answers: 3-1. adaptive, reproductive, resources, baby-faced **3-2.** ingroup, outgroup **3-3.** may not be, selection.

ATTRIBUTION PROCESSES: EXPLAINING BEHAVIOR

4. Explain what attributions are and why we make them.

4-1. Why are you reading this book? The search for causes of events and of our own and others' behavior is termed _____ . For example, you might _____ your reading behavior to an upcoming test (or to personal interest, lust for knowledge, fear, etc.).

4-2. Attributions are inferences that people make about the _____ of events and about the their own and others' behavior.

4-3. Why do we make attributions? We seem to have a strong need to _____ our experiences.

Answers: 4-1. attribution, attribute **4-2.** causes (origin, source, explanation) **4-3.** understand.

5. Describe the distinction between internal and external attributions.

5-1. Which of the following involve internal and which external attributions? Label each sentence with an I or an E.

_____ He flunked because he's lazy.

_____ Our team lost because the officials were biased against us.

_____ The accident was caused by poor road conditions.

_____ He achieved by the sweat of his brow.

_____ Criminal behavior is caused by poverty.

_____ His success is directly derived from his parents' wealth and influence.

Answers: 5-1. I, E, E, I, E, E

6. Summarize Kelley's and Weiner's theories of attribution.

6-1. See Figure 16.3. Kelley's theory is tough to follow, but here's a sample problem. Ralph cried when he watched the Santa Claus parade. *No one else* seemed to be crying, so according to Kelley's model Ralph's behavior would be *low* in (<u>consistency/distinctiveness/consensus</u>). Further, Ralph *always cries* when he watches parades, so Ralph's crying is *high* in (<u>consistency/distinctiveness/consensus</u>). Ralph also cries when he watches a movie, attends the ballet, watches a sporting event, or on almost any other occasion; thus, Ralph's crying is *low* in (<u>consistency/distinctiveness/consensus</u>).

6-2. According to Kelley, *low* consistency favors an external attribution. *High* consistency is compatible with either an external or internal attribution: internal if distinctiveness and consensus are low and external if distinctive and consensus are high. So, people will tend to attribute Ralph's crying to _____ factors.

6-3. Weiner proposed that attributions are made not only in terms of an internal-external dimension but also in terms of a stable-unstable dimension. Suppose that Sally makes a high score on an exam. She could attribute her score to her ability, an (<u>internal/external</u>) factor that is also (<u>stable/unstable</u>). If she attributed her success to her good mood, the attribution would be (<u>internal/external</u>) and (<u>stable/unstable</u>).

6-4. Or, Sally may think she did well because these types of test are easy, an (<u>internal/external</u>) and (<u>stable/unstable</u>) attribution. If she attributes her score to luck, the attribution would be (<u>internal/external</u>) and (<u>stable/unstable</u>).

Answers: 6-1. consensus, consistency, distinctiveness **6-2.** internal. (I said this was a tough theory. The idea is that if Ralph cries on many occasions, regardless of the event, when no one else is crying—then we begin to think it's something about Ralph.) **6-3.** internal, stable, internal, unstable **6-4.** external, stable, external, unstable.

7. Describe several types of attributional bias and cultural variations in attributional tendencies.

7-1. Define or describe the following:

(a) fundamental attribution error:

(b) actor-observer bias:

(c) defensive attribution:

(d) self-serving bias:

7-2. Recent research has indicated that the attributional biases described above may not apply to all cultures. Since collectivist societies emphasize accomplishing the goals of the group over individual achievement, collectivist cultures are (less/more) likely to attribute other's behavior to personal traits. In other words, people from collectivist cultures tend to be (less/more) prone to the fundamental attribution error.

7-3. Some evidence also indicates that people from collectivist societies would be more likely to attribute their *successes* to (the ease of a task/unusual ability). Similarly, they would be more likely to attribute their *failures* to (bad luck/lack of effort). Thus, in contrast with people from individualistic societies, people from collectivist cultures appear to be (less/more) prone to the self-serving bias.

Answers: **7-1.** (a) the tendency for observers to attribute an individual's behavior to *internal* rather than *external* factors (b) the tendency for observers to attribute an actor's behavior to internal rather than external factors *and the tendency for actors to attribute their own behavior to external causes* (Yes, there is overlap between these two concepts. The fundamental attribution error is part of the actor-observer bias.) (c) the tendency to attribute other people's misfortunes to internal causes, that is, the tendency to blame the victim (d) the tendency to attribute our *successes* to internal factors and our *failures* to situational factors **7-2.** less, less **7-3.** the ease of a task, lack of effort, less.

CLOSE RELATIONSHIPS: LIKING AND LOVING

8. Summarize evidence on the role of physical attractiveness in attraction.

8-1. What factors influence liking, friendship, and love? The key determinant of romantic attraction for (males/females/both sexes) is physical _____.

8-2. While everyone might prefer to have a relationship with the most attractive person, people take their own attractiveness into account. What is the matching hypothesis?

Answers: **8-1.** both sexes, attractiveness **8-2.** The matching hypothesis asserts that people tend to date and marry others of the opposite sex who are *approximately equal* to themselves in physical attractiveness.

9. Summarize evidence on the role of similarity and reciprocity in attraction.

9-1. Do opposites attract, or do birds of a feather flock together? An overwhelming amount of research supports the idea that we are attracted to others who are (similar to/different from) us in attitudes, personality, social background, etc.

9-2. We also tend to like others who like us, the principle of _____. In many cases we are particularly fond of those who exaggerate our good characteristics and overlook our bad. For married or dating couples, for example, the happiest couples seem to be those who have an (accurate/idealized) view of their partners.

Answers: **9-1.** similar to **9-2.** reciprocity, idealized.

10. **Describe various distinctions regarding love set forth by Berscheid and Hatfield.**

   10-1. Hatfield and Berscheid divide love into two types: _____ love, which involves a complete absorption in another and is characterized by intense emotion, and _____ love, described as a warm, tolerant, and trusting affection.

   10-2. Sternberg further divides companionate love into two subtypes: _____, characterized by closeness and sharing, and _____, an intention to maintain a relationship in the face of difficulties.

   10-3. Of Sternberg's three factors, _____ love appears to peak early and drop off rapidly, while _____ and _____ gradually increase over time.

   Answers: 10-1. passionate, companionate **10-2.** intimacy, commitment **10-3.** passionate, intimacy, commitment.

11. **Summarize the evidence on love as a form of attachment.**

   11-1. In Chapter 11 we discussed types of attachment styles between infants and their caregivers. What *general* conclusion did Hazen and Shaver reach concerning the association between types of infant attachment and the love relationships of adults?

   11-2. Write the names of the three infant attachment styles next to the appropriate letters below.

   S: _____

   A-A: _____

   A: _____

   11-3. Using the letters from the previous question, identify the types of romantic relations predicted by the infant attachment styles.

   _____ As adults these individuals tend to use casual sex as a way of getting physically close without the vulnerability of genuine intimacy and commitment.

   _____ These people experience more emotional highs and lows in their relationships, find conflict stressful, have more negative feelings after dealing with conflict.

   _____ These individuals easily develop close, committed, well-adjusted, long-lasting relationships.

   Answers: 11-1. The three types of infant-caretaker attachments (also described in Chapter 11) tend to predict the love relationships that children have as adults. **11-2.** secure, anxious-ambivalent, avoidant **11-3.** A, A-A, S.

12. Discuss cross-cultural research on romantic relationship and evolutionary analyses of mating patterns.

12-1. While there is considerable cross-cultural overlap in what the two sexes want in mates (e.g., kindness, intelligence, dependability), David Buss has found nearly universal differences as well. Buss's data indicate that _____ want mates who can acquire resources that can be invested in children, while _____ want mates who are beautiful, youthful, and in good health. These gender differences in mate preference appear to occur (in virtually all/only in Western) societies.

12-2. There are also differences among cultures in their views on the relationship between romantic love and marriage. The idea that one should be in love in order to marry is in large part an 18th-century invention of (Eastern/Western) culture. Arranged marriages, in which romantic love is less important, tend to be characteristic of (collectivist/ individualist) societies.

12-3. If men emphasize physical attractiveness and women resources, how does this affect *tactics* that the sexes use in pursuing the opposite sex? In support of the evolutionary perspective, Buss has found that men tend to use tactics that emphasize their (looks/resources) and women tactics that emphasize their (looks/ resources). For example, _____ might talk about their jobs or display what they own while _____ would try to enhance their makeup or clothing.

12-4. A recent study by Schmitt and Buss further specifies that the tactic used by the two sexes may depend in part on the type of romance they are looking for. Signals of sexual availability (e.g., dressing seductively) were rated as most effective for women seeking a _____ -term relationship. Signals of sexual exclusivity (e.g., rejecting overtures from other men) were considered most effective for women seeking a _____-term relationship. For men an immediate display of resources was rated the most effective tactic for a _____ -term relationship and an emphasis on potential for acquiring resources as most effective for a _____ -term relationship.

12-5. With regard to the use of tactics involving deception, (males/females) anticipate more deception from prospective dates and underestimate men's potential commitment, perhaps as an _____ strategy for protection against consenting to sex and being abandoned. Men tend to overestimate women's _____ interest, perhaps as an evolved tactic of not overlooking sexual opportunities.

Answers: **12-1.** women, men, in virtually all **12-2.** Western, collectivist **12-3.** resources, looks, men, women **12-4.** short, long, short, long **12-5.** females, evolved (adaptive, survival), sexual.

ATTITUDES: MAKING SOCIAL JUDGMENTS

13. Describe the components and dimensions of attitudes and correlates of attitude strength.

13-1. Attitudes are positive or negative _____ of objects of thought. Objects of thought may include *issues* (e.g., gun control), *groups* (e.g., Irish people), or _____ (e.g., your best friend).

13-2. Attitudes may include three components: cognition (thought), affect (emotion), and behavioral predispositions. People may have attitudes toward any object of thought—political views, art, other people, cottage cheese. Take cottage cheese. List the three possible components of attitudes next to the examples below.

_____ He hates cottage cheese.

_____ If cottage cheese touches his plate he scrapes it into the garbage.

_____ He thinks: "Cottage cheese seems kind of lumpy."

13-3. Attitudes also vary along various dimensions, as follows.

_____ The importance, vested interest, or knowledge about the attitude object.

_____ How easily the attitude comes to mind.

_____ The degree to which the attitude includes both positive and negative aspects.

13-4. Attitude strength is a function of several factors, including how _____ the attitude is to the person, the extent to which the attitude involves a _____ interest that directly affects them, and the degree of _____ that they have about the attitude object.

Answers: **13-1.** evaluations, individuals **13-2.** affect, behavior, cognition. (Note that the components may be remembered as the ABCs of attitude.) **13-3.** strength, accessibility, ambivalence **13-4.** important, vested, information.

14. Discuss the relations between attitudes and behavior.

14-1. As LaPiere found in his travels with a Chinese couple, attitudes (are/are not) consistently good predictors of behavior. One reason involves a failure to account for attitude _____, the importance of the attitude for the person. In general, the stronger the attitude the better it will predict _____.

14-2. In addition, the actual situation is likely to present new information: possible embarrassment, pressure from others, the unanticipated pleasant or unpleasant aspects of the situation, and so on. In other words, the behavioral component is just a _predisposition_ that may change as a function of norms or other constraints of the _____.

Answers: **14-1.** are not, strength, behavior **14-2.** situation.

15. Summarize evidence on source factors, message factors, and receiver factors that influence the process of persuasion.

15-1. If you are the _source_ of a communication, the message giver:

(a) What factors mentioned in your text would you use to make yourself more _credible_? _____ and _____

(b) What else would you hope to emphasize about yourself? _____

15-2. With regard to _message_ factors:

(a) Which is generally more effective, a one-sided message or a two-sided message? _____

(b) In presenting your argument, should you use every argument that you can think of or emphasize just the stronger arguments? _____

(c) Is simple repetition a good strategy, or should you say something just once? _____

(d) Do fear appeals tend to work? _____ When? _____

15-3. With regard to *receiver* factors in persuasive communications:

(a) If you know that someone is going to attempt to persuade you on a particular topic you will be (harder/easier) to persuade. This is the factor referred to as _____

(b) Resistance to persuasion is greater when an audience holds an attitude incompatible with the one being presented. In this case the receiver will also tend to scrutinize arguments longer and with more skepticism, an effect referred to as _____ bias.

(c) In addition, in part because they may be anchored in networks of other beliefs that may also require change, _____ attitudes are more resistant to change.

Answers: 15-1. (a) expertise, trustworthiness (b) likability (for example, by increasing your physical attractiveness or emphasizing your similarity with the message receiver) **15-2.** (a) In general, two-sided (That's the kind of speech Mark Antony gave over the body of Caesar in Shakespeare's *Julius Caesar*.) (b) stronger only (c) repetition (causes people to believe it's true, whether it is or isn't) (d) yes, *if* they arouse fear (and especially if the audience thinks the consequences are very unpleasant, likely to occur, and avoidable) **15-3.** (a) easier, forewarning (b) disconfirmation (c) stronger.

16. Discuss how learning processes can contribute to attitudes.

16-1. Following are examples that relate learning theory to attitude change. Indicate which type of learning—classical conditioning, operant conditioning, or observational learning—matches the example.

_____ Ralph hears a speaker express a particular political attitude that is followed by thunderous applause. Thereafter, Ralph tends to express the same attitude.

_____ Advertisers pair soft drinks (and just about any other product) with attractive models. The audience likes the models and develops a stronger liking for the product.

_____ If you express an attitude that I like, I will agree with you, nod, say "mm-hmm," and so on. This will tend to strengthen your expression of that attitude.

Answers: 16-1. observational learning, classical conditioning, operant conditioning.

17. Explain how cognitive dissonance can account for the effects of counterattitudinal behavior and effort justification.

17-1. (Dissonance is a truly complicated theory, but the following exercise should help. First read over the text, then see how you do on these questions. Here's a hint: Both problems that follow are contrary to common-sense ideas of reward and punishment; dissonance theory prides itself on making predictions contrary to these common-sense ideas. Item 17-1 indicates that we like behaviors accompanied by less, not more, reward; item 17-2 indicates that we like behaviors accompanied by more, not less, discomfort.)

Ralph bought a used car. However, the car uses a lot of gas, which he doesn't like because he strongly supports conserving energy. He rapidly concludes that conserving fuel isn't so important after all.

(a) Ralph has engaged in counterattitudinal behavior. What were the two contradictory cognitions? (One is a thought about his *behavior*. The other is a thought about an important *attitude*.)

(b) Suppose the car was a real beauty, a rare antique worth much more than the price paid. Alternatively, suppose that the car was only marginally worth what was paid for it. In which case would dissonance be stronger? In which case would the attitude about gas guzzling be more likely to change?

17-2. Suppose Bruce decides to join a particular club. (1) One possible scenario is that he must travel a great distance to attend, the club is very expensive, and he must give up much of his free time to become a member. (2) Alternatively, suppose that the traveling time is short, the club is inexpensive, and he need not give up any free time. In which case (1 or 2) will he tend to value his membership more, according to dissonance theory? Briefly, why?

Answers: **17-1.** (a) I know I bought the car. I'm against the purchase of cars that waste gas. (b) The additional reward in the first situation produces less dissonance and will tend to leave Ralph's original attitude about gas consumption intact. Ralph's attitude about gas consumption will change more when there is less justification (in terms of the value of the car) for his action. As described in your text, we tend to have greater dissonance, and greater attitude change, when *less reward* accompanies our counterattitudinal behavior. **17-2.** According to dissonance theory, he will value the membership more under alternative 1, even if the benefits of membership are slight, because people attempt to *justify the effort* expended in terms of the benefits received. (While dissonance is a genuine phenomenon with many of the characteristics that Festinger described in 1957, several other variables are operating, so it is difficult to predict when dissonance will occur.)

18. Relate self-perception theory and the elaboration likelihood model to attitude change.

18-1. At a cocktail party Bruce eats caviar. When asked whether he likes caviar he responds, "I'm eating it, so I guess I must like it." This example illustrates _____ theory.

18-2. According to self-perception theory, people infer their attitudes by observing their own _____. Thus, if people engage in a behavior that is not accompanied by high rewards, they are likely to infer that they (enjoy/do not enjoy) the behavior.

18-3. To illustrate the elaboration likelihood model: Suppose that you are to travel in Europe and must decide between two options, renting a car or traveling by train (on a Eurailpass). In the blanks below indicate which persuasive route, central (C) or peripheral (P), is referred to in these examples.

_____ On the basis of train brochures showing apparently wealthy and dignified travelers dining in luxury on the train while viewing the Alps, you opt for the train.

_____ Your travel agent is an expert who has advised many of your friends, and she strongly recommends that you take the train. You decide on the train.

_____ A friend urges you to consider details you hadn't previously considered: traffic, waiting in line, additional cab fare, and so on. You seek additional information, and after weighing the relative expenses and conveniences for four traveling together you decide to rent a car.

18-4. In the elaboration likelihood model, the route that is easier, that involves the least amount of thinking, is the _____ route. The route in which relevant information is sought out and carefully pondered is the _____ route. Elaboration, which involves thinking about the various complexities of the situation, is more likely to occur when the _____ route is used.

18-5. Elaboration leads to (more enduring/transient) changes in attitudes. In addition, elaboration (i.e., the more central route) is (more/less) likely to predict behavior.

Answers: 18-1. self-perception **18-2.** behavior, enjoy **18-3.** P, P, C **18-4.** peripheral, central, central **18-5.** more enduring, more.

CONFORMITY AND OBEDIENCE: YIELDING TO OTHERS

19. Summarize research on the determinants of conformity.

19-1. Briefly summarize the general procedure and results of the Asch line-judging studies.

19-2. Conformity increased as number of accomplices increased, up to a point. Conformity seemed to level off, so that increasing the number of accomplices beyond _____ has relatively little effect.

19-3. Suppose there are five accomplices, one real subject, and another accomplice who dissents from the majority. What effect will this "dissenter" have on conformity by the real subject?

19-4. Several factors affect conformity, as you may have observed. For example, people are more likely to conform in _____ situations, when the "correct" answer is very unclear. Not surprisingly, people also tend to conform more to individuals who have high _____ and to members of their (ingroup/outgroup).

Answers: 19-1. Subjects were asked to judge which of three lines matched a standard line, a judgment that was actually quite easy to make. Only one of the subjects was a real subject, however; the others were accomplices of the experimenter, who gave wrong answers on key trials. The result was that a majority of the real subjects tended to conform to the wrong judgments of the majority on at least some trials. **19-2.** 4 **19-3.** Conformity will be dramatically reduced, to about one-fourth the frequency without a dissenter. **19-4.** ambiguous, status, ingroup.

20. Describe the Featured Study on obedience to authority and the ensuing controversy generated by Milgram's research.

20-1. Two individuals at a time participated in Milgram's initial study, but only one was a real subject. The other "subject" was an accomplice of the experimenter, an actor. By a rigged drawing of slips of paper the real subject became the _____ and the accomplice became the _____. There were a total of _____ subjects, or teachers, in the initial study.

20-2. The experimenter strapped the learner into a chair and stationed the teacher at an apparatus from which he could, supposedly, deliver electric shocks to the learner. The teacher was to start at 15 volts, and each time the learner made a mistake the teacher was supposed to _____ the level of shock by 15 volts—up to a level of 450 volts.

20-3. At 300 volts, the learner pounded on the wall and demanded to be released. Of the 40 subjects, how many quit the experiment at that point? _____ How many subjects had quit prior to that point? _____ What percentage of the subjects continued to obey instructions, thereby increasing the shock all the way up to 450 volts? _____

20-4. What is the major conclusion to be drawn from this study? Why are the results of interest?

20-5. As you might imagine, Milgram's studies on obedience were controversial, producing both detractors and defenders. Reasonable issues were raised about both the generality of the studies and whether or not they were ethical. Beneath each of the following examples are possible *counter-arguments* asserted by either Milgram or his supporters.

(a) "Subjects in an experiment expect to obey an experimenter, so the results don't generalize to the real world."

The flaw in this argument, according to Milgram's defenders, is that in many aspects of the real world, including the military and business worlds, obedience (is not/is also) considered appropriate. So, Milgram's results (do/do not) generalize to the real world.

(b) "Milgram's procedure, by which subjects were allowed to think that they had caved in to commands to harm an innocent victim, was potentially emotionally damaging to the subjects. Milgram's experiment was unethical."

Milgram's defenders assert that the brief distress experienced by the subjects was relatively (slight/ great) in comparison with the important insights that emerged.

Answers: 20-1. teacher, learner, 40 **20-2.** increase **20-3.** 5, none, 65 percent **20-4.** The major conclusion is that ordinary people will tend to obey an authority even when their obedience could result in considerable harm (and perhaps even death) to others. The result is of interest because it suggests that such obedience as occurs in war atrocities (e.g., in World War II, at Mi Lai in Viet Nam, in Cambodia, Rwanda, Yugoslavia, and throughout history) may not be due so much to the evil *character* of the participants as to pressures in the *situation*. (Milgram's results are also of interest because most people would not expect them: even psychiatric experts predicted that fewer than 1% of the subjects would go all the way to 450 volts.) **20-5.** (a) is also, do (b) slight. (Many psychologists today share the critics' concerns, however, and the study has not been replicated in the United States since the 1970s.)

21. Discuss cultural variations in conformity and obedience.

21-1. As with other cross-cultural comparisons, replications in other countries yield some similarities and some differences. Indicate true (T) or false (F) for the following statements.

_____ The obedience effect found by Milgram seems to be a uniquely American phenomenon.

_____ In replications of the Milgram studies in several European countries, obedience levels were even higher than those in the United States.

_____ Replications of the Asch line-judging studies have found that cultures that emphasize collectivism are more conforming than are those that emphasize individualism.

Answers: 21-1. F, T, T.

BEHAVIOR IN GROUPS: JOINING WITH OTHERS

22. Discuss the nature of groups and the bystander effect.

22-1. The word *group* doesn't have the same meaning for social psychologists that it does for everyone else. As I look out across my social psychology class on a Tuesday morning, I might say to myself, "Hm, quite a large group we have here today." Actually, my class is *not* a group in social psychological terms because it lacks one, and perhaps two, of the essential characteristics of a group. A group consists of two or more individuals who (a) _____ and (b) are _____.

22-2. Which of the following are groups, as defined by social psychologists?

_____ A husband and wife.

_____ The board of directors of a corporation.

_____ A sports team.

_____ Spectators at an athletic event.

_____ Shoppers at a mall.

22-3. What is the bystander effect?

22-4. Why does the bystander effect occur? In part because the presence of onlookers not doing anything produces an _____ situation (no one seems to be upset, so maybe it's not an emergency). In addition, the presence of others causes a _____ of responsibility (we're all responsible, or else someone else will do it.)

Answers: 22-1. (a) interact (b) interdependent **22-2.** The first three are groups and the last two are not. **22-3.** When people are in groups (or at least in the presence of others), they are less likely to help than when they are alone. Or, the greater the number of onlookers in an emergency, the less likely any one of them is to assist the person in need. **22-4.** ambiguous, diffusion.

23. Summarize evidence on group productivity, including social loafing.

23-1. Individual productivity in large groups is frequently less than it is in small groups. Two factors contribute to this decreased efficiency: a loss of _____ among workers in larger groups (e.g., efforts of one person interfere with those of another) and _____ loafing.

23-2. Social loafing is the reduction in _____ expended by individuals working in groups as compared to people working alone. Social loafing and the bystander effect seem to share a common cause: diffusion of _____.

23-3. In some situations in which members are convinced that individual performance is crucial and that excellent group performance will be rewarded, social loafing is (<u>less/more</u>) likely to occur. factors may also have an effect; social loafing is less common in (<u>collectivist/individualistic</u>) societies.

Answers: **23-1.** coordination, social **23-2.** effort, responsibility **23-3.** less, collectivist.

24. Describe group polarization and groupthink.

24-1. This problem should help you understand the concept of group polarization. Suppose that a group of five corporate executives meet to decide whether to *raise* or *lower* the cost of their product, and by how much. Before they meet as a group, the decisions of the five executives (expressed as a percentage) are as follows: +32%, +17%, +13%, +11%, and +2%. After they meet as a group, which of the following is most likely to be the result? Assume that group polarization occurs.

a. +30%, +10%, +3%, +3%, and +2%

b. +34%, +29%, +22%, +15%, and +20%

c. -3%, -1%, 0%, +9%, and +11%

d. –10%, –7%, –3%, 0%, and +2%

24-2. What is group polarization?

24-3. Have you ever been in a group when you thought to yourself, "This is a stupid idea, but my best friends seem to be going along with it, so I won't say anything." If so, you may have been in a group afflicted with groupthink. Groupthink is characterized by, among other things, an intense pressure to _____ to group opinions accompanied by very low tolerance for dissent.

24-4. According to Janis, the major cause of groupthink is high group _____, the degree of attraction group members have for the group. Other possible causes include _____ leadership and high decision _____.

24-5. Recent evidence has also found that group members tend not to pool information. That is, they tend to:

_____a. discuss information that is commonly known among members.

_____b. explore information that is unique to individual members.

24-6.   While the groupthink theory has intuitive appeal, research support for Janis' conclusions has been (strongly supportive/mixed).

Answers: 24-1. b **24-2.** Group polarization is the tendency for a group's decision to shift toward a *more extreme position* in the direction that individual members are *already leaning*. **24-3.** conform **24-4.** cohesiveness, directive (strong), stress **24-5.** a **24-6.** mixed.

PUTTING IT IN PERSPECTIVE

25.   Explain how the chapter highlighted three of the text's unifying themes.

25-1.   This chapter again illustrates psychology's commitment to empirical research. When people hear the results of psychological studies they frequently conclude that the research just confirms common sense. Dispute this view by listing and describing *at least one study* with results that are not predictable from common sense assumptions.

25-2.   Cross-cultural differences and similarities also reflect one of the unifying themes. People conform, obey, attribute, and love throughout the world, but the manner and extent to which they do so are affected by cultural factors. Important among these factors is the degree to which a culture has an

_____ or _____ orientation.

25-3.   Finally, the chapter provides several illustrations of the way in which our view of the world is highly subjective. For example, we tend to make ability and personality judgments based on people's physical

_____; see what we expect to see as a result of the cognitive structures termed social _____; distort judgments of physical lines based on pressures to _____; and make foolish decisions when we become enmeshed in the group phenomenon known as _____.

Answers: 25-1. This chapter has described at least three studies that defy the predictions of common sense or of experts. (1) Concerning *Milgram's studies*, Psychiatrists incorrectly predicted that fewer than 1% of the subjects would go to 450 volts. (2) Results from *cognitive dissonance* studies are frequently the opposite of common sense. For example, subjects liked tasks *more* when they were paid *less* or else when they suffered in order to participate. (3) Common sense might predict that the larger the number of people who see someone in need of help, the more likely any one is to offer help. Research on the *bystander effect* consistently finds the opposite result. **25-2.** individualistic, collectivist **25-3.** attractiveness, schemas, conform, groupthink.

APPLICATION: UNDERSTANDING PREJUDICE

26.   Relate person perception processes and attributional bias to prejudice.

26-1.   Prejudice is a negative _____ toward others based on group membership. Like other attitudes, prejudice may include affective, _____, and behavioral components.

26-2.   The cognitive component of prejudice may be comprised of schemas about groups. This type of schema is frequently referred to as a _____.

26-3. Stereotypes are part of the *subjectivity* of person perception. People tend to see what they expect to see, and when stereotypes are activated people see and remember information that (<u>is/is not</u>) congruent with their stereotype.

26-4. Stereotypes are highly accessible and frequently activated automatically, so that even though people reject prejudiced ideas, stereotypes (<u>can not/may still</u>) influence behavior.

26-5. Our *attributional biases* are also likely to maintain or augment prejudice. For example, observers tend to attribute success in men to (<u>ability/luck</u>) but success in women to (<u>ability/luck</u>).

26-6. People may also attribute other people's behavior to internal traits, the bias referred to as the _____ attribution error.

26-7. When people experience adversity such as prejudice, we are also likely to attribute their misfortune to character flaws, a predisposition referred to as defensive attribution or _____.

Answers: **26-1.** attitude, cognitive **26-2.** stereotype **26-3.** is **26-4.** may still **26-5.** ability, luck **26-6.** fundamental **26-7.** victim blaming.

27. Relate principles of attitude formation and group processes to prejudice.

27-1. Attitudes are to a large extent learned. For example, if someone makes a disparaging remark about an ethnic group that is followed by approval, the approval is likely to function as a _____ that increases that person's tendency to make similar remarks in the future. This is the learning process known as _____ . Or, if someone simply *observes* another person making such a remark, the observer may acquire the tendency to make similar remarks through the process known as _____.

27-2. Ingroup members view themselves as different from the outgroup in several ways. First, they tend to see themselves as superior to outgroups, a tendency known as _____ . In addition, they seem themselves as relatively heterogeneous and outgroup members as relatively _____.

27-3. In other words, ingroup members see outgroupers as highly (<u>dissimilar/similar</u>) to one another in appearance as well as behavior. In fact, studies have found that (<u>blacks/whites/both</u>) have difficulty distinguishing the faces of the other group. This important difference in the perception of outgroups by ingroups is termed the illusion of outgroup _____.

Answers: **27-1.** reinforcer, operant conditioning, observational learning (modeling) **27-2.** ethnocentrism, homogeneous **27-3.** similar, both, homogeneity.

CRITICAL THINKING APPLICATION

28. Discuss some useful criteria for evaluating credibility and some standard social influence strategies.

28-1. We are constantly bombarded with information designed to persuade. Sometimes we are persuaded and happy about it and sometimes we regret the outcome. How can we resist attempts at manipulation? Two tactics are discussed in this section: evaluating the _____ of the source, and learning about several widely-used social _____ strategies.

28-2. To assess credibility, consider these questions: Do they have a _____ interest? If so, information they provide may not be objective. What are the source's _____? Although degrees do not certify competence, they may indicate relevant training.

28-3. Is the information inconsistent with _____ views on the issue? If not, one should ponder why others haven't arrived at the same conclusion. Finally, what was the _____ of analysis used? One should be particularly skeptical if the source relies on anecdotes or focuses on small inconsistencies in accepted beliefs.

28-4. In addition, learn to recognize social influence strategies. Following are several scenarios. Identify each with one of the four strategies discussed: *foot-in-the-door*, *reciprocity*, *lowball*, and *scarcity*.

_____ Scenario 1: Mail solicitation for a magazine subscription. "Enclosed is a packet of seeds, free of charge, just for you. We hope you enjoy the beautiful flowers they produce! Also, you will benefit from subscribing to Outdoor Beauty magazine. We've enclosed a free copy."

_____ Scenario 2: Newspaper ad. "This weekend only—mammoth blowout car deals!! These beauties will go fast!!!! Don't miss this once-in-a-lifetime opportunity!!"

_____ Scenario 3: A college development office calling alumni. First week: "We don't care about the amount, perhaps $5, just so that we can ensure full participation." You commit to $5. Next week: "Would you become one of our member donors with a contribution of $100?"

_____ Scenario 4: On the phone with a wholesale camera salesman. "Yes, we do have the XXY Camera at $499.00 plus tax. We'll ship that this afternoon. Now, did you want the new lens or the old lens with that? The new lens would be an additional $99. Did you want the carrying case also?" (Your assumption was that the so-called extras were included in the original price.)

_____ Scenario 5: Mail solicitation. First week: "Would you answer this brief survey for us? There are only 12 questions." Next week: "Thanks for responding to our survey! We desperately need money for this worthwhile (candidate, school, charity, etc.)."

_____ Scenario 6: At the car dealer. "We've got a deal, $22,900 plus tax! You'll be very happy with this car! Let me check with my manager to see if that price includes the radio and CD player." (Fifteen minutes pass while the salesman supposedly checks.) "Well, I tried, but the manager won't budge. Fortunately it's not much additional!"

Answers: 28-1. credibility, influence **28-2.** vested, credentials **28-3.** conventional, method **28-4.** reciprocity, scarcity, foot-in-the-door, lowball, foot-in-the-door, lowball.

REVIEW OF KEY TERMS

Attitudes	Group	Obedience
Attributions	Group cohesiveness	Outgroup
Bystander effect	Group polarization	Passionate love
Channel	Groupthink	Person perception
Cognitive dissonance	Illusory correlation	Prejudice
Collectivism	Individualism	Receiver
Commitment	Ingratiation	Reciprocity
Companionate love	Ingroup	Reciprocity norm
Conformity	Internal attributions	Self-serving bias
Defensive attribution	Interpersonal attraction	Social loafing
Discrimination	Intimacy	Social psychology
Ethnocentrism	Latitude of acceptance	Social schemas
External attributions	Lowball technique	Source
Foot-in-the-door technique	Matching hypothesis	Stereotypes
Fundamental attribution error	Message	

_____ 1. The branch of psychology concerned with the way individuals' thoughts, feelings, and behaviors are influenced by others.

_____ 2. The process of forming impressions of others.

_____ 3. Clusters of ideas about categories of social events and people that we use to organize the world around us.

_____ 4. Widely held beliefs that people have certain characteristics because of their membership in a particular group.

_____ 5. Error that occurs when we estimate that we have encountered more confirmations of an association between social traits than we have actually seen.

_____ 6. Inferences that people draw about the causes of events, others' behavior, and their own behavior.

_____ 7. Attributing the causes of behavior to personal dispositions, traits, abilities, and feelings.

_____ 8. Attributing the causes of behavior to situational demands and environmental constraints.

_____ 9. The tendency of an observer to favor internal attributions in explaining the behavior of an actor.

_____ 10. The tendency to blame victims for their misfortune so that we feel less likely to be victimized in a similar way.

_____ 11. The tendency to attribute our positive outcomes to personal factors and our negative outcomes to situational factors.

_____ 12. Liking or positive feelings toward another.

_____ 13. Getting people to agree to a small request to increase the chances that they will agree to a larger request later.

_____ 14. The observation that males and females of approximately equal physical attractiveness are likely to select each other as partners.

_____ 15. Liking those who show that they like us.

_____ **16.** A conscious effort to cultivate others' liking by complimenting them, agreeing with them, doing favors for them, and so on.

_____ **17.** A complete absorption in another person that includes tender sexual feelings and the agony and ecstasy of intense emotion.

_____ **18.** A warm, trusting, tolerant affection for another whose life is deeply intertwined with one's own.

_____ **19.** Warmth, closeness, and sharing in a relationship.

_____ **20.** The intent to maintain a relationship in spite of the difficulties and costs that may arise.

_____ **21.** Positive or negative evaluation of objects of thought; may include cognitive, behavioral, and emotional components.

_____ **22.** The person who sends a communication.

_____ **23.** The person to whom the message is sent.

_____ **24.** The information transmitted by the source.

_____ **25.** The medium through which the message is sent.

_____ **26.** A range of potentially acceptable positions on an issue centered around one's initial attitude position.

_____ **27.** A tendency to evaluate people in outgroups less favorably than those in one's ingroup.

_____ **28.** Situation that exists when related cognitions are inconsistent.

_____ **29.** Yielding to real or imagined social pressure.

_____ **30.** Involves getting someone to commit to an attractive deal before its hidden costs are revealed.

_____ **31.** A form of compliance that occurs when people follow direct commands, usually from someone in a position of authority.

_____ **32.** Involves putting group goals ahead of personal goals and defining one's identity in terms of the group one belongs to.

_____ **33.** Involves putting personal goals ahead of group goals and defining one's identity in terms of personal attributes rather than group memberships.

_____ **34.** Two or more individuals who interact and are interdependent.

_____ **35.** The apparent paradox that people are less likely to provide needed help when they are in groups than when they are alone.

_____ **36.** A reduction in effort by individuals when they work together as compared to when they work by themselves.

_____ **37.** Situation that occurs when group discussion strengthens a group's dominant point of view and produces a shift toward a more extreme decision in that direction.

_____ **38.** Phenomenon that occurs when members of a cohesive group emphasize concurrence at the expense of critical thinking in arriving at a decision.

_____ **39.** The group one belongs to and identifies with.

_____ **40.** People who are not a part of the ingroup.

_____ **41.** The strength of the liking relationships linking group members to each other and to the group itself.

_____ **42.** A negative attitude held toward members of a group.

_____ **43.** Behaving differently, usually unfairly, toward the members of a group.

44. The rule that we should pay back when we receive something from others; may be used in an influence strategy.

Answers: 1. social psychology **2.** person perception **3.** social schemas **4.** stereotypes **5.** illusory correlation **6.** attributions **7.** internal attributions **8.** external attributions **9.** fundamental attribution error **10.** defensive attribution **11.** self-serving bias **12.** interpersonal attraction **13.** foot-in-the-door technique **14.** matching hypothesis **15.** reciprocity **16.** ingratiation **17.** passionate love **18.** companionate love **19.** intimacy **20.** commitment **21.** attitudes **22.** source **23.** receiver **24.** message **25.** channel **26.** latitude of acceptance **27.** ethnocentrism **28.** cognitive dissonance **29.** conformity **30.** lowball technique **31.** obedience **32.** collectivism **33.** individualism **34.** group **35.** bystander effect **36.** social loafing **37.** group polarization **38.** groupthink **39.** ingroup **40.** outgroup **41.** group cohesiveness **42.** prejudice **43.** discrimination **44.** reciprocity norm.

REVIEW OF KEY PEOPLE

Solomon Asch
Ellen Berscheid
David Buss
Leon Festinger

Elaine Hatfield
Cindy Hazen and Phillip Shaver
Fritz Heider
Irving Janis

Harold Kelley
Stanley Milgram
Bernard Weiner

_____ **1.** Was the first to describe the crucial dimension along which we make attributions; developed balance theory.

_____ **2.** Devised a theory that identifies important factors relating to internal and external attributions.

_____ **3.** With Hatfield did research describing two types of romantic love: passionate and companionate.

_____ **4.** Originator of the theory of cognitive dissonance.

_____ **5.** Devised the "line-judging" procedure in pioneering investigations of conformity.

_____ **6.** In a series of "fake shock" experiments studied the tendency to obey authority figures.

_____ **7.** Developed the concept of groupthink.

_____ **8.** Under the name of Walster did early study on dating and physical attractiveness; with Berscheid, described types of romantic love.

_____ **9.** Concluded that attribution has not only on internal-external dimension but a stable-unstable dimension.

_____ **10.** Proposed an evolutionary view of attraction; did cross-cultural research on priorities in mate selection.

_____ **11.** Did research on infant-caregiver attachment patterns as predictors of adult romantic relationships.

Answers: 1. Heider **2.** Kelley **3.** Berscheid **4.** Festinger **5.** Asch **6.** Milgram **7.** Janis **8.** Hatfield **9.** Weiner **10.** Buss **11.** Hazen & Shaver.

SELF-QUIZ

1. Which of the following characteristics do we tend to attribute to physically attractive people?
a. low intelligence
b. friendliness
c. unpleasantness
d. coldness

2. Cognitive structures that guide our perceptions of people and events are termed
   a. attributions
   b. stigmata
   c. schemas
   d. denkmals

3. Inferences that we make about the causes of our own and others' behavior are termed
   a. attributions
   b. stigmata
   c. schemas
   d. denkmals

4. Bruce performed very well on the examination, which he attributed to native ability and hard work. Which attributional bias does this illustrate?
   a. the fundamental attribution error
   b. the actor-observer bias
   c. the self-serving bias
   d. illusory correlation

5. According to this viewpoint, men emphasize physical attractivenss in mate selection while women emphasize the ability to acquire resources. Which theory does this describe?
   a. evolutionary theory
   b. cognitive dissonance
   c. sexual propensity theory
   d. attribution theory

6. Which of the following could be an example of the fundamental attribution error?
   a. Ralph described himself as a failure.
   b. Ralph thought that the reason he failed was that he was sick that day.
   c. Jayne said Ralph failed because the test was unfair.
   d. Sue explained Ralph's failure in terms of his incompetence and laziness.

7. Which influence technique involves asking for a small request in order to increase the likelihood of the target complying with a larger request later?
   a. foot-in-the-door
   b. feigned scarcity
   c. reciprocity norm
   d. lowball

8. Which of the following is, in general, likely to reduce the persuasiveness of a message?
   a. The receiver's viewpoint is already fairly close to that of the message.
   b. The receiver has been forewarned about the message.
   c. A two-sided appeal is used.
   d. The source is physically attractive.

9. Subjects in Group A are paid $1 for engaging in a dull task. Subjects in Group B are paid $20 for the same task. Which theory would predict that Group A subjects would enjoy the task more?
   a. balance
   b. cognitive dissonance
   c. self-perception
   d. observational learning

10. In making a decision you rely on the opinion of experts and the behavior of your best friends. According to the elaboration likelihood model, which route to persuasion have you used?
    a. central
    b. peripheral
    c. attributional
    d. 66

11. Which of the following is the best statement of conclusion concerning Milgram's classic study involving the learner, teacher, and ostensible shock?
    a. Under certain circumstances, people seem to enjoy the opportunity to be cruel to others.
    b. People have a strong tendency to obey an authority even if their actions may harm others.
    c. The more people there are who observe someone in need of help, the less likely any one is to help.
    d. Aggression seems to be a more potent force in human nature than had previously been suspected.

12. Which of the following is most likely to function as a group?
    a. shoppers at a mall
    b. the audience in a theater
    c. the board of trustees of a college
    d. passengers in an airplane

13. Someone witnesses a car accident. In which of the following cases is that individual most likely to stop and render assistance?
    a. Only she saw the accident.
    b. She and one other individual saw the accident.
    c. She and 18 others saw the accident.
    d. The other observers are pedestrians.

14. Suppose the original decisions of members of a group are represented by the following numbers in a group polarization study: 9, 7, 5, 5, 4. The range of numbers possible in the study is from 0 to 9. Which of the following possible shifts in decisions would demonstrate polarization?
    a. 2, 3, 3, 4, 5
    b. 7, 7, 6, 5, 5
    c. 5, 4, 0, 2, 3
    d. 9, 9, 7, 7, 5

15. According to Janis, what is the major cause of groupthink?
    a. strong group cohesion
    b. weak group cohesion
    c. the tendency of group members to grandstand
    d. group conflict

Answers: 1. b 2. c 3. a 4. c 5. a 6. d 7. a 8. b 9. b 10. b 11. b 12. c 13. a 14. d 15. a.

Appendix B
Statistical Methods

REVIEW OF KEY IDEAS

1. **Describe several ways to use frequency distributions and graphs to organize numerical data.**

    1-1. Identify the following methods that are commonly used to present numerical data.

    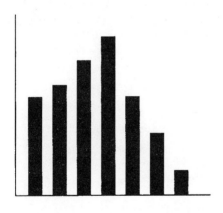   

    (a) _____   (b) _____

    1-2. What data are usually plotted along the:

    (a) horizontal axis?

    (b) vertical axis?

    Answers: 1-1. (a) histogram (b) frequency polygram **1-2.** (a) the possible scores (b) the frequency of each score.

2. Describe the measures of central tendency and variability discussed in the text.

2-1. Tell which measure of central tendency—the mean, median, or mode—would be most useful in the following situations.

    (a) Which measure would be best for analyzing the salaries of all workers in a small, low-paying printshop that includes two high-salaried managers? Explain your answer.

    (b) Which measure would tell us the most common shoe size for men?

    (c) Which measure would be best for pairing players at a bowling match, using their individual past scores, so that equals play against equals?

    (d) Where do most of the scores pile up in a positively skewed distribution?

Answers: 2-1. (a) the median, because the high salaries of the two management persons would distort the mean (b) the mode (c) the mean (d) at the bottom end of the distribution.

3. Describe the normal distribution and its use in psychological testing.

3-1. Answer the following questions regarding the normal distribution.

    (a) Where do the mean, median, and mode fall in a normal distribution?

    (b) What is the unit of measurement in a normal distribution?

    (c) Where are most of the scores located in a normal distribution?

(d) Approximately what percentage of scores falls above 2 standard deviations in a normal distribution?

(e) If your percentile ranking on the SAT was 84, what would your SAT score be (see Fig. B.7 in the text)?

Answers: 3-1. (a) at the center (b) the standard deviation (c) around the mean (plus or minus 1 standard deviation) (d) 2.3% (e) 600 (approximately).

4. **Explain how the magnitude and direction of a correlation is reflected in scatter diagrams and how correlation is related to predictive power.**

   4-1.   Answer the following questions about the magnitude and direction of a correlation as reflected in scattergrams.

   (a) Where do the data points fall in a scattergram that shows a perfect correlation?

   (b) What happens to the data points in a scattergram when the magnitude of correlation decreases?

   (c) What does a high negative correlation indicate?

   4-2.   Answer the following questions regarding the predictive power of correlations.

   (a) How does one compute the coefficient of determination?

   (b) What does the coefficient of determination tell us?

(c) What could we say if the sample study used in the text showed a correlation of -.50 between SAT scores and time watching television?

Answers: 4-1. (a) in a straight line (b) They scatter away from a straight line. (c) High scores on one variable (X) are accompanied by low scores on the other variable (Y). **4-2.** (a) by squaring the correlation coefficient (b) It indicates the percentage of variation in one variable that can be predicted based on the other variable. (c) Knowledge of TV viewing allows one to predict 25% of the variation on SAT scores (.50 x .50 = .25).

5. **Explain how the null hypothesis is used in hypothesis testing and relate it to statistical significance.**

   5-1.   Answer the following questions regarding the null hypothesis and statistical significance.

   (a) In the sample study correlating SAT scores and television viewing, the findings supported the null hypothesis. What does this mean?

   (b) What level of significance do most researchers demand as a minimum before rejecting the null hypothesis?

   (c) What is the probability of making an error when a researcher rejects the null hypothesis at the .01 level of significance?

Answers: 5-1. (a) We cannot conclude that there is a significant negative correlation between SAT scores and television viewing. (b) the .05 level (c) 1 in 100.

REVIEW OF KEY TERMS

Coefficient of determination
Correlation coefficient
Descriptive statistics
Frequency distribution
Frequency polygon
Histogram
Inferential statistics

Mean
Median
Mode
Negatively skewed distribution
Normal distribution
Null hypothesis
Percentile score

Positively skewed distribution
Scatter diagram
Standard deviation
Statistics
Statistical significance
Variability

_____   1.   The use of mathematics to organize, summarize and interpret numerical data.

_____   2.   An orderly arrangement of scores indicating the frequency of each score or group of scores.

_____	**3.** A bar graph that presents data from a frequency distribution.
_____	**4.** A line figure used to present data from a frequency distribution.
_____	**5.** Type of statistics used to organize and summarize data.
_____	**6.** The arithmetic average of a group of scores.
_____	**7.** The score that falls in the center of a group of scores.
_____	**8.** The score that occurs most frequently in a group of scores.
_____	**9.** A distribution in which most scores pile up at the high end of the scale.
_____	**10.** A distribution in which most scores pile up at the low end of the scale.
_____	**11.** The extent to which the scores in a distribution tend to vary or depart from the mean.
_____	**12.** An index of the amount of variability in a set of data.
_____	**13.** A bell-shaped curve that represents the pattern in which many human characteristics are dispersed in the population.
_____	**14.** Figure representing the percentage of persons who score below (or above) any particular score.
_____	**15.** A numerical index of the degree of relationship between two variables.
_____	**16.** A graph in which paired X and Y scores for each subject are plotted as single points.
_____	**17.** The percentage of variation in one variable that can be predicted based on another variable.
_____	**18.** Statistics employed to interpret data and draw conclusions.
_____	**19.** The hypothesis that there is no relationship between two variables.
_____	**20.** Said to exist when the probability is very low that observed findings can be attributed to chance.

Answers: 1. statistics **2.** frequency distribution **3.** histogram **4.** frequency polygon **5.** descriptive statistics **6.** mean **7.** median **8.** mode **9.** negatively skewed distribution **10.** positively skewed distribution **11.** variability **12.** standard deviation **13.** normal distribution **14.** percentile score **15.** correlation coefficient **16.** scatter diagram **17.** coefficient of determination **18.** inferential statistics **19.** null hypothesis **20.** statistical significance.

Appendix C

Industrial/Organizational Psychology

REVIEW OF KEY IDEAS

1. **Discuss the settings, procedures, and content areas of I/O psychology.**

   1-1. In a humorous commentary a few years ago psychologist Jerry Burger said he longed to hear, just once, someone in a theater asking, "Is there a social psychologist in the house?" (Burger, 1986). Burger's comments reflected not only his wish that psychology be recognized somewhere outside the halls of academia but his desire for application. Of course, the settings for the four applied fields of psychology (Chapter 1) frequently are outside university settings—clinical psychology and counseling psychology take place in mental health settings, school psychology occurs in educational settings, and I/O psychology is conducted in _____ settings.

   1-2. While research and application of I/O psychology may occur in the work place, many of its principles derive from academic fields such as social psychology. I/O psychologists also use (<u>much the same/very different</u>) research methods and statistics as the other fields of psychology.

   1-3. There are three primary areas of interest for the industrial psychologists. Write the names of these subareas in the blanks below next to the initial letters that represent them.

   P: _____ psychology

   O: _____ psychology

   HF: _____ _____ psychology

   1-4. Below are descriptions of the three subareas of I/O psychology. Match the subareas with the descriptions by placing the letters from the previous question in the appropriate blanks.

   _____ Examines the way human beings fit the work environment; concerned with the interface between human beings and the tools and resources they use.

   _____ Tests and selects employees, tries to match the abilities of the person to the job requirements.

   _____ Concerned with job satisfaction, relationships among employees, social adaptation of the worker to the workplace.

1-5. Below are possible problems encountered in a workplace. Match the subareas with the problems.

_____ The employees intentionally work at a slow pace.

_____ Several employees unintentionally push the wrong buttons on the machines in their work environments.

_____ Ralph tests out poorly in accounting but has potential for working with the gyroplex machine.

Answers: **1-1.** work (employment, industrial, business) **1-2.** much the same **1-3.** personnel, organizational, human factors (or human engineering) **1-4.** HF, P, O **1-5.** O, HF, P.

2. Discuss how the systems approach relates to the subfields of I/O psychology.

2-1. The three subareas of I/O psychology do not operate independently. For example, using email in place of interoffice memoranda affects not only the way employees interface with machines (the _____ _____ subarea), but also the fit between employee characteristics and the job (the _____ subarea) as well as the way interaction of employees with one another (the _____ subarea).

2-2. Thus, changes in one part of the sociotechnical system affect other parts. For this reason the approach of I/O psychology is termed a _____ approach.

Answers: **2-1.** human factors (human engineering), personnel, organizational **2-2.** systems.

3. Describe how the three subfields of I/O psychology emerged historically.

3-1. The first of the three subareas of I/O psychology to appear historically was _____ psychology. This field emerged as a result of several cultural influences. Sir Francis Galton, Darwin's cousin, developed the first psychological _____ of abilities; Binet developed the first recognized _____ test; and Munsterberg developed ability tests for a variety of applications (e.g., testing for ship captains, telephone operators, trolley drivers, etc.).

3-2. Two major historical events of the twentieth century spurred the use of ability testing on a massive scale and enhanced the importance of personnel psychology. What were these two events?
_____ and _____

3-3. Prior to 1930, the cost-benefit theories of Frederick _____ dominated industry's thinking about behavior in the workplace. Productivity was thought to be determined solely by identifying efficient movements, finding employees capable and willing to work, and paying amounts that were exactly proportionate to rate of _____.

3-4. In 1930 a now-famous study at a Western Electric plant near Chicago found that productivity was affected by workers' _____ toward their supervisors. This result was surprising because it had previously been thought that only physical factors, such as pay and working conditions, would affect productivity. This experiment marks the beginning of the _____ _____ movement in industrial psychology.

3-5. The subarea directed toward developing workplace environments that fit the human beings who use them is known as _____ _____ psychology.

3-6. Human factors developed in large part in response to the need to understand the best and safest ways for human beings to interact with airplanes and other weapons of war. What historical event may be used to mark the beginning of human factors psychology? _____.

Answers: **3-1.** personnel, test, intelligence **3-2.** World War I and World War II **3-3.** Taylor, production (work) **3-4.** attitudes, human relations **3-5.** human factors (human engineering) **3-6.** World War II.

4. Discuss job analysis and psychological testing in personnel psychology.

4-1. The function of personnel psychology is to match the abilities of people with the requirements of the job. This fitting process involves three steps: determining the most important or _____ characteristics of the job, deciding what human _____ are needed to accomplish the job, and developing a way of _____ those attributes.

4-2. Characteristics of the job are not always obvious, however. We know that accountants do accounting and managers do managing and so on, but these rough descriptions are not specific enough to permit prediction from tests. A more precise description is provided by the process known as job _____, a method for breaking a job into its constituent parts.

4-3. Job analysis determines not only what tasks a person does for a particular job but which of the tasks are _____ to the job and which are not. Once the analysis has determined the components of the job and the skills needed, the personnel psychologist administers psychological _____ to assess those skills.

4-4. Tests used must be both consistent and measure what they are supposed to measure. That is, the tests must show an appropriate level of _____ and _____ (Chapter 9).

4-5. In part as a result of the popularity of the "_____" theory of personality, the last few years has seen renewed interest in using _____ tests (Chapter 12) in addition to ability tests.

4-6. Although standardized tests are frequently used, the most widely used procedure in personnel selection is the _____. The _____ interview uses non-standardized questions with no clear right and wrong answers.

4-7. The _____ interview uses standardized questions, asked of all candidates, which are scored for the adequacy of the answers. Of the two types of interview, only the _____ interview has been found to be reliable and valid.

4-8. At some point in the process it is important to verify the reliability and validity of a standardized test as it applies to the job being analyzed. The process of demonstrating that a test is a good predictor of job performance is known as _____ . If the test score is found to _____ with some reliable measure of job performance, then the test is defined as having validity.

4-9.   People of different races, ethnicities, and genders may not perform at the same level on personnel tests, so their use in employee selection creates controversy. One possible solution is to administer a _____ of tests in which relatively high performance on one attribute may compensate for low performance on another.

5. Summarize I/O psychologists theories of work motivation.

5-1.   Herzberg proposed that motivation in the workplace depends on the nature of (<u>the work itself/extrinsic rewards</u>). This point of view, known as job _____ theory, asserts that workers are motivated by (<u>challenges/money</u>) associated with a particular job.

5-2.   Skinner's reinforcement theory is described as the viewpoint which maintains that job interest is created only when the work is followed by sufficient and meaningful _____ , such as money or other extrinsic entities.

5-3.   Expectancy theory contends that people estimate the probability that a particular task will produce a desired _____ . Under this theory, managers must make sure that workers understand the likelihood or _____ that particular rewards will follow particular types of work.

5-4.   Work motivation may also depend on employees' confidence that they can accomplish the task, a point of view referred to as _____ theory. Implementation of this theory involves selecting workers who believe that they can do a job and providing conditions that will enhance this feeling.

5-5.   Finally, another theory asserts that it is important for workers to determine in advance specific objectives, the viewpoint know as _____ theory.

6. Summarize research on job satisfaction.

6-1.   What do people want in a job? Place check-marks next to those items below which appear to be major factors associated with job satisfaction.

_____   interesting and challenging work

_____   pleasant co-workers

_____   adequate salary

_____   opportunities for advancement

_____   effective and supportive supervisors

_____   acceptable company policies

6-2. To assess job satisfaction most organizations distribute questionnaires that ask employees to rate their jobs. Results indicate that satisfaction is correlated with three factors: absenteeism, turnover, and productivity. Employees who are happy with their jobs tend to be absent less often, look for new jobs less frequently, and be more productive. These correlational data do not indicate causal direction, however. While it is probably the case that satisfaction reduces _____ and _____, it may not increase _____.

6-3. Managers might hope, and it would seem reasonable to expect, that job satisfaction would result in greater productivity. Decades of research have failed to find this to be the case. There is some evidence, however, that the reverse is true, that greater _____ leads to increased _____.

Answers: **6-1.** Thousands of studies have found that all of these are primary sources of job satisfaction! **6-2.** absenteeism, turnover, productivity **6-3.** productivity, job satisfaction.

7. **Discuss the concepts of work teams, transformational and charismatic leadership, and organizational culture.**

7-1. The past 15 years or so has seen an increased use of work teams in American companies, an outcome of the downsizing of the 1980s. Which of the following resulted from this change? (Mark T or F.)

_____ Fewer people are expected to do more work with less supervision.

_____ Feelings of accountability and ownership increased at lower levels.

_____ Work motivation and job satisfaction increased.

7-2. In recent years I/O psychologists have become interested in two leadership styles in companies, *transformational* and *charismatic* leadership. Differentiate between these somewhat overlapping concepts by indicating which style is described in each of the following. (Use T or C.)

_____ Succeeds through a vision of what should be accomplished, how the company should change.

_____ Succeeds through the sheer force of the leader's personality.

_____ Makes clear to employees the importance of they are doing.

_____ Persuades workers to put the organization ahead of self-interest.

_____ Appeals to achievement and mastery (self-efficacy) needs of employees.

_____ Are willing to take personal risks.

_____ Are particularly sensitive to others' needs.

_____ Are able to get followers to accept challenges they would normally reject.

7-3. Companies, like people, have differentiating characteristics or personalities. For example, a company might emphasize innovation, or quality, or time urgency. In current I/O psychology jargon, these company traditions or characteristics are referred to as the organizational _____. Since these norms have a critical impact on the way employees work together, I/O psychologists are interested primarily in the way the (employee/customer) experiences the organizational culture and how it is developed, maintained, and changed.

Answers: 7-1. T, T, T **7-2.** T, C, T, T, T, C, C, C **7-3.** culture, employee.

8. Discuss how human engineering can enhance work environments.

8-1. Human factors or human engineering is the study of the interaction or _____ between humans and machines. There are two parts of this system, the _____ part, which conveys information to the operator, and the _____ part , which involves action or inaction by the human operator. Actions create new displays and interfaces, and the process of adjustment occurs in a continual _____ loop.

8-2. For example, dashboards in cars provide the _____ part of the system. Based on that information, the human being operates the pedals and knobs that provide the _____ part of the system, which in turn changes the display.

8-3. The major problems encountered in using machines result from confusion that may involve either the _____ or the _____ parts of the system. To reduce these interface problems, human factors specialists design display panels that are easily understood at a glance or control components shaped like the functions they control. For example, after World War II the knobs that operated the flaps on airplanes were redesigned to be shaped like _____.

8-4. Most people have certain expectations about the way things work. For example, people generally expect to unscrew things in a counterclockwise direction. Thus, a major design principle is to build controls that take into account response _____, people's natural expectations about the way controls work.

8-5. As I sit here writing the last paragraph of this study guide, I am well aware that my computer and software are user-friendly. Probably some nice human factors psychologist designed them that way, and for that I am grateful. They make my life easier. How can human engineering enhance work environments? Well designed machines permit greater efficiency and are less confusing and less frustrating. Thus, they reduce _____ in the human operator, a potential cause of both health problems and _____ in the workplace.

Answers 8-1. interface, display, control, feedback **8-2.** display, control **8-3.** display, control, flaps **8-4.** stereotype **8-5.** stress, accidents (mistakes).

Reference: Burger, J. M. (1986) Is there a Ph. D. in the house? *APA Monitor, 17,* 4.